CARDINAL MANNING

CARDINAL
MANNING
A BIOGRAPHY

ROBERT GRAY

St. Martin's Press
New York

Library of Congress Cataloging in Publication Data

Gray, Robert,
  Cardinal Manning.

  1. Manning, Henry Edward, 1808–1892.   2. Cardinals—England—Biography.
3. Catholic Church—England—History—19th century.   4. England—Church
history—19th century.
I. Title.
BX4705. M3G73   1985   282'.092'4   [B]   85–10687
ISBN 0–312–12032–X

First published in Great Britain by George Weidenfeld & Nicolson Ltd.

First U.S. Edition

10 9 8 7 6 5 4 3 2 1

For Hatty
first of my Catholic friends

Contents

GENEALOGICAL TABLE   X
PROLOGUE   I

  1 A Decided Character   9
  2 Marriage and Churchmanship   36
  3 Promotion and Powerlessness   67
  4 An Essay in Development   98
  5 The One True Fold   121
  6 A Forward Piece?   142
  7 The Unnamed Coadjutor   174
 ⋏8 Archbishop of Westminster   197
  9 Infallibility at Rome and Westminster   226
 ⋋10 Private Life and Public Character   269
 11 The Pitcher at the Fountain   294

EPILOGUE   322
SOURCE NOTES   328
INDEX   357

It is not now known, what never needed proof or statement before, that Religion is not a doubt; that it is a certainty, – or else a mockery and horror.

Thomas Carlyle: *Life of John Sterling* (1851)

There is no man that is not in some measure twofold; and that simply because there is no man who is willing to be known by his fellow men as he knows himself, and as none knows him beside, but God only.

Manning: *Sermons*, volume I (1842)

'Priests are sometimes very disagreeable people, in fact they often are,' he said with a smile.

Manning in conversation with Mrs Crawford, *Dublin Review* (Autumn 1967)

Si hominibus placerem, non essem servus Jesu Christi.

Early Christian maxim cited by Manning

Manning did seem to me (and still seems to me) much the greatest Englishman of his time.

Hilaire Belloc: *Cruise of the Nona* (1925)

Family Tree of Henry Edward Manning

(Italics indicate Catholics, whether by conversion or birth)

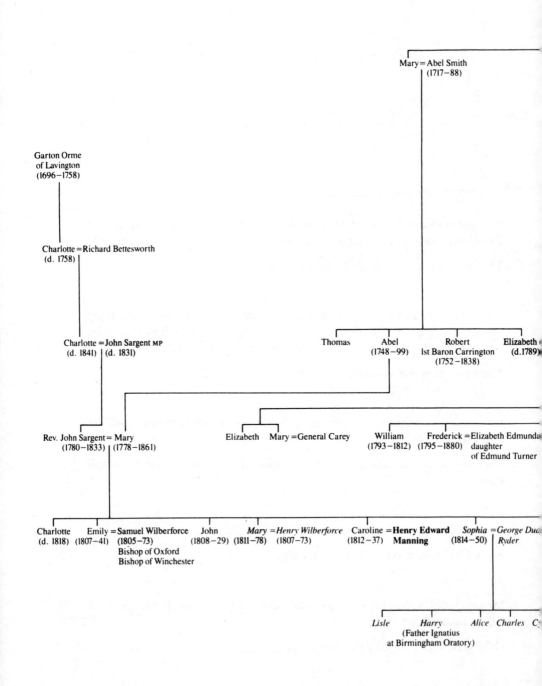

Mary = Abel Smith
(1717–88)

Garton Orme
of Lavington
(1696–1758)

Charlotte = Richard Bettesworth
(d. 1758)

Charlotte = John Sargent MP
(d. 1841) | (d. 1831)

Thomas   Abel   Robert   Elizabeth
(1748–99) 1st Baron Carrington (d.1789)
(1752–1838)

Rev. John Sargent = Mary
(1780–1833) | (1778–1861)

Elizabeth   Mary = General Carey

William   Frederick = Elizabeth Edmunda
(1793–1812) (1795–1880) daughter
of Edmund Turner

Charlotte   Emily = Samuel Wilberforce   John   *Mary = Henry Wilberforce*   Caroline = **Henry Edward**   *Sophia = George Dud*
(d. 1818) (1807–41) (1805–73)   (1808–29) (1811–78) (1807–73)   (1812–37) **Manning**   (1814–50) | *Ryder*
Bishop of Oxford
Bishop of Winchester

Lisle   *Harry*   *Alice*   *Charles*   *C*
(Father Ignatius
at Birmingham Oratory)

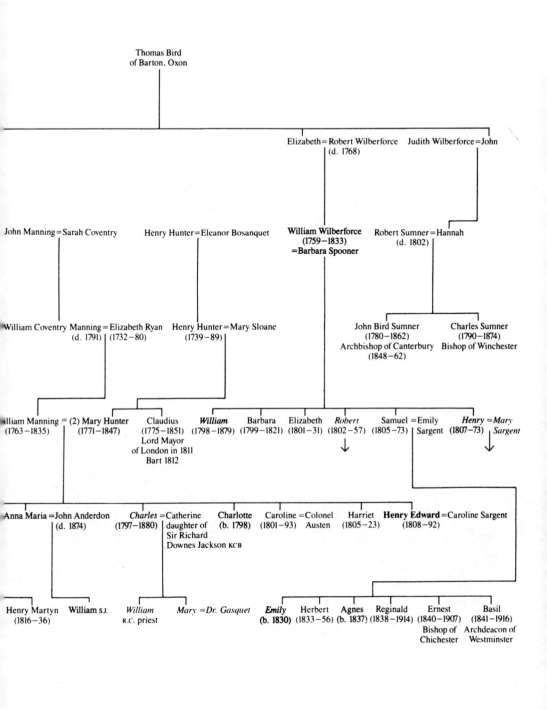

Thomas Bird
of Barton, Oxon

Elizabeth = Robert Wilberforce   Judith Wilberforce = John
            (d. 1768)

John Manning = Sarah Coventry   Henry Hunter = Eleanor Bosanquet   **William Wilberforce**   Robert Sumner = Hannah
                                                                            (1759–1833)   (d. 1802)
                                                                            =**Barbara Spooner**

William Coventry Manning = Elizabeth Ryan   Henry Hunter = Mary Sloane   John Bird Sumner   Charles Sumner
                (d. 1791) (1732–80)   (1739–89)   (1780–1862)   (1790–1874)
                                                                                      Archbishop of Canterbury   Bishop of Winchester
                                                                                      (1848–62)

William Manning = (2) Mary Hunter   Claudius   *William*   Barbara   Elizabeth   *Robert*   Samuel = Emily   *Henry* = Mary
(1763–1835)   (1771–1847)   (1775–1851)   (1798–1879)   (1799–1821) (1801–31)   (1802–57)   (1805–73) | Sargent (1807–73) | Sargent
                                     Lord Mayor   ↓   ↓
                                     of London in 1811
                                     Bart 1812

Anna Maria = John Anderdon   *Charles* = Catherine   Charlotte   Caroline = Colonel   Harriet   **Henry Edward** = Caroline Sargent
               (d. 1874)   (1797–1880) | daughter of   (b. 1798)   (1801–93) Austen   (1805–23)   (1808–92)
                                         | Sir Richard
                                         | Downes Jackson KCB

Henry Martyn   William S.J.   *William*   *Mary* = *Dr. Gasquet*   *Emily*   Herbert   Agnes   Reginald   Ernest   Basil
(1816–36)   R.C. priest   (b. 1830)   (1833–56)   (b. 1837)   (1838–1914)   (1840–1907)   (1841–1916)
                                                                                                                            Bishop of   Archdeacon of
                                                                                                                            Chichester   Westminster

Prologue

For mercy will soon pardon the meanest; but mighty men shall be
mightily tormented.

WISDOM OF SOLOMON, vi v.6

More than that of any other great public figure in English history, Manning's
reputation has been ruined by a biography. It almost seems as though he had
struck some bargain with his Creator, whereby the position and honour
conferred by this world, which he theoretically despised, should be
transmuted into contempt and mockery after his death.

For no reputation ever appeared more secure. His death and funeral
evoked extraordinary scenes of popular grief. This was the more remarkable
as he died on the same day, 14 January 1892, as the Duke of Clarence and
Avondale, the eldest son of the Prince and Princess of Wales. It might be
expected that the loss of a youth born to be king would have entirely
monopolized the British public's capacity for mourning. Yet, while the
leader writers groped for phrases in which to extol the lost monarch –
'unassuming modesty' was about the limit of their success – and while Lord
Tennyson and Alfred Austin tuned their poetic lyres to mark the passing of
this sprig of royalty –

> Hope of a people's heart; your promised
> King, and mine

sang Mr Austin – the masses in London showed themselves perversely
determined to concentrate their sorrow upon a man who represented to an
extreme degree all that John Bull was supposed to regard with instinctive
loathing: papistry, priestcraft and Romish presumption.

For two days the Cardinal's body remained in his tiny bedroom (sixteen
feet by twelve) at the top of the vast mansion in Victoria which he had
inhabited. By 16 January, a Saturday, it had been moved to one of the huge
reception rooms, and an item in *The Times* of that date announced that the
public would be allowed to view the Archbishop's mortal remains on the

following Tuesday. Whether or not that was the original plan, it quickly became evident that a single day's access would be altogether insufficient to meet the demand. In the event, Manning lay in state from the Saturday to the Tuesday, from eleven o'clock to five o'clock each day. *The Times*, an ancient enemy, could scarcely credit the extent of the crowds which availed themselves of this opportunity. Traffic in Victoria was brought to a halt. On Sunday afternoon the queue stretched, four or five in width, for nearly half a mile, from Archbishop's House in Carlisle Place to Vauxhall Bridge, though every effort was made to keep it moving as quickly as possible. *The Times* found the numbers 'difficult to estimate, and not easy to exaggerate'; it reckoned, nevertheless, that on the Sunday more than 100,000 people filed past Manning's body. Many of them had come up specially from the country. On Monday, though a working day, the crowds were even greater. Privileged visitors were escorted upstairs to view the cell-like bedroom, with its narrow iron bed, but privilege did not prevent the room being rifled of its meagre contents by devotees anxious to carry off some relic of the dead Cardinal.

Assuredly he had been a holy man; either that, or he had played the part uncommonly well. The ascetic features were now somewhat softened and, perhaps through the undertaker's art, less pale and emaciated than in life, but who among those paying their respects to the gorgeously arrayed cadaver as it lay in the shadow of a massive crucifix, the head bedecked with a mitre, the hands folded as if in prayer, who among those processing thousands would have dared to affirm that Henry Manning was not a saint? Elsewhere in the capital, too, particularly in the poorer areas, at the Italian church in Hatton Garden, at St Patrick's, Soho, throughout the East End, his death called forth the same impassioned response; and the intoning of the *De Profundis* was interspersed with the tears and the sobs of the bereaved faithful.

On Tuesday evening the body, now sealed in its coffin, was moved from Archbishop's House to the Brompton Oratory for Thursday's Requiem Mass. Wednesday was the day of the Duke of Clarence's funeral, but Londoners flowed into the Oratory, ignoring the services for a chance to be near the coffin. The Requiem Mass, tickets only, was a supreme piece of ecclesiastical theatre: the congregation in blackness, the coffin on a catafalque surrounded by candles, an address by Bishop Hedley, a choir of priests (no women, as the Cardinal had always insisted) performing their dirges in plainsong (the only *really* religious music, the Cardinal had also insisted).

The most impressive of all the tributes was the last. The coffin was borne in procession from the Oratory to Kensal Green cemetery. The route was four miles, along the Cromwell Road, striking north by Warwick Gardens and Addison Road to Holland Park Avenue, into Ladbroke Grove by way of Clarendon and Cornwall Roads, and then along the Harrow Road for the last few hundred yards. Visibility was restricted by the London fog. Yet all the way the route was lined with mourners. Near the Oratory and again at Notting Hill the pavements were overflowing. It was the same for a whole mile down Ladbroke Grove, where in addition every window and every doorstep were crammed with spectators. At the Harrow Road the press was such that the progress of the procession was halted while the police struggled to cut a way through the throng. Here, as at the lying in state, many among the crowds were Irish, but with them, for once, were Englishmen of every class and every creed.[1] Mr Gladstone, reading about the obsequies of his old friend in the South of France, commented on how much deeper and more extended an impression had been made by Manning's death than by that of Cardinal Newman seventeen months before. 'This caused me some surprise,' Gladstone wrote[2] in an aside pregnant with implications for the future of Manning's reputation. But the crowds in the streets were not surprised; they knew simply that one of the greatest men of their times had gone. Their reaction constituted perhaps the most striking, certainly the most spontaneous, demonstration of mass emotion that occurred in the capital during the late Victorian period.

Unhappily, though, there were few, if any, literary men among the enthusiasts who lined the streets. The task of producing the official biography was claimed by a Catholic journalist named Edmund Sheridan Purcell, who maintained that the Cardinal himself had appointed him to this labour. This was at best a half truth. Purcell had been editor of a Catholic journal called the *Westminster Gazette*, which Manning had founded in 1866. At that time, at least initially, he had been a wholehearted supporter of Manning's, especially in the matter of the Pope's temporal power, concerning which the paper had taken a strong Roman line, as distinct from the more moderate approach of Newman. Evidently, though, there had been differences between Manning and Purcell, for at the end of 1880 Manning wrote to Vaughan, his closest ally among the bishops, recalling that 'we were continually annoyed by the *Tablet* in Wallis's hands and by the *Westminster Gazette* in Purcell's.'[3] Indeed, as early as April 1867 Purcell had taken rebellion so far as to sign the open letter in which the laity of England, or at least the better connected of them, expressed their loyal devotion to Newman (see page 215). Thereafter the *Westminster Gazette* had lost official support, though Purcell kept the paper going until 1878, when it disappeared. Three years later Purcell reported that he was 'exclusively engaged in writing for non-Catholic papers'.[4]

In 1886, however, he was involved in some scheme to re-establish a Catholic journal, for which he prepared a sketch of Manning. When plans for this journal fell through, his work appeared to be wasted, until Manning offered consolation. 'The loss of your m.s. is a blessing in disguise,' he told Purcell (or so Purcell remembered); 'publish the Life in volume form. I should like you, if you can, to write the first volume in my lifetime.'[5] Probably Manning only meant to throw a lifeline to a struggling journalist by offering the chance of a lucrative potboiler. 'I am telling him nothing which he could not find for himself in the back files of the *Tablet* or the *Dublin Review*,'[6] he told an anxious enquirer, and he also assured Gladstone that his letters would not be shown to Purcell.[7] Manning wanted J. E. C. Bodley, Sir Charles Dilke's private secretary, to be his official biographer, and had begun to assist him in the task. Since Bodley was a Protestant, Manning suggested the co-operation of a Catholic priest, Father Butler, to help in elucidating the mysteries of Roman Catholicism. It was necessary to 'set a thief to catch a thief',[8] the Cardinal thought.

He did, however, allow Purcell to see a carefully expurgated journal of 1848, which contained a mainly factual account of his stay in Rome during that year; he also let the importunate journalist read portions of other documents and make copies of them.[9] Purcell was inclined to interpret this limited permission as a warrant to delve freely into whatever he could find. Manning never intended to accord any such liberty, and when he discovered on one occasion that Purcell had made off with one of his private diaries, he evinced the greatest anxiety, sending message after message to recover the lost item.[10] It is to the credit of the Cardinal's forbearance, if not his judgement, that after this episode he allowed Purcell to continue his work in any form at all. Perhaps he imagined that he had protected himself sufficiently through his understanding with Bodley.

In any case, Purcell would by this time have taken a great deal of stopping. He had correctly apprehended that he had stumbled upon a potential goldmine and had no intention of allowing the opportunity to slip. After Manning's death he acted forcefully and accomplished a major scoop. He managed to persuade the gullible curators of Manning's papers at the church of St Mary of the Angels in Bayswater that the Cardinal had authorized him as official biographer and that he might therefore carry off whatsoever documents he wished.[11] In fact, as Manning had not mentioned him in his will, he had no right at all to any of the papers.[12] It was in this knowledge that Purcell bundled as much material as possible into a cab and carted it off from Bayswater before any awkward questions could be asked. As luck would have it, Bodley was on an extended trip abroad when Manning died. When he heard what had happened, he described it as the hardest blow of his life.

Purcell now had about half the Manning papers. When he applied for the other half, he was refused by custodians too late grown wise. Still, if Purcell had been well disposed or even neutral towards his subject, his skulduggery would not have greatly mattered, at least in the long term. Word soon got about, however, that he meant to cause a sensation, and the publication of his book in 1895 did not disappoint these rumours. The portrait he drew of Manning, thinly disguised by a dressing of unctuous flattery, was of an ecclesiastic consumed by ambition and the will to dominate, prepared to gain his ends by any means, however unscrupulous. Father Ignatius Ryder, who, though Manning's nephew, succeeded Newman as Father Superior of the Birmingham Oratory, believed that Purcell was not consciously activated by ill-will; Ryder rather convicts him of literary incompetence.[13] That is a very Christian, perhaps one should say a very Newmanite, judgement. To this reader it seems incontestable that the whole work is pervaded by malice. In particular Newman, 'the illustrious Oratorian', is continually presented as a hero who resists the insidious scheming of his Metropolitan. Purcell had certainly changed his spots since the first days of the *Westminster Gazette*.

Although his book was carelessly thrown together, the documents inaccurately transcribed, the structure non-existent, it would be idle to deny that it makes fascinating reading. Manning's letters alone were enough to ensure that. Moreover Purcell, whatever the literary failings discerned by Father Ryder, wrote with great facility. Inevitably, the biography became a best-seller. 'I hope that no word of mine,' Manning had recorded on that new invention the phonograph, 'whether written or spoken, will do harm to anyone when I am dead.'[14] His wish was granted with the single exception of the harm which his letters and journals did to himself. His private writings lent sufficient substance to Purcell's insinuations to make the general thesis of a designing prelate stick as the complete truth in minds that were only too eager to see a popular idol exposed. The English establishment greeted with relief the knowledge that the man who had consistently shown up their selfishness and indifference through his work for the dispossessed was, after all, simply a power-hungry hypocrite.

Particularly interesting, although for quite different reasons, was the reaction of Gladstone to Purcell's work of demolition. 'I was not merely interested in your biography but even fascinated and entranced,' he wrote to Purcell. 'You have so pierced into Manning's innermost interior that it really seems as if little more remained for disclosure in the last day and when the books are opened.' This was a surprising verdict from a man whose friendship with the Cardinal dated back more than sixty years, particularly when taken in conjunction with the final judgement that he delivered on

Manning. 'The immense gifts of his original nature and intense cultivation,' Gladstone considered, 'his warm affections, his lifelong devotion, his share in reviving England, but above all his absolute detachment, place him on such a level that, from my place of thought and life, I can only look at him as a man looks at the stars.'[15] It appears that the memory of Manning produced considerable confusion in Gladstone.

The delight of the Protestant establishment in Purcell's book was perhaps predictable. What may be thought strange is that no Catholic sprang to the rescue of his traduced and departed leader. There were only a few snorts of protest. Vaughan, Manning's successor at Westminster, wrote an article describing the publication of Purcell's book as 'almost a crime'[16], but as he then proceeded to express the opinion that Manning had been senile in his last years, his defence, though strenuous, only shifted the grounds of hostile speculation. No large-scale retort to Purcell appeared. Catholic history at that epoch was nearly all Newmanite history, and no Catholic man of letters was anxious to hazard his intellectual credentials in defence of the man who had now been identified as Newman's great persecutor. As for the Catholic hierarchy in England, if the bishops ever formulated any official policy towards Purcell's Life it was simply to let the book fade into obscurity and to leave the work of restitution to the next generation. After all, the materials were still available. Purcell died in 1898, when most of the papers he had used were returned to Bayswater. (Some, however, were lost, for when Mrs Purcell died in 1901 three collections of Manning's papers were offered for sale. Whoever bought them, they have never been seen or heard of since.)

The hierarchy's inactivity might have qualified as wisdom but for the mischance of Lytton Strachey's happening upon Purcell's volumes. 'Such is my low ebb', he told a friend in 1910, 'that I am reduced to reading a life of Cardinal Manning.'[17] It was always embarrassing to admit even the most tenuous connection with organized religion, but to his delight Strachey discovered that the weighty Victorian tomes were crammed with good sniggering material. The study of Manning which he subsequently wrote became the first and the longest essay in *Eminent Victorians*, the book with which he made his name in 1918. Strachey's account of Manning was hardly more than a collection of the spicier bits in Purcell, tricked out with Bloomsbury art and additional Bloomsbury malice, but the readership of the time, largely unfamiliar with the earlier biography, was delighted by his revelations and innuendos.

It would be difficult to imagine anyone less likely to be fair to Manning than Strachey, who was wholly out of sympathy with the religious impulse, and who regarded this antipathy as one of the many signs of his obvious superiority. True, as his own death hovered near, he began composing poems addressed to some undefined, albeit capitalized, Deity. His reverent biographer, hardly knowing what to make of so embarrassing an aberration, but always full of resource, designates one such effort as 'really a hymn to sexual passion and love', adding (lest we should fail to grasp the point) that it 'acts as a satirical mockery of the orthodox Christian concept of a God of platonic love'.[18] That is all right, then. But Strachey's acquaintance with the Almighty, whatever it was, came far too late to save Manning, whom he never made the least attempt to understand. There was hardly a reference to anything so tedious as social work. It was more amusing, and simpler, to produce an elegant piece of persiflage. Thus was the Purcell version handed on to another generation.

This time, though, there was a Catholic defence. As soon as Shane Leslie read Strachey's essay he posted down to Bayswater to investigate the Manning papers. His Life, published in 1921, is a *tour de force* of crisp phrasing and brilliantly handled anecdote. Unfortunately it is also such a chaos chronologically and schematically that the author's sympathetic intentions tend to be buried under the brilliant surface. It was, nevertheless, a hard act to follow, at any rate for a decade or so. Astonishingly, though, *six* decades have now passed since Leslie's book, and still no further biography of any substance has been published. (Leslie himself, however, produced a revised edition in 1953, containing some new material.) During that time hordes of historians have traversed the Victorian period, desperately burrowing into ever obscurer corners in search of a Ph.D. thesis, unearthing statistics about everything from pig iron to pig farming; hardly any of them, though, have been tempted to approach the colossal and unexploited figure of Manning. Presumably they considered Roman Catholicism less attractive, less *relevant*, than the pig iron. An honourable exception must be made of Professor McClelland, whose able, informative and most resolutely non-Newmanite study, *Cardinal Manning, His Public Life and Influence 1865–92*, was published in 1962. There is, of course, any number of books and articles in which Manning appears, but by and large English historians have shied away from the man himself.

The task, never ungrateful to a Frenchman, of enlightening the obtuse Anglo-Saxon mind has been assumed in this instance by the Abbé Alphonse Chapeau of L'Université Catholique de l'Ouest. The Abbé Chapeau arrived in London after the Second World War and soon uncovered further cause for English shame. Up to 1939, despite Shane Leslie's carelessness and (it must be said) destructiveness with the papers, a large collection still remained at St Mary of the Angels in Bayswater. During the blitz those responsible for air raid precautions transferred the entire hoard into a vast cellar under the church sacristy and adjoining school. They omitted, however, to take any precautions against neglect, decay and wanton destruction in the cellar. Local children playing therein soon transformed the papers into piles of rubbish. By the time that the Abbé Chapeau came to Bayswater the collection was in an advanced state of disintegration. He rescued what he could, picking rotting, charred, crumpled and torn fragments out of the dirt, in some cases even out of dustbins. For thirty-five years now he has been the leading, for much of that time the only, specialist in Manning. This author records with deep gratitude the kindness which the Abbé Chapeau showed in giving up time during a recent visit to London to divulge some of his encyclopaedic knowledge of Manning, including, incidentally, the melancholy history of the papers and their destruction. The Abbé Chapeau has long been working on a full biography, a project which he now shares with Professor McClelland. The first volume, dealing with Manning's Anglican years, will be completed in 1986.

Further gratitude is due to Jacqueline Clais, who has written under the Abbé Chapeau's guidance a lengthy thesis entitled *Le Cardinal Manning et la question sociale*, which she generously made available to the present writer. It is an impressive and scrupulously documented account of Manning's social work, clear, readable and comprehensive. Its translation and publication in England would do much to show Manning's fellow countrymen what a notable figure they have chosen to neglect. But they are not to be dissuaded from reading this book too.

1 A Decided Character

No, when the fight begins within himself,
A man's worth something. God stoops o'er his head,
Satan looks up between his feet – both tug –
He's left, himself, in the middle: the soul wakes
And grows. Prolong that battle through his life!
Never leave growing till the life to come!

ROBERT BROWNING: *Bishop Blougram's Apology*

Henry Edward Manning was born at Copped Hall, Totteridge, in what was then Hertfordshire, on 15 July 1808,[1] the youngest of eight children from the second marriage of William Manning, MP. From the worldly point of view the boy's prospects could hardly have been bettered, unless by changing places with his eldest brother. The future Cardinal was not obliged, in Lady Bracknell's phrase, to rise from the ranks of the aristocracy; he was born into the purple of commerce.

In fact he turned out to be one of two cardinals sprung from City of London families in the first decade of the nineteenth century. But whereas Newman's father was merely a partner in a bank, William Manning was a veritable merchant prince. In such circumstances ancestors were a superfluous luxury which, to do him justice, William Manning made no effort to acquire. As for his famous son, when he was asked about his Manning forebears, he was inclined to refer the enquirer to St Paul's warning against genealogies. He did not, however, always heed this counsel himself. In particular, he displayed interest in his grandmother Elizabeth Ryan. 'All Ryans are papist,' he would affirm;[2] Irish too, he liked to believe. His grandfather William Coventry Manning, who married Miss Ryan in 1751, may have been more impressed by the fact that she owned two estates on the West Indian island of St Kitts.[3]

It seems likely that this grandfather had been involved with the West Indies even before making this fortunate match, and that he encountered Miss Ryan, who had been born in St Kitts, on her own ground. The Cardinal suspected that his paternal ancestors had been deported to the West Indies by Cromwell.[4] The immediate forebears of William Coventry Manning, however, seem to have inspired some reticence in his descendants. Dr Gasquet, who married the Cardinal's niece, assures us that William Coventry's mother was 'of the family of Lord Coventry of North Cray Place, Kent',[5] an offering which conveys a distinct rasp of genealogical barrel-scraping. Several weeks' correspondence in the *Tablet* after the Cardinal's death failed to elicit anything of note or certainty about William Coventry's father, although there was an item in *Notes and Queries* recording that he 'is said to have come from Bristol and to have been of Jewish blood'.[6] Similar speculations have been made about Cardinal Newman's racial origins, though Wilfrid Ward, in his biography of Newman, defiantly insists that his subject's nose was *Roman* not Jewish.[7]

The obscurity to which William Coventry's father has been consigned, together with the report of his Bristol origin, prompts the thought that he may have been a slave-trader. No matter; William Coventry himself, with his two estates on St Kitts, courtesy of Miss Ryan, stood on the verge of better things. The Manning business, based in the West Indian sugar trade, prospered; William Coventry moved the centre of his financing operations to the City of London; the family acquired a substantial house that formed the west side of Billiter Square, near the Tower. George Basevi, Disraeli's grandfather, lived in the same square and became a friend.[8] Curiously, though, when Elizabeth Manning (née Ryan), the *fons et origo* of all this good fortune, died in 1780, it was left to her son, rather than the still surviving William Coventry, to signify the family gratitude. He erected a tablet extolling her exemplary virtues in the City church where she was buried. If she had ever been a Catholic, the Mannings of that epoch saw no cause to mention the fact.[9]

From the 1780s this son, William Manning junior, who had been born in 1763, gradually took over the business from his father and succeeded so well that by the end of the century the firm was pre-eminent among West Indian merchants in the City.[10] The Manning wealth, moreover, was being translated into sober influence. As early as 1790 William Manning became a Tory MP, the start of a continuous thirty-nine-year stint in the Commons. Although he never attained ministerial office, the great merchant found himself gradually drawn into the realms of public finance. Shortly after his youngest son's birth his career reached its zenith. As Deputy Governor and then (1812–3) Governor of the Bank of England he was at the centre of the heated monetarist controversies that attended the financing of the Napoleonic wars.[11] There was even a Court connection: his son Charles was a page to the Prince Regent.[12]

Inevitably this swift family ascent had been consecrated by the acquisition of a country estate. Although Copped Hall was scarcely more than ten miles from the City, near enough for William Manning to travel to his business in a coach and four,[13] it was still, at that period, sufficiently distant to escape any metropolitan taint. The Mannings were in residence there just in time to provide William Coventry, who died in 1791, with a country gentleman's grave in Totteridge churchyard. Thereafter the family had to rely on their West Indian servants for any touch of exotica.

William Manning aimed at more than respectability; he sought virtue. Indeed, he espoused virtue, not once but twice, on each occasion acquiring a wife whose excellence had been well tried by the stresses of prosperity. The first, Elizabeth Abel Smith, was a banker's daughter, sister of that Robert Abel Smith who financed, among other causes, the Prime Minister William Pitt, ending as Lord Carrington for his pains. More to our point, the first Mrs William Manning was also a first cousin of William Wilberforce, and although she died in 1789, only two years after Wilberforce had conceived his ambitious design of reforming the morals of the nation, her husband had been brought into contact with the innermost sanctum of the Evangelical Movement.

Cardinal Manning lived to describe his family's religion as of the 'high and dry' school of Anglicanism.[14] 'High' it may well have been in one sense, for Wilberforce himself, as he grew older, found himself less and less in sympathy with his ungentlemanly allies among the Dissenters.[15] But 'dry'! If the word be understood in its accepted sense, as implying a distinct wariness about anything approaching a good work or a public display of virtue, it would be difficult to imagine a term less applicable to William Manning. The man was a perfect daemon of philanthropy. It was not just that Wilberforce relied on his support for the party of 'saints' in the Commons. William Manning belonged to what has been called the 'directorate' of Evangelicalism. He was one of that group of rich men – Samuel Whitbread, Thomas Baring, Zachary Macaulay and Henry Hoare among them – whose patronage and purses were sure to be solicited in any good cause. Few others were so active. William Manning's name appears as a member of forty philanthropic societies; he was vice-president of ten, governor of nine and on the committee of thirteen. Wilberforce himself only managed another twenty-nine societies.[16]

The upper-class Evangelicals possessed a keen sense, which William Manning's youngest son would also manifest, not just of the necessity of good works, but also of those who might be in a position to advance the cause of true religion. The enlisting of the rich and influential was a fundamental part of Wilberforce's strategy. He had an instinct for 'those who count', for 'useful people', who were by no means always the same as

the godly or even the beneficent people. Alexander Wedderburn, Lord
Loughborough, for instance, was the most conspicuous political rat of his
generation, as Wilberforce well knew. 'Going away because Lord Loughborough coming,' he recorded when staying with Pitt at Wimbledon in 1793.
But second thoughts were cannier: 'on the whole thought it best to stay,
considering that he is to be made chancellor'.[17] And certainly Loughborough was to prove worth the trouble that his cultivation entailed: again
and again he appointed Evangelical clergy as Wilberforce directed.

Whether the kingdom of heaven is to be established by such means is
questionable. There were certainly contemporaries who reacted against
Wilberforce's bland acceptance of the mechanics of influence. 'Mr Wilberforce's humanity will go to all lengths that it can with safety and discretion,'
wrote William Hazlitt, 'but it is not to be supposed that it should lose him his
seat for Yorkshire, the smile of Majesty, or the countenance of the loyal and
pious.'[18] To such criticisms the abolition of slavery may be deemed a
sufficient human response. The Evangelical leadership beat the world at its
own game. 'Never omit any opportunity, my dear Samuel,' Wilberforce
wrote to his son in 1823, 'of getting acquainted with any good man or any
useful man (of course I mean that this usefulness, in any one line, should not
be countervailed by any qualities of an opposite Nature, from which
defilement might be contracted). More perhaps depends on the selection of
acquaintances than on any other Circumstance in life, except I mean of
course still more close and intimate Unions. Acquaintances, indeed, are the
raw Materials, from which are manufactured friends, wives, husbands,
etc.'[19] So the Wilberforce circle found that their crusades for the poor and
oppressed often involved them in marriages of the very best kind. Like many
of their descendants, spiritual and actual, among today's meritocracy, they
kept one eye upon the wrongs of the world and the other upon the main
chance. None of William Manning's children would make any superficial
error in their matrimonial choice.

But then the second Mrs William Manning, whom he married in 1792, also
came from a family with more than its share of practical acumen. She had
been born Mary Hunter. The Cardinal would explain that the Hunters came
from Italy (as papist as Miss Ryan, no doubt) and that their name was an
anglicized version of Venatore.[20] The fact that one of the Cardinal's sisters
was called Anna Maria might seem to bear him out. Other sources,
however, suggest that Mary Hunter, like Newman's mother, was of French
Huguenot stock: in this account Veneur takes the place of Venatore.[21]
Certainly the Hunters had intermarried three times with the unquestionably
Huguenot Bosanquets; certainly Mary's younger brother Claudius received
a Protestant education in Switzerland. This Claudius became another

prominent Evangelical, perhaps partly through the influence of William Manning, though he married money on his own account. While still a young man, he became solicitor to Wilberforce's Society for the Promotion of Religion and Virtue and the Suppression of Vice, and thereafter his name appears among the subscription lists almost as frequently as William Manning's. In 1811 he became Lord Mayor of London, an event celebrated with more than usually magnificent pageantry; and at the end of his term of office he was created a baronet.[22] Sir Claudius's usefulness was not in doubt. Besides, his mother had been Mary Sloane, the great niece of Sir Hans Sloane. Sir Hans had been a famous doctor, Newton's successor as President of the Royal Society and an antiquarian whose collections, bequeathed to the nation, had formed the basis of the British Museum. He had also bought the manor of Chelsea. Decidedly, there was talent in the Hunter family.

The children born of the Manning-Hunter marriage, however, appeared at first to be unexceptionable enough to suit the most conservative taste. The first, William, born in 1793, died young in 1812, thus allowing Frederick, born in 1795, to assume the role of eldest brother, in which he was to prove himself odiously well qualified. Anna Maria followed in 1796; another boy, Charles John, in 1797; then came three more girls, Charlotte[23] (born and died November 1798), Caroline (1801) and Harriet (1805), before the arrival of Henry Edward in 1808.

It was a large family, and Henry (henceforward, and more suitably, 'Manning') was very much the youngest. From the very beginning he seems to have been solitary. In his memories of childhood his brothers and sisters never featured very largely. There are some decorous references to the love and devotion of his family background, but precious few instances, either in childhood or thereafter, of love and devotion in practice. The denizens of Copped Hall were a straight-backed crew, not much given to displays of emotion or sentiment. 'My dear father', Manning recalled, 'was one of the justest, most benevolent, most generous men I ever knew.'[24] It may have been so. To the boy, however, he was a distant and preoccupied figure, obviously worthy of respect but with little time for anything so trivial as bringing up his own children. Of course he knew his duty: his friend Viscount Sidmouth, former Prime Minister and now Chancellor of the Exchequer, was trotted out to be the youngest boy's godfather; and the Bishop of Bath and Wells, 'a man who did not neglect the opportunities which his bishopric afforded him of forwarding the interests of his family',[25] baptized the infant Manning in St Martin-in-the-Fields on 25 May 1809. (Mr Manning had taken a house nearby to fulfil his parliamentary duties.) A little later there were pony rides in the park with the Bishop of Lincoln.[26] What more could a father do?

Human relations were delegated to Mrs Manning, who would, indeed, have had to be quite other than human not to have doted on her youngest child, with his wide-set eyes and curling blonde locks, especially as he so resembled his mother. 'She loved me too much as the youngest,' remembered the Cardinal, who regretted that 'our talk was not on topics of education'.[27] Mrs Manning begins to appear as far the most sympathetic member of the family. Oscar Browning, whose grandfather lived in Totteridge, remembered hearing that she had been 'very beautiful, and beautifully dressed, and a leader of society'.[28] She was a voracious reader ('but not of the higher subjects', lamented the Cardinal); loved gardening and making the house look pretty; and even took delight in making little shoes for her child,[29] a rare amusement for a woman in her position. The same kind of marginally eccentric practicality is evident in a story that she had sheets spread over a field at Copped Hall in order to decide upon the best position for a lake.[30]

For all that, her views on upbringing were rigidly Evangelical. She never allowed her son to forget his duty towards the poor. 'All the time I had a sense of the interval between my family and the household, and between that and the poor of the village,' Manning recalled in his old age.[31] Mrs Manning also insisted upon absolute truthfulness. 'I remember that one day I came in from the farmyard, and my mother asked me if I had seen the peacock. I said yes, and the nurse said no, and my mother made me kneel down and beg God to forgive me for not speaking the truth.' Another incident also struck deep. 'A cousin of mine, about two years older, when I was about four, told me that God had a book in which he wrote down everything we did wrong. This so terrified me for days that I remember being found by my mother sitting under a kind of writing-table in great fear. I never forgot this at any time in my life, and it has been a great grace to me, and kept me from the greatest dangers.'[32] Manning's mind rarely prognosticated any dangers less than the greatest, either in this world or the next. Total ruin, utter chaos, deepest iniquity, eternal damnation – such extremes of horror constantly recur in his thinking; eventually they were to demand no less absolute an antidote. Meanwhile, when he was eight, his mother gave him a New Testament. It did not take him long to discover his favourite passage. 'I remember that I devoured the Apocalypse, and I never through all my life forgot "the lake that burneth with fire and brimstone".'[33]

Here on earth, however, the Mannings appeared to be singularly blessed. Since the turn of the century American competition had been making the sugar trade steadily more difficult, but in 1812 the outbreak of war with the United States, involving the limited number of American ships in fighting rather than trade, temporarily restored the English monopoly and doubled the price of sugar.[34] It was probably the profits that resulted during 1813 and 1814 which caused William Manning to sell Copped Hall and remove in 1815 to an estate called Combe Bank in Sundridge, near Sevenoaks in Kent. The following year Christopher Wordsworth, younger brother of the poet, was installed as Rector of Sundridge, an appointment which, William Manning gallantly opined, much enhanced the value of his property.[35] The youngest Manning son profited from his early acquaintance with the extraordinarily talented Wordsworth boys, Charles and Christopher, who were destined to end as bishops respectively of St Andrews and Lincoln. Manning used to enjoy recounting how the three of them once stole some grapes: 'probably the only case on record where three future Bishops were guilty of larceny'. Even the young Manning's rogueries were committed in the very best company. 'I frankly admit I was mischievous,'[36] the Cardinal recalled.

Soon after the move to Combe Bank he was sent away to a school in Streatham, where, as the Cardinal noted, the moral tone had unfortunately been lowered by a bad (not mischievous) boy who had left a train of immorality behind him.[37] After less than two years Manning was invalided home, probably on account of the asthma which continued to plague him until he took the cure of Rome. A year's convalescence followed, and then he returned to Totteridge, to a school run by a stern disciplinarian called the Revd Abel Lendon. 'I will not say that he was harsh, but he was austere and we were afraid of him, with a wholesome fear.' Here, happily, 'the friendships were good, and had a higher tone'.[38] While at this school Manning was confirmed by the Bishop of Lincoln, he of the pony rides in the park. 'I remember that he recognised me and shook hands with me there and then, his kindness overcoming his dignity.'[39] Bishop Pelham, in fact, was the very type of the time-serving, place-seeking, nepotistic Hanoverian bishop.[40] In 1827 he was to confirm William Gladstone at Eton, an experience which he did not survive by many days.[41] The schoolboy Manning, however, did not take religion nearly as seriously as the future Prime Minister.

At the Totteridge school Manning mounted his first assaults on the classics, beginning in the process to develop the iron self-discipline on which his subsequent achievements would be built. Progress in Latin was not initially encouraging, but in the holidays it was possible to rectify matters. 'I got up every morning at five, or before, and lighted my fire, and made my breakfast, and read till eight o'clock, then got my pony and rode to the curate of Sundridge, the priest of Combe Bank, and read with him both Latin and Greek. It made me like getting up in the dark for the rest of my life; and it was the beginning of self-education.'[42]

And so, in 1822, to Harrow. The choice of such a school, whither his brother Charles had preceded him (although he failed to last the course), represents a break with the Evangelical pattern of Manning's youth. Even by their own high standards of barbarism this was an age of spectacular savagery in English public schools. The headmaster of Eton, Dr Keate, once flogged eighty boys in a single day, and received an admiring cheer from the whole school for *his* pains.[43] Extra-curricular activities at Eton evoked similar enthusiasms: in 1825 the future Earl of Shaftesbury's brother was pummelled to death in a fist fight while the rest of the scholars egged on the two brandy-sodden combatants.[44] For a time it seemed that the English ruling classes could not take the pace, and William Wilberforce's example helped set the fashion, reinforced by the post-war economic depression, of educating children privately. Harrow was quite up to the mark for brutality, with its own speciality of pitched battles with the local townsfolk. Numbers in the school halved from 295 in 1816 to only 128 in 1828.[45] But William Manning was not deterred.

The headmaster of Harrow, the Revd George Butler, was accounted a civilizing influence, having introduced science into the curriculum. He was certainly remarkably versatile, a Senior Wrangler at Cambridge, fluent in French, German and Italian, a fine draughtsman, an athletic god. These talents, however, had not prevented a difficult start at Harrow. Lord Byron, then (1805) a senior boy in the school, had taken a sharp dislike to him, to the extent of laying a train of gunpowder in the passages through which the headmaster was to pass.[46] By the time Manning arrived at Harrow seventeen years later Butler was an institution and Byron a living legend. When, in 1824, Byron became a dead legend (or so it seemed) the headmaster addressed the school on the abuse of great natural gifts. It is doubtful if the Harrow boys were much impressed. Manning was self-confessedly under Byron's spell. As for Dr Butler, 'I only remember one thing he said, but it did me good, that when we were laughed at for religion's sake, angels were rejoicing over us.'[47] It was a sentiment destined to take deeper root in him than the whole of *Childe Harold* and *Don Juan*.

Manning survived Harrow well enough; not for him the depths of misery endured at that time by the unkempt, badly dressed and obviously poor day-boy Anthony Trollope. George Richmond, the painter, who was not in the school, went so far as to say that Manning was 'a buck of the first water', who sported, among other adornments, Hessian top-boots with tassels, 'rather an extreme piece of foppery in a Harrow boy'.[48] Among the Mannings this footwear became something of a family joke, symbolizing Mrs Manning's passionate adoration of her favourite child, who was already, under this treatment, beginning to develop an alarmingly assertive character. 'The mistake his mother made was to give Henry those Hessian boots,' recalled an elder relation.[49] Dean Merivale, a contemporary at Harrow, remembered him as a 'handsome, well-mannered, but mightily affected boy, giving himself airs of fashion and patronage, but generally agreeable and even fascinating'.[50] Another contemporary, Bishop Oxendèn, recounted that Manning was 'steady and well-conducted', though 'he did not then appear to be a boy of unusual promise'.[51] Always, in the case of those who obtain reputation in later life, there are former schoolfellows pushing forward to explain how very ordinary (beside themselves) the object of admiration appeared in youth. Manning's Harrow career gave plenty of opportunity to such people. Yet the standard of distinction in classics was alarmingly high. Merivale succeeded in committing to memory the *Eclogues* and *Georgics* of Virgil, Catullus, Juvenal, and almost the whole of Lucan.[52] Charles Wordsworth, the boy from Sundridge who was now the star of Harrow, could learn a hundred and twenty Latin lines in an evening.[53] Even so, it *is* strange, in the light of later events, that Manning did not make more mark at Harrow. Were those five o'clock risings to no avail? A portrait of the time reproduced in Shane Leslie's biography displays no lack of confidence. The tilt of the head, the level gaze, the supercilious smile, even (could it be?) the paunch, all betoken a proper sense of self-satisfaction, if not more. He was, however, quite aware of his academic shortcomings, attributing them in the first place to the use of a different Greek grammar at his previous school, and then (rather more convincingly) to the absence of any intellectual stimulation or encouragement in his home life. 'My danger was always doing things too easily.'[54]

On the other hand, he was good at games, which counts for quite as much as scholarship in schoolboy lore. No one, according to Harrow tradition, ever directed a more accurate stone in the direction of the unhappy townsfolk. (A more fitting version of the future Cardinal's early ventures into community relations has him organizing a collection for an apple-woman whose barrow had been overturned – but by whom? – in the mud.)[55] The stone-throwing talent found a more acceptable outlet on the cricket ground. The Cardinal apparently believed that he had been captain of the Harrow team,[56] but this seems highly unlikely with Charles Wordsworth, five years in the XI, a near contemporary. Manning played for the school in 1825, a year in which Harrow were comprehensively beaten by both Eton and Winchester. Against Eton, batting No. 9, he was bowled 0 in the first innings; bowled Pickering 1 in the second. He does not appear among the wicket takers. Against Winchester his scores were 6 and 0.[57] In after years the Cardinal's cricketing reminiscences became an occupational hazard for the priests in Archbishop's House,[58] and it seems that his performances, like those of Lord Byron, did not suffer anything in the telling. At Harrow,

Manning knew the score. When Charles Wordsworth presented him with a
cricket bat, Manning, in writing a doggerel verse of thanks (fourteen stanzas
of it!), concentrated on modesty:

> The bat that you were kind enough to send
> Seems (for as yet I have not tried it) good;
> And if there's anything on earth can mend
> My wretched play, it is that piece of wood.

It was really remarkable, Wordsworth thought, that he should have
preserved this verse, for there had been no reason at all to suppose that the
writer would rise to distinction, let alone *eminence*.[59]

Two noteworthy features of Harrow in Manning's time, which may or may
not have been related, were the almost total absence of religious instruction
or observance, and the remarkable output of ecclesiastics. Dean Merivale
remembered an inter-house match around 1823 in which, besides himself,
two future archbishops (Trench of Dublin, and Manning) and three future
bishops (Wordsworth, Oxenden and Terry) all played.[60] Two boys who
followed Manning in the school, Faber and Coffin, were also destined to
become prominent Catholic converts. And Lord Shaftesbury, no ecclesiastic but perhaps the greatest Christian of all, had been at Harrow only a few
years before him. For a school which did not even possess a chapel of its
own,[61] it was an astonishing record, one that might give the devotees of
institutional Christianity pause for thought. There does not even seem to
have been any very rigorous enforcement of attendance at Harrow parish
church; a few years after Manning left, Frederick Faber was said to be the
only boy at Sunday communion.[62] Up to 1825 the school had attended the
church on saints' days, but the Revd George Butler put a stop to this
dangerously popish practice. Manning looked back on his schooldays as 'my
greatest danger', 'the least religious time of my life'.[63] But for the lake that
burneth with fire and brimstone, and the prayers which his mother had
taught him, he would, he later considered, have been lost. 'God held me by
His will against my will. If I had fallen I might have run the full career of
evil.'[64] No half-way house for this sinner.

Like many a younger son, Manning had been earmarked from birth for
the Church. In childhood his brothers and sisters had dubbed him 'the
parson', a drollery from which he apparently derived little amusement. The
same nickname reappeared at Harrow, along with 'the general',[65] which
suggests that his schoolfellows had spotted a love of command. They did not
require any special penetration. 'You know that my motto is *Aut Caesar,
Aut Nullus*,'[66] Manning is supposed to have told his friends in explanation of
his silence at the dinner-table of John Cunningham, the Evangelical vicar of

Harrow. Perhaps he was right to be wary of Cunningham, whom Mrs Trollope considered a toadying hypocrite, though Faber fell under his spell.[67] The interesting point of this anecdote, however, is that Nullus, hitherto so well adapted to his role, was entertaining the possibility of becoming Caesar.

Manning's brother-in-law John Anderdon, husband of Anna Maria and business partner of William Manning, played a large part in this development. Perhaps it had been Anderdon's idea that Manning should go to Harrow; he had been in the school himself and was now a sufficiently fanatical old boy to pay for a cricket professional from Lords to coach the XI, albeit with no discernible effect except possibly the selection, and even conceivably the captaincy, of Manning. In any case, Anderdon was the first man of consequence to discern potential in the boy, whom he determined to take in hand. Here was the intellectual mentor whom Manning required. It was not that the older man taught him to believe in himself – Manning was probably never prone to self-doubt – but Anderdon did widen the boy's concept of what he might achieve by determination and will-power. In a teenager expectation and achievement are closely related, and Anderdon made sure that expectation was high. 'Time waxeth on, melteth like wax,' he warned in 1826, 'and I want to see you take your first class degree at Oxford.'[68] At that time there was no warrant for such an ambition; the idea would have appeared laughable to Manning's Harrow contemporaries. It did not, however, appear laughable to Manning.

Had Anderdon merely inspired pipe-dreams he would have been a disastrous influence. In fact, he was a stern realist, who never spared Manning's self-esteem in continuously emphasizing the need for more intensive and concentrated effort. However good-humoured the letters that flowed between them might be in form, they were always serious in content and purpose. Anderdon was a natural pedagogue, ready with advice and information on every subject under the sun, to the point of stuffiness and way beyond. But his pupil, though eager to learn, was never cowed: if Anderdon became tedious or pompous, Manning was always ready with chastising banter. 'You talk of severer studies,' he wrote after one lecture, '. . . my leisure hours at Oxford will not be thrown away, you old Zeno; go to a nunnery, go!'[69]

Perhaps the greatest intellectual service which Anderdon rendered was to teach a proper command of English. Himself the author of a life of Bishop Ken, who was the model of his own High (but not dry) Church views, he extolled the virtues of economy and accuracy in style. Sometimes Manning's letters were returned with corrections, inflated passages cut down to size, superfluous matter erased, choice of words rejected. 'Even your hasty notes must be *in order*; it is a mere habit – a knack! Your Johnson.'[70] It was a hard treatment, but Manning had the good temper and the talent to profit. Gradually his cumbrous schoolboy facetiousness was honed down to sharp pointed phrases, and he became endowed with exceptional verbal facility. Manning would never be capable of imaginative flights, nor in general was his thinking troubled by those counter-currents that draw the mind away from certainty into subtlety, irony and qualification. He liked to be on firm ground and to tread hard upon it. Later in life his arguments would be summarily marched across the page in well-drilled and often numbered squads; the effect could be daunting rather than convincing. But Anderdon was not to blame for that. He taught Manning to express himself with precision, clarity and speed without any loss of natural verve.

In 1826, however, Manning's powers still had not developed sufficiently to inspire him with any serious misgivings about the preordained family plan that he should enter the Church. This arrangement meant that, unlike his brothers, he was bound for Oxford. 'That I should enter Oxford at Whitsuntide or October is not very material,' he told Anderdon, 'as I cannot take Orders till twenty-three, and therefore have upwards of four years before me.'[71] There was time to make up some of the ground that had been lost at Harrow. Manning, already very much the master of his own fate, urged the necessity of a crammer to put him on a level with the best of his contemporaries. His father suggested a Mr. Wright who took pupils in Northamptonshire, but that was not at all what Manning had in mind. 'I should consider the six months lost, were they to be spent with a houseful of pupils, with any tutor. Harrow would be far preferable'.[72] The indulgent Mr Manning complied with his son's wishes: the boy was sent as sole pupil to Canon Fisher at Poulshot, near Devizes. The Canon was the miracle-worker of his age: Lord Shaftesbury had gone to him hardly able to construe Xenophon, yet even that unpromising material had been crammed up into a First Class.

Manning duly profited. 1827 was the year 'I ceased to vegetate'. 'I began to know both Latin and Greek more critically. I gained the method of study and self-education which, dunce as I am, I have never left off.'[73] Although Canon Fisher's programme of studies was rigorous, Manning would still sit up into the small hours firing off verses, quips and quiddities to his brother-in-law. Anderdon experienced the greatest difficulty in stopping the flow of Manning's poetry. 'You are to be a reasoner, whether Parson, Lawyer or Senator, not a poet,' he pleaded. 'Why Law?' responded Manning. 'Your Honour, I never thought of no such thing, but "doing as you tells I so" – why, I will be if I can.'[74] The political ambition, be it noted, was not denied. He was swiftly gaining a sense of all things being possible.

Anderdon's fussing became increasingly irritating. 'I collect from your hurried, worried and disjointed sentences that you suppose my French and Italian would prevent some of my other reading. In case you should think that I waste my time here on what you compliment by calling poetry and in writing jargon to you, I can only say that for five months I have rarely had more than six hours' sleep a night. How to squander the remaining eighteen hours I know not. But perhaps you may inform me.'[75] At other times Manning had ideas that would have finished off a less dedicated mentor. 'I have a proposal to make. Let your part be to write me a paper on whatever first occurs to you, of which I am uninformed (a large field, i' faith). Let yours be a series of *Noctes Urbanae*, mine *Noctes Rusticae*. I shall give you my opinions upon languages and my reasons for wishing to attack French and Italian.[76] But let them be papers, not letters.' Poor Anderdon. And then Manning would switch back into defensive banter that made a mockery of their joint endeavours: 'I trust to be able to take a second class at Oxford, which, if well done, confers much greater honour than fifty middling *firsts*.'[77]

Anderdon stuck to the task. In September 1827, with Manning about to go up to Oxford, he brought his heavy armament into play. This was a collection of essays by John Foster entitled *Decision of Character*, a work which might have been written to describe the qualities which Anderdon was instilling into his protégé. Foster himself had been conspicuously lacking in the decisiveness which he extolled; a Baptist minister, he was rumoured to entertain serious doubts about baptism. He had been a minister in Dublin, where, he admitted, 'the congregation had been small when I commenced, and almost nothing when I voluntarily closed'.[78] Yet Foster's purpose was to explain not so much how decisiveness may be acquired, as how it proceeds in action, and with what profit to its practitioners. The virtues he admired were those of the will: courage, single-mindedness, commitment, persistence. 'It is a poor and disgraceful thing', he begins, 'not to be able to reply, with some degree of certainty, to the simple questions, What will you be? What will you do?' An effective character will not only make up his mind speedily on such points; he will bend every effort to put his conclusion into practice. In Foster's pages, however, the type often appears like a nineteenth-century anticipation of Stephen Potter's one-upmanship. 'In consultation his manner will indicate that when he is equally with the rest in possession of the circumstances of the case, he does not at all expect to hear any opinions that shall correct his own. . . . This difference will be apparent between him and his associates, that *their* manner of receiving *his* opinions is that of agreement or dissent; *his* manner of receiving *theirs* is judicial – that of sanction or rejection.' Foster admits that such a character, whose natural style will be 'high-toned, laconic, and careless of pleasing', may not be entirely popular. He seemed puzzled, however, that the exemplars of decisiveness whom he selected from history did not generally exhibit any outstanding goodness. This defect he attributed to the faults in his own memory. For while it is evident that the decisive character without humanity or principle will be a dangerous misanthrope, Foster insists that 'if he be of great humanity and principle, he may become one of the noblest of mankind'.[79]

Manning expressed enthusiasm for this work. Even before reading it he had concluded in 1826: 'I am not *undecided* or *irresolute*.'[80] Three years later he told Anderdon, 'Foster's essays have been a real comfort to me lately, yet do not think that I read them for the first time . . . I am afraid (no, not *afraid* – pardon the parenthesis) I am throwing for high stakes, and giving my adversary odds; but a letter of Foster's generally inspirits me, especially as a friend of mine some time ago, when asked, held me up as a decided character. My only corollary is, "Do it!" I'll get up, or die in the breach; so there we'll leave it.'[81]

The worship of the will might be reckoned to consort ill with Oxford at any epoch, and more especially with the institution that Manning entered in October 1827. The university was only just beginning to shake off its eighteenth-century torpor, and if it clung to its role as the bastion of Anglicanism, this was because any other justification for its existence would have been hard to come by. Dissenters and Roman Catholics were excluded by the necessity of subscribing to the Thirty-Nine Articles and of receiving communion in the college chapel at least once a term. The undergraduates were taught and governed entirely by Anglican clergymen. Fellows of colleges had to be not merely in Orders, but celibate; when they wanted to marry, they were put out to grass in a college living. There was no requirement that they should live in Oxford, nor that they should be qualified for the instruction of youth. The appointment of fellows, as Mark Pattison, who became Rector of Lincoln in harsher times, explained, was 'done under conditions which left no place for any qualification of learning, even if learning had existed at all at the university'.[82]

Some tentative efforts at reform had been made. In 1800 a proper examining board was established and it became possible to take an Honours degree in which candidates were graded in bands of merit, though few undergraduates at first shared Manning's eagerness to avail themselves of this privilege, and no subjects were on offer save the classics and mathematics. At Oriel, however, where, exceptionally, open fellowships had always been available, strenuous efforts were made to appoint fellows of talent, instead of hard readers or privileged numbskulls. This policy was revolutionary enough to secure the college for a time the leading place in the university and, incidentally, to save the career of John Henry Newman. Manning's college Balliol was also in the vanguard of reform. In 1828 it followed Oriel in throwing open its scholarship exam to general competition, the original cause of an intellectual pre-eminence that has never since been lost. Manning kept good memories of his Balliol tutors; all the same, when the pressure of Schools began to tell he went to his boyhood friend Charles Wordsworth at Christ Church for private tuition. As an added bonus, in Wordsworth's rooms he encountered William Gladstone, another young man from a rich commercial background.[83]

Manning did not devote himself entirely to study at Oxford. A friend called him 'the idlest hard-reading man and the hardest-reading idle man'[84] that he had ever known. It was true. His early hours and disciplined habits left him with time for leisure. He was no ascetic. While still at Harrow he had launched a campaign to persuade his father that he could scarcely live in a fitting style at Oxford on less than £350 p.a. This sum was about five times that on which many curates were required to keep their families, and about ten times that on which some Roman Catholic priests survived. But what could be done? 'I spoke to Poulshot (a Balliol man) today. . . . He said that living as close as he could, having no pursuit, no hobby, no *book-collecting*, he lived at about £260 a year.' Mr Manning, however, was distressingly slow on the uptake, and Anderdon's good offices were required. 'You will do me *a kindness* to mention this subject to my father,' the schoolboy urged. 'He will require the most succinct explanation on every point since he has no idea, not the most remote conception, of Oxford affairs.'[85]

The worldly-wise Harrovian duly prevailed over the ignorant financier. Manning's leisure pursuits at Oxford, however, fell considerably short of wild abandon. He rode, played cricket, became an oarsman, even boxed. This last activity, he reflected, 'will make one careful of picking a quarrel with a small cad, who might be more than a match for our skill'.[86] Such caution was warranted; Manning was acknowledged to be one of the handsomest men of his day. On his Balliol contemporaries, however, he left little impression. The Revd E. B. Wickham, who had lived on the same staircase, remembered him as 'very quiet and well-conducted'.[87] It is difficult to imagine how he got through his £350 a year, though a penchant for pink silk riding breeches must have helped. Neither the high jinks of the bloods nor the high thinking of the student philosophers ever deflected him from his allotted task of securing a First. He made no close friends in Balliol; indeed, friendship for its own sake, as something to be enjoyed quite innocently of any cause or reputation, never held much appeal. His sister Harriet, the nearest to him in age and so religious that he called her a Methodist, had been his closest companion, and she died in 1826. Manning arrived home from Harrow just as she drew her last breath. 'Her death was a great loss to me and left me alone; the others being so much older as to be no companions to me.'[88] It would not have occurred to him that a replacement might be found from outside the family circle. Intimacy implies a dropping of the guard. It is born of self-abandon not self-control, confesses weakness, acknowledges vulnerability. It is not at all the kind of relation that the decisive character will seek.

Sir Francis Doyle, in his *Reminiscences*, told an anecdote which, though it may be apocryphal, shows how Manning's Oxford contemporaries regarded him. Gladstone, in a speech at the Union, had referred to the duty on barilla. What could that be, someone asked Manning. 'Dear me,' responded the Balliol sage, 'not know what barilla means? I will explain it to you at once. You see in commerce there are two methods of proceeding. At one time you load your ship with a particular commodity, such as tea, wine or tobacco, at other times you select a variety of articles suitable to the port of destination. And in the language of trade we denominate this latter operation barilla.' Manning's questioner went away fully satisfied with this explanation, and it was a week before he discovered that 'barilla' is a kind of seaweed burnt in the manufacture of soda, soap and glass.[89]

Whether this story shows Manning as a humorist or a con-man, there is no question but that he impressed some people. 'Manning is very unassuming and perhaps the best informed man in Oxford,' enthused James Milnes Gaskell, who considered him 'with the exception of [Sidney] Herbert . . . more deservedly popular than anyone I know'.[90] This observation does not really conflict with what has been said about Manning and friendship. Gaskell was much involved with the recently founded Union debating society, and it was in that context, rather than a purely social one, that he made his judgement. In the Union, among the luminaries of Christ Church and Oriel – Gladstone, Samuel and Henry Wilberforce, Acland, Hope, Charles Wordsworth – the anonymous Balliol man took on quite another personality. Manning took no part in Union debates until March 1829, half-way through his Oxford career, but when he did begin to speak it was immediately evident that he had found his element. He became renowned for his ability to discourse extemporarily and impressively on any subject, regardless of ignorance. He never missed an opportunity to speak and, once launched into his theme, there was no telling when the flow of well-turned phrases might end. When someone suggested cutting down on the number of American newspapers at the Union, Manning jumped up and improvised an hour's oration on the necessity of maintaining the closest possible links with the brave New World.[91] His most celebrated feat was in a debate between the Oxford and the Cambridge Unions. The Cambridge men

(Monckton Milnes, Sunderland, Arthur Hallam) arrived in Oxford to urge the then highly unorthodox view that Shelley, who had been expelled from Oxford, was a greater poet than Byron, who had not cared to conclude his Cambridge studies. In contesting his motion the Oxford orators were rather handicapped by their total ignorance of Shelley. When, therefore, the Cambridge case had been put with a force and eloquence hitherto unknown on the banks of the Isis, there was a prolonged and awkward pause. 'We cowered like birds, and ran like sheep.'[92] Even Gladstone did not feel constrained to speak.

It was Manning who stepped into the breach. His effort was perhaps more remarkable for courage than for literary criticism. Byron is a great poet, he asserted; we have all read Byron. If Shelley had been a great poet we should have read him too, but we have not done so. *Ergo*, Shelley is not a great poet; *a fortiori*, he is not so great a poet as Byron.[93] This argument, one might think, would have required not a little natural authority in the presentation to pass muster. Yet Manning's tall spare form already radiated command; he carried the day with the Oxford audience. Byron's ascendancy was maintained by 78 to 45 votes. And Oxford men began to read Shelley.

Manning's performances in the Union were the first real successes of his life. Encountering there the most formidable of his Oxford contemporaries, he proved himself not only their equal but their master. He had joined the Union when Wilberforce's son Samuel had been the dominant figure; he left it as Gladstone's star was beginning to rise. Between these two Manning was the unrivalled leader in debate. The experience was intoxicating. He began to forget his career in the church, and became caught up in political ambitions. 'The thought of being a clergyman had . . . utterly passed from me.'[94] He took to reading Adam Smith, Burke and Bolingbroke as a preparation for future responsibilities. His dreams, though, were of power and triumph rather than of political economy. He began to pay regular visits to the House of Commons. In his imagination he would take up some great cause and alone subdue the opposition of the House by sheer force of will and advocacy.[95] And who knows how different the Victorian age might have been if Gladstone had stuck to his original ambition of becoming a clergyman and Manning had achieved a seat in parliament? The two men came from similar mercantile backgrounds. At Oxford they were both Tories, though Manning was far in advance of Gladstone in showing his independence. He supported Huskisson's free trade policies that so alarmed the die-hards. Though reprobating democracy, he was prepared to countenance some measure of parliamentary reform, which the young Gladstone regarded with horror. Radicalism did not, however, stretch quite as far as supporting Roman Catholic emancipation, which he considered (quite correctly) would undermine the position of the Church of England. Nor could he altogether concur with a motion that 'the present state of Slavery in our Colonies is one of injustice and crime, and (however distant the period of final emancipation may be) more immediate measures ought to be taken for its abolition than have yet been proposed to the country'.[96] Manning agreed with the second part of this proposition, but as a son of William Manning he could hardly subscribe to the first.

The firm of Manning and Anderdon, unfortunately, had fallen on evil days since the flourish of profits in 1813–14. On the return of peace the French and the Americans came back into the sugar trade with a vengeance, while, to make matters worse, new sources of supply were being exploited in the East. The result was a glut on the market and tumbling prices: Peel's tight monetary policies were no help. According to another West India merchant, Manning and Anderdon compounded their difficulties by not adequately supervising their estates.[97] By 1829 it was clear that the family business was on the brink of collapse. When Manning came of age in that year his father gave him £700 in Consols with a clear warning: 'I cannot at present do more for you, as your uniform good conduct has entitled you. Your future success in life must depend entirely upon your own exertions.'[98]

The threat of financial insecurity ahead redoubled Manning's determination to achieve First Class honours. Elected President of the Union in November 1829, he declined the office as likely to interfere with his preparation for Schools. His hard-pressed father was persuaded to stump up further funds for extra tuition. At first the effort to cram seemed hopeless;[99] a few days before the exam, however, a mood of extraordinary buoyancy came over him. Assuredly there would be no danger of his suffering the kind of collapse that Newman had experienced in the Schools nine years before, when, the best hope for a Double First that Trinity has ever produced, he failed completely in mathematics and achieved only a pass 'under the line' in classics. Manning, by contrast, approached the ordeal as John Foster might have ordained. 'I do not expect so much as to falter in Schools; this is a moral, not an intellectual, principle. I have seen many men pleading ill-health, or nervelessness, or such like pretexts. I will none of them. To say so and to do so is equally an act of volition. No false estimate shall be made of me. If I fail, I will fail in Livy, not in steadiness of principle.'[100] He did not fail in Livy. There were six First Classes in the list that Michaelmas term, and Manning was among them.

What next? Ideally there would be a month or so resting on hard-earned laurels; some suitable employment – a private secretaryship, perhaps – on the fringes of public life; and then that effortless passage into the House of Commons that a young man of means and proven talent might expect.

The problem was that the means were now much reduced, as his father had made clear in 1829. But Manning would not acknowledge the need for any change of course: his ambitions had taken too deep a root to be easily plucked up. The political economy studies continued. Now, though, reality asserted itself in unmistakable terms. Early in 1831 the firm of Manning and Anderdon finally collapsed. Manning remembered going with his father to the Guildhall, and watching him, the former Governor of the Bank and lord of commerce, symbolically lay down his watch and seals as tokens of his last possessions. 'I have belonged to that class of men with whom bankruptcy was synonymous with death,'[101] the old man murmured pathetically. Fortunately that class of men – the very rich – are rarely entirely ruined. Friends bought out his life interest in Mrs Manning's marriage settlement and provided him with an income. Mrs Manning retained some resources of her own. The bankrupt man retired to a house in Gower Street, which many might consider a fate rather better than death. Mr Manning, however, was a broken man. 'My reputation, Iago, my reputation. I have lost the immortal part of myself, and what remains is bestial.' He died in 1835, and was buried at Combe Bank, the estate which in life had been torn away from him.

Manning had attended his father's disgrace in the Guildhall, but he still failed, or rather wilfully refused, to understand its significance for his own future. A parliamentary career was now out of the question. No-one was at hand to support the proud and lonely Manning, as Lord Lincoln found rich young Mr Gladstone a seat the year after he came down from Oxford. Manning's father, Anderdon and brother Frederick combined to urge on him the necessity of trimming his sails to the unfavourable winds. He must renounce all political ambition. Preferably he should enter the Church, a point on which brother Frederick was particularly emphatic. Or, since Manning objected to that course, let him forthwith find some employment that might give him a proper start in life. Anderdon, notwithstanding the collapse of the business, was able to offer a clerkship at £80 a year.[102] The days of the pink silk riding breeches were well and truly gone.

Manning would have none of his relations, neither of their jobs nor of their counsel. Did not the philosophy that Anderdon had taught him proclaim that a man must make his own circumstances, must bend reality to his will? Yet now here was that same Anderdon prosing on about the necessity of serving an apprenticeship in the world – sound and sensible claptrap for ordinary insects. 'I thank you for your advocacy, not omitting to estimate "your convictions",' Manning wrote to him in bitter exasperation. 'Supposing I was to begin twaddling about convictions – not another word.'[103] This high-handed rejection of Anderdon's platitudes is understandable enough in a youth who had grown conscious of exceptional abilities and who now felt all his hopes slipping away. This was the critical moment. He knew that the only training for a statesman was to enter parliament, so why this waffle about qualifications? To corner himself in some derisory employment would be to abandon his star. Rather than that, he would be prepared to gamble, to live on such slender capital as remained to him, and seek the miraculous chance.

If my family, I will not say my father, from a knowledge of his character, will lend their aid to my endeavours; in asking which I only ask what a man unintroduced in life may expect; I shall cheerfully abide by the result. I ask no sacrifice from any individual member of the stock. I only wish a cordial sanction; and a sincerely exerted influence among those they are capable to incline in my behalf. But if in the place of sanction, I meet disapprobation, if when I ask for encouragement I am hindered by opposition, I may be excused from abstaining to solicit their opinion with their assistance; and from considering such conduct a liberation from consulting further with them on all matters individually my own.[104]

There was no doubting the temper of Manning's steel. Anderdon switched his attack: 'You have no idea of your deficiency in writing English.' But the protégé now knew better. 'I have been paying considerable attention to English composition, and think I am improving.'[105]

Desperately he cast around for expedients. A fellowship at Merton, Oxford, would help him to gain the time that he required. Manning forced himself to go through the humiliating process of seeking testimonials, although, he defiantly asserted, 'I had rather forgo a Fellowship than solicit a favour thus purely gratuitous.' But the fellowship was a wild hope for a layman to indulge. 'The Warden of Merton . . . asked whether I had decided upon a profession. I said I had decided negatively against the Church.'[106] That was admirably honest and honourable because policy demanded, if not a positive commitment to take Orders, at least a degree of prevarication about his intentions. No Orders, no fellowship; and so it proved. Even while he was rejecting a clerical vocation Manning showed that he did not consider it something to be trifled with.

Some Oxford contacts applied on his behalf to Lord Goderich, the Colonial Secretary, and managed to get him a supernumerary clerkship in the Colonial Office. It did not amount to much. He was to attend when specifically required, not otherwise. The work, when there was any, bored him to distraction. And he was beginning to discover the ways of the world which had allured him so much. 'I am glad to hear that your brother writes a good hand,' observed Lady Stanhope to his sister Caroline apropos the new employment. 'Yes, and knows a little arithmetic,' Caroline had sweetly replied.[107] Was it really only a few months since Manning had achieved his

First? To make his plight worse, he found, or so Charles Wordsworth would remember in old age, that his attentions to a Miss Defell were rejected on grounds of his negligible prospects.[108] It is mere conjecture, but conceivably matrimony had occurred to him as a way out of his impasse. Miss Defell lived in Grosvenor Street.

Manning spent many days in that early summer of 1831 mooning about the still unsold Combe Bank, where he fished and poeticized and 'dabbled to an infinitesimal shallow degree in multitudinous books on manifold topics'.[109] The beauty of the place, now that it was to be taken away from him, seemed overwhelming. In other circumstances and to other men such a means of passing a summer might have seemed idyllic, but Manning was eaten up by frustration at his lot. 'I am very cynical and resolute,' he wrote to Anderdon, 'without which virtues never could I outlive my present routine of nonentitous existence. . . . Faith, I have an half mind to inflict certain scourges of thy cuticle, to the end of expelling somnolency. . . . Six months of this rustic vegetation, and my cerebellum would put forth mustard and cress. If I abide here much longer *je deviendrai bientôt fou.*'[110] But what was the alternative? Lectures from Anderdon in Upper Harley Street; lectures from Frederick in Wyndham Place: Manning tried both and fled both alike. It was preferable, he concluded, to expend £2 a week on rooms in Mount Street. He would live in style, even *in extremis*.

From this new abode he continued the epistolary persecution of Anderdon. Insults rained upon his mentor without any consideration that he was addressing a man who had recently been ruined. Manning's ego-centricity was unrelenting. Yet there was a Byronic dash as well as a Byronic spleen in his prose:

I have not a single particle of application. How long I may remain so, I dare not contemplate, but of this I am assured, that my present services are not worth the minutest fraction of the national coin. I am splenetic, sick, savage, sour, rabid, indolent, useless, and ill at ease. I want to be anywhere but where I am, do anything but what I do, see anybody but whom I see, hear anything but what I hear, recollect anything but what I recollect, hope anything but what I hope, feel anything but what I feel, know anything but what I know, care for anybody but whom I care for (there you go); in fine, be anything, body, monster, beast or creature, but what I am. If for this you think me discontented, you will at least acquit me of self-love . . . I can do nothing under heaven but rail, rail, rail. Now for a *requiem*. My watch says it is half-past three, but I would not believe it on its oath. All things are false, whether made of body and soul, or cog-wheels and claptraps. Deceitful, proud, and desperately wicked.

Why look ye now, there's philosophy, *vitae Magistra, doctrinarum excultrix, artium indagatrix*, with as many superincumbent polysyllables of collaudation as His Imperial Mightiness of Ava, Siam, and Regia. When all is snug and warm and comfortable, she's the trustiest friend, companion, counsellor, comforter, and protector; but when matters take an angry aspect – whiff, she's off with her tail in the air, like a rumbustious cow in sultry weather.

Timon will to the woods.[111]

As with Timon, nothing stimulated contempt for the world so effectively as the world's contempt. Manning had refused to enter the Church of England because he had been conscious of no vocation strong enough to counter his political ambitions. But where had these ambitions led but to indolence and frustration? Conscious now of great abilities running to seed, Manning began to look back on what he had rejected. To someone of his temperament, instinctively attracted to power and influence, this thwarting of profane desires was a necessary preliminary to the acceptance of a religious vocation. To that extent it is permissible to speculate that if he had had some break in 1831 – a rich wife, a political patron, some support from the family – he would never have entered the Church.

Yet the connection between the blighting of Manning's political hopes and his call to Orders should not be made too slickly. It is not as though the sole alternative to being a politician was to become a clergyman. Mr Manning, despite his bankruptcy, must have had many City contacts who might have smoothed his son's path into commerce; and there was always Anderdon's old idea of the Law. Mrs Manning was still giving her youngest son an allowance of £100 p.a.[112] It is difficult to believe that, notwithstanding the odds stacked against him, a man of Manning's talents and character would have remained for ever obscure in secular employment. Consider the obstacles which Disraeli overcame.

The vital difference, though, was that Disraeli's entire being was penetrated with an inextinguishable belief in the romance and excitement of power. Manning danced to the same tune, but in his nature there was also an insistent, spiky counterpoint, discernible even before he encountered any serious setback:

Ambition and Avarice [he wrote while still at Oxford] differ only in the selection of means. The former is as unmixedly selfish as the latter, and in the generality of instances incalculably more pernicious and destructive to others. Vanity is the mainspring. Vanity, boundless, blind, empty, insatiate vanity. It was vanity that first made me desirous of becoming a speaker. It is vanity that keeps me to the object. I can trace vanity in every word I utter, possibly in every word I now commit to paper. Is it not the duty of man to mortify so contemptible a propensity?[113]

An undergraduate capable of writing in this vein is obviously not wholly suited in politics. The prickings of conscience were always as essential a part of Manning as the will to power. And while these two characteristics are hardly reconcilable in one man, there can be no doubt that an archbishop is considerably better placed than a prime minister to make this attempt.

However eagerly Manning strove to become an accomplished man of the world, his Evangelical inheritance was always liable to break through his polished exterior. The self-denial that had enabled him to gain a First might equally well be marshalled to unwordly ends. During a continental holiday in the long vacation of 1828 he visited Paris and went to a play. The piece was apparently harmless enough, but Manning resolved never to visit a theatre again.[114] (Newman made a similar vow at the same age, but Newman subsequently relented.) Although Manning's reminiscences are not always reliable, he was probably right to look back upon Oxford, no less than the succeeding years, as the time of his conversion. It is important, in giving prominence to his secular ambitions, not to ignore the first fumblings of the other side of his nature. In old age he would recall how he had delighted in the services in Balliol chapel, how he had studied the Greek Testament, read sermons and pondered weighty tomes of theology. The company he kept was godly as well as political: witness Newman's diary for 12 September 1830: 'HW[ilberforce], Manning and Acland with RW[ilberforce].'[115] This is the first indication that Newman was aware of Manning's existence. Mr Manning's first marriage gave his son a natural entrée into this set. In the long vacation of 1830, much of which Manning spent in Oxford preparing for Schools, he used to attend St Mary's, where Newman was beginning to acquire a reputation. 'Having once seen and heard him,' Manning would recount sixty years later at Newman's memorial service, 'I never willingly failed to be there.'[116] That autumn Newman preached a sermon on Jeremiah, waxing eloquent on the inevitability of worldly disappointment to the true Christian.[117] It is odd to think of Manning, to whom Newman would one day feel indebted, but not grateful, for the fulfilment of this prophecy in his own life, sitting attentive and unnoticed among the congregation.

The most important religious influence in Manning's life at this time, however, was once more Evangelical. One of his Harrow contemporaries had been Robert Bevan, whose family was involved in the banking firm of Barclay, Bevan & Co. Shane Leslie has described the Bevans as 'probably as sure as their accounts in one world as in the other'.[118] Not the least pious among them was Miss Favell Lee Bevan, the second daughter, who, six years older than Manning, had devoted herself to founding schools on her father's Hertfordshire estate. When Manning went to stay with Robert Bevan in an Oxford vacation he quickly fell under the notice of this sister, who divined his need for her spiritual ministrations. She suggested that they should read the Bible every day after breakfast, and she was sure that her

brother Robert would want to join them. When Manning returned to
Oxford the same system of reading (minus Robert) was continued by
correspondence. Perhaps this was the stimulus behind the Greek New
Testament studies mentioned earlier. At any rate, Miss Bevan became well
acquainted both with Manning's ambitions and with the foils that checked
them. When he was at a loose end in 1831, he naturally sought refuge in this
stronghold of virtue. 'Robert is improved by his friendship with Manning,'
thought Miss Bevan, who noted with surprise that 'the total ruin of his
[Manning's] fortunes does not lessen him in his [Robert's] esteem'. But
there was other encouragement to be drawn from Manning's state. 'I think a
work of grace is going on in his heart. He is deeply convinced of the vanity of
the world and the sinfulness of sin. He is much interested in the Scriptures,
from which he has formed a very high standard of religion. It is delightful to
see him so humbled and sanctified, but he does not for a moment think
himself religious; he looks very poorly, and is not happy. He remains at the
gate knocking; reflecting on his conversation, I perceive he is in bondage to
the law.'

Being in bondage to the law was a decidedly parlous condition in
Evangelical theology, as implying a lack of confidence in the saving power of
faith alone. St Paul had written sternly to the Galatians on this subject: 'If
righteousness come by the law, then Christ is dead in vain.' The implications
of St Paul's letter were the same to the Evangelicals as they had been to
Luther: 'If I, wretched and damnable sinner, through works or merits could
have loved the Son of God, and so come to him, what needed he to deliver
himself for me?' Any conviction, or even suspicion, of personal merit, or of
the possibility of salvation through works, implicitly denied the need for
Christ's sacrifice and so dammed up the channels of redeeming grace. That is
why Luther spoke of 'the dung of one's merit', and 'the filthy puddle of
righteousness', because it was unrighteous mankind that Christ had died to
save. Hence, too, Miss Bevan's delight in Manning's unhappiness and sense
of sin. Such symptoms were classic preliminaries to the kind of Evangelical
conversion which she herself had experienced four years previously. Only
when the soul had accepted both its own utter corruption and the
impossibility of any human cure was it in proper condition to find assurance
in the free bestowal of grace. By November 1831 Miss Bevan found cause for
confidence. 'HM is in the hand of One who can guide by His counsel and fit
for His own work by His Spirit. Who knows but that after being tempest-
tossed for a season he may seek the service of his Master?'[119]

Henry Fielding, writing in more cynical times, had remarked that 'as
sympathies of all kinds are apt to beget love, so experience teaches us that
none have a more direct tendency this way than those of a religious kind

between persons of different sexes'.[120] It cannot be said that Manning's conduct towards Miss Bevan lent any support to this worldly philosophy. As for Miss Bevan, she was dispassionate enough when she came to assess the character of her brother's handsome friend. 'I know of no power in which he is deficient,' she began, promisingly enough. But she could not help seeing further:

Pride is the natural accompaniment of talent. This is the ruling passion of HEM. One characteristic, however, of a truly great mind is also his – namely an ardent love of truth . . . [which] gives a peculiar colouring to his proud, ambitious desires. He seeks not only praise, but *deserved* praise, praise doubly deserved because hardly earned. . . . He covets *every* gift from the highest to the lowest, the admiration of every creature from the highest to the lowest. So towering an aim, so grasping an ambition, can never be gratified. Convinced of this fact . . . he prefers the more substantial to the more showy portion, and forgoes the praise of the undiscriminating multitude for the approbation of the discerning few, and especially for his own.

But there, according to Miss Bevan, was the rub. Manning was no kind of judge in his own cause. 'He is liable to be mistaken in his review of his own past conduct, in his view of his present position, and in his anticipation of his future course. With regard to himself he is a theorist, though in respect to abstract truth he is a trampler on theories.'

Miss Bevan's keen eye discerned his double nature:

Do you judge him to be a stern, firm character from the outline I have drawn? Know that he struggles with a temperament of a most susceptible, excitable, I may say morbid kind. . . . His kind feelings and his self-love continually hinder the exercise of his sagacity. When these do not interfere he acts admirably, with a steadfastness and a self-denial to be rarely met with. He has strength of mind and decision of character, but he has more to contend with than other men. The hallucinations of ambition, the morbid scruples of a sensitive nature, the closely entwined associations of a feeling heart, are sometimes arrayed against him.

In the end Miss Bevan, like many after her, confessed herself unable to pin down a character with so many contradictions. There seemed to be no consistently applicable description. 'If I called him great and daring you would not believe in his sensitive points and fits of despondency. Well, I do declare him capable of braving public opinion. What should you say when you saw him full of anxiety to please, and solicitous to gain every suffrage?' For understanding of Manning's complexity, few observers have matched Miss Bevan. She was more accurate in her prophecy than many commentators have been in their hindsight:

He is a complicated creature, and calculated to disappoint expectation in some respects and at some seasons. Yet he may take flight beyond the warmest hopes of those who wish him well. I fear he will occasion his friends to lead an unquiet life, if they give full scope to the interest they may feel. He will himself need the exercise of no ordinary vigilance to steer his course right, of no common degree of faith to enjoy a moderate share of repose.[121]

'No common degree of faith', however, was just what Manning had been constituted to sustain. His mind was impatient of half measures, moved naturally to extremes. Also, as Miss Bevan had noted, he was more than capable of bringing experience into line with his preconceptions. The great difficulty, with such temperaments, is not so much with the demands of faith as with its attainment, not with the long and troublous journey, but with the first step. It is not easy to step on to a path from which there is no return; harder still if it leads away from all preceding hope. The temptation to shy away was all the stronger because Manning envisaged vocation in such demanding terms. His conception of the Anglican priesthood had little to do with the conventional understanding of that institution. Would it be necessary, he asked Anderdon, to sell all his goods and give them to the poor?[122] This was a distinctly unusual question to ask at a time when many entered the Church of England precisely to assure themselves of a comfortable livelihood.

Nor, in that agonizing period of decision, was there any sudden, blinding illumination that left Manning with no choice but to take up his cross. It was conscience, not certainty, that initially drove him into a life of faith, conscience that would never cease throughout his life to grapple with worldly ambition. As to whether this motive force came from God through prayer, from the Evangelicals through his family, from Miss Bevan through correspondence, or simply from within through bafflement and frustration, these are questions that each will answer according to his own convictions. Manning himself knew only the reality of a sharp and painful internal struggle. On the one hand, 'My doubt was whether God had called me; and I had a great fear of going uncalled.'[123] On the other hand, 'this feeling that God was calling me worked continually. I spoke of it to no one. I could not lay it. Every day it grew upon me and I found myself face to face with this choice: to leave all that I was attracted to, and to take up all that I shrunk from. If ever I made a choice in my life in which my superior will controlled my inferior will, it was when I gave up all the desires, hopes, aspirations after public life at the dictate of my reason and my conscience.'[124]

That was hardly conversion as Miss Bevan understood the term, an immediate and irresistible overpowering of the old Adam through an involuntary reception of God's grace. Nothing came free to Manning. He had never been undividedly religious in the way of Newman, who, as a boy, conceived that 'life might be a dream, or all this world a deception, my fellow angels by a playful device concealing themselves from me, and deceiving me with the semblance of a material world'.[125] No, Manning had found the material world real enough; he had to stamp on its allurements at the cost of much suffering before he could begin to realize his spiritual nature. Renouncement, it has been said, is not joy, but only sorrow that is willingly born. There was, moreover, little that attracted him in the Church of England. Many years later, when he was a Cardinal, he would recall that even as a young man he had thought it secular, pedantic and unspiritual. 'I remember the disgust with which I saw a dignitary in Cockspur Street in his shovel and gaiters.'[126] It may have been so: all good Evangelicals recoiled from ecclesiastical pomp, and no doubt the young Manning would have thought even less well of a Cardinal. In truth, though, the fundamental issue at stake in 1831 had little to do with ecclesiastical forms and preferences. The question was simply whether Henry Manning should live for this world or the next. And when what he called his 'superior will' gained an ascendancy, there was but one way to go. How was it that John Foster instructed the decisive character to act? 'If the judgement is *really* decided, let him commit himself irretrievably, by doing something which shall oblige him to do more, which shall lay on him the necessity of doing all.'[127]

And so, towards the end of that fateful year, standing in a bookshop leafing through a book of Wesley's sermons, Manning communicated to the long-suffering Anderdon his decision to take Orders.[128]

2 *Marriage and Churchmanship*

What do I not owe him? No living man has so powerfully
affected me; and there is no mind I have so reverenced.

MANNING, AS AN ANGLICAN, ON NEWMAN[1]

The reservations which Manning felt about the Anglican Church before he
took Orders were widely shared in England during the 1830s, though
perhaps the most common reaction was rather apathy than outright
hostility. The popular view was succinctly expressed by a soldier whom the
young Gladstone heard arguing with a comrade on top of the London–Eton
coach. 'Come now,' said the more godly of the two, a man who liked to
define his terms, 'what is the Church of England?' 'A damn large building
with an organ in it,'[2] his companion unceremoniously returned.

To radicals, though, the Church of England was something much more
sinister than a spiritual desert; it was a system of patronage and property
ruthlessly manipulated by the ruling classes to their own privilege and profit.
One pamphlet, 'The Extraordinary Black Book', which sold over fifty
thousand copies between 1831 and 1835, claimed that the revenue of the
Church of England was £9.5 million a year, more than that of Austria or of
Prussia. 'The clergymen of the Church of England', the writer thundered,
'receive, in the year, more money that all the rest of the Christian world put
together.'[3] However exaggerated these claims, there was more than enough
evidence to support the general case. The richer bishops lived like medieval
princes, even to the extent of keeping open table; the sees of Canterbury and
Durham were each worth over £19,000 a year, a sum which should be
multiplied at least sixty times to gain a present-day equivalent. The
cathedral chapters contained many a golden stall the blessings whereof were
also counted in thousands; and scattered around the country were rectories
that had been left no less fabulously provisioned by the chances of history.

Equally vulnerable to radical attack were the means by which these plums
were distributed. The bishops were appointed on blatantly political
grounds, a practice which called into question the whole concept of an
Established Church. In many livings also, the right to present the clergyman

(called the advowson) was in lay hands, and treated as a species of property to be bought and sold on the open market. In consequence, where once the advowson had belonged to the local squire, it had often fallen, whether by purchase or inheritance, into the possession of someone who had no other connection with the parish. That advowsons were valuable is not to be wondered at; if the living were rich, the patronage bestowed the power to set up a member of the family in comfort, perhaps in luxury, for life. The classic procedure of those obtaining rich benefices was to install a curate to discharge the religious obligations, and so retire to enjoy the plenty. Doddington Rectory, in the diocese of Ely, provided an extreme example of what might be achieved. Patron: Sir H. Peyton. Rector (absentee): Algernon Peyton. Value: £7,306 p.a. Duties: performed by two curates who together cost the Rector £385 p.a.[4] Ecclesiastical patrons exploited curates just as ruthlessly, and were quite as mindful of the Christian duty to provide for their families. The son-in-law of Manners-Sutton, Archbishop of Canterbury from 1805 to 1828, held an archdeaconry, a chancellorship, two prebends, two rectories and one curacy, a collection which brought him £10,000 a year.[5]

Pluralism and non-residence were not isolated vices; they were the conditions under which the Church of England existed. In 1832, of the 11,913 clergy who were available to fill 12,200 preferments, 3,806 held two or more titles, and 4,254 were curates. Yet the abuses were more often the consequence of poverty than of greed. A quarter of the livings were worth less than, in some places much less than, £100 p.a.[6] The Anglican Church attracted all the odium of a rich corporation even while many of its clergy were reduced to an existence of apostolic simplicity. Clerical indigence was a far more widespread problem than clerical indulgence. Failing some wholesale measure of reform to make stipends more equal, pluralism was a necessary evil that in many cases represented the only means of providing for a family.

It is not surprising that a Church organized on such principles should have given rise to some scandalous behaviour. Sensational stories abounded. There was the bishop who conducted an ordination examination in a cricket pavilion during the match;[7] there was the eighth Earl of Bridgewater, who drew £3,000 a year as a canon of Durham for forty-nine years while he lived in Paris;[8] there was Edward Watson, absentee Bishop of Llandaff from 1782 to 1816, who explained how, 'having no place of residence within my diocese, I turned my attention to the improvement of land'.[9] The Rector of St Buryan in Cornwall, however, capped all other absentees by installing a lunatic to provide Sunday services. The man was secured to the altar rail by a chain which allowed him to move between altar and reading desk, but no further.[10]

Of course, the horror stories were not typical. It would be possible to match every example of corrupt or outrageous conduct with an edifying tale of pastoral zeal. In truth, though, the prevailing tone of Anglicanism was neither especially godly nor especially debased; it was simply *gentlemanly*, with all the virtues and all the limitations which that word implies. A good parson acted as a kind of second squire, as ready with material as with spiritual counsel. The majority of the clergy was kindly and respectable; a minority was outstandingly learned. Spread throughout the country their value as a civilizing influence was undeniable. The question was, what did they have to do with Christianity? The image of the parson living in a comfortable rectory with his large family, or even of the curate struggling to make ends meet, was far removed from the stern New Testament ethic that prescribed contempt for the world, and a joyful acceptance of the pains of sanctity. 'If any man come to me, and hate not his father, and mother, and wife, and children, and brethren, and sisters, yea, and his own life also, he cannot be my disciple. And whoever doth not bear his cross, and come after me, cannot be my disciple.'

The Evangelical revival had been a sign that the Church of England might finally, in old age, be getting some form of religion. It had proved impossible, though, to keep John Wesley's Methodists within the fold. Wesley always professed himself a loyal son of his native Church, but he ended by setting up the Methodist Conference and ordaining his own ministers. The unabashed emotionalism of his appeal to the poor was profoundly antipathetic, for all his conservative social philosophy, to the Anglican tradition. 'Sir,' wrote Bishop Butler to Wesley, 'this pretending to extraordinary revelations and gifts of the Holy Ghost is a horrid thing; yes, sir, it is *a very horrid thing*.'[11] Much more acceptable to, and much more accommodating towards, the Established Church were the upper-class Evangelicals who enlisted under Wilberforce's standard. These men affected a remarkable change in the English consciousness. The movement to abolish slavery was not just a noble cause in itself, but a symptom of a new moral strain which, well before the Victorian age dawned, threatened to make virtue almost as fashionable as vice. But the Evangelicals, even when Anglicans, were not *primarily* Church of England men. The essence of their belief was that the Holy Ghost acted directly on each individual soul. Their characteristic devotion was family prayers rather than Church services; their preferred mode of action philanthropic societies rather than parochial care. The Church might be convenient to them as a sign of fellowship, but it could hardly render any more intimate their communication with the Almighty.

It is an eloquent commentary on the state of Anglicanism in the eighteenth century that the Evangelicals, to whom in theory the idea of a Church represented little, should nevertheless have been the principal instigators of improvements in Church practice. The irony of their reforming influence is most of all striking in the case of the communion service, which, by their theology, was not so much a sacrament as simply a commemorative rite. In the eighteenth century even Catholics received communion only rarely. The place of the rite in Anglican worship may be gathered from an instruction which the Bishop of Oxford gave to his clergy in 1741: 'One thing might be done in all your parishes,' he gently suggested, 'a sacrament might easily be interposed in that long interval between Whitsuntide and Christmas. If afterwards you could advance from a quarterly communion to a monthly I have no doubt that you will.'[12] The Bishop's wishes seem modest enough, but he did not live to see them widely fulfilled. It was the Evangelicals who, despite their 'low' views, set the example of more frequent celebrations. By the 1830s a quarterly communion, at least, was common practice. The custom could be confusing for the older generation of clergy. The ancient vicar of Bloxham, though he remembered to put a loaf of bread and a bottle of wine on the altar table, suddenly realized during the consecration that a vital detail was missing. Did anyone have a corskcrew, he asked the congregation.[13]

'Whenever you meet a clergyman of my age,' remarked Sydney Smith towards the end of his life (1771–1845), 'you may be quite sure he is a bad clergyman.'[14] The judgement is too harsh. Smith himself, though an unabashed worldling, and much handicapped by wit in maintaining the dignity of his calling, was a fine example of his own generation of clergymen. With his irrepressible high spirits, robust good sense and unaffected kindliness he was perfectly equipped to relieve at least the pains of this life. His observation was just, however, in so far as it implied that a new spirit was abroad. As a young man it had seemed to him that:

Religion is much like Heraldry, an antiquated concern; a few people attend to the one and the other, but the world laugh [sic] at them for engaging in such a superannuated pursuit. In fifty years more the whole art of going to church – how the Squire's lady put on her best hat and cloak, and how the Squire bowed to the parson after church and how the parson dined with the Squire, and all these ceremonies of worship – will be in the hand of the antiquarian, will be elucidated by laborious investigation, and explained by appropriate drawings.[15]

This prophecy proved premature. Yet what did occur in the early nineteenth century was almost worse to a mind constituted like Sydney Smith's. The Evangelical revival succeeded in proving that the Church of England was not altogether impermeable to religious enthusiasm. Under its

influence the era of the country gentleman in Orders, of the parson who rode
to hounds, and shot, and danced, 'and often did worse things', was passing.
It would be an exaggeration to say that a young man like Manning, with his
determination 'not to be a clergyman in the sense of my old destiny, but to
give up the world and to live for God, and for souls,'[16] was a typical
candidate for ordination, but he was by no means as untypical as he would
have been fifty years earlier.

It required more than sporadic outbreaks of religious fervour, however,
to mollify critics of the Church. The Anglican Church might have been
staffed exclusively by saints without diminishing the case for administrative
reform. The distribution of parishes was as glaring an abuse as the
inequalities of income. No attempt had been made to cater for the shift of
population into the towns during the industrial revolution. In 1824
Parliament was informed that there were four million souls in England
without any place of worship. Manchester, for instance, had a population of
187,000 but church seats for only 22,468; Birmingham, with 100,000
inhabitants, offered but 16,000 places to worshippers.

All might agree on the need to tackle such problems. But where would
Parliament, once it had begun, lay off? Radicals nursed a particular hatred
of Church rates: 'You may as well propose a national medical establishment,
and oblige everyone to pay for its support.'[17] An extremist like Cobbett
advocated confiscating Church revenues and setting them against the
National Debt. Such a measure would certainly have been popular. During
the Reform Bill crisis the Church of England appeared more than ever the
bastion of conservative reaction. Twenty-one bishops voted against Lord
Grey's Reform Bill in 1831, and only two for. For a while the bishops
required courage to venture out in public. Archbishop Howley became a
target for brickbats and cabbage stalks in the streets of Canterbury.[18] In
Bristol the bishop's palace was ignited.[19] The Bishop of Cork, paying a visit
to Bath, was set upon by the crowd; nor did he improve matters for himself
by frantically protesting that he was the Roman Catholic and not the
Anglican prelate of that diocese.[20] As for Sydney Smith, 'I bought a blue
coat, and did not despair in time of looking like a Layman.'[21]

With the Whigs duly returned to a reformed House of Commons in 1832–
3, it seemed that the day of reckoning had come. 'The Church, as it now
stands, no human power can save,'[22] Dr Arnold pronounced in 1832, a
reflection which did not inhibit him from publishing his *Principles of Church
Reform* in the following year. In this work he proposed that the dissenting
sects should be united by Act of Parliament into a comprehensive Church of
England. As for doctrine, there need be none, beyond a general assent to
the divinity of Christ. It was up to each Christian to decide what he believed.

Unfortunately, though, neither Anglicans nor Dissenters seemed keen to believe in Dr Arnold. 'It is with me a matter of deep, serious religious conviction,' explained the Rev Thomas Binney in October 1833, 'that the Established Church is a great national evil; that it is an obstacle to the progress of truth and godliness in the land; that it destroys more souls than it saves; and that therefore its end is devoutly to be wished by every lover of God and man.'[23] Few shared quite the depth or the seriousness of Mr Binney's religious conviction, but few also, whether in the Church or out of it, would have dismissed the possibility that disendowment and disestablishment of the Church were imminent.

Neither prospect would have alarmed the young Manning, disgusted with the sight of shovel hats and gaiters. At this stage he still regarded religion as an essentially personal matter between a man and his Creator. No priest had been required to effect the change from bumptious ambition to unflinching religiosity that had occurred with such startling rapidity and completeness in his own life. Just possibly there was a moment of uncertainty before his mind closed for ever upon his choice. Purcell prints part of a letter to Anderdon dated 9 March 1832 which he interprets as showing that Manning suffered from early doubts about his vocation. 'I think the whole step has been too precipitate. I have rather allowed the instance of my friends, and the allurements of an agreeable curacy in many respects, to get the better of my sober judgement.'[24] It is not clear, however, whether Manning refers in this quotation (all that Purcell cites from the letter) to his decision to devote his life to religion or to the narrower question of how quickly he should obtain a curacy. The second interpretation seems much the more likely. Manning's intensely earnest view of the religious calling made him hesitant about taking up his duties too quickly.

The formal qualifications demanded of a university man who wanted to take Orders were not onerous. A candidate merely had to subscribe to the Thirty-Nine Articles, obtain a curacy, and convince the bishop, or the bishop's chaplain, that he was fit for the position. Manning required much more of himself. 'From what I have seen of my own attainments in theology, although I might satisfy the Bishop of London's chaplain, I should by no means satisfy myself by June next,' he wrote to Anderdon. 'I do not think I can possibly enter upon a profession of such responsibility without a much more mature preparation.'[25] Fortunately, doors which had been closed to the budding politician now swung open to admit the fledgling clergyman. A quick canvass among his Wilberforce connections easily secured the fellowship at Merton which had been denied him in the previous year. That meant another £200 p.a. The sudden shift of fortune inspired appropriate Evangelical reflections. 'God has indeed been bountiful to us all from the hour in which our former resources were annihilated,' he informed his mother. 'I have watched the gradual return of prosperity with feelings of reverence, and now that I myself am thus happily provided for, I am anxious still to preserve in my mind a due gratitude and thoughtfulness of the Giver. It is a hard task: and unhappily the easier our lot the less we think of Him that disposes it.'[26]

Years later in Rome Manning would remember the intoxicating happiness he had experienced in this first freshness of his commitment. 'My past then seemed to be pardoned – 23 years blotted out, and I had a sort of lightness of heart and simple trust in the love of God. Heaven seemed blessed and near, and Holy Scripture heaven upon earth.'[27] At Merton he settled down to read 'acres of Anglican writers'. The college library registers show how diligently he pursued his studies: Hooker, Donne, Hammond, Hall, Bull, Tillotson, Berkeley and Butler all came under his scrutiny. All these authors were men of vast learning and intellect, but together they make up a curious hotch-potch representative of nothing except the doctrinal uncertainties of Anglicanism. In the sixteenth century Hooker's *Laws of Ecclesiastical Polity* laid the foundations of Anglicanism on the basis of compromise, fusing national Church with national State, combining original Catholic truth with later Protestant reform. The Caroline Divines leaned more distinctly on Catholic claims of authority, setting forth high sacramental doctrine and presenting the Church of England as the single faithful heir of the apostolic legacy. Bishop Tillotson, by contrast, put forward a broadly-based ethical Protestantism that proved so acceptable to the Whigs of the Glorious Revolution that he became Archbishop of Canterbury. Bishops Berkeley and Butler were eighteenth-century religious philosophers who pitted their reason against the rationalism that rejected supernatural revelation. As Bishop Tait would proudly proclaim in the 1860s, the Church of England 'has never committed itself to the dogmatism of one school of thought'.[28]

So Manning read, and puzzled, and came to no conclusions. At this stage his mind was still as innocent as his Church of any closely defined convictions; Miss Bevan had inculcated zeal not doctrine. Nevertheless, there were other influences at hand. Manning did not fail to profit from the proximity of Merton to Oriel. His name crops up several times in Newman's 1832 diary. 'Manning of Merton dined in hall with me [2 June] . . . dined with Manning at Merton [7 July] . . . called on Manning [19 September].' Perhaps at these meetings Manning began to glimpse the possibility of grounding his faith more securely on dogma enunciated by a divinely appointed Church. He did not, however, look back on this period as one of intellectual excitement. 'It was a quiet time, and Merton is the most perfect resting place in the natural order.'[29]

His major concern was the practical one of finding a curacy, a problem compounded by continuing worries about his health. There was talk of a parish in the Chester diocese, but Manning was careful about committing himself. 'The number of inhabitants I believe to be about 1700,' he told John Anderdon. 'It is very material in what rank of life they may be. Such a population of poor would be far more than any man, and very far more than one with my health and strength, could undertake.' This same health and strength, he added, was 'far less that I have hitherto had, and some time will have to elapse before I am qualified to discharge any office of much labour'. As usual it was asthma that was giving him trouble, asthma that was apparently exacerbated by the noxious air of the country. 'I think it highly questionable whether for some years I shall be able to live out of London.'[30] It would, in fact, be seventeen years before he lived *in* London. For a year from November 1832 good fortune came upon Manning at such a pace that the asthma was unable to keep up.

Once more the Wilberforce connection proved its value. William Wilberforce had four sons, of whom the youngest, Henry, was closest to Manning in age and (at that time) in acquaintance. Many found him the most attractive of the four. William, the eldest, 'never was endurable'[31] according to Marianne Thornton; he did not even enter the Church. Robert was an intellectual heavyweight, and a social one also. Samuel, though copiously blessed with charm, energy and talent, already gave evidence of that calculating worldly streak which would later earn him the soubriquet of 'Soapy Sam'. Henry, however, no one ever accused of being either ambitious or boring. He was certainly hopelessly extravagant, and capable of appearing arrogant and overbearing to outsiders. To his friends, though, he was an irresistible source of amusement and gossip. Newman, not a man easily lured from his work, professed himself incapable of self-discipline when Henry was around with his 'nonsensical chat'. For his part Henry became one of Newman's most ardent disciples, and it was very much under this influence that he decided, in the summer of 1832, to enter the Church.

For a Wilberforce the difficulty of finding a suitable curacy was somewhat less pressing than for ordinary mortals. In 1829 Henry's brother Samuel had married a distant cousin called Emily Sargent, whose father was Rector of Lavington and Graffham, near Chichester in Sussex. Now, in 1832, the Revd John Sargent sought a curate who would also serve the tiny hamlet of Upwalden (population under a hundred) nearby. Naturally the call went out to Henry Wilberforce, but Newman, who had heard something of the attractions of the three remaining Sargent sisters, and who knew Henry's susceptible nature, counselled caution. 'I fear the ladies of the house will make you idle,' he wrote to Henry. 'You will be lounging and idling with them all day – There is this mischief attends all familiar society between our sex and the fair – we cannot talk without being idle, whereas ladies are employing their fingers in ten thousand ways all the time they are encouraging idleness in us.'[32] Henry began to have doubts about his calling. 'As to Lavington,' he wrote to his brother Robert in November 1832, 'I do not find my mind so far settled that I can comfortably take orders at Christmas.' Perhaps the offer might be delayed? 'I had thought that possibly they might take a *locum tenens* till Easter, and it occurred to me that *Manning* would be a very fit man if he would accept it. I sounded him (of course I could do no more without authority from Mr Sargent) and I am sure that he would gladly take it from Christmas to Easter.'[33] So Manning was ordained deacon on 23 December 1832, and early in the New Year proceeded to Sussex to undertake the Upwalden curacy. The ensuing months were among the most decisive in his career.

John Sargent was an exceptionally distinguished country rector. His family presents another instance of outstanding Evangelical virtue bred out of the well-merited prosperity of preceding generations. His grandfather had been a director of the Bank of England; his father Joint Secretary to the Treasury; both worthies had been MPS. The Sargent connection with Lavington had been formed in 1778, when the Revd John's father, another John, married Charlotte Bettesworth, only daughter of the manor. Charlotte's ancestry included one coal-black sheep, her grandfather Garton Orme, who had appeared to qualify on all counts as the archetypal wicked squire. He lost half the Lavington estate through gambling, while his achievement as a seducer was such that the father of one of his victims called down a surprisingly effective curse on the male line of her descendants. As his *pièce de resistance* Garton Orme had been widely suspected of having stuck his first wife down a well in order to marry the rector's daughter. The discovery in 1845 of a coffin full of stones in Lavington church did nothing to clear his name.[34]

The Sargent genes, however, proved more than a match for any degenerate element in the Orme inheritance. The only moral ill that seemed to have survived Garton Orme was the curse upon the male descendants; no Sargent son ever succeeded to the Lavington property. Otherwise the line was utterly satisfactory, and the Revd John Sargent a particularly fine specimen. Educated at Eton and King's, Cambridge, he became a Fellow of the latter college. While at Cambridge he fell under the spell of the Evangelical Charles Simeon, whose disciples were no less devoted and considerably more numerous than those of Newman at Oxford.[35] Simeon found places for many of them by means of a trust fund which he set up to buy advowsons, the aim being to establish Evangelicals in as many important parishes as possible. No such assistance was required in the case of John Sargent. When he decided to take Orders his father expended £2,000 buying back the advowson of Lavington and Graffham, which had been sold by the wicked Garton Orme.[36] John Sargent became Rector of Graffham in 1805 and Lavington in 1813. His flock was small (Lavington in 1831 had a population of only 338, Graffham 372),[37] but all the better tended for that.

The rector's perfections, moreover, had been crowned in 1804 by his marriage to Mary Abel Smith, as handsome, clever and rich as Emma Woodhouse, besides being considerably more virtuous and agreeable. She was a niece of the first Mrs William Manning, and a first cousin once removed of William Wilberforce, who regarded her as 'almost my daughter'. Naturally the advice of the great man was sought as to her projected marriage with John Sargent. Wilberforce was obliged to confess that 'a clergyman with £1000 a year is not a necessitous man', more especially when he had the prospect of double that sum. 'Still, I confess frankly that I wish you had more – and much more – and why? Because, my dear Mary, I think so highly both of you and Mr. S. as to be sure that the largest fortune if you had it would be expended to the glory of God and for the benefit of your fellow creatures.' But then, Wilberforce consoled himself, 'a moderate sufficiency and the middle station of life are the most favourable to happiness'. As to the proposed bridegroom, 'from the uniform account I have received from those who know Mr. S. best I have not the smallest doubt that he is a man of good understanding, of warm affections, of extraordinary proficiency as a Christian, and eminently formed for domestic life'.[38]

And so it proved. The Sargents had seven children, of whom five were still surviving when Manning came to Sussex. There were four daughters (Emily, Mary, Caroline and Sophia), and a son, Henry Martyn, named after the missionary who had been John Sargent's intimate friend. Contemporary accounts are unanimous on the beauty of the girls. It must be said, though, that a photograph of Mary, 'the most beautiful woman in the world' to her adoring spouse, hardly gives that impression to the detached observer, though admittedly it was taken when the bloom of youth was well past. The sketch which George Richmond made of Emily just after her marriage to Samuel Wilberforce[39] presents a face which is attractive, but lively and witty rather than classically proportioned. People spoke of the girls' perfect complexions, a form of compliment often inspired by those with imperfect features. With the Sargents the 'peach bloom' in their cheeks denoted a tubercular strain. Perhaps it was the cheerful and happy atmosphere in the Sargent household, as much as their beauty, that generated the copious encomia which the girls received. John Sargent might not allow cards or dancing in the house[40] but, contrary to the image bequeathed to posterity, the Evangelicals were not gloomy – at least not upper-class Evangelicals.

John Sargent senior had rebuilt Lavington Manor house in the Georgian style, and hung it with Dutch and Italian masters picked up at the Duc d'Orléans's sale in 1804. Until 1831 the Revd John Sargent and family were installed in Graffham rectory. Neither Sargent daughters nor Dutch pictures ever prevented visitors from delighting also in the charms of the surrounding country, lying, beech-clad, in the shelter of the Sussex Downs about fifteen miles north of Chichester. A beautiful family living in a beautiful place: it would have required very much more cynicism than Henry Manning possessed to avoid being captivated. Lest the scene should cloy on fallen spirits, though, let it be immediately said that this same beautiful English countryside was for many a savage hell. The sharp fall in wheat prices after the Napoleonic wars put landowners under heavy pressure, which they hastened to pass on to their workers through lower wages. While the Sargents got by on their 'moderate sufficiency' of £1,000 a year, local labourers experimented with survival on casual work that paid, when available, ten shillings a week.[41] This level of remuneration was justified on the overoptimistic theory that additions from the parish poor rate would prevent actual death from starvation. The position was the worse because eighteenth-century Enclosure Acts had taken into private ownership all common land from which a cottager might have scratched a subsistence. Unlike his continental counterpart, the English agricultural labourer had no ground of his own; and therefore no independence.

In 1829 and 1830 the sullen discontent in the countryside flared into alarming revolt. 1830 was the autumn of the Captain Swing riots: throughout the southern counties desperate men burnt hay-ricks, destroyed machinery and terrorized the propertied classes with the cry of 'Bread or Blood'. Manning used to recall having seen the fires when he lived at Combe Down: 'Madness had been infused into the minds of our simple agricultural population.'[42] It was his first introduction to the 'condition of England' question. Even the Sargents had not been entirely insulated from the troubles. 'This morning after breakfast', Caroline Sargent wrote to her sister, 'a party of Graffham men . . . came to the kitchen door and Papa went to speak to them. They were tolerably civil, and after Papa had given them a lecture they walked off.' Clearly the Revolution still had some way to go in Graffham, in itself a tribute to Mr Sargent's stewardship. Yet one of the men had carried a lantern, 'which Papa has no doubt was a sign that he meant to burn the stacks if he did not get what he wanted.' The parson was frequently singled out as a special target of the rioters on account of the tithe, a tax owing to the Church which was levied on one tenth of the yearly produce of land and stock. 'We heard the other day,' reported Caroline, 'that some of the people said they should be contented if they could but have the parson's head.' Mr Sargent took the threat seriously enough to earn his family's ridicule. 'Papa is very much laughed at by all except Grandmama: he would not let Mama or Mary go to the meeting the other night, and he stopped Mama from going with Aunt Rosamund to New Grove this morning to fetch Sophie: we expect soon that he will barricade us into the house for the winter.'[43]

The high-spirited writer of that letter, possessed for good measure of beautiful eyes,[44] was destined, three years later, to become Mrs Henry Manning. The new curate from Merton certainly made his mark quickly. He arrived in Sussex on 3 January 1833; he was engaged to Caroline Sargent by Easter. Beyond that bald statement nothing can be said, because nothing is known. It is hardly surprising that in after years the Cardinal, though never forgetful, should have been unforthcoming on the subject of his youthful romance. What does seem strange is that the Anglican curate should have been equally tight-lipped. S. F. Wood, a godly and well-connected young barrister who had carried on an intimate correspondence with Manning during 1832, was obliged to discover the news of his confidant's engagement from Henry Wilberforce.[45] (But then a lot of people discovered a great many things from Henry Wilberforce.) From the start Manning shrouded his relations with Caroline in total privacy. Contemporaries found him close on every subject; his marriage is only exceptional in that it constitutes one of the rare secrets that he has contrived to keep from posterity also. Where facts are lacking, legend thrives. A story of Manning's proposal technique – 'Caroline, I have spoken to your mother'[46] – used to circulate in W. G. Ward's family. Ward, however, was not on close terms with Manning until twenty years later; clearly the tale was invented to suit the austere Catholic dignitary. All the same, it is difficult to imagine even young Mr Manning on his knees before Caroline.

No sooner was the engagement settled than the rector, Manning's prospective father-in-law, was dead. He was, in fact, the third John Sargent to die in four years; the elder boy had been lost in 1829, and the rector's father, the squire, in 1831. His own end was extremely sudden. A gentleman to the last, the rector had given up his inside place on a coach. He caught a severe chill and expired three days later, on 3 May 1833.[47] Although Manning had been in Lavington only four months, as a temporary stand-in for Henry Wilberforce, old Mrs John Sargent, the squire's widow, who held both the property and the advowson, decided immediately that he should be the new rector. The love match had turned out to be a marriage of convenience as well. Perhaps also Manning's Evangelical views appealed to the Sargents more than Henry Wilberforce's discipleship of Newman.

Besides, as Mrs Sargent wrote to Henry Wilberforce, a bachelor could hardly live in a house that contained two unmarried daughters.[48] And so in the summer and autumn of 1833 a succession of ceremonies marked the changes in Manning's life. On 9 June, in Lincoln's Inn, he was ordained priest by Bishop Maltby of Chichester, a prelate who owed his elevation to his Whiggish politics, and who would one day play his part in helping Manning out of the Anglican Orders into which he now consecrated him. In the same month the new Rector of Lavington was formally inducted by Samuel Wilberforce, who returned again on 7 November to make his sister-in-law Mrs Henry Manning.[49]

It is interesting that Manning remembered the exalted state of mind that followed his conversion as continuing only 'down to the summer' of 1833.[50] This rather odd limitation may have been related to the fact that the course of true love did not, in the latter stages of the engagement, run altogether smooth. Caroline, it appears, had begun to be uneasy about the prospect of marriage to this intensely serious young man. After the wedding Manning took her to his brother's London house at 23 Chester Street. Next day, 8 November, he wrote to Mrs Sargent contrasting Caroline's happy mood with her previous disposition. 'She bore the journey surprisingly well, and has been more like herself, with the vigour, and activity she used to show, than I have seen for many, many months. [He had only known her for ten months.] It really seems as if a weight of uncertainty and depression had been removed, and her mind had reassumed a perfectly natural tone.' The same letter also conveyed Manning's exalted hopes for his marriage. 'Ask for us that our union may comprehend both time and eternity and that our sincere, our single, aim in all things may be the glory of God in our holy and devoted life.'[51] This ambitious programme commenced with visits to Manning's family. From London they went to the home of one of his sisters in Sevenoaks, before returning to Lavington at Christmas. After all, it appeared that Caroline's sisters would not be living with them. Sophia, the youngest, had become engaged to George Ryder, son of the Evangelical Bishop of Lichfield, in August; and Mary to Henry Wilberforce (none other) in December. These Sargent connections would henceforth play a very much more significant part in Manning's life than his own more secular and less intelligent relations.

Henry Wilberforce, in particular, provided a close link with Newman and the Oxford Movement, but he was not alone. All the Sargent girls had married upper-class Evangelical husbands who were becoming conscious of the limitations of the individualistic and emotional faith in which they had been raised. The trouble with such a religon was that it appeared no more secure than the individual and no more enduring than the emotion. Whereas in its first flowering the Evangelical revival had produced men of genuine spiritual power, the movement now seemed to be foundering through its very success. What had once been inspiration had become dangerously like fashion. Mere lip-service on Sunday now afforded self-satisfaction in plenty, whereas once a lifetime of struggle against evil had seemed an insufficient token for the privilege of conversion. Words and phrases which in their freshness had awakened powerful religious emotion had now become empty formulae parroted endlessly to no noticeable effect. The certainty of being predestined to salvation, which had once kindled a fierce moral passion, now undermined the will to make any effort at all. As Thomas Mozley put it in his *Reminiscences of Oriel*: 'The Evangelical preacher very quickly discovered that his vocation was not in cottages and hovels, or in farm houses, or in garrets and cellars far up or down, in . . . dirty lanes and courts.'[52]

Newman, who loathed the doctrine of assured salvation, attacked Evangelical smugness at all turns: 'To look at Christ is to be justified by faith; to think of being justified by faith is to look away from Christ and to fall from grace.'[53] What Newman objected to above all in the Evangelicals was their *vulgarity*. He shrank fastidiously from their habit of addressing the Lord of Creation as though he were a cosy familiar. He despised those who acted as though religion could be achieved without holiness, or holiness attained without painful striving The contempt which the Oxford leaders felt for Evangelicals is well conveyed in the terse description which Hurrell Froude gave of them: 'Fellows who turned up the whites of their eyes and said "Lawd".'[54] Samuel Wilberforce, Emily Sargent's husband, though never really a disciple of Newman or Froude, shared the same sentiments on this score. Replying indignantly to his father's entreaties that he should keep in with the godly set, he wrote: 'The men generally who are most religious belong (I believe) to Wadham and St. Edmund Hall and are very very low by birth and equally vulgar in manners, feelings and conduct. Would you have me form acquaintances with these?'[55]

Manning was never a snob, and it is noteworthy that at Oxford his inherited Evangelical sympathies actually intensified. As he remembered matters forty years later it was the experience of practical work at Lavington that first raised difficulties for which the kind of religion he had learnt from Miss Bevan supplied no answers. 'The first question that rose to my mind was, What right have you to be teaching, admonishing, reforming, rebuking others? By what authority do you lift the latch of a poor man's door and enter and sit down and begin to instruct or correct him? This train of thought forced me to see that no culture or knowledge of Greek or Latin would suffice for this. That if I was not a messenger sent from God, I was an intruder and impertinent.'[56]

Yet perhaps Manning, looking back, rather put the cart before the horse. To his temperament the idea of being a messenger sent from God would have appealed on its own account. The picture of his hovering uncertainly outside the poor man's cottage does not convince. Authority had been a personal characteristic well before it became a religious principle; John Foster's *Decision of Character* long preceded any apprehension of Catholic doctrine. Manning never had any doubts that he belonged to God's officer class, however sincerely he strove for humility in the discharge of his commission. What he needed from theology was a warrant for his natural predilections.

In September 1833 Newman provided just that with the first of his *Tracts for the Times*. This very first *Tract*, with its pungent, dramatically phrased challenges, went straight to the heart of the question of authority. Newman was fearful of Whig designs upon the Church.

Should the Government and Country so far forget their God as to cast off the Church, to deprive it of temporal honors [sic] and substance, *on what* will you rest the claim of respect and attention which you make upon your flocks? . . . There are some who rest their divine mission on their own unsupported assertion; others, who rest it upon their popularity; others, on their success; and others, who rest it upon their temporal distinctions. This last case has, perhaps, been too much our own; I fear we have neglected the real ground on which our authority is built, – our APOSTOLICAL DESCENT.[57]

Manning read and was evidently entranced; within two months he was helping to distribute tracts in West Sussex. Henry Wilberforce, down in Lavington for the rector's wedding, reported back to Newman the news of a new convert. 'Manning has revised his opinions and adopts the Apostolic Succession.'[58]

There was nothing new about Anglicans claiming the Apostolic Succession: it had always been the principle, however questionable, upon which High Churchmen rested their case for a divine mandate. What *was* new was the fervour and urgency with which Newman embraced the doctrine. For as Evangelicals had degenerated into religious gushers, so High Churchmen had tended to recoil into a cold and barren formalism. Newman, however, fused devotion with dogma; on the one hand, he sought to remove the 'dry' element from the 'high and dry' school, on the other, to introduce doctrinal rigour into religious enthusiasm. It is significant that so many of those who proved susceptible to Newman's teaching came from Evangelical backgrounds. The 'high and dry' party, though closer to Newman in doctrine, was further removed in spirit. However fierce Newman might be against Evangelicals (and he *was* fierce), the Oxford

Movement which he led was not so much a reaction against the religious revival of the eighteenth century as an attempt to reanimate it on sounder principles. Gladstone put this more elegantly: 'The Evangelical movement filled men so full with the wine of spiritual life that larger and better vessels were required to hold it.'[59] That, too, was how Manning saw the matter when he looked back in the 1860s. For him the Oxford Movement was a synthesis, 'which readily sympathised with the interior personal religion of the Evangelicals, distinct from their heterodoxies, and with the hierarchical and sacramental principles of the High Church, distinct from their Erastianism'.[60] It was in this context that, as a young Evangelical parson, he was open to Newman's influence. By his own admission, he had no definite ideas about the role of the Church when he went to Lavington. Having accepted the Apostolic Succession, however, he discovered that the doctrine did not stand in isolation: it was part of a comprehensive religious system that Newman was developing. Since this system would eventually lead Newman, Manning and many others into the Roman Church, it is necessary to consider the issues involved.

The conscious impulse behind Newman's search for authority sprang from his acute awareness that an ill-defined mish-mash of pious sentiment and private judgement such as the Evangelicals indulged in could never, in the last analysis, stand against the secularizing tendencies of the times. If Christianity were to survive (and Newman was quite prepared to concede that the issue seemed doubtful), Christians needed firmly and objectively fixed propositions into which they could fasten their mental hooks. In a word, they needed dogma, which would curb the intellect just as morality curbed the will; it was all part of the same process. The increasingly fashionable alternative view, that every man might construct his own belief, implied a denial that absolute religious truth was attainable, or even that it existed. On that account Newman saw liberal and individualistic principles as the most dangerous threat that Christianity had ever had to encounter, a recipe for infidelity and moral chaos. A faith that depended upon reason was always liable, nay likely, to be swept away by reason; there could be no saving grace of reverence for ideas that came out of the mind of man. Whenever reason was made sole judge of religious truth, Newman admitted with that frankness which makes him such an attractive controversialist, faith was weakened and in logical minds destroyed.[61] The human mind possessed a natural tendency towards unbelief: 'No truth, however sacred, can stand against it, in the long run.'[62]

But then, Newman insisted, the mind played no essential part in the genesis and maintenance of faith. As Pascal had used his genius to destroy the pretensions of human vanity, so Newman bent his prodigious intellectual resources towards exposing the limitations of human intellect. Reason was merely a critical faculty, not a creative one; it might justify belief, as a judge may declare a man honest, but it could no more create a living faith than a judge could make a man honest.[63] Newman taught that faith is given, not discovered, given to those whose moral dispositions and wills are correctly ordered. Those who live solely for this life can hardly expect to gain any knowledge of the next. A holy life and an untroubled faith go together; so do a selfish heart and a sceptical temper. Faith, in fact, is a branch of morality. That was the somewhat smug principle that lay at the root of the stern ethical strain in Newman's sermons, of his relentless demand for other-worldly standards of conduct. It was also the reason that he detested Bentham's utilitarianism, with its guiding principle of the greatest happiness for the greatest number. For Newman this was simply 'the science of selfishness'. To make an ideal out of earthly gratification seemed to him monstrous blasphemy, the negation of the spiritual and mystical essence of human personality. That way lay the shortest route to hell, both now and hereafter. Any kind of credulity appeared preferable to the rampant self-sufficiency of the liberal intellect.

Newman saw this life in Platonic terms, as the shadow of a supernatural reality which none but the spiritually prepared could hope to contemplate. Whereas intellectual brilliance was given to few, the holiness which brought true sight was within the compass of all. Conversely, those who did not strive for sanctity would never grow in faith. 'If we but obey God strictly,' Newman proclaimed, 'in time (through His blessing) faith will become like sight.'[64] It was no good following the Evangelical pattern and waiting for some dramatic experience of conversion. Rather, 'let us venture to believe, let us make trial before we see, and the evidence which others demand before believing, we shall gain more abundantly by believing'.[65] If the argument seems circular that is just another point of stupid logic. The first movement must come from the heart not the intellect. 'Everyone must begin religion by faith; he must take for granted what he is taught and what he cannot prove; and it is better for himself that he should do so, even if the teaching he receives contains a mixture of error.'[66]

Where was this teaching to be found? If faith was inextricably associated with obedience, it was vital to be quite clear where religious authority lay. Throughout the 1830s Newman laboured to convince himself and others that the Church of England was a divinely appointed instrument for the interpretation of revealed religion. His disgust with continental Catholicism helped to fortify this belief. 'I begin to hope', he wrote to his mother from Naples in February 1833, 'that England after all is to be the "Land of Saints" in this dark hour, and her Church the salt of the earth'.[67] For the moment it did not seem relevant that this same Church, far from being in any obvious sense God-ordained, had been created by a sixteenth-century political compromise designed to prevent the English people squabbling about religion; nor that it now bore so many tokens of shambling decay. God moves in a mysterious way his wonders to perform.

Just recently He had been moving more mysteriously than ever. The repeal in 1828–9 of laws which had kept those refusing to subscribe as Anglicans out of public office destroyed the claim that, though the Church of England might be governed by Parliament, Parliament consisted of Churchmen. Now that dissenters, atheists, even Catholics might be involved with decisions affecting the constitution and doctrines of the Church, its bondage to the godless State was incontestable. The purely nominal Anglicanism of many leading politicians also raised difficult questions. Was a man like Lord Melbourne, who considered that things had come to a pretty pass when religion was allowed to interfere with private life, properly qualified to appoint bishops and to direct the course of the Apostolic Succession? Newman's every fibre resisted the idea. Yet it would need more than political facts to persuade him to abandon the high claims which he made for the Anglican Church. That became evident in 1833 when the Whigs legislated to abolish ten Anglican bishoprics in Ireland, and projected turning the revenues to purposes that would benefit the Catholic population. The measure was obviously just, but that, to Newman, was not the point. He protested wildly that it was sacrilege for the State to interfere in such a matter, to act as though God's Church was simply another department of the Home Civil Service. For all his misgivings, though, he never, at this stage, contemplated abandoning the Anglican Church. If he saw a way out of the impasse it was through disestablishment rather than through secession.

As to doctrine, Newman recognized that a Church which claimed to represent the voice of God on earth must speak with a single voice. The Anglican Church hardly qualified on this ground. Newman determined, however, that an apostolical institution must convey apostolical doctrine, that is, the teaching and traditions found in the writings of those who lived nearest to the time of the apostles, the Fathers of the Church. Here might be discovered the true Catholic faith, as distinct from that promulgated by the Church of Rome, which, Newman considered, had made unwarrantable doctrinal additions and alterations – purgatory, indulgences, communion in one kind only – at the Council of Trent. The Church of England, therefore, should rejoice 'that she was able to escape from pollution, and from the bondage and sin to which a continued stay within the venerable walls would have condemned her'. At the same time Newman also felt a profound distaste for the sixteenth-century reformers. What he called the *Via Media*

of Anglicanism was not a compromise between Catholicism and Protestantism. His case was rather that the Church of England, at least as he envisaged
it, constituted the sole remaining healthy branch on the original Catholic
tree. It was 'the Catholic Church in England,' providentially charged with
the task of maintaining Apostolic Christianity. This mission implied the
possession of sacramental powers, those 'keys and spells', as Newman called
them, 'by which we bring ourselves into the presence of the great company
of saints'.[68]

The claim that the rickety, rotten and decidedly terrestial Anglican
Church had been favoured in this way might seem to open up a credulity gap
unbridgeable even by the doctrine of the Apostolic Succession. For
Newman himself the difficulty did not obtrude until the late 1830s. He had
lived almost all his adult life in Oxford: the exotic growths that flourished in
the hothouse of his mind were rarely exposed to the cold reality of the native
climate. Though he acknowledged and regretted the contrast between the
austere simplicity of the primitive Church and what Sydney Smith called the
system of prizes and blanks under which Anglican clergymen carried out
their apostolic duties, this kind of practical consideration never shook his
ideas at root. Newman was a man who started with theories and found the
facts to fit, rather than the other way about. That he convinced himself was
not surprising. The remarkable thing about him was the genius he possessed
for making other people share his beliefs. That Catholic ideas should have
made the least headway in the almost wholly alien environment of the
Anglican Church is the greatest possible testimony to his moral force and
controversial brilliance. In the 1830s he was at the height of his powers. Over
his disciples he exercised a mesmeric personal fascination: Credo in
Newmanum was *their* creed. In the pulpit of St Mary's he left his listeners in
no doubt of their need for the offices of the Church if they were to aspire to
salvation. That the *Tracts* found their mark we have already observed.
There were, nevertheless, significant exceptions to the rule of Newman's
triumphant course. In particular, his superiors remained unconvinced.
When, for example, he pronounced that the cause of religion in England
might be forwarded if the Anglican bishops were to suffer spoliation of
goods and martyrdom,[69] somehow the bishops were not entirely impressed.

Extreme pronouncements were Newman's stock-in-trade at that time. 'It
would be a gain to this country', he reckoned, 'were it vastly more
supersticious, more bigoted, more gloomy, more fierce in religion, than at
present it shows itself to be.'[70] Newman was as good as his word; in the 1830s
he was a raging fanatic. This point needs to be stressed in view of the
Strachey version, which presents him as a lachrymose and ineffectual
dreamer, an easy victim, later in life, for Manning's wiles. It was the

Newmanites who spoke of their master's extreme sensibility; opponents discovered a prickly combativeness. Supporters noted his burning religious conviction; critics discerned only an unhealthy preoccupation with the drama of his own soul. His sister once remarked that 'to become his friend, the essential condition is, that you see everything along his lines, and accept him as your leader'.[71] That was, after all, the logical position for one convinced of his duty to bear witness to apostolic truth. How could there be a compromise between right and wrong? Newman's remarks upon the conduct of the Jews at the siege of Jericho are revealing in this context. The children of Israel, it will be recalled, 'utterly destroyed all that was in the city, both man and woman, young and old, and ox, and sheep, and ass, with the edge of the sword'. 'Doubtless, as they slew those that suffered for the sins of their fathers,' reflected Newman, 'their thoughts turned, first to the fall of Adam, next to that unseen state where all inequalities are righted, and they surrendered themselves as instruments unto the Lord, of mysteriously working out good through evil.'[72] Doubtless. Perhaps Newman's thoughts also turned in some such direction as he savaged opponents with his biting irony, attempted to hound a liberal professor of divinity from office, cut his old mentor dead in the street because of a doctrinal disagreement. Like the Jews at Jericho he surrendered himself as an instrument to the Lord. Henri Brémond has written thus of Newman's polemics against the Roman Catholic Church in the 1830s: '*Je ne me rappelle pas avoir rien lu de plus suavement perfide, de plus spécieux ni, au fond, de plus violent contre nous.*'[73] As for opponents at the other end of the religious spectrum, Newman himself wrote the truth: 'I am aware that I deserve no mercy from your Protestants, and if they read me, shall find none.'

The doctrines that evoked so much controversial bile in their chief expositor found an equally zealous advocate in the Rector of Lavington. In his old age, when relations with Newman had soured, Manning would claim that he had read his own way into the Church, that he had, in the sporting metaphor that he adopted, become a Catholic 'off my own bat'.[74] It is true that he was never at the centre of the Oxford Movement; how could he be when he did not live in Oxford? As he himself acknowledged, however, 'the influence which went out from it [the University] spread all over the country. It penetrated into every diocese, and almost into every parish.'[75] It certainly penetrated into Lavington. If Manning read his way into the Church, it was because he had begun by following the prescribed Newmanite texts.

The shepherds of Sussex soon became aware that they had an apostolic successor in their midst. Manning was an indefatigable parish visitor who reckoned to call on every house at least once a fortnight. In that respect, of course, the messenger of God did not differ from his Evangelical pre-

decessor; and the presence of Caroline Manning, who had taught in the
parish school in her father's time, must have increased the sense of
continuity. Manning, however, wore a cassock on his daily rounds, in order
to emphasize that he was a servant of no earthly master; and it was this sense
of the greatness of his calling that sharply distinguished him from Mr
Sargent. 'We magnify our office,' he explained, 'not to exalt ourselves, but
to abase; for it is ever seen that they who lay least stress on the commission,
lay most on the person; and they that esteem lightly the derived authority of
Christ's ministers, exalt their personal qualifications, intellectual and
spiritual, into credentials of their ministerial office.'[76] That sounded very
well, but somehow in practice meekness never appeared a distinguishing
characteristic of Henry Manning; he chastised in the name of the Lord, but
he chastised just the same. It was plainly his duty to rebuke irreverence, but
was it tactful, was it wise, to enter a gentleman's home unbidden in order to
admonish his servants for their behaviour at church? The gentleman, a Mr
Holford, thought not.[77] Again, it may well be that lateness in church implies
disrespect to the Almighty; and perhaps the rector was justified in stopping
the service while offenders made their way to their pews. But what is to be
made of this? 'The Church door opened one day. Mr. Manning stopped. An
old lady was heard slowly tottering to her pew. There was a terrible fall. It
was Mr. Manning's own mother, who had vainly endeavoured to hurry her
pace during the reader's awful pause.'[78] The only possible defence is that
Tom Mozley's *Reminiscences*, from which that anecdote comes, is a
notoriously unreliable work.

    Where John Sargent had made church services more frequent, Manning
established daily Matins and Evensong, in emulation (as he saw it) of early
Christian practice. 'When once the Church has restored the solemn days of
fast and festival, the stated hours of daily prayer, there will be an order
marked out for all men of goodwill to follow.'[79] The rector, however, often
found himself without a congregation. There was no tradition of daily
worship in the Church of England; and even Sunday worship could not
always be taken for granted. Not long before Manning arrived in Lavington,
four Sussex clergymen discovered playing cards on a Sunday afternoon
explained that the weather was too bad to allow them to go to their
churches.[80] Nothing that the English climate could produce ever kept
Manning from church, and once there he liked to draw attention to his
exalted position. 'I am now beginning a course of sermons upon the Liturgy,
the ministerial office, and the doctrine and discipline of our Church,'[81] he
told Samuel Wilberforce in January 1834. Later that year Henry Wilberforce reported to Newman that Manning was '*exceedingly* improved since he
left Oxford', a remark which in that circle naturally referred to Manning's

ecclesiastical opinions rather than to his social quality. 'I am glad about Manning,'[82] Newman tersely replied. By 1836 even a Newman disciple like John Bowden was beginning to feel that Manning was getting a trifle obsessional about his mandate. 'It is all very well', Bowden considered, 'to bring in the Church now and again, but *he* never preaches a sermon without it.'[83]

Manning's estimate of the Church's powers grew with his conception of its mission. When he went to Lavington, only two sacraments, baptism and Holy Communion, both specifically commended by Christ and therefore acceptable to Evangelicals, commanded his assent; and Holy Communion he would have regarded more as an act of remembrance than as a means of supernatural grace. In 1834, under Samuel Wilberforce's auspices, he imbibed the doctrine of the Real Presence from Hooker. Next year, 1835, Manning found himself 'convinced that neglect of confirmation is one of the great and efficient causes of our present low state of religion in the Church';[84] two more winters, and it was rather 'neglect of apostolical censures, and absolution' which claimed his attention as an explanation for 'the mystery of our weakness'.[85] There was the case of Jones, whose 'parish is in a state very unsatisfactory to himself . . . out of about 1200 he has 40 or 50 communicants. The whole is solved when you hear that he never preaches on the Eucharist, and expresses, I believe, a wish that his curate should also be silent about it. This seems to me like trying to build Stonehenge single-handedly, and without any mechanical power. And is this not very wilful when the Church has appointed the apparatus?'[86]

The first years of Manning's ministry, then, saw him increasingly devoted to Catholic faith and practice. The question, not yet consciously formulated, but bound sooner or later to arise, was whether the Church of England could possibly bear the weight of such ideas. Jones and his like were an all too common phenomenon that continually pressed, uninvited, awkward, but insistent, into Manning's rarefied theological speculations. Even at their best the English clergy appeared as simply 'a number of good men in black kerseymere, and our usefulness is not so much ministerial as *ordinary, i.e.* such as any man good, and clad in black kerseymere, could do'.[87] By the later 1830s Manning was showing signs of exasperation. 'We are no better than a pack of Protestant, self-willed, self-wise Presbyterians. Nine-tenths of our priests and people neither know nor care more for a Bishop's wig than for a broccoli head.'[88]

Even the Lavington and Graffham communion figures fell short of what the rector might have wished. Weekly celebrations were not introduced until 1839. Over Christmas 1836 some eighty persons from the two villages received the sacrament. 'I do not think there are many of a very high reach of faith,' Manning wrote of these communicants, 'but I hope there is a healthy religion.' Ever conscious of his responsibility for the moral welfare of the flock committed to his charge, he wondered whether the virtuous eighty might not be used as a task force to raise the tone of the parish, 'a sort of reflector to report and spread abroad the light of the Church'.[89] Such quasi-inquisitorial methods appealed strongly to Tractarian clergymen, and did a lot to keep the movement unpopular. Manning never introduced this scheme, but he was well informed about his parishioners' failings, of which he kept careful record in Latin. James H– was 'inebrietati addictus'; James S– less specifically and more tantalizingly 'actibus pessimis deditus'. Sarah Webb had a trade that compelled the use of the vernacular: 'sells gingerbread – deceitful'.[90] Perhaps before the end of the 1830s Manning had begun to use the sacrament of penance as a way of enforcing moral discipline, another practice which excited the direst suspicions in English minds. The thought of a married woman in the confessional never failed to give the solid Victorian male a *frisson* of disgust.

Lord Chichester described Manning as the most exemplary clergyman he had ever known, alike for his parochial zeal and his personal holiness.[91] Gladstone, from an even greater distance, reached a similar judgement. In the parishioners themselves, however, Manning seems to have instilled respect and admiration rather than affection. No one could fail to recognize the excellence of his intentions, or the depth of spirituality from which they sprang, yet no one felt any closer to him for that knowledge. He did his best to be companionable. Under the influence of Henry Wilberforce he might try amusing his nephews and nieces by jousting on ponies.[92] Occasionally he displayed his cricketing skills: 'The parson, he be the best cricketer in the village next to me,' the local champion adjudged.[93] But these attempts at camaraderie were never quite convincing. Manning's youth always strove in vain against his dignity. 'People said he was cold,' remembered one of his parishioners. 'He would do anything for the children, but we were afraid of him, tho' we knew he was very much taken up with children. He were very strict. But you should ha' seen him in Church. He were a wonderful Churchman. He looked like an Archangel when he prayed.'[94]

It is a revealing picture, that of a man 'very much taken up with children' who cast fear into children's hearts. To be fair, other Tractarian clergymen were also severe, and even the universally loved John Keble would lay a stick across the back of any boy who failed to touch his cap to the vicar.[95] Manning was not alone in wanting to instil respect; he was just somewhat over-qualified for achieving his aim. He was so very self-consciously a man of the Lord. Through prayer and conscience he invariably discovered a Christian response in himself; through faith and will he was capable, far beyond ordinary human clay, of Christian heroism in turning that response into action. What eluded him was any spontaneous Christian joy in the performance of his task. He loved Lavington; he only cared for its inhabitants. Whereas Keble's villagers were never allowed to discover that their vicar was one of the foremost scholars of the day, Manning's parishioners were left in no doubt that their rector was wrestling with problems way beyond their ken. 'He was an out-of-the-way serious man. Always reading and walking up and down in front a-reading as if seemingly he couldn't find no rest. . . . [He] always drove a pair of greys. Old John Tribe he used to have to stop 'em half an hour together while he got out and sat down somewhere and took no notice of no one.'[96] Manning's theological musings were indeed far removed from the duties that fell to his lot as a Sussex country clergyman. Once, when visiting a sick parishioner, he was obliged to spreadeagle himself against the bedpost in order to illustrate the meaning of crucifixion.[97]

From the beginning of his ministry he knew himself called to wider responsibilities than a village parish could provide. Before long others knew it too. In July 1835 he was invited to preach the visitation sermon in Chichester Cathedral to the assembled clergy of the diocese. What should he choose as subject but . . . the Apostolic Succession? Having established by means of a necessarily somewhat sketchy historical introduction the application of this doctrine to the Anglican Church, the twenty-seven- year-old clergyman proceeded to lecture his reverend elders on the awesome responsibilities of their office. The high claims of God's ministers, he told them, could not possibly be convincing unless upheld by an example of personal sanctity. Should they fail to measure up to their apostolic calling in their lives their lot would be certain – to 'dwell with everlasting burnings'. 'Woe to the covetous and greedy steward, woe to the careless and insensate minister, woe to the loitering and unprofitable servant, woe to him whom the gain, the honour, and the ease of the world, whom a trifling temper, a selfish heart, and an unspiritual mind shall make a cumberer of Christ's ministry, a hinderer of the Lord's service, and a blight upon his church.'[98] Manning's presence, physically enhanced by premature baldness, was quite impressive enough to carry off this sort of thing. Henry Wilberforce, who was a year older, used to complain that when he went to a meeting with Manning he was always told to give way to his seniors. Evidently the Archdeacon and clergy of Chichester felt the same, for the sermon, 'The English Church' was published by their request. Manning despatched a copy to Newman, who considered the work a 'bold, clear, and (cannot but be) effective statement of a truth now in jeopardy'.[99] This opinion was not astonishing considering the whole thrust of the sermon had been derived from Newman's own teachings.

In the same letter, dated 8 September 1835, the earliest extant of those he wrote to Manning, Newman took advantage of the opportunity to issue instructions about finding a bookshop to sell the tracts. He took nothing for granted in his country lieutenant. Manning was told that he would have to provide a sign, that is, 'a bit of wood painted black with an inscription in paint (of *another* colour) to the following effect, "Tracts of the Times sold here" – the said board to be suspended by two strings meeting in an angle and connected with a nail in the wooden frame of the window pane in his shop'.[100] It was as footling as epistle as ever issued from an Oxford academic, and it was written to one of the most competent men of business that the Victorian era produced. In reply Manning, understandably enough, ventured on some practical advice. He urged that Newman should not give up the lighter kind of tract. Dr Pusey had recently declared his allegiance to the movement; and Dr Pusey appeared to imagine that several hundred pages heavily weighed down with intellectual apparatus was the very least that a reader could respectably be asked to undertake. Manning, always practical, knew better. 'If you have only heavily armed [tracts] they will not scour half the country.'[101] His excellent counsel went unheeded.

By 1835 Manning had become, like any self-respecting Newman follower, immersed in a study of the Fathers. 'These are the witnesses of the mind of the Church at all times,' he had learned. 'How far am I in harmony with them?'[102] He undertook translation work for Newman, who found it a godsend to have such an accomplished and willing acolyte. Manning's labours on Justin were pronounced 'very good and impressive'[103], and the pupil was delighted to receive the master's commendation. 'You have not altered my article as I expected – pray do so without scruple or explanation.'[104] Since there was some question of Manning's writing a tract, he had been careful to keep Newman abreast of the state of his researches. 'I have been reading Vincentius Lerinensis, and I have thought of trying to put something together about tradition, showing how much we necessarily and unconsciously depend upon it, while we anathematise it in Popery.'[105]

These were, as Manning implied, dangerous waters for an Anglican clergyman to fish in: it was not easy to reconcile the provincialism of the Church of England with Vincentius's maxim that Catholic truth must be that which has been believed '*everywhere, always, by all*'. Newman, though, was delighted, declaring, 'It was the very next subject I meant to have taken.'[106] Manning eventually helped to prepare a list of extracts from the commentaries of English divines on Vincentius's rule, which appeared as part of *Tract LXXVIII* in February 1837. The year previously Newman had written to Pusey including Manning's name in a list of the movement's inner circle.[107]

Manning proved his loyalty by coming up to Oxford to vote against Hampden, an inoffensive divine whom Melbourne had appointed Professor of Divinity at Oxford, and whom Newman had determined, unsuccessfully as it turned out, should be removed on account of his liberal theological views. Ryder and Samuel Wilberforce were also in Oxford for the vote, and Manning was with them one evening when they witnessed the phenomenon of Newman in full flood. 'It really was most sublime as an exhibition of human intellect,' wrote Samuel Wilberforce, by no means an uncritical Newman admirer, 'when in parts of our discussion Newman kindled and poured forth a sort of magisterial announcement of truth, in which Scripture, Christian antiquity, deeply studied and thoroughly imbibed, humility, veneration, love of truth and the highest glow of poetical beliefs, all impressed their own picture upon his conversation.'[108]

Manning's Evangelicalism was not, however, instantly annihilated by Newman's elevated view of the Church of England, if indeed this early habit of mind ever entirely died in either man. Manning took the Evangelical journal *The Record* regularly until 1835. He also objected at first to the attack on Evangelical confidence about salvation that he found in Newman's first volume of sermons, published in 1834. Newman's stress upon the requirement of holiness seemed too daunting. 'The more I read them,' Manning wrote of the sermons to Samuel Wilberforce, 'the more I feel that it is the hardest book to criticise that I ever met with . . . because it contains so much truth, and because the fault is rather defect than disease. . . . It exhibits religion most fully and pointedly as a system of *requisitions*, but seems to cramp the attractive, encouraging the cheering spirit of "our better hope".'[109] Manning dropped these reservations soon enough; his own first volume of sermons, published in 1841, sets forth the cheering spirit of our better hope as well and truly cramped. The titles of his sermons alone: 'Salvation a Difficult Work', 'Obedience the Only Reality', 'Suffering the School of Obedience', 'A Severe Life Necessary for Christ's Followers', suffice to make the point; and the content is likewise shot through with echoes from Newman's work.

Before 1836, though, Manning was in a theological muddle. It was one thing to adopt the Apostolic Succession; quite another to forfeit the subjective notions of religion that Miss Bevan had instilled. Apparently at the request of Bishop Maltby, Manning undertook some administrative work for the SPCK (Society for the Propagation of Christian Knowledge); and according to Gladstone, whose recollections date from more than thirty years after the event, he supported the Evangelical faction against the High Church men in one of the many disputes which rent that quarrelsome organization.[110] It would be wrong to make too much of this point, which only reflects what has already been observed, that the line between Evangelicals and Tractarians was not drawn as distinctly as tidy-minded historians might wish. Newman looked for Evangelical converts to the Tracts, and the Evangelicals, like Manning, supported him in his campaign against Hampden.

The most significant point about Manning's SPCK activities was that they brought him back into touch with Gladstone, whom he had not met since Oxford. The would-be politician turned clergyman, and the would-be clergyman turned politician, found a natural affinity. 'Politics would become an utter blank to me,' Gladstone informed Manning, 'were I to make the discovery that we were mistaken in maintaining their association with religion.'[111] As Manning expressed no reciprocal view, it followed that their correspondence – they rarely met – should be mainly upon ecclesiastical and spiritual topics. That, in their joint estimation, was the highest level any friendship could reach. By 1851 some four hundred letters had passed between them. Their relations were the more satisfactory because Gladstone was also, in the late 1830s, rejecting his early Evangelicalism for High Church views. The correspondence puts some strain upon the uncommitted reader. Nevertheless, Manning's close contact with the likeliest young politician in the country gave him a link with the great world that he had forsaken when he took Orders. Already in 1835 Gladstone, who was a year the younger, had become a junior Lord of the Treasury. By 1840 his opinion of the rector of Lavington was so high that he appointed him godfather to his eldest son.

Manning's public identification with the Evangelicals, such as it was, proved short-lived. After the publication of his sermon 'The English Church', he was clearly committed to Newman's view of Anglicanism. Indeed his message was rather too clear for a certain Mr Osburn, who, not being a whit apostolical, launched a hot offensive against the sermon. Uncharacteristically, Manning showed himself insecure enough in his views to be disturbed by this first public experience of hostility, and turned to Newman for support. The hardened controversialist of Oxford made light of the affair. 'I condole with you amid your numerous antagonists, though I do not think they are very frightful ones . . . Mr. O. is too vile and abominable (reviewed as an author) to touch with a pair on tongs *in propria persona*.'[112] That was satisfactory. All the same, Manning preferred to remain incognito when he himself entered the polemical fray against a Roman Catholic opponent. In the summer of 1836 Dr Wiseman gave a course of lectures in London which set forth Roman Catholic doctrine and introduced the English intellectual world to the novel idea that a popish priest might yet retain some vestiges of a vigorous mental endowment. Newman, it is true, saw nothing in the performance: 'Dr Wiseman will do us no harm at all.'[113] But Manning discerned matter fit for chastisement. Wiseman's lectures were 'the most precious piece of Jesuitism I ever met'.[114] It was outrageous that he should have classified members of the Anglican Church as biblical Protestants. Manning wrote to the *British Magazine* to correct this calumny, signing himself 'A Catholic Priest'[115] lest any should be deceived by Wiseman's arrogant Roman claims.

Yet even while Manning was thus embroiled in the cause of truth, Newman somewhat tactlessly wrote to ask if he knew anyone at *The Record*, the extreme Evangelical journal, who might manage to get an article inserted in that paper.[116] Perhaps it was partly Manning's need to make his position absolutely clear that caused him to declare to Newman his heartfelt admiration for the work that the Oxford leaders were accomplishing. 'My dear Manning,' Newman replied in April 1837, 'I ought long before this to have acknowledged your last very kind letter, for which I sincerely thank you. . . . Such expressions it is always a privilege to receive – and considering how much one has to go through, which perhaps persons like you partly escape from your country life, not lightly to be prized.'[117] Did the country rector's firm jaw perhaps tighten a little as he read these lines?

Down in his remote Sussex fastness, though, Manning now suffered a loss that it was not given to the celibate of Oxford to comprehend. Samuel Wilberforce, who saw Manning on 22 June 1837, knew at a glance that something was seriously amiss. What was wrong was that Caroline Manning was dying of consumption. The onset of the crisis had been sudden, its course rapid and relentless. On 23 July Mrs Sargent wrote to prepare her daughter Sophia for the worst. 'Our beloved Caroline is not in a suffering state. She is perfectly tranquil, her pain all past and sinking most gradually. The cough is rather better last night and today. There is no delirium but a great weakening of her mind, and no power of attending to anything but the present bodily wants. She is not aware that she is worse.'[118] Next day Caroline was dead. She was only twenty-five.

There has been no more vicious, but unfortunately no more enduring, calumny against Manning than Lytton Strachey's snide insinuation that he came to regard Caroline's death as a deliverance from an alliance that would otherwise have held him back from the Catholic priesthood. For many people it is the sole thing that they remember about Manning. That Strachey deliberately perverted his sources to achieve this libel will become evident in Chapter Four. He also stated, for good measure, that in after years the memory of Caroline 'seemed' – what an abyss of ignorance that 'seemed' may cover – to be blotted from Manning's mind. This may be taken to signify no more than that Manning failed to adopt the Bloomsbury habit of sending an emotional bulletin by every post. Strachey also lifted from Purcell's biography a story that the Cardinal showed little concern that his wife's grave in Lavington churchyard was falling into ruin;[119] he does not, however, mention the window that Manning gave to Chichester Cathedral in her memory.[120]

Perhaps no outsider ever knows much about any marriage; even insiders sometimes learn only retrospectively and indistinctly. Certainly no one can hope to penetrate into the domestic life of a Sussex rectory of one hundred and fifty years ago. It may or may not be significant that Caroline, unlike her sisters, never gave birth to any children. It is interesting that so few visitors disturbed the Mannings' matrimonial seclusion, though as the Sargents had always lived very much *en famille* Caroline may well have felt no desire for a wider social life. It is odd that, outside the home, Manning mentioned Caroline as little when she was alive as he did after she was dead; Gladstone, for instance, could not recall his friend's making any reference to his wife until he wrote to announce her death.[121] It is, finally, undeniable that in one sermon Manning lumped together 'children, women, poor and uninstructed souls'[122] as being incapable of judging for themselves, and thus perhaps saved by invincible ignorance. He was, however, refering to the Eastern Church.

After all these points have been made, the fact remains that every scrap of hard evidence available suggests that the marriage had been a success. After Caroline's death the Sargents all remained devoted to Manning. Mrs Sargent, who had been in the same house throughout the marriage, and who now stayed on in obedience to Caroline's dying instruction to 'do all you can to take care of Henry',[123] treated him as though he were her own son. Mary Wilberforce, Caroline's sister, became his most intimate confidante. Father Ignatius Ryder, Sophia's son, remembered all his life how his mother had brought him up in affection for Uncle Henry.[124]

The best source on the marriage is Manning himself. In the aftermath of Caroline's death he remained calm, but it was the calm of acceptance, not indifference. 'All I can do now is to keep at work,' he told Newman a month or so after Caroline's death. 'There is a sort of rush into my mind, when unoccupied, I can hardly bear.'[125] Again, to Samuel Wilberforce on 25 September 1837: 'I feel that I cannot trust myself to dwell on the past except in direct acts of devotion – at these times, in church, but especially day by day at home – I both can, and do, fully and fixedly – and these are the most blessed moments of my present life. At all other times I feel the absolute need of full employment.'[126] This concentration on work was no mere palliative; it was an essential part of the cure. He was a distant, proud man of an already impenetrable dignity; henceforward his deeper needs would find no human solace. It meant nothing that, in future years, he would enjoy the witty conversation of the widowed Mary Blunt (mother of Wilfrid Scawen Blunt) at Petworth Rectory;[127] or that, in Lavington Manor, which her family rented in the 1840s, pretty Marianne Byles would dream her dreams of the handsome rector to the edification of local gossips.[128] Manning never showed the least intention of marrying again. This was not, at first, a matter of religious principle. For the next ten years, at least, he continued to defend the concept of clerical marriage, arguing that celibacy involved a contradiction of instinct that all too often proved unachievable, and that the parson could set a fine example of family life.[129] For himself, though, there could be no replacement for Caroline. Looking back some forty-three years later he recorded that he had lived as a widower 'without ever wavering in the purpose of living and dying as I now am'.[130]

Instinctively he sought, immediately he found, a spiritual meaning to his affliction. The answer appeared self-evident: he was being scourged into a still more intense dedication to God's service. Only three days after Caroline's death he wrote to Gladstone: 'God has been graciously pleased to lead me into a way that is desert, and to bid me to serve Him with entire surrender of myself.' Gladstone had just been re-elected to parliament, 'a very different and perhaps severer trial,' warned Manning, 'for I have ever found the time of our tribulation safer than the time of our wealth'.[131] Four years later, writing to Samuel Wilberforce, whose own wife had just died, Manning offered a more developed version of this theme. 'For my part, I doubt if anything else [but Caroline's death] would have made me so love and yearn for the unseen world as to counterpoise the stifling hold with which the world we see and act in weighs one down.'[132]

It is, unquestionably, an egocentric reaction to consider that one's wife has been taken off for the express purpose of improving the condition of one's own soul; to that extent Strachey's sneers are understandable. A sceptic might also judge that Manning appeared quite sufficiently detached from terrestial values before the tragedy of Caroline's death. Yet every man, surely, may claim some charity as to the manner he contrives of living with his griefs; and the reaction which Manning adopted, for all its self-absorption, did not show any lack of feeling for Caroline. Quite the contrary: Manning was not a man to make a public parade of his feelings, but each year, he confessed to a friend, that fateful week of July was 'like a churchyard path'[133] to him. Mrs Sargent described him as being 'in quite an agony of tears'[134] on the second anniversary of Caroline's death. Two years further on, and he was still recalling his trauma in obsessional detail. 'Yesterday four years (then a Monday) at 5.00, and Wednesday next (then a Friday) at the hallowed hour of burial towards the going down of the sun are sainted hours with me.'[135]

Always it was upon Caroline's death and not her life that his feelings were fixated. To think of her alive would have been to risk the thought that they had both been victims of a blind and insensate chance; to stand fast by his interpretation of her death was to bestow meaning upon his sorrow. All his griefs were ruthlessly marshalled into the place that he had ordained for them: the sense of desolation *had* to be doing him good, otherwise it was not to be endured. His determination on this point quite transcended lesser demands, such as those of human tact. 'May you be blessed as I have been,' he wrote to Archdeacon Hare on the latter's engagement in 1844. 'May you be blessed much longer. And yet, if sorrow be as good for you as for me, may your lot be as mine.'[136] Was there ever a more invidious note of congratulation? What fun Strachey might have made of it. Yet the same thought was capable of more noble expression. Far from being a deliverance, Caroline's death, from its very sharpness and painfulness, should be a spur urging him forward still more resolutely into the paths of God's calling. 'Before we met,' Manning wrote to that same Archdeacon Hare in 1841, 'what I once was had been abolished. You have only known me a sadder and, God grant, a better man. Between this and that glad morning when we shall sit down with our sainted ones in our Father's Kingdom there lies only one thing, toil for Christ's Church in warfare here on earth.'[137]

3 Promotion and Powerlessness

> In truth I once said that it would be a disaster to be the captain of a ship which, as Lord Dundonald said of his first Frigate, sailed like a haystack.[1]
>
> CARDINAL MANNING, LOOKING BACK ON HIS ANGLICAN CAREER

Like so many radical expectations in English history, the attack on the Church of England, which raised such exaggerated hopes and fears in prospect, proved in the event to be a damp squib. Having reached office and carried the Reform Act, the Whig aristocrats in the Cabinet soon concluded that their dissenting allies were hardly the sort of people to be further encouraged. It might be argued, too, that the efforts of the Tractarians had done something to stiffen the resolve of Anglicans to resist encroachments, though this factor probably did less to rally waverers to the Establishment cause than the presence of Irish Catholic MPs among those who were eager to despoil the Church of England. Even the most bitter Dissenters hardly liked to share a crusade with company like that. Then there was the King, William IV, in whom the least mention of any plan to touch the Church was apt to produce apoplexy.[2] So by the time that Lord Grey, having discovered that running an administration was not entirely to his taste, resigned in July 1834, the threat of plunder and disestablishment of the English Church had receded. The Whigs stumbled on for a few more months under Lord Melbourne, who showed no inclination to rekindle radical fervour. He was, as he remarked after a particularly good dinner with Archbishop Howley, 'all for a *rich* and *lazy* Church, against a *poor* and *active* one'.[3] Melbourne's Government drifted on to the rocks when he suggested that Lord John Russell might become Leader of the House of Commons. Lord John was not merely clever and arrogant, a combination of qualities that made no appeal whatever to William IV; he also proposed putting the revenues of the established Irish Church to uses that might benefit Roman Catholics; and it was by no means certain that the rest of the Cabinet possessed the backbone to prevent his committing this outrage. The King knew his duty. Ignoring the large majority which the Whigs commanded in the House of Commons, he summarily dismissed them, a decision which appeared to afford Lord Melbourne some satisfaction. The only ecclesiastical measure of any importance that the Whigs had achieved was the abolition of ten Protestant bishoprics in Ireland.

Traditionally, the Tories were defenders of the Church. Sir Robert Peel, who led the minority Tory Government which ruled between November 1834 and April 1835, wisely decided that the most effective long-term protection would be to undertake moderate reforms. He set up a Commission to investigate the Church of England, a defensive ploy which proved wholly successful. When the Whigs returned to power, they felt bound to act through the machinery which Peel had established; indeed in 1836 they reconstituted the commission as a permanent body. But where Peel had zealously attended every meeting, the Whig politicians on the Commission soon began to absent themselves. No one, Melbourne complained to Archbishop Whateley, had any notion what a deal of trouble it was reforming a Church.[4] In consequence, the Church once more escaped spoliation. There was an Act to make bishops' stipends more equal and to create two new sees; there was another Act which limited the number of benefices held by one person to two, and those to be within ten miles of each other with a combined population of under three thousand and a joint income of under £1,000. In addition the Dean and Chapter Act of 1840 abolished all non-resident prebends and limited resident canonries to a norm of four for each cathedral. And that was the end of the Whig reform of the Church.

For Manning this tinkering represented the worst of all possible worlds. Temperamentally he would have preferred a full-blooded and successful onslaught on the Church, which could then have stood forth like the apostles of old, shorn of all material accoutrements, offering uncorrupted spiritual truth in defiance of the materialism of the age. The Whig measures at once denied him this satisfaction and asserted unequivocally that Parliament was ultimately in control of the Church of England. The Ecclesiastical Commission appointed by Peel had included five bishops, but they had been outnumbered by lay politicians. This was a grievance that Bishop Otter, who had succeeded Maltby at Chichester in 1836, felt strongly; and Manning was quite ready to take up the cudgels on his behalf. The result was his 'Principle of the Ecclesiastical Commission Examined in a Letter to the Bishop of Chichester' (1838). In this pamphlet Manning attacked the Commission as 'nothing less than a virtual extinction of the polity of the Church'. This authority, he declared, had been granted by God Himself to his apostles and was therefore quite beyond the reach of human power. Yet here was the

Commission, openly secular in origins, leanings and policy, presuming to trespass upon the rights of the Lord's appointed. The implications were disturbing. 'The Ecclesiastical Commission is so constituted as to transmit the popular will to the whole framework of the Church, and to make it yield with unerring subserviency to every vote in Parliament. The Church will be its *organ* for religion . . . . We shall have exchanged the reality of truth for the impressions of the multitude.' Then, in a passage which closely echoed Newman, and which expressed a concept vital to his own religious development, Manning continued: 'Men cannot long believe that they may have fellowship with God through a Church and Priesthood of their own appointing. This is beyond even the credulity of unbelief. They must seek out some Church exhibiting divine credentials, or let go the faith at last.' Manning did not despair of the Church of England, but he predicted that the dilemma which he had outlined 'must one day bring the separation of Church and State . . . for the present line of policy must make it, sooner or later, impossible to communicate with the established religion'.[5]

The unacknowledged flaw in Manning's position was that there was not the remotest chance that the Church of England, even if left to control its own destiny, would adopt the Tractarian principles to which he subscribed. Convocation, the provincial synod of the Church which had not met, save formally, since 1717, would have reflected the predominantly Evangelical bias of the lower clergy. Perhaps some realization of this was behind Manning's suggestion that the recommendations of the Ecclesiastical Commission should be sent, not to Convocation, but to the bishops, for ratification before Parliament legislated thereon. Yet even the bishops could hardly be relied upon when so many of them were Whig appointments. Nevertheless, Manning's pamphlet was a success. Once more a copy went to Oxford; once more the master awarded praise. 'I like your pamphlet much, and so does Pusey, and trust and believe it will be useful.' Enthusiasm made the writer 'ever yours affectionately, J. H. Newman'.[6] Manning could point to some other effects. In 1840 an Act changed the membership of the Commission, which thereafter included all the bishops. The ecclesiastical element thus became a majority, although still itself appointed by the State.

At the behest of Bishop Otter, Manning also became involved in the education question, which was to loom so large both in his own life and in national politics for the rest of the century. The reader may sympathize with Manning's claim that originally the subject held no attraction for him. The Prime Minister felt the same sense of recoil: he did not believe in education, he said, 'the Pagets got on so damned well without it'.[7] Lord Melbourne's affectation of indifference, however, was a sure indication that the matter had assumed a crucial importance. The fundamental issue at stake during the 1830s, and for long afterwards, was whether education should be the responsibility of the Church or of the State. With a decision of that kind at stake it was most unlikely that Manning would maintain his lack of interest. It was equally unlikely, though, that the Anglican cause which he championed could succeed.

Universal education, already widely accepted as an ideal, was never going to be a practical proposition without substantial assistance from the State. And such money, if provided, must surely be made available to all denominations; for how could the Government, which drew taxes from subjects of all beliefs and none, justify spending these takings to the exclusive benefit of one particular sect? The notion that the State might enforce Anglicanism as the national religion had perished in effect with Catholic emancipation and with the abolition of many of the civil disabilities affecting dissenters. Yet the *theory* of the confessional State outlived the reality of its abandonment. This was especially true of education, where some basis for an alliance between Church and State was actually in existence. Two societies received the education grant from the Privy Council: the Anglican National Society for Promoting the Education of the Poor in the Principles of the Established Church, and the non-denominational British and Foreign Schools Society. Since the meagre £20,000 which the Government allotted to education each year was distributed in proportion to the amounts these societies expended on their own account, the rich Anglican society ended up with 70% of the State grant. Zealous Churchmen like Gladstone and Manning were, therefore, encouraged to entertain hopes that the Church of England might assume control of the country's school system.

The theoretical basis of their claim was a view of education as essentially a spiritual trust. Manning developed this theme in a sermon on 'National Education' which he delivered in Chichester Cathedral in May 1838. 'The one predominant idea of Christian education', he asserted, 'is a remoulding of the whole nature, a rooting out of evil, a ripening of good, and a shaping of the inward character after a heavenly example.' The idea of education without religion was a contradiction in terms, like that of religion without a creed. In a rare display of open-mindedness Manning was prepared to admit that if the doctrines which the Church preached were false, then Christian education would be a 'most blighting, withering infection, filling the young mind with moral pestilence'. This possibility did not, however, survive his mature consideration. The doctrines were not false; and so the Church was charged with a sacred duty to instil them into each new generation. Manning recognized that there was some idea abroad that every man should form his own religion by weighing and sifting the evidence for himself. As to this, he echoed Newman's view that life is too short for inferences. 'Believing comes first and, by purity, understanding afterwards.' Those who were educated in dogma by the Church were blessed with a tremendous privilege: 'While others are looking about for arguments, they are building upon conclusions; while others are seeking, they are being sanctified through truth.' The Church should not be modest in its claims. 'To whom did our Blessed Saviour say, "All power of Heaven and Earth is given unto me, *go ye therefore*"? Was it to civil rulers that Chirst said, "Feed my sheep"? Surely this solemn charge was given to none but the Apostles and to their successors after them: and that, not to break in upon, or to overwhelm, any natural or civil duties, but to control and sanctify them all.'[8]

Manning's practical suggestions were necessarily somewhat more hazy than his enunciations of principle. The hope of the group to which he belonged was that the cathedral should become a centre for education in every diocese. To this end, twenty-four diocesan or sub-diocesan boards of education were formed in the country during 1838 and 1839; and Manning always claimed that the Chichester Board, of which he was secretary and moving spirit, had been the first in existence. In his 'National Education' sermon he drew particular attention to the need for teacher training colleges, and suggested that the resources of the cathedrals, on which radicals looked so greedily, be committed to this purpose. For the rest, Manning could only point to the need for 'an extension of our existing institutions, and a great multiplication of their number, by new foundations and endowments in populous towns'.[9] The key question, which he did not tackle, was who was going to pay. The Church of England might finance the odd teacher training college from its own purse, but even Manning did not delude himself that its members would voluntarily subscribe sufficient sums to educate an entire nation. It was just not, as he must have been beginning to realize, that kind of Church.

Manning probably found it congenial to turn from evidence of the Church of England's functional impotence to consideration of its privileged position as a witness of Christ's teaching. Only a fortnight after his address on 'National Education' he preached another sermon in Chichester Cathedral. This one, 'The Rule of Faith', attempted to analyse where, amidst all the warring voices and jarring sects, authentic Christian doctrine was to be found. The sermon displayed an impressive familiarity with the writings of the Fathers, but the argument once more appeared to owe much to Newman. In particular, Manning followed him in insisting on a standard of truth that was external to the individual mind. He reiterated also the connection between faith and morality. In the eighteenth century – Manning said nothing of the nineteenth – the Church of England had been beset by 'the heavy, stifling action of politics and worldly wisdom', and as a result doctrine gave place to opinion, and truth resolved itself into the *views* of this or that person. Manning was not disposed to judge lightly those who vaunted their own private judgement over the facts of revelation. 'The doctrinal errors of the cold, earthly mind, of the indolent and unconcerned heart, much more of the self-wise and incredulous intellect, have their graduated measures, and those, not small, of positive moral guilt.'

Men needed some certain rule by which they might know the will of God. The sixth of the Anglican Articles refers enquirers to the Bible, which 'containeth all things necessary to salvation'. Manning did not deny that, but he would not admit that the Bible could of itself be sufficient. There would always be problems of clarity and differences of interpretation. The solution of these difficulties, he considered, might be deduced from the way in which Christianity had grown. The Gospels had been written some decades after the Gospel revelation; they were understood by their composers and by their earliest readers in the light of the apostolic teaching that had already been received. It was the creeds which, embodying truths that pre-dated Scripture, provided what Tertullian called 'the one sole rule of faith, never to be changed or remodelled'. And beyond the creeds the Church remained as a living witness to antiquity, ever ready to define old truths and to condemn false novelties on the authority of its universal, unchanging, never-failing traditions. 'The first axiom of Apostolic truth is, what ever is new is not of Christ.' The Church of England Manning judged to be especially favoured as an exponent of antiquity. It had been compelled at the Reformation to reassess traditions at their source. Cranmer and Ridley had looked to the primitive Church as their guide against the unwarranted innovations of Rome.[10]

The sermon was published, and Newman yet again responded favourably to the receipt of his indefatigable disciple's prose, albeit with a scholarly query: 'Are you quite safe in the note on page 28?'[11] Others were less impressed. Samuel Wilberforce worried that 'some of my dear brother-in-law's statements' might 'lead men to regard the Romish view of tradition without suspicion and dread'.[12] The Evangelicals were hopping mad, scarcely knowing whether to be more outraged that the supreme authority of the Bible had been called into question or that the authority of the Church should have been exalted. In defence Manning prepared a lengthy 'Appendix' in which he sustained his argument with an even more formidable array of scholarly references. Bishop Otter grew alarmed. 'I cannot but think that, unless you are quite convinced that your Appendix is very important under some large view, you had better reserve it for some more convenient season. You have yourself taken much pains to bring the

Evangelical party in this part of the diocese into a more harmonious co-operation with the rest. Are we not now undoing this good, and that, too, without necessity?'[13] The large view to which the bishop referred evidently prevailed with Manning, for he went ahead and published. The consequences were as the bishop had predicted. The Chichester brethren gathered in knots and conclaves to express their horror to one another. 'They say it is *all* verbiage,'[14] one of their leaders was overheard to pronounce. The *Record*, the national journal of extreme Evangelicalism, was more forthright. 'The Sermon was bad enough; the "Appendix" was abominable.'[15] But some reactions were favourable. 'I have read the last part out aloud to the ladies,' reported one especially loyal friend, 'and was not disappointed in my expectations of finding there very pithy reading.'[16] The Appendix does not appear ideally suited to the beguilement of womankind. In the story of Manning's life, however, it does acquire a certain interest as containing some of his earliest pronouncements on a subject with which his name was to become closely associated – papal infallibility.

In his sermon Manning had made claims for the Church as the guardian of apostolic tradition that seemed to imply something very near to infallibility. Once it has been granted that an institution has been given a divine mission to bear witness to the doctrines of antiquity, it becomes difficult to entertain the idea that the Almighty should allow his chosen instrument to err in the discharge of this duty. When the initial premise of a supernatural Church has been accepted, the question becomes not so much whether infallibility exists as where it resides, how it is expressed, and what are its limits. At this stage Manning was not prepared to allow that the Church possessed any infallible powers if it went beyond its appointed task of expounding the ancient doctrines which had been entrusted to its keeping. There could be no changes, no adaptations, no growth, no additions, when the matter at stake was truth that had been divinely revealed once and for all time. In 1838 Manning believed that infallibility was static, attaching rather to the traditions themselves than to the Church which expounded them.

As to the doctrine that infallibility was vested in the Pope, Manning explained that even within the Roman Church this was 'the Italian doctrine, the Gallican and British Romanists placing it in the Church assembled in council'. He permitted himself some scorn for the absurdity of papal pretension. 'It is plain, that the meaning of a mute document, if it be tied to follow the utterance of a *living* voice which shall claim the supreme right of interpretation, must vary with its living expositor. And in this lies the real danger of the Roman doctrine of papal infallibility.' The Pope might doctor antiquity to suit the needs of the moment. Newman had berated the Roman

Church on that score, and now Manning eagerly cited his words: 'Of Antiquity it [Rome] accepts so much as is in accordance with its existing system; of the rest, some it explains away, some it rejects, some it utterly condemns . . . . Antiquity is no *rule* to the Church of Rome; it is not even a *proof*, but a pretext.' Further to illustrate the dangers inherent in papal infallibility Manning commented disparagingly on the ridiculous lengths to which the doctrine might be stretched: there was a bishop of Bitonto, for instance, who had declared at the Council of Trent that he 'would rather credit one pope, in matters touching the Faith, than a thousand Augustines, Gregories or Jeromes'. It was erroneous thinking of that kind, Manning declared, which had misguided the council into pronouncing doctrines which had no basis in the primitive Church and which were therefore unjustifiable additions to Catholic dogma. Such Roman presumption was as liable to undermine faith as 'the new rule' of private judgement. 'Indifference already prevails, and the end is not doubtful . . . . For as the Roman rule, by *superseding* universal tradition, had brought in particular and unwarranted tenets upon the Church, so the new rule, by *rejecting* universal tradition, had taken away many doctrines of the gospel, had rendered all more or less uncertain, is, in fact, undermining the very canon of Scripture, and will, in due time, when that which letteth is taken out of the way, bring in the Antichrist of Infidelity.'[17]

Yet what, in the end, did Manning's espousal of tradition as the rule of faith depend upon if not upon his private judgement? The Church of England offered no consistent guidance. How else but through his own intellect was he interpreting tradition? How else but through his own intellect was he so certain that the Council of Trent had gone beyond the teachings of the apostles? If it was fixed religious certainty that Manning sought, he had no choice, finally, but to seek an external authority that took all doctrinal decision away from the individual, no choice but to make one conclusive act of private judgement in its favour, and then rest for ever secure in the barque of St Peter.

He was not yet prepared to contemplate this step. Indeed, he resisted the Church of Rome on the very same grounds that ultimately induced his surrender. 'It is the assumption of supremacy on earth, and of freedom from all controlling authority in religion that makes the Church of Rome and the modern school unteachable and wilful.'[18] Nevertheless, the preparation of this sermon and Appendix, following on his controversy with Dr Wiseman in 1836, had given Manning some introduction to Roman Catholic theology. The grain of mustard seed had been planted, though as yet it grew among the tares.

The intense activity into which Manning had plunged in the year after

Caroline's death took its toll. As well as his intellectual work he had all his parish duties. In addition he had been appointed a Rural Dean in 1837, an insignificant office, but not one that Manning was disposed to take lightly.[19] In August and September 1838 he was laid low by severe attacks of asthma, the effects of which he did not speedily shake off. Alarming rumours began to circulate. 'Pray tell me soon, my dear Manning, how you are,' wrote S. F. Wood, himself within five years of death from consumption, 'for I feel very uneasy at some things people have said about you.'[20] Bishop Otter also showed concern. 'I am sincerely anxious about your health, which requires tranquillity. Try to consider this, for there are many who estimate your services at a high price . . . . I hear you are going to preach two sermons on Sunday. You are doing too much. Will you come to luncheon at 2 p.m., and to sleep?'[21] In the upshot, Manning reported that 'friends and relations have conspired against me, and have sentenced me to transportation'.[22] The destination was Rome, which tempted Bishop Blomfield of London to essay a joke; 'he thought Manning had been there ever since his last volume of sermons was published.'[23] Actually Rome was probably chosen for no more sinister reason than that Gladstone would also be there. Others expressed warmer sentiments than the Bishop of London. 'First, how I rejoice that you are going abroad; next, how I envy your going to Rome; thirdly, how I hope you will thoroughly convert Rose whom you will meet there . . . . And now *vive valeque*, my dear Manning, as wishes and prays yours affectionately, John H. Newman.'[24]

The first of Manning's twenty and more journeys to Rome was undertaken in the company of his sister Caroline and her husband Colonel Austen; it occupied a leisurely twenty-five days, 'sleeping in our beds every night'.[25] Travellers discover what they set out to find, and since Manning was not yet looking for any spiritual revelation in Rome, no spiritual revelation occurred. It was not, in any case, a propitious period for visitors stamped with English preconceptions to warm to the claims of Rome. In his temporal role as ruler of the Papal States Gregory XVI appeared as the head of an antiquated, ramshackle system of government that had set itself squarely against all liberal dreams, whether of a united Italy or simply of a free society. In the first years of his reign Gregory had put down risings in the Romagna with the help of Austrian troops and Rothschild finance: now his government maintained order through a police system that employed spies and informers in quite the manner prescribed for repressive regimes in liberal horror stories. Papal theory provoked as much outrage as papal practice. The Abbé Lamennais, the French precursor of quite another kind of Catholicism, had begged Gregory to place the Church in alliance with the people at the head of the newly emerging social order; in a free society, he assured the Pope, Catholic truth would be certain to prevail. Gregory did not share his confidence. The encyclical *Mirari Vos* (1832) reprobated freedom of conscience, freedom of the press and disobedience to princes. No doubt these anathemas were consistent with the age-old Catholic principle of the Church as the source of all earthly authority. It was not to be expected that Rome should overnight become a subscriber to the social contract. On Manning, however, the Church's reactionary stance did not yet produce the stimulating effect which it would later have. He had made large claims for the Church, but in 1838 he was not ready to ignite in sympathy with the Pope's rearguard action against the modern world.

At least, though, the city came up to the mark as a Mecca for tourists.

I hope to see Rome thoroughly [he wrote to his brother Frederick]. In fact I care more to see Rome completely than all other places. The city as a whole quite fulfils my anticipations, except only that the hills are not, and do not appear, sufficiently marked to satisfy one's classical notions of the site. . . . I have seen St Peter's twice. The outside disappointed me, and I do not get over it. The façade is heavy and hinders the dome's being seen, but the inside is beyond anything one can imagine; I cannot, however, admit even its splendid interior into a comparison with the Gothic of the north of Europe.[26]

In company with Gladstone, Manning went sermon-tasting, a diversion enhanced by the fact that at Oxford he had providentially cast an eye over an Italian grammar while shaving every morning.[27] Though not by any means convinced by what he now heard, he found it hard to rise to quite the level of horror that Romish superstition and idolatry evoked in his companion. Sometimes he even approved. At Epiphany, for example, the two friends went to the Caravita, where Manning noted of the sermon: 'Christ suffered for us. If Christ is our Saviour then our Example. Patience in duty. Purity in tongue, eyes and ears. Very good.'[28] Immediately on coming out of the church he rebuked Gladstone for buying apples on a Sunday. That was brave, if hardly Catholic. Nevertheless, they went together to see the English College for training priests, where they were welcomed by Dr Wiseman, who may or may not have been aware that one of his visitors was the 'Catholic priest' who had assailed him in the *British Magazine*. Wiseman 'was not even a bishop', recalled Manning many years later. 'How little we thought that he and I should have the first two palliums in the hierarchy of England.'[29]

How little indeed. In 1838 Manning's head was buzzing with comparisons between Anglicanism and Roman Catholicism, and he was still clear that the Church of England had the better of the argument as the authentic upholder of Catholic truth. 'Both Churches have committed irregularity,' he reflected. 'The English in discipline which is essentially mutable. The Roman in doctrine which is essentially immutable. If either, which vitiates the succession of the Church?' He ran into English converts and noted with surprise that

really pious people may be converted to Rome without perceptibly, perhaps actually, losing anything of their personal piety. The occasional conversion of a serious person hides the taint of the system. I have known four people tampered with by the Romanists: (1) Ignorant disputatious. (2) Devout instructed. (3) Nervous uninstructed. (4) Rather conceited . . . . The present converts to Romanism may be a provision for mitigation of their system; *per contra*, converts always rabid.

As for the Romans, they received short shrift. 'There are two sorts of men in Rome. The one devoted to the Government, the other to religion. The latter are sent on foreign missions.' Foreign missions – that was another point. Had the British been permitted to subdue one-eighth of the world without some divine purpose in view? 'The English Church – the skeleton of an irresistible spiritual power,' he noted mysteriously. 'Adequate to the mastery of the world, therefore destined to it.'[30] This remote but intoxicating prospect would take increasing hold of Manning in the next few years. If he could not feel adequately inspired by Anglicanism as an insular sect cut off from the universal Church, then he must invent something better. 'We must answer for the heathenism of India, for the destitution of Canada, for the degradation of the West Indian slaves, for the Tophet we have made in Australia. We are now on trial as Tyre.'[31] It was a pity, then, that the Church of England possessed only six bishoprics outside the mother country. No wonder that, on his return from Rome, Manning threw himself into the organization of a Colonial Bishoprics Fund. His enthusiasm for imperial Christianity only stopped short of accepting the headship of Bishop's College, Calcutta, which was apparently offered to him.[32]

Years later Manning would claim that the effect of observing Roman Catholic services and devotions on his first visit to Rome had been 'highly repulsive'.[33] Nevertheless, by the late 1830s his own ministrations were producing Romeward leanings among the more susceptible of those who came under his care. He may not at this stage have begun acting formally as a confessor giving absolution for sins, but he was already sharply aware that his apostolic office conferred the duty of becoming a spiritual director. The great privileges which he now associated with the priesthood, in particular the infusion of grace through the sacraments, suggested to some of his flock, if not yet to himself, the need for sacerdotal credentials rather more impressive than those bestowed by the Church of England. In the summer of 1839 Manning found it necessary to write to Newman for advice about how to deal with a case of 'Roman fever' among his charges. The reply, dated 1 September 1839, was disquieting:

My dear Manning, I feel very anxious about such a case as you mention; from the consciousness that our Church has not the provisions and methods by which Catholic feelings are to be detained, secured, sobered, and trained heavenwards. Our blanket is too small for our bed . . . we are raising longings and tastes which we are not allowed to supply – and till our bishops and others give scope to the development of Catholicism externally and wisely, we *do* tend to make impatient minds seek it where it has ever been, in Rome. . . . I think nothing but *patience* and dutifulness can keep us in the Church of England.[34]

Clearly, Newman was losing confidence. The manner in which this occurred illustrates the sealed-off nature of his thinking. His faith in the Church of England had depended upon his representation of that Church as the guardian of Early Church doctrines, whereas in fact Anglicanism was Erastian in organization and predominantly Evangelical in feeling. Despite the spread of Tractarian ideas, the mass of Englishmen remained indifferent to Newman and all his works. If enthusiasm was shown it was as likely to be that of Mr Lane Fox, MP for Yorkshire, who talked of wading in blood up to his horse's bridle to put down the popery of the Oxford school,[35] as it was to be the ardent discipleship of Manning. Newman's catholicized Anglicanism was, as he himself recognized, a paper religion. Therein lay its weakness and its security. It existed most effectively in Newman's own brain, a magnificently appointed abode bristling with intellectual armament that was more than capable of warding off all external attack. He had dreamed of the *via media* in despite of reality; he was safe against all objections rooted in reality. A faith that had survived Lord Melbourne would surely survive anything.

Yet there might be a threat from within. The witness of antiquity upon which Newman relied might be undermined by antiquity itself, the artificial theory finally destroyed by an artificial objection. In the summer of 1839 Newman began to study a fifth-century sect called the Monophysites, who had been condemned at the Council of Chalcedon (451) for their view that there was but one, divine, nature in Christ. Subsequently a splinter group of Monophysites had adopted a kind of *via media*, rejecting their former extreme position without accepting the blanket condemnation of Chalcedon. The effect of this ancient, and far from compelling, controversy on Newman was shattering. 'I saw my face in that mirror, and I was a Monophysite.' If the Monophysites were heretics because they had rejected the Council of Chalcedon, then, it suddenly dawned on Newman, might not the Anglicans be heretics because they had rejected the Council of Trent?

'The shadow of the fifth century was on the sixteenth.'[36] The analogy between Anglicans and Monophysites was tenuous in the extreme, and in any case Newman could have fallen back on his former objection to the Council of Trent, that the Church had long been split before it was convened. But the time for such saving distinctions was past. Newman's mind had broken loose from its moorings. In September 1839 he received a further jolt when he read an article by Wiseman on the Donatist schism – fourth century, this time. Wiseman had given him, he said, 'the first real hit from Romanism'.[37]

It was some time before Newman's doubts became widely known. Not until 1841 would he throw down a public challenge with *Tract xc*, which attempted to prove that the Thirty-Nine Articles were open to Catholic interpretation. This Tract earned Newman an episcopal rebuke, after which his dissatisfaction with Anglicanism became common knowledge. In 1839, however, neither Manning, nor perhaps Newman himself, understood how far matters were going. Manning was aware that Newman felt the shortcomings of Anglicanism, but he did not doubt for a moment that 'patience and dutifulness' would keep him in the Church of England. Indeed, Newman's advice for dealing with the Romewardly inclined subject of whom Manning had written had concluded with a series of questions designed to combat this tendency:

Can she deny that the hand of God is with our Church, even granting for *argument's sake* Rome has some things which we have not? Is it dead? Has it the sight of death? Has it more than the signs of disease? Has it not lasted through very troublous times? Has it not from time to time marvellously revived, when it seemed to be losing all faith in holiness? Is it *to be given up*? – for her step would be giving it up – would be saying, 'I wish it were swept away, and the Roman developed in its territory,' not 'I wish it reformed – I wish it corrected – I wish Rome and it to be one.'[38]

Manning, at least, was quite sure he did not wish that. Later that autumn he urged Newman to take up the controversial cudgels against Rome, and sent him a reading list for the purpose. ('I am sending owls to Athens,'[39] he graciously remarked.) He could still afford, in November 1840, to jest with those who reproached him with any attraction to Rome. 'I protest that when I was in Rome they did not offer me the first tonsure, nor so much as a pair of red stockings.'[40] Yet his feelings were ambivalent. 'I abhor and tremble at Romish error,' he wrote to Gladstone in 1841 (abhorring and trembling being the very least that was required when addressing this particular correspondent on this particular topic), '. . . but I cannot refuse to sympathise with what is high and true and lovely in their system. And as for the hollow false soulless no-system of Protestantism I can yield to it neither the homage of reason nor of affection. The English Church is a real substantive Catholic body capable of development and all perfection – able to lick up and absorb all that is true and beautiful in all Christendom into itself – and this is our problem.'[41]

So Manning continued to work energetically for this real substantive Catholic body. In 1839 he took on a curate at Lavington the better to devote himself to a wider stage. When the Whigs produced their Bill to abolish non-resident canonries, a measure which Bishop Otter heartily deplored, the rising star of the diocese provided another of his public letters to meet the occasion. Take away the revenues of the cathedral stalls if you must, he argued, but at least leave the canons to fulfil their duties. As to what these duties might be, he was unavoidably a little vague; nevertheless, he insisted,

To any serious mind the idea of the cathedral church, with its daily sacrifice and perpetual Eucharist, has a deep and sacred character. . . . I should feel that I had grievously slandered any twenty-eight of my brethren [there were twenty-eight non-resident canons at Chichester] were I to imagine for one moment, that the joint partaking in the yearly benefits of those poor prebends could exercise over their minds a thousandth part of the influence which is wielded by the spiritual dignity of the Mother Church, the soul and centre of Apostolical authority.[42]

No doubt this confidence was justified; in any case Bishop Otter was delighted with the letter. He now leant increasingly on Manning, who was clearly marked for promotion. Already the eager young rector had taken over most of the work of Webber, Archdeacon of Chichester, an ecclesiastic who languished between senility and retirement. 'He is most kind to me, but the grasshopper to him is a burden,' Manning explained.[43] At least, though, there was little doubt whom Bishop Otter would appoint as Webber's successor.

Then in August 1840 Bishop Otter suddenly died. 'I feel to have lost in my time two fathers,' Manning fulsomely informed the Archdeacon of Lewes.[44] The Dean of Chichester shared his grief, but came swiftly to the point – 'Who are we likely to have? I can hardly bear to think of it.'[45] This worry proved abundantly justified. Lord Melbourne, after offering the see in vain to Lord John Russell's brother, reluctantly chose Shuttleworth, the Warden of New College. 'I know little of him,' the Prime Minister wearily explained, 'and what I know I do not very much like.'[46] At Chichester they knew all too much. The new bishop was a Whig in politics and an Evangelical in theology. He had recently published a book entitled, as if in answer to Manning's rule of faith, *Not Tradition but Scripture*. At the time it had sufficed that Newman had dismissed this work as 'very superficial, retailing old objections',[47] but of what comfort were such strictures now? Shuttleworth's other distinctions included having persuaded New College to provide him with a large increase in salary, and having invented a railway for passing the port round the senior common room. To make matters worse, he had a sense of humour. 'Washing-day', he would head his letters, in parody of the Tractarian habit of dating their communications by saints' festivals. He was very much not Manning's kind of person.

'When I think about the diocese,' the Rector of Lavington informed a friend at this time, 'I feel as a man does on an autumn afternoon when the sun has gone in. . . . But, thank God, it is His ordinance. . . . Perhaps we have had our day's growth, and a night's check may be what we need as a discipline and a trial.' For himself, 'I could not brook to be thought forward, or indeed careful, to be employed by Shuttleworth.'[48] It was fortunate, then, that the new bishop should have been present at a meeting in Brighton, where Manning spoke with all his accustomed effectiveness. Such evident ability, allied to the reports of the rector's unflagging zeal, lifted the bishop's judgement out of the mire of Anglican party politics. When, at the end of 1840, Archdeacon Webber finally signified his intention to retire, Shuttleworth did not hesitate to appoint Manning to the vacant post. The decision was the more remarkable because it apparently threw Mrs Shuttleworth, plainly a forerunner of Mrs Proudie, into high dudgeon with her spouse.[49] Manning's friends were torn between delight and amazement. Gladstone judged that his promotion was 'a sure sign of an enlarged and far-sighted spirit in your new bishop, of whom I shall now, with great confidence, anticipate everything that is good'.[50] Unfortunately Bishop Shuttleworth was not destined to fulfil these hopes. He dropped dead as he was about to deliver his first Charge to the diocese, an event which Dr Pusey, who apparently did not share Gladstone's confidence, described as a 'token of God's presence in the Church of England'.[51] Newman was inclined to agree with Pusey.[52] It would, however, have required the liquidation of almost the entire episcopal bench to reconcile the Church of England to his ideas. Bishop Shuttleworth's successor at Chichester, Dr Gilbert of Brasenose, had been prominent in Oxford as an opponent of the Tractarians.

During the Middle Ages an archdeacon had been a considerable figure, administering the diocese for the bishop and often reckoned to be his natural successor. He had presided over his own court, in which he heard cases concerning moral delinquencies among both clergy and laity; he also decided disputes over wills. These were not duties likely to gain popularity; and the archdeacons' use of secret informers, together with their habit of charging extortionate fees, gave an unsavoury reputation to the office. By 1840, though, the archdeacon's powers had been much diminished: in that very year an Act removed the last vestiges of his jurisdiction. What remained was a general supervisory role over the clergy; some responsibility for the condition of church buildings; and a special concern for minor officials like parish clerks and churchwardens. The diocese of Chichester contained two archdeaconries.

Predictably, Manning brought the deepest sense of responsibility to the discharge of his new duties. He set himself to visit every parish in his archdeaconry as soon as possible. He emphasized that the claims of Apostolic Succession would redound as a mockery if the clergy did not lead lives worthy of their divine commission. Even parish clerks were exalted and exhorted in terms that must have occasioned astonishment in the holders of this unremarkable position. 'It is greatly to be lamented', Manning told them, 'that an office of so much sacredness should have fallen into so low esteem. Next to the clergyman no one bears a charge of more public example, or one more nearly related to the highest blessings, than the clerk who is appointed to take part in the services of parochial worship. The very name is witness that he is the Lord's servant.'[53] Manning showed better proportion and sense in his advice on the restoration of churches, pointing out that it would cost no more to remain faithful to the building's original style than to flout it. His own efforts with Graffham church, however, were not successful; presumably as a result of his enthusiasm for Gothic, the interior was obscured in an impenetrable gloom. 'See how an archdeacon with the best intentions can spoil a church,' he told visitors.[54]

Every year Manning delivered to his clergy an address or 'Charge' in which, according to the custom, he set forth his reflections on matters of moment affecting the Church. His first Charge (1841) more than reciprocated the confidence which the Church of England had shown in him. He noted how those countries most successful against the Reformation, Spain and France for instance, were now the most destitute of any active Christianity. *Per contra* the English Church 'has now more than ever shown a vivid and inextinguishable life, which quickens with an even pulse the whole of her extended system: she has retained what they have visibly lost – her hold upon the nation as a people, and her mastery over the highest intellectual natures'. He returned to this agreeable theme of vaunting the Anglican Church in his peroration. 'Who can ponder these things and not feel a consciousness returning stronger than all reasoning, that if she be loyal to her heavenly Lord, she shall be made more glorious in His earthly kingdom, as the regenerator of the Christendom that seems now dissolving, and the centre of a new Catholic world?'[55] The prospect was sublime, inspiring; and about as close to reality as the Monophysites were to nineteenth-century Anglicans.

The reception of Manning's views was not to be confined to the clergy of the Chichester archdeaconry. His Charges were carefully wrought set-pieces to be published and sent forth into the land, more particularly to the homes of influential friends and colleagues. Manning now had a platform on which to build a national reputation, and one part of him was swept up into the role of rapidly rising ecclesiastic. 'He were a wonderful man,' remembered one of his Lavington flock, 'but he wasn't such a man for the parish, after they made him Archdeacon.'[56] His house was no longer the stronghold against the world that it had been in Caroline's day. During the 1840s invitations sped out to the great and the good, to the Wilberforces, to Whewell, the Master of Trinity; to F. D. Maurice, one of the founders of Christian socialism, to Keble.[57] The talk was lofty, although the cuisine was unpredictable.[58] At the same time the archdeacon was seen more and more in London, particularly in the winter when the cold and the damp of the country imposed unacceptable strains upon his health. (George Richmond recalled visiting him in June and finding big fires in every room.)[59] In town Manning discovered an effortless entrée into the spheres of influence. 'I see you are coming to town again,' Gladstone would write. 'On Tuesday the Archbishop of York, the Bishop of London, and Dr Hook are engaged to dine with us, and if you would come in about nine your company would be very acceptable.'[60]

Even without Gladstone, Manning's success would have been ensured. The combination of his polished social manner, his growing reputation and his ascetic appearance made him an irresistible force in the circles of fascination. Saints are a capture for any hostess, especially when they know how to behave. In Manning's case his easy flow of anecdote was perfectly offset by the clear, steady gaze emanating from a countenance that suggested, in its handsome but taut features, the most rigorous mortification. It was obvious that the man was going to be a bishop, at the very least. There were three men to whom the country had to look, declared Bishop Phillpotts of Exeter: 'Manning in the Church, Gladstone in the State, and Hope in the Law.'[61] 'No power on earth', Phillpotts added for good measure, 'can keep Manning from the Bench' (of bishops).[62]

And why should it not have been so? The Church of England has never been so well supplied with outstandingly able men that it could afford to let them fester in country rectories, even if they were besotted with religion. The witnesses of Manning's impressiveness at this period are diverse and unanimous. F. D. Maurice, writing oddly enough to Lytton Strachey's uncle, described him thus after a visit to Lavington in 1843:

Manning is one of the completest, perhaps the completest man I ever met with; there are doubtless deficiencies, which completeness itself implies, seeing that the incomplete is that which is ever seeking the infinite and eternal to fill up its hollows; and in him there is a logical rotundity which I should not wish for. But it is united with so much appreciation of everything good, such great refinement, tolerance and kindliness, that I do not know where one would look, rather, for a wise and true bishop in these times.[63]

Essentially similar testimony is provided by a very different man, James Sterling, a minor literary figure who had once been in Orders but resigned when he lost his faith. He met Manning in Rome early in 1839 and reported to a friend:

He is one of the most finished and compact specimens of his school of manhood and of theology that I have ever fallen in with, and it was amusing to see how by faultless self-command, dialectical acuteness, coherent system, readiness of expression, and a perfect union of earnestness and gentleness, he always seemed to put in the wrong the gentlemen of the so-called Evangelical class, who muster strong here, and whom he frequently met with. He could not play quite the same game with me, for I knew better than most of them what I meant by my words. I conceive him to be, in his own place and generation, one of the most practically efficient and energetic men I have ever known, and in a state of freer and more fluent life in the ecclesiastical polity he would rise high and do considerable things.[64]

That was a detached view. Those who shared Manning's religious sympathies threw aside all restraint. William Lockhart was an undergraduate when he first saw Manning in the archdeacon's stall in Chichester cathedral. 'His face was to me some first dim revelation of the *supernatural in man*.'[65] It was a dim revelation that was to lead Lockhart into the Catholic Church well before the archdeacon. Another worshipper was Aubrey de Vere, something of a poet. He first met Manning in 1849 and soon concluded that this was the most ecclesiastical man he had ever seen. 'You would think that a saint of old had stepped out of a picture by Raphael or Perugino. His manners are not less interesting, including a marvellous union of grace, decisiveness, and sanctity.'[66] By the time that he wrote his *Recollections* (published 1897) the memory of these early encounters with Manning had become sacred. 'The intensity of his nature . . . could not be doubted by anyone who had seen him in Church or at prayer. . . . I see a word written on the forehead of that man, and that word is *sacerdos*.' De Vere's final judgement, committed to verse, was that Manning appeared as a combination of Dante and St Thomas Aquinas: 'These two great minds in him are one.'[67] It is not necessary to go quite that far to see that Manning had potential in his chosen profession.

The Bishop of Exeter was wrong, however, when he opined that no earthly power could keep Manning from becoming a bishop. On the contrary, there was a succession of earthly powers, Prime Ministers, only too likely to do just that. Any connection with Newman or Pusey was a well-nigh fatal handicap to aspirants for a bishopric. Even a Tory like Sir Robert Peel, Prime Minister from 1841 to 1846, and determined to promote worthy men without undue regard for political advantage, drew the line well short of Tractarians. One day, perhaps, Gladstone would be Prime Minister, but that must have seemed (indeed it turned out to be) a distant hazard on which to rest any hopes. For the foreseeable future the position was absolutely clear. 'No chance,' Manning replied to a speculation that he might become a bishop, 'unless some crisis comes and they require me to quiet it.'[68] He would have been more than human if these considerations had not increased his distaste for the secularity of the English Church.

Of course he wanted to be a bishop; he even (later) admitted to having fantasized about how he would discharge the role.[69] He knew very well from instinct, upbringing and experience how he should act to fulfil these dreams. Nevertheless, the jeers of Lytton Strachey about his ambition entirely miss the point. The striking thing about Manning was what he would *not* do to achieve promotion. He had, after all, adopted one of the few religious lines that must effectively cut off his way of advance. 'People were expecting and predicting all things for me, and I was making them impossible.'[70] If he was never quite capable of becoming a fool for Christ's sake, at least he resisted becoming an Anglican bishop. In theology he was intransigent. 'I am too much of a Platonist to hold truth moderately,' he said. 'I should as soon think of holding the multiplication table in moderation.'[71] It is true that he tried to live in peace with the Evangelical clergy of the Chichester diocese. Conciliation, however, is quite distinct from concession.

He had only to look to his brother-in-law Samuel Wilberforce to see what policy might achieve. Wilberforce held unexceptionably moderate High Church views, cultivated connections at Court, and became Bishop of Oxford in 1845 at the age of forty. After the death of John Sargent's mother in 1841, Wilberforce, whose wife, Emily Sargent, died the same year, became the owner of the Lavington property, so he and Manning stayed very much in touch. They never really got on. 'I think he always feared me,' Manning recollected in old age, 'and I never fully trusted him. I saw that he pursued worldly interests, and that he was losing simplicity.'[72] When Samuel Wilberforce remarked of someone that he was 'one of those men who had abilities to rise if he had not conscience enough to make it impossible', Manning thought how closely this judgement applied to his own case.[73] That Samuel's rapid elevation piqued him is suggested by the tone of sorrowful superiority in which he wrote to Robert Wilberforce of 'our dear brother'.[74] He did not like the emotions that the dear brother aroused in him, though he would occasionally try to do penance. 'Forgive me all my faults towards you,' he would write to Samuel in 1850, 'and give me not as much love as I deserve, but as much as your loving heart can bestow.'[75]

This was typical of the way in which Manning valiantly strove to bring his natural human feelings into conformity with his high ideal of Christian duty. Inevitably, since the same exceptionally strong will served both his secular and his spiritual aspirations, the tension between these two disparate elements was extreme. It was relieved by endless self-analysis. Manning has been condemned for his ambition, yet most of what is known of this failing comes from the journals in which he recorded his struggles against it. He could not enter a drawing-room without some internal voice starting up an insistent counterpoint under his urbane manner: 'What doest thou here, Elias?'[76] He longed for position, but he taught that the meek shall inherit the earth. He felt the urge to dominate, but he held that the Christian should turn the other cheek. He was an Anglican archdeacon, but he was committed to eternity.

Manning, who had begun by forcing religion upon himself, gradually discovered that it had taken possession. The experience brought him little joy. To make any serious attempt to follow the New Testament ethic is to embrace suffering, as his congregations were constantly informed:

The world is . . . bitter, treacherous, and full of enmity against God. The law, that every man that will live godly in Christ Jesus must suffer persecution, is still unrepealed in this fallen earth. Every faithful man will have the grace-tokens of the Cross upon his inmost soul. By temptation, by wrestling against evil, by crucifixion of self, by wrongs and snares from without, by sorrow and afflictions from above, every brother of the First-born in the family of man will bear His likeness, and be perfected by the keen edge of pain.[77]

Repeatedly in his sermons he returned to this theme of the necessity of suffering, until it appears that he is seeking not so much to convince his congregation as to keep his own resolve up to the mark. So many passages seem to have a directly personal bearing:

What a life of disappointment, and bitterness, and aching fear, and restless uncertainty, is the life of the ambitious, and covetous, and self-indulgent: merchants, trading at a thousand hazards; statesmen, climbing up to slippery places; men of letters catching at every breath of fame; men of the world, toiling to sustain a great appearance, – how anxious, and craving, and sensitive, and impatient of an equal do they become! How saddened, how ill at ease, how preyed upon by the fretting of unrest; and therefore how far from the calm inward shining of the love of God![78]

Again, 'the habit of mind which is formed in us by society is so unlike that in which he speaks with God in solitude, that it seems to wear out of us the susceptibility of deeper and higher energies. Much more true is this when to the love of society is added . . . a love of power, or a craving after rank and dignities.'[79] If it hurt to give up these things, so much the better: 'They that have no fellowship with the Man of Sorrows have no share of His Cross, no promise of His Crown.'[80]

The sermons in which Manning so eloquently denounced the world sold excellently, further enhancing both his reputation and his dilemma. He was a first-rate preacher, capable of a well-regulated and apparently effortless flow of language on any subject, from the spiritual agonies of expiring harlots (intense, apparently) to the mechanics of the resurrection, on which he appeared equally well informed. As a Catholic Manning would criticize his Anglican sermons as being over-studied in content and monotonous in delivery, but clearly he gave satisfaction at the time. In 1841 he was appointed a Select Preacher at Oxford University, where he became one of the few besides Newman who could fill St Mary's on a weekday. Manning's appeal was rather to the heart than to the head, and there was never any lack of unction in the style. Occasionally people complained of obscurity.[81] Nevertheless he was effective at making congregations aware that the highest standards of holiness would be required on Judgement Day.

Yet Manning never, like Newman, regarded the quest for salvation as an end which utterly transcended the fact of earthly suffering. The best part of him, humanly speaking, and the key to much that he achieved, was his deep and passionately felt sympathy for the victims and underdogs of this life. However much he learnt from Newman in theology, in this respect he was his own man. His campaign against the world was not, like Newman's, conducted at a comfortable distance from the material sufferings that the world inflicted.

Newman was disgusted by the unfettered capitalism of the nineteenth century, but his mind was exercised principally with the moral dangers that afflicted the wealthy rather than with the appalling hardships that attended the poor. His aesthetic sensibility was outraged by the worship of Mammon, so 'dreary', so 'low'.[82] 'It is a very fearful consideration', he thought, 'that we belong to a nation which in good measure subsists by making money.'[83] Manning quite agreed with him that the country was parlously placed on that score. 'Of all the chilling and isolating spells of the world, none are more deadly to the Christian life than politics and trading: they are the foster-fathers of self-will and self-interest, and these lie at the root of our modern English character.'[84]

Manning's distaste for the commercial spirit, however, was combined with an instinctive sympathy for the dispossessed, whose distress Newman forbore to investigate. Towards individual cases of need Newman might be charitable; by the spectacle of mass suffering which the 1840s presented he remained wholly unmoved. The material problems of humanity were just not his field. Fifth-century religious controversies appeared to him not merely a more entertaining, but even a more relevant, study than nineteenth-century philanthropy. He adopted the uncompromising and not wholly inconvenient standpoint that 'the human race is implicated in some terrible aboriginal calamity',[85] that the world by its very nature was irretrievably lost, that his proper concern was, therefore, with the destiny of men's eternal souls, not with how their short-lived bodies fared. 'The Catholic Church', he proclaimed after his conversion, 'holds it better for the sun and moon to drop from heaven, for the earth to fail, and for all the many millions on it to die of starvation in extremest agony, as far as temporal affliction goes, than that one soul, I will not say, should be lost, but should commit one single venial sin, should tell one wilful untruth, or should steal one poor farthing without excuse.'[86] Manning might have approved such a sentiment as abstract theology, but he was far too practical, and far too compassionate, to distance himself from the distress of the poor. What could be more likely to make a man steal and lie than starvation? Such a commonplace reflection, however, aroused no enthusiasm in Newman. For a while in 1833, under the influence of Hurrell Froude, he had toyed with the idea that the Church might be an ally of the people. But this notion was more an expression of Froude's anarchic nature than an earnest of any sympathy with the oppressed. It did not survive in Newman's mind for more than a month or two. 'I have left off being anti-aristocratical,' he soon announced. 'I do not feel the time has come.'[87] For him it never did.

Manning, by contrast, was anti-aristocratical whenever justice demanded as much. When the Duke of Richmond pressed too hard upon his tenants for rent, the young rector of Lavington did not hesitate to chastise 'the sin of exacting the largest rent and doing the least repairs'.[88] 'The possessors of land,' he declared, 'are the natural guardians of the poor who live and die upon their soil. The laws of property are altogether second in the scale of God's providence, compared with these laws of local and personal obligation.' That was a decidedly radical statement for the 1840s. Already Manning was insisting that the welfare of the people must come before the dictates of the market-place. 'There is a grace of life which is more real than political economy, more living, active and beneficent than efficient management and statistical exactness.'[89]

So Manning spoke out for the poor and the outcast. His sympathies were deep and far-reaching. Very few Englishmen concerned themselves, as he did, with the fate of convicts transported to Australia. 'Our convict population', he thundered, 'is a phenomenon of carnal and spiritual wickedness, such as, I believe, this earth has never seen. . . . It is not enought to say "This system will henceforward be abandoned." The blood of souls cries to heaven against us . . . works meet for repentance must be done.'[90] Manning was not, however, one of those philanthropists who prefer to concentrate attention on causes well removed from home. He saw misery and distress where the privileged classes have invariably found it hardest to discern, under their own noses, masquerading as unalterable facts of existence. Even the beauty of the Sussex countryside, Manning realized, was horribly flawed. 'We have a people straitened by poverty – worn down by toil; they labour from the rising to the setting of the sun; and the human spirit will faint or break at the last. It is to this unrelenting round of labour that the sourness so unnatural to our English poor, but now too often seen, is chiefly to be ascribed.'[91] The rural labourers, however, Manning considered to be more fortunate than 'the poor sicklied workman in the manufactory', for whom 'life is an uncheered, grating toil, which jars and galls the whole man in soul and body. Life has for them few gleams, little or nothing of gladness or of freedom: even wife and children, which make the natural heart to spring, give to a wearied and saddened people but little happiness. In them they see their own toil-worn life, as if it would never end, beginning over again.'[92]

Manning's remedies for these ills were at this stage essentially paternal-istic, very much the same kind of solutions as were being propounded by the 'Young England' group of Tories under Lord John Manners. As the Oxford Movement imagined the medieval Church to have been an ideal spiritual authority, so the Young Englanders looked back on the feudal order as a paradigm of social responsibility.[93] Which of these two points of view was further from the truth would be hard to determine; still, it would be churlish to demand historical accuracy of any theory which succeeds in inducing social conscience into ambitious and well-connected young men. One of the 'Young England' calls that Manning took up was that the lower classes should be accorded more holidays. The language he used was typical of that movement:

Time must be redeemed for the poor man. The world is too hard upon him and makes him pay too heavy a tale out of his short life. Except Sunday and one or two other days – such as Christmas Day, Good Friday, and Ascension Day, which through Christian kindness of many landlords and farmers in this neighbourhood, has of late, without loss of wages, been given to their labourers – our poor have no days of relaxation for body and mind. Those who have lived as it is our blessing to do among the agricultural poor will know that with some rudeness of address and with faults not to be denied, they are still a noble-hearted race, whose sincerity, simplicity, and patience we should buy cheap at the cost of our refinements. But little is needed to make their holiday. The green fields and tools idle for a day, the church bell, an active game, simple fare, the sport of their children, the kindly presence and patient ear of superiors, is enough to make a village festival.[94]

That was certainly a romanticized view of the poor, but it was not a callous one. Manning cannot be blamed for having failed, in the 1840s, to foresee that the State might become a universal provider. He *had* seen, however, that in the face of widespread destitution 'the irregular efforts of private charity will not suffice'.[95] This realization was combined with a sense that it might not be desirable to relieve the poor entirely of responsibility for their own betterment. His attachment to the philosophy of self-help was reflected in his curious practice of giving one shoe to poor children in the village and leaving the mother to provide the other.[96] He also advocated the development of village friendly societies. In theory these organizations existed to provide members with relief during sickness and old age, to be distributed from the pennies which they had subscribed in better times. In practice those in charge frequently blew the funds on an annual binge. Manning, paternalistic as ever, wanted the societies placed under the control of the parish clergyman, who might be trusted to take a longer and a soberer view of members' interests.

If irregular private charity did not suffice, it would have, in the absence of the welfare state, to be made more regular. Only the Church, Manning held, could achieve this miracle, and what opportunities the task presented:

It was the design of the Legislature [he explained in his 1842 Charge] and I think a wise one, to call into life a larger energy of voluntary almsgiving, by throwing more upon the principle of private charity. I believe this has been done; and the moral strength of that change is ours. Well may we accept this sacred burden with a forward and ready will, for it has made the Church once more the centre of poor men's hearts, and has endowed it with functions of consolation, which surround it with its mightiest defences, the prayers of the sick and needy.[97]

Once more, as with education, as with the plans for the conversion of Empire and the regeneration of Christendom, the programme sounded magnificent as Manning outlined it. Once more the ideal was utterly beyond the Church of England's capacities. It is difficult, but essential, to remember, when reading Manning's confident pronouncements, that his message was that of a small and unpopular sect. As for the Church becoming 'once more the centre of poor men's hearts', how could that be when it sanctioned and reinforced social distinctions? Even in the very churches themselves the rich secured the best seats through buying or renting private pews, while the poor were obliged to find such inconvenient and distant places as they might. Manning vigorously supported the campaign to abolish this practice, marshalling his archidiaconal concern for church buildings in the good cause. 'Not only are the aisles and passages of the church and chancel choked by pews, but I have seen screens of beautiful carved work cut to pieces; wrought capitals and bases of columns hacked and broken; shafts of the finest stone, the piers of arches, and the very arches themselves, altogether cut away, to make room for the backs and corners of private pews.' But of course Manning's main objection to private pews was that they destroyed the trust of the poor in the Church, and confirmed the rich in their unwarranted arrogance. He wanted to return to the free and open benches of former times, when the church interior had served as 'a pathetic witness against the self-elevation and self-preference of one above another, a rebuke of the exacting vigilance of private rights, and a manifestation that in Christ all things are united; that in Him "there is neither bond nor free".'[98] Manning's hopes were not realized: the number of private pews declined, but they were not obliterated.

Men of great energy and practical ability do not care to find themselves reduced to practical impotence. Though Manning might explain in a sermon that the Christian conquers through that which the world deems weak,[99] he was never reconciled to the ineffectiveness of the Anglican *Church*. 'We have exchanged our spiritual weapons for secular powers,' he grumbled to Gladstone, 'and they fail us in contending against the world of which we have borrowed them.'[100] Powerlessness in this world might just be acceptable to him as a token of a commission from another, infinitely powerful order. Conversely, though, the more evident the terrestial weakness of the Church of England, the more Manning needed to be sure of its divine credentials. Caught in this dilemma, he published in 1842 a large volume entitled *The Unity of the Church*, dedicated to Gladstone. It is a curious production. The argument tells entirely against Anglicanism; the conclusion comes down resoundingly in its favour.

Manning's contention was that division from God's Church must end in heresy and sacramental impoverishment as certainly as division of each individual from God must end in sin. He depicted the predicament of the disunited soul in a simile that may have sprung from his own struggles with ambition. 'As a flame, beaten down in its ascent, is severed into many flames, and turns every way; so the will of man, averted from God, reaches out around, and is drawn out on all sides by objects of sense, and becomes the slave of many lusts.' The remedy was plain to see. 'It is in the One True Church alone', Manning proclaimed, 'that there is a revealed way of salvation in the Name of Christ.' Outside that Church virtue could only be a limited concept:

Among those that are severed from the unity of the Church may often be found a rigid morality, but little of the unearthly temper which marks the Catholic Saints. We often see strict truth, integrity, and benevolence, but little of the conscious awe of God's invisible presence, the subjugation of passion, and denial of self, which distinguish a Saint from a Philosophic Moralist. We shall often see, likewise, much zeal, forwardness and energy in action, but little of the meekness, self-withdrawal and devout humility which is the crowning glory of Christ's example.[101]

Manning had cast his life upon the search for holiness, and here he was expressing the conviction that the Catholic Church alone possessed the means to its attainment. While working on his book, Manning expressed in a letter to Gladstone the dilemma which this belief raised. He was still determined (no doubt under the influence of *Tract xc*) that the Church of England was 'Catholic in dogma and in polity', but, he complained, 'the subjective, the internal, ascetic, contemplative, devotional, moral, penitential elements are wasted down to a meagreness which is nigh unto death'.[102] What did that catalogue leave uninfected? In reply, Gladstone could only recommend that the way to restore Church discipline was 'to do it permissively and as it were in a corner'.[103] That hardly suggested the Church Militant.

Yet Manning was unable, or unwilling, to make the obvious deduction. He still clung doggedly, in *The Unity of the Church*, to the opinion (it was now more like a hope) that Anglicanism was the true branch of the Catholic Church in England. 'The suspension . . . of communion between the Churches of England and Rome is no hindrance to the obtaining of salvation on both sides.' The Reformation required some explaining, but Manning's phrasing was equal to the task. 'The Church of England . . . released its Apostolical powers from the oppression of a foreign and uncanonical jurisdiction.' Catholic faith and doctrine had remained intact. The Church of England had merely followed the example of the Eastern Church and 'rejected the arrogant pretence of a universal pontificate rashly alleged to be of divine right, imposed in open breach of Apostolical traditions, and the canons of many councils'.[104]

In a private treatise written at this time, however, he admitted his admiration for the 'majesty, grandeur and reality' of Rome even while maintaining his sentimental attachment to the Church of England.[105] Then, in the autumn of 1843, his hard-maintained faith in Anglicanism received another jolt. Newman, who had retired to Littlemore outside Oxford after the hostile reception accorded to *Tract xc*, marked another stage in his religious odyssey by resigning the living of St Mary's. Manning immediately wrote to ask what could have precipitated such a step. His own lack of sympathy with *Tract xc* had prompted him to tell Gladstone that 'in some things I thoroughly agree with Newman, in some things partially, in some not at all'.[106] Now he intended, with his query about St Mary's, to find out where Newman stood. In reply Newman complained of having been treated as 'foreign material'[107] in the Anglican church. He was not yet expounding the papal case quite as effectively as Karl Marx, who wrote in 1842 that 'if . . . there is no supreme head of the Church, the domination of religion is nothing but the religion of domination, the cult of the will of the government',[108] but he had lost for ever his trust and hope in the Church of England:

I fear I must confess [he elaborated] that in proportion as I think the English Church is showing herself intrinsically and radically alien from Catholic principles, so do I feel the difficulties of defending her claims to be a branch of the Catholic Church. It seems a dream to call a communion Catholic, when one can neither appeal to any clear statement of Catholic doctrine in its formularies, nor interpret ambiguous formularies by the received and living Catholic sense, whether past or present. Men of Catholic views are too truly but a party in our Church.[109]

Newman the sober realist was a new apparition. The archdeacon essayed a rebuke. 'Has not God prospered you in these last ten years in a measure which makes it – may I venture to say – impatience something like Jonah's to ask or look for more?'[110] This remonstrance merely had the effect of drawing Newman further from his cover. 'It is not from disappointment, irritation or impatience, that I have, whether rightly or wrongly, resigned St Mary's,' he returned, 'but because I think the Church of Rome the Catholic Church, and ours not part of the Catholic Church, because not in communion with Rome.'[111]

This alarming letter Manning immediately forwarded (with Newman's permission) to Gladstone. The reaction was all that might have been expected. 'I stagger to and fro like a drunken man and am at my wits' end,'[112] reported the President of the Board of Trade, in imitation of the psalmist. Yet his 'good angel',[113] as he called Manning, might still save the situation by explaining to Newman the flaws in his argument. (Gladstone had a singular trust in Manning's abilities: that May he had sought the archdeacon's opinion before agreeing to accept a place in the Cabinet.[114] Manning had sent a most satisfactory answer, seizing the occasion to reciprocate his friend's high opinion: 'I know of no one man, not in Holy Orders, on whom the Providence of God has laid so much of the burden of the English Church at this time.')[115] But Manning hesitated to grapple with Newman, even at Gladstone's behest. The most he would venture was to invite Newman down to Lavington, that he might witness at first hand the living evidence of God's presence in Anglican parish life. Newman declined this opportunity, which might not, in any case, have served the end which Manning intended. The Sussex agriculturist took a decidedly down-to-earth view of religious mystery. 'I see Elijah the prophet once,' declared one of them. 'I tell ye I see him just over agan that woodstack. I told the Archdeacon too. He knowed very well all about Elijah. He said I should see him again one day, but I ha'n't!'[116]

The fact was that Newman's confession had badly shaken Manning, as he explained in a letter to Pusey:

I feel to have been for four years on the brink of I know not what; all the while persuading myself and others that all was well; and more – that none were so true and steadfast [as Newman] to the English Church; none so safe as guides. I feel as if I had been a deceiver speaking lies (God knows, not in hypocrisy), and this has caused a sort of shock in my mind that makes me tremble. Feel for me in my position. Day after day I have been pledging myself to clergymen and laymen all about me that all was safe and sure. I have been using his books, defending and endeavouring to spread the system which carried this dreadful secret at its heart.

Manning had written that letter in reply to Pusey's complaint about a sermon which he had delivered before the University of Oxford on Guy Fawkes Day 1843. The occasion demanded an anti-Roman rant, and Manning duly obliged. For this he has been accused, both posthumously and by contemporaries, of deliberately betraying his convictions in order to identify himself with the broad – and promotable – mainstream of the English Church. The suggestion is too Machiavellian. Manning was acting by instinct not calculation, attempting in the immediate aftermath of Newman's revelation to draw back from an abyss he was not yet ready to contemplate. The guide had proved treacherous: let the fortress be secured at its weakest point. Manning felt himself bound to speak out or to lose credibility:

There remains for me nothing but to be plain henceforward on points which hitherto I have almost resented, or ridiculed the suspicion. I did so because I knew myself to be heartily true to the English Church, both affirmatively in her positive teaching, and negatively in the rejection of the Roman system and its differential points. I can do this no more. I am reduced to the painful, saddening, sickening necessity of saying what I feel about Rome.[117]

Manning's error was to imagine that he had any distinct feelings about Rome; on that subject his mind was still a confused mixture of conventional English prejudice and nascent religious attraction. His Gunpowder Plot sermon was not, by the standards of the time, a particularly ferocious rant. Such animus as appeared was mainly concentrated upon the Pope's assumption of temporal powers, and especially upon his claim to possess the right to depose princes – all routine polemic for 5 November. Manning only caught fire when he described how Providence, in foiling the Plot, had worked to protect the Church of England. Surely there must have been some special purpose in this – and once more Manning galloped off on his hobby-horse of God's plans for Anglicanism. 'All the phenomena of the world warn us that the latter days have set in,' he pronounced in his most apocalyptic vein.

It may be, that our highly favoured Church, amid much chastisement and rebukes of heavenly discipline, shall be fashioned and corrected until it become a principle of reconciliation between east and west, and a law of unity and peace to mankind. It may be, that our task shall be to cast up the camp of the saints against the day when the nations of Antichrist shall, for the last time, go up and compass it about. We may be called to bear and to break the last assault of the kingdom of evil.'[118]

What emerges from this performance is not so much any detestation of Rome as a desperate need to be convinced, through no matter what exaggeration, of the validity of Anglicanism.

Having delivered himself of this sermon Manning, quite unabashed, betook himself next day to Littlemore to see Newman. Throughout his life he maintained the optimistic view that there was no earthly reason why any difference of opinion should interfere with friendship. Presumably on this occasion he wanted to hear some first-hand explanation of how Newman had reached his present pass. An account of what occurred upon his arrival at Littlemore appeared in *The Century* forty years later:

The door was opened by one of those young men, then members of the quasi-monastic community, who had to convey to the Archdeacon the unpleasant intimation that Dr Newman had declined to see him. So anxious was the young man to cover the slight, and to minimise its effect, that he walked away from the door with the Archdeacon, bareheaded as he was, and had covered half the way to Oxford before he turned back, unaware, as was his companion, of his unprotected state, under the November sky.[119]

The story seems to have lost nothing in the telling. At all events, the correspondence between the two men continued, and the tone became even more affectionate. When Manning wrote a worried letter asking how things stood between them, Newman replied (24 December 1843) in his most charming vein:

How can I thank you enough for your most kind letter received last night, and what can have led you to entertain the thought that I could ever be crossed by the idea which you consider may have been suggested to me by the name of Orpah*? Really,

* 'She who turns her back,' *vide* Ruth, I, IV, 14.

unless it were so very sad a matter I should smile; the thought is as far from me as the antipodes. Rather I am the person who to myself always seem, and reasonably, the criminal. I cannot afford to have hard thoughts which can more plausibly be exercised against myself . . . it would be strange if I had the heart to blame others, who are honest in maintaining what I am abandoning. It is no pleasure to me to differ from friends, no comfort to be estranged from them, no satisfaction or boast to have said things which I must unsay. Surely I will remain where I am as long as I can. I think it right to do so. If my misgivings are from above I shall be carried on in spite of my resistance. I cannot regret in time to come having struggled to remain where I found myself placed. And, believe me, the circumstance of such men as yourself being contented to remain is the strongest argument in favour of my own remaining. It is my constant prayer that if others are right I may be drawn back, that nothing may part us.[120]

Manning hastened to send this letter also on to Gladstone, who concluded that 'a most formidable contingency is in the distance, more or less remote'.[121] Who better to keep it more remote than Manning? Gladstone proffered some advice on tactics. 'By one word he gives you an excellent ground of approach – the word "contented". Starting from that word you may, though with a light touch, avow that you are – (1) Not contented, but obliged; perhaps it might be dangerous to add, (2) Not contented, but thankful. Such writing might be a parable to him.'[122] It was not through parables, however, and certainly not through lightness of touch, that Manning would gain influence over Newman's destiny.

Meanwhile his own restlessness about the Anglican case did not abate. 'If our position be tenable,' he wrote to Gladstone, 'let us work onward with all hope. If not, let us abandon it. I cannot consent nor endure to be going back in the midst of work to root up first principles to see if they are alive, like children gardening.'[123] Clearly Manning's difficulties had as much to do with his own psychology as with objective theological argument. And now, just as his doubts about the Church of England were beginning to breed, he suffered a disappointment which emphasized how difficult promotion would be for anyone tainted with Tractarianism. The Preachership of Lincoln's Inn had fallen vacant, not a great office in itself, but one which offered the successful candidate a prominent pulpit in London, and which would mark him down as a potential candidate for episcopal honours. Gladstone was keen that Manning should apply, and sanguine about his chances. 'You may take the vacancy for a certainty,' he wrote to Manning on 18 November 1843.[124] With much seemly protestation about his determination not to canvass, Manning allowed his name to go forward. Gladstone, while professing to respect his friend's scruples, drummed up as much support as possible. His optimism, however, was not universally shared. 'They say Manning is too high for the Lincoln's Inn men,'[125] noted James Mozley. And certainly this was not a time – but when was it ever the time? – for a High Churchman to be seeking promotion. Newman's resignation of St Mary's had set the Benchers sniffing suspiciously for the least sign of papistry. In January 1844 the post was awarded to some wholly undistinguished, but correspondingly safe, protégé of Queen Adelaide.

Gladstone could only attempt to soothe his friend's disappointment with expressions of esteem. He had been guilty of a political error, he admitted, but he had believed that the Benchers would be guided by a sense of comparative fitness. The appointment was highly disparaging to them. 'Your character is part of the property of the Church, and must be husbanded for the sake of its association with that truth.'[126] Manning was not to be consoled. He felt humiliated out of all proportion to his failure. Three years later he would write in his journal that from 1827 to 1844 God had preserved him 'from great public shame'.[127] It was, apparently, the Lincoln's Inn affair that had marked the end of this happy state of affairs, though the event cannot have caused the least ripple outside the narrowest of ecclesiastical circles. It was never Manning's way, however, to minimize the importance of events in which he was involved. And by 1847, when he made that reflection, he had become obsessed with the idea that he was being led through pain and chastisement into a better path. After the desertion of Newman, Manning would never again find any peace or security within the Anglican Church.

4 An Essay in Development

It is difficult exactly to say what I am resting upon. I think it is partly the esteem of others, chiefly founded on what I have written; and on the expectation of something to come. Suppose I were left here alone, or with an uncomfortable neighbour; that my books were to leave off selling, and I were publicly attacked; that the prospect of elevation were at an end, and that nothing were left me but to stay myself on God in prayer and parish work – should I feel as I do now? If God were really my stay now, I should. But I think I should not do so, and therefore I doubt whether He is so.[1]

MANNING'S JOURNAL, 15 FEBRUARY 1846

It is easier to give an external account of the steps which Manning took towards Catholicism than to understand the inner development that underlay the process. Manning needed certainty; Manning relished authority; Manning rejected the secularism and impotence of the State Church: such explanations are valid, but they are also insufficient. 'Catholicism is a deep matter,' said Newman, 'you cannot take it up in a teacup.'[2] Why, for instance, did Manning become absorbed not just by Roman Catholic claims of authority, but also by Roman Catholic devotions? No doubt he owed something on this score to Pusey, who reintroduced the Church of England to Catholic devotional works and practices. But that does not explain their appeal, or account for Manning's finding deep satisfaction, in his latter days as an Anglican, in Roman Catholic rites such as the Adoration of the Blessed Sacrament or the veneration of relics. A psychologist might think in terms of self-induced brainwashing; a Catholic might wonder at the operation of divine grace. Both, perhaps, would subscribe to the Sermon on the Mount: 'Ask, and it shall be given you; seek, and ye shall find; knock, and it shall be opened unto you.' But the mystery still remains.

Manning asked and sought and knocked most earnestly, and we have seen that he did not confine himself to prayer and theological study. His life reflected his acute awareness both of the moral dimension of faith and of the extreme difficulty of salvation. Like Newman, he had a Calvinist's sense of the predestined Elect of God, but (again like Newman) none of the Calvinist's assurance that he himself was counted among the fortunate few. He cited the meagre reckoning given in the seventh chapter of Revelations, that a mere 144,000 are sealed among the Elect. It was typical of him that he omitted to mention that this number refers only to the Jews. A succeeding verse, which brings the more comforting news that 'a great multitude which no man could number' was additionally raised to glory, he did not find compelling enough to quote.[3] These were times when English clergymen could discern the Almighty's purpose quite as distinctly as St John. Over on the other side of Sussex, at Alfriston, there was a Revd Charles Bohun Smyth who was wonderfully gifted in this respect. 'It is a sad thing', he would declare from the pulpit, 'that out of the whole congregation here present only six will be saved – and I could name them too.'[4] Manning, by contrast, was reduced to trembling uncertainty by the prospect of the Last Judgement. In 1840 he composed a prayer to the Holy Ghost that he recited every day for the rest of his life; its kernel was, 'Make me to be of quick understanding in the fear of the Lord.'[5] The prayer was answered. There was but one way, Manning concluded, by which a man might allay this fear and win some hope of Election. 'Not by any external signs, nor by any supernatural intimations, nor by resting upon absolute decrees and the like; but by deep inward marks of the work of God in us, by the correspondence of our spirit with the will and working of the Spirit of God.'[6]

In the 1840s Manning found that the Church of England afforded insufficient means for the attainment of that security. He was caught on both sides. As an Anglican he risked not only that he would not become a bishop, but, much more serious, that he would not save his soul. His episcopal ambitions were foundering on his beliefs; his hopes of salvation increasingly appeared to be prejudiced by the Church of England's lack of belief. Anglicanism did not set men on fire with the love of God nor persuade them to venture their paltry terrestial existence for an eternal reward. There were no Anglican saints. Learned and judicious divines, even those who wrote such excellent English as Jeremy Taylor or William Law, could not inspire Manning like the mystical theology of St Francis de Sales or the heroic charity of St Vincent de Paul. Anglicanism, as befitted English state religion, limited itself to the humanly possible. In the words of W. G. Ward, the most critical of the Oxford men, it 'watered down Christianity to what seemed more practicable for the average Christian than Christ's own teaching'. Ward became a Catholic in September 1845, after the publication of his *Ideal of the Christian Church* the previous year. He loved to outrage and mock the Anglican Establishment, and had taken especial delight in the solemn ceremony by which Oxford University condemned his book and deprived him of his fellowship. Manning was not amused. 'The situation seems to me, Mr Ward, to be one of the utmost gravity. Let us not at such a time give way to a spirit of levity or hilarity.'[7] Nevertheless he shared Ward's need for a severer religious ideal than the Church of England propounded, an ideal that could only be realized through supernatural aid. And the more he reflected the more he also tended to agree with Ward that the Roman Catholic Church had been ordained as the channel of that divine assistance.

This was not an opinion shared by the English public at large. 'Down with Popery' came second only to 'Queen and Country' as a cry for uniting all classes. It was also treasured as the one principle on which, at least before Newman, all members of the Anglican Church might unite. Even today the anti-papal strain has not been extirpated from the English character; in the middle of the nineteenth century the disease was still virulent. Newman, after his conversion, recorded the kind of experience that a Catholic priest might expect to undergo:

Our very persons, not merely our professions, are held in abhorrence; and we are spat at by the malevolent; we are passed by with a shudder of contemptuous pity by the better-natured; we are supposed to be defiled by some secret rites of blood by the ignorant . . . we are regarded as something unclean, which no one would touch, if they could help it: and our advances are met as would be those of some hideous baboon, or sloth, or rattlesnake, or toad, which strove to make itself agreeable.[8]

Even Catholic laity might encounter this treatment if they presumed to treat their faith as other than a guilty secret. Pugin, the architect, once made the mistake of crossing himself in a railway carriage. The woman opposite began screaming for the guard. 'You are a Catholic, sir,' she declaimed. 'I must get into another carriage.'[9]

The intense hostility generated by the confessional has already been mentioned. A surprising number of Victorians seemed incapable of believing that a priest might listen to a woman confessing without making improper suggestions. Clergymen debated how the rite might be stamped out. 'Transportation would not satisfy me,' wrote one, 'for that would merely transfer the evil from one part of the world to the other. Capital punishment alone would satisfy me. Death alone would prevent the evil. That is my sober conviction.'[10] Convents worried stout English hearts almost as much as confessionals:

Fellow Britons [the Revd Michael Augustus Gathercole declared in the mid-1830s], keep your little daughters from the popish schools, for they are nurseries out of which the handsomest may be selected for the seraglios of the Popish priests called nunneries. . . . Freedom is the Briton's noble birthright, rescued from Popish tyranny, at the expense of the heart's blood of our valiant Christian forefathers, bravely shed amidst the racks, tortures, and the fires of the bloody popish inquisition; and shall any of our countrywomen be confined in nunnery prison-houses, to be the victims of licentious priests, and without one hope of escape but through the gloomy portals of death?[11]

Victorian pornography abounded in tales of unwilling nuns, more especially lovely girls from the upper classes, being incarcerated in subterranean cells and mercilessly whipped by way of penance. The *pièce de resistance* often involved the ritual murder by priests of infants who had been conceived in the convent, the same kind of slur, ironically enough, that the Catholics used to cast at the Jews in the Middle Ages. Even respectable opinion was not prepared to forgo all sexual innuendo; it registered manly shock at clerical celibacy. William Wordsworth, no less, was much exercised over this matter:

I reckon the constrained celibacy of the clergy the monstrous root of the greatest part of the mischiefs of Popery [he wrote in 1840]. If that could be got rid of, most of the other evils would gradually melt away. If we would truly spiritualise men, we must take care that we do not do so by unhumanising them, which is the process in respect of all those who are brought up with a view to the making of that unnatural vow.[12]

Anti-Catholicism, in short, was a weird and unpleasant national psychosis. Its roots tracked back to the burnings of Mary's reign; its growth had been nurtured by a propaganda that identified Catholicism with tyranny and foreign threat, Protestantism with liberty and patriotic sentiment. The case was self-evident: why, look at Ireland, where even the benefits of English rule had not succeeded in overcoming the degrading effects of papistry.

Most of the time the prejudice against Catholics festered in private places, content with mindless slander and vicious penal laws. By the 1840s it required the most advanced paranoia to take the old religion seriously as a threat to the national fabric. Yet the old animus still smouldered, and there was no surety that another rogue like Titus Oates or another crackpot like Lord George Gordon might not once more fan it into mob fury. The passing of Catholic Emancipation had only intensified John Bull's vigilance against the enemy within. Only men of the world were indifferent, like Charles Greville, who deplored Protestant bigotry on the grounds that religion was not a subject which any gentleman ought to make a fuss about. This level of sophistication was rare. The Protestant consensus left no one tempted to become a Catholic on whim. Conversion meant expulsion from the mainstream of English life, and very likely ostracism even from one's own family.[13]

Those like Manning and Newman, who had been under early Evangelical influence, were especially aware of the virulent and implacable nature of the English prejudice towards Rome. Newman, indeed, had fanned its flames; and he would admit in the *Apologia* that he was past forty before he succeeded in ridding himself completely of the conviction that the Pope was Anti-Christ.[14] As a man who rejoiced in his Englishry, he knew as well as any the tensions and strains that a drawing towards Rome involved. Perhaps it was partly Manning's need to feed on this knowledge, almost as though he subconsciously recognized that he too would be called upon to tread the abhorred path, which caused him to take such a keen interest in Newman's progress.

In November 1844 he wrote a letter of affectionate sympathy to Newman, who politely described it as 'a great gift'. Newman's reply, however, brought no comfort. He still held to his 'deep, unvarying conviction that our Church is in schism and my salvation depends on my joining the Church of Rome'. Even more worrying, he now spoke of 'contemplating a change'. He did not pretend that this prospect was pleasant on any worldly view; indeed, he would be giving up all his dearest associations for an unknown future. 'I have no existing sympathies with Roman Catholics; I hardly ever, even abroad, was at one of their services; I know none of them; I do not like what I hear of them.' Yet, Newman confessed, nothing but a fear that he might be under some delusion kept him in the Anglican Church, and that seemed a slim possibility, for his 'conviction' remained firm in all frames of mind. 'And this most serious feeling is growing on me, viz. that the reasons for which I believe *as much* as our system teaches, must lead me to believe more, and not to believe more, is to fall back into scepticism.'[15] This last argument appealed powerfully to Manning, who would use it time and again in ensuing years.

For the moment, however, Manning still refused to accept Newman's contention that the Catholicity of the English Church was a lost cause. 1845 saw the archdeacon producing a Charge in which he professed his loyalty to Anglicanism in his most lavish manner. After reviewing with some satisfaction the divisions and discontents in continental Catholicism he turned by way of contrast to the happy state of affairs at home. 'Every year, both by its prosperous and its adverse events, has deepened, with a force for which I can find no adequate expression, the belief – if I dared I would rather say the consciousness – that the Divine Presence and Power is with us in our pastoral office, in our sacraments, and in our whole spiritual being; restoring us, I trust, to a higher and holier life, and moulding this branch of the Catholic Church to be the channel of a great effusion of God's love not only to ourselves, but to the nations entrusted to our spiritual charge.' After a few more paragraphs of this heady stuff, Manning positively gave way before the press of emotion: 'I humbly thank God that He has permitted me to be a member of a Church in which I am not worthy to keep the door.'[16]

All the same, private doubts were niggling behind the public face. With Newman no longer available as an Anglican mentor, Manning felt the need of another intellectual guide to whom he could take his problems. His choice fell on Robert Wilberforce, and during the later 1840s an affectionate correspondence, albeit largely confined to theological matters, flourished between the two men. After Henry Wilberforce at Oxford, and Samuel during the years of Anglican ambition, it was finally with Robert, the eldest of the three brothers, that Manning established the most intimate friendship. But Robert, for all his vast theological knowledge, was prey to self-doubt and self-questioning; he was never capable, as Newman had been, of dominating an intellect so trenchant and decided as Manning's. The influence went the other way, with Robert Wilberforce's cumbersome mental apparatus being drawn down paths cut out by Manning's clear, efficient mind.

That was not what Manning had envisaged when he wrote to Robert on 30 June 1845 about his continuing problems with penitents attracted to Rome:

I have longed greatly to see you in quiet and to have the benefit of your judgement on some of the heavy events which are hanging over us. The extent to which unsettlement has extended itself is a serious matter. At the moment (let this be kept to yourself) I am directly or indirectly in contact with not less than seven cases. And I deeply feel that, with my little reasoning and constant active work, it is impossible for me, even if I were by nature able, to deal with the merely intellectual questions which are coming on us. I especially desire to join with you in this because some of the ablest and dearest of those round us fail to satisfy me in some of the conditions necessary for dealing fairly and solidly with the realities of our relation to the Roman Church.[17]

This letter was penned at much the same time as his wildly optimistic Charge.

Wilberforce attempted reassurance, but the same worries were still nagging away at Manning that autumn:

It seems to me that our theology is a chaos, we have no principles, no form, no order, or structure, or science. It seems to me inevitable that there must be a true and exact *intellectual* tradition of the gospel, and that the scholastic theology is (more or less) such a tradition. We have rejected it and substituted nothing in its room. Surely divine truth is susceptible, within the limits of revelation, of an expression and a proof as exact as the inductive sciences.[18]

Manning did not mean Wilberforce to take any undue alarm. 'My anxiety does not extend to doubts, for nothing can shake my belief of the presence of Christ in our Church and sacrament. I feel incapable of doubting it: again, the saints who have ripened round our altars for 300 years make it impossible for me to feel it a question of safety.'[19] But the Anglican saints, whoever they were, did not always bring Manning such security. Henry Wilberforce, taxed about this time with Manning's inordinate opinion of the Anglican Church, reassured his interlocutor that Manning, in fact, possessed a very deep sense of its corruption.[20]

Manning was also gaining a very deep sense of the Church's reduced constitutional status. The impracticality of his views on the education question has already been noted. Yet as late as 1838 his ally Gladstone published *The State in its Relations with the Church*, in which he urged the Government's duty to foster and favour the established Church, if not quite to the point of aggressively persecuting other denominations, at least (the distinction was fine) to the extent of discriminating actively against them. Gladstone's book was shot to pieces by Macaulay, but the author was still loyal to his principles in 1841, when he voted in the Commons against removing the restrictions barring Jews from Parliament. By that time, however, an issue had arisen which was to bury the ideal of the confessional state for ever.

The question of whether the Roman Catholic seminary at Maynooth, near Dublin, should receive an increase in its annual grant hardly seems of earthshaking moment. In fact, no other topic occupied so much parliamentary time from 1838 to 1845.[21] So many different interests were at stake. The Prime Minister, Sir Robert Peel, proposed an increase of £17,000 a year in the grant because he hoped to detach moderate Irish Catholics from O'Connell, who was demanding that the Act of Union should be repealed. Stalwart Protestants like the Revd William Brock found themselves unable to credit that 'whilst the Constitution shudders from its extremities to its heart at the damnable doctrines which are inculcated at Maynooth, Maynooth itself should be sanctioned with its patronage, and provided with a princely income from its funds'.[22] Manning and Gladstone were concerned at the measure's import on relations between Church and State. 'What we pay', Gladstone explained, 'I do not consider to consist chiefly in the £17,000 a year, but in the cession we make of the most important parts of the argument for the maintenance of the [Established] Church in Ireland.'[23]

For the Maynooth grant, carried in 1845 by a Tory Government supposedly committed to the defence of Anglicanism, was a clear admission that exclusive endowment of a State Church had ceased to be practical politics. As long as government had claimed to derive its authority from God alone it could logically prefer one religion to another on the optimistic assumption that the Almighty was assisting his rulers to distinguish between religious truth and error. Establishment could be justified on a kind of Erastian infallibility theory. But now that government was demonstrably created by human choice, it inevitably existed to express the will of the voters. There were those who believed that *vox populi* and *vox Dei* were one and the same, but Manning, for all his social radicalism, was never among them. He had no relish at all for the idea of divinely revealed doctrine being redefined by Act of Parliament. The fury which Peel's grant provoked had once more shown that the popular prejudice was overwhelmingly Protestant. Manning felt that the support which the Church of England received from the State would be dearly purchased if it meant exposing dogma to democratic correction. Better by far that the Church should forfeit its privileged position, and be left free to carry out its mission without any assistance from Members of Parliament.

Manning's views on the Maynooth question only developed slowly. He began by opposing any increase in the grant, and encouraged Gladstone to resign from the Cabinet as his book had committed him against the measure in the public mind. Gladstone agreed and left office; but he did so as a matter of honour rather than conviction. He now recognized that his youthful ideal of State and Church was unsustainable. Having paid his debt to the principle of political consistency, he proceeded to speak and vote in favour of Peel's bill. This exhibition of scrupulousness led both Peel and Disraeli to conclude that he had no future in politics. Yet his behaviour was intelligible enough to Manning, who performed the same volte-face on his own account over Maynooth. After the grant was carried in 1845, the archdeacon showed that he perfectly grasped the wider implications. He became considerably warier of invoking the divine mission of the Church of England against political realities, as he had done in the education question. Indeed, in 1846, he told Sidney Herbert, another friend in the Cabinet, that 'on grounds of political justice'[24] he was fully prepared to assent to the endowment of the Roman Catholic Church in Ireland.

Yet the prospect of a Church of England which could no longer rely on an alliance with the State, however unavoidable as a fact and however desirable for the security of Catholic doctrine, filled Manning with misgivings as to the future. No longer securely underpinned by the civil government, Anglicanism would perforce stand or fall by its popular appeal, a state of affairs which Manning could not but view with alarm. 'Its [the Church of England's] hold on the people, I firmly, and from experience, believe to be more nominal than real. If any distinctive and testing Church question should arise in 1848, as in 1648, I believe the population would fall off as a landslip . . . .'[25] This was a far cry from the heady confidence Manning had displayed in his 1841 Charge, when he had exulted in the Church of England's 'hold upon the nation as a people'.

This period 1845–6 was crucial in Manning's religious development, the time when his doubts about the Church of England crystallized, and when the lure of Rome first began to appear menacingly strong. It was surely not coincidence that this unsettlement coincided so closely with Newman's conversion. That long-expected event had finally occurred on 9 October 1845. Manning was one of the privileged few to receive a personal note from Newman conveying the news of his admission into what he now called, after St. John, the 'One True Fold' of Christ.[26] The uncompromising phrase must have seemed like a challenge to a mind of Manning's extremist cast. His inner turmoil is suggested by the extraordinarily emotional note which he struck in reply:

> If I knew what words would express my heartfelt love of you, and keep my own conscience pure, I would use them. Believe me I accept the letter you wrote me, at such a moment, as a pledge of your affection. I shall keep it among many memorials of past days and lasting sorrows.
>
> Only believe always that I love you. If we may never meet again in life at the same altar, may our intercessions for each other, day by day, meet in the court of Heaven. And if it be possible for such as I am, may we all, who are parted now, be there at last united.[27]

Not often, surely, have a correspondence devoted to theological matters, and the odd brief meeting, produced such exaggerated an expression of affection.

His letter dispatched, Manning made a determined effort to be unaffected by Newman's desertion. On 28 October he regaled Edward Coleridge, an Eton master of Tractarian sympathies, with his unconcern: 'Natural as it is, that one to whom we owe so much, should powerfully affect us by every step he takes, yet our probation before God is so severely distinct and personal that I dare not look anywhere but to my own conscience. Being unable to find there the dictates on which he has acted, I feel that the case is closed.' Manning even tried to believe that Newman's loss had been providentially intended to produce a better spirit in the Church of England. 'To rely on individual minds has been a strong temptation to many of late . . . we have perhaps all been too intellectual, too much related to persons, or to a school of opinions: too little to the Church and to the Person and Presence of our only true Master. I trust that this sorrow may humble us, and turn us back to Him with a firm and fervent attachment.'

True to these reflections Manning shortly afterwards noted in his diary: 'I feel that I have taken my last act in concert with those who are moving in Oxford. Henceforward I shall endeavour, by God's help, to act by myself as I have done hitherto, without any alliance. . . . My duty is to live and die striving to edify the Church in my own sphere.'[28] For his own benefit, as much as for Coleridge's, he now rehashed the message of the Charge that he had delivered the previous summer:

Certainly there has never been in my memory, any moment when the Church of England has put forth such tokens of life and power. It is almost incredible that a body which fifteen years ago was elated at being an Establishment should now be conscious of being a Church. . . . What may not be hoped from a body that has even conceived such works of Faith? It is not the nature of severed or barren branches to blossom after three hundred yerars, except 'an Aaron's rod that budded'.[29]

This proved to be one of the last occasions on which Manning could bring himself to deliver such a generous judgement. Writing to Robert Wilberforce on 3 November he adopted quite a different tone. 'What shall I say of our dear friend Newman? My heart is very heavy. I still seem to see great difficulties before us; and wish I could read and talk with you, for we shall have to give plain answers and firm to many hard questions. Not the least part of the difficulty will be to show why principles are safe so far and no farther.'[30] And in a letter to Gladstone (29 October) his perplexities drove him to take refuge in the flimsiest of hopes. 'I often think that all will be reduced at last to the simple opposition of negative and affirmative principle, and that Rome and we shall be thereby united.'[31]

Precious little encouragement was given to that notion in the work which Newman published shortly after his conversion, his *Essay on the Development of Christian Doctrine*. Newman's principal purpose was to justify the Roman Catholic Church in holding doctrines which apparently found no warrant in the practices of the early Church, but in tackling this difficulty he did not eschew some hefty side swipes at the inadequacies of Anglicanism. Gladstone began worrying about Newman's book before it had even appeared, fearing that it might spark off a whole rush of conversions. An answer was required. Who should stand forth as the new champion of Anglo-Catholicism? There was Dr Pusey, but Gladstone had his doubts about Pusey, whom he deemed guilty of 'one-sidedness' as to the Church of Rome.' Manning, on the other hand, was almost as learned in theology, sounder in judgement, and certainly far more lucid in exposition. On 21 November Gladstone wrote to him asking if he would undertake to reply to Newman's book.[32] Manning was delighted to accept the task. He read the *Essay on Development*, which he immediately recognized as a work of genius. It was, he told Gladstone, as though 'the doubts, difficulties and problems of the last ten years were suddenly brought into focus. . . . The whole book exhibits an intellectual compass and movement belonging to an order of mind which lives in a region above the reach of all except a few. I am afraid it will open a running sore in our poor body.' Nevertheless, 'in the end I feel where I was. On the whole, then, the great debate is where it was, with this gain. Even Newman has not moved its limits in advance against us.'[33] Gladstone was well pleased. 'I augur that you will find your confidence grow as you proceed,' he returned.[34] Yet somehow Manning's manuscript did not materialize, a strange hesitation in one who usually wrote with such dispatch.

The fact was that, even before reading Newman's book, Manning had been feeling severely at odds with himself. His letters to Robert Wilberforce were a truer reflection of his innermost worries than those to Gladstone. Doubts about his career in the Anglican Church had surfaced again early in December 1845 when he was offered the post of Sub-Almoner to the Archbishop of York. The position conferred more honour than duty (though sermons were required on five feast days each year); as with the Lincoln's Inn Preachership the holder was generally expected to be on the way to higher things. Indeed, the vacancy had appeared because Samuel Wilberforce, the last Sub-Almoner, had been appointed Bishop of Oxford. But Manning, instead of accepting with alacrity, was thrown into an agonized internal debate. The entry in his journal for 8 December, when he rehearsed the pros and cons of accepting, ought to suffice by itself to dispose of the slander that he was crudely or uncomplicatedly ambitious:

FOR	AGAINST
1. That it comes unsought.	1. Not therefore to be accepted. Such things are trials as well as leadings.
2. That it is honourable.	2. Being what I am, ought I not therefore to decline it – (i) As humiliation (ii) As revenge on myself for Lincoln's Inn (iii) As a testimony?
3. That it is an opening to usefulness.	3. All I have is pre-engaged.
4. That it may lead to more.	4. Therefore, at least for that reason, not to be accepted. It is a sphere of temptation to which I am akin, and have been.
5. That it has emolument.	5. But this is dearly bought with five sacred days, and anything ethically wrong.
6. That I owe it to my friends.	6. Supposing the reasons good.
7. That it is due to the Archbishop.	7. The same.[35]

The last of the reasons for accepting was rather scraping the barrel, whereas he listed a further ten points against taking the post. The seventh shows that he already anticipated that there was a struggle to come: 'Anything which complicated my thoughts and position may affect the *indifference* with which I wish to resolve my mind on the great issue. Visions of a future certainly would.' What could this great issue have been but the need to assess the rival claims of Anglicanism and Roman Catholicism? A week later Manning had steeled himself to refuse the Sub-Almonership. A whole new set of numbered paragraphs set forth the reasons for his refusal. Number Two is of interest. Manning's growing reputation had won him presentation at Buckingham Palace, and he felt that the Sub-Almonership might have pushed him over the brink into just the kind of worldliness that he deprecated in his 'dear brother' Samuel Wilberforce. '. . . (2) I am afraid of venturing out of the Church into the Court. . . . If I am to go, then I shall be called again, not less surely for having now refused. My course has been afar off and I have seen a stronger man than I damaged. "Wine is a mocker, strong drink is raging." ' Manning felt that the time had come to act his professions, not merely state them. '. . . (4). I have *prayed* against "pride, vanity, envy, jealousy, rivalry and ambition" but have done nothing to attain humility. (5) I would fain deny myself as an offering to Him who pleased not Himself, and perhaps in a distinction and an honour having worldly estimation, such a denial is better for me than in money and the like.' The gyrations of his mind were endless. Was he perhaps being virtuous for the wrong reasons? 'Satan tells me I am doing it to be thought mortified and holy; or out of pride, as wishing to slight what others value and assume I should gladly accept.' Away in London for a few days his self-denial looked like plain stupidity. 'I have, since I left home, been deprived of my supports; have not found others confirm my view. The associations of the world came about me, and made me feel that I had played the fool and lost a great opportunity, etc. I cannot deny that in the region of the world, even of the fair, not irreligious, view of self-advancement, also of command and precepts, I have made a mistake.' He pulled himself together with an effort. 'But in the regions of counsels, self-chastisement, humiliation, self-discipline, penance, and of the Cross, I think I have done right.' This conclusion was strengthened when he returned to Lavington. 'Mistake or no, it is a good thing I have mortified my vanity. . . . I have been both ambitious and designing, and it is good for me to be mortified by the act of others as in Lincoln's Inn, or by my own as now.'[36]

Manning knew only too well how hard it is for a man to change his own nature. 'Could I be content to live and die no more than I am? I doubt it.'[37] His ambition remained. The Christian might aspire to virtue but (as

Manning noted in a sermon) 'the sap of the old stock rises into the graft, and lowers the quality of the fruit. . . . A person who before his repentance was proud, will, after he has become religious, often insensibly grow to be self-confiding, or self-complacent.'[38] Forewarned is forearmed; his Lenten diary for 1846 kept up a continual flow of self-criticism. He castigated himself for 'ostentation of learning and mean concealment of ignorance'; for 'envy, especially in spiritual offices and state' (Samuel Wilberforce again, no doubt); for 'vainglory and self-flattery'; for 'censuring others with an aim'; for 'anger, especially with J. L. Anderdon'. (Alas, poor Anderdon.) 'To this I must add, Fearful want of love towards God; fearful want of repentance; fearful absence of mind in prayer. Dead, sluggish, obstinate unwillingness to pray. It is a feeling like nightmare when one cannot move.'[39] Notwithstanding the above catalogue he still managed to accuse himself of self-complacency, a charge so evidently unjust that it rather detracts from one's belief in his other sins.

This state of spiritual anguish and theological uncertainty was no condition in which to attempt an answer to Newman's book. Manning found himself paralysed, and his usually self-possessed and masterful nature cannot have relished the experience.

Newman had argued that Roman Catholic doctrines and practices, even if apparently unsupported by the earliest records of Christianity, were in fact developments of conceptions found in embryo from the first, in the same way as the character of a fully grown man is different from, but may be referred back to, that of the boy he once was. So the exaltation of the Virgin Mary, for instance, grew out of the reverence in which the disciples had held the Mother of Christ. So the veneration of relics derived from the devotion inspired by the saints in their lives. So the monastic ideal stemmed from the high value which had always been placed upon the holy single life. It was the principle of evolution applied to theology, and that some fourteen years before Darwin published his *Origin of Species*. (When he did, Newman found no difficulty at all in accepting his argument.) Under this view the Catholic Church was not an inert institution but a living organism which had, through divine guidance, adapted itself to bear witness to an unchangeable faith at all times and in all places. The *Essay on Development* was itself a development. There had been anticipations in Wiseman's writings,[40] in Gladstone's *Church Principles* (1841),[41] and doubtless in many other places, not least in the parable of the mustard seed. Newman, however, expressed himself with matchless resource and fertility. He explained how Catholic truth had been preserved and expanded through the guardianship of the Church:

It is indeed sometimes said that the stream is clearest near the spring. Whatever use may fairly be made of this image, it does not apply to the history of a philosophy or sect, which, on the contrary, is more equable, and purer and stronger, when its bed has become deep, and broad and full. . . . In time it enters upon a strange territory; points of controversy alter their bearing; parties rise and fall about it; dangers and hopes appear in new relations, and old principles appear under new forms; it changes with them in order to remain the same. In a higher world it is otherwise; but here below to live is to change, and to be perfect is to have changed often.[42]

   Such fluid thinking was not Manning's vein. Instinctively he preferred the downright dogmatic statement of fixed principles: 'Whatever is new is not of Christ.' He quite rightly saw that Newman was venturing on to slippery ground. Once the idea that doctrines evolve is accepted, who knows but that they may eventually evolve themselves out of existence? As Gladstone wrote to Manning, Newman 'places Christianity on the edge of a precipice; from where a bold and strong hand would throw it over'.[43] Manning agreed, telling Robert Wilberforce that 'Newman's mind is subtle even to excess, and to us certainly seems to be sceptical'.[44] That was the first statement of an opinion that was eventually to degenerate into an obsession.
   The theory of development did not challenge Manning so decisively as the arguments with which Newman had accompanied it. His book showed a compelling awareness of the many vicissitudes from which, time and again throughout history, the Roman Church had emerged as the immovable rock on which the Christian world was grounded. Did not this remarkable survival carry all the signs of divine protection and purpose? Newman made the ordainment of a Church by God seem not merely possible but likely. 'Some authority there must be if there is a revelation. . . . If Christianity is both social and dogmatic, and intended for all ages, it must, humanly speaking, have an infallible expounder.' Again, 'either an objective revelation has not been given, or it has been provided with means for impressing its objectiveness upon the world'.[45] Such statements were meat and drink to Manning. Five years later he told Robert Wilberforce that Newman's book had 'opened my eyes to one fact, namely, that I had laid down only half the subject. I had found the *Rule* (in the traditions of the Church), but not the *Judge*. It was evident that to put Scripture and Antiquity into the hands of the individual is as much private judgement as to put Scripture alone.'[46] An infallible authority: that, ultimately, was the only secure basis for faith.
   Manning could bring himself to believe that the Anglican Church showed signs of Christ working in its midst, but he could not, with the best will in the world, imagine that it constituted an infallible authority. There were far too many Evangelicals on the episcopal bench for that to be possible. Newman

pressed the attack further and ridiculed the claim, which he had once so eloquently maintained, that the Anglican Church might be more representative than the Roman of the teaching of the Fathers:

Did St. Athanasius, or St. Ambrose come suddenly to life, it cannot be doubted what communion they would mistake [Newman was being ironic] for their own. All surely will agree that these Fathers, with whatsoever differences of opinion, whatever protests, if we will, would find themselves more at home with such men as St. Bernard, or St. Ignatius Loyola, or with the lonely priest in his lodgings, or the holy sisterhood of Charity, or the unlettered crowd before the altar, than with the rulers and members of any other religious community.[47]

Newman's book did not effect a dramatic change in Manning, but it did strike home on the very points where Manning himself had already found the Church of England most vulnerable. And now there came another shock. Early in May 1846 Manning heard that his sister-in-law Sophia and her husband, George Ryder, had gone over to Rome. That month was a critical one for Manning. The impressions that had been lurking in his subconscious for years suddenly bobbed to the surface:

I am conscious to myself of an extensively changed feeling towards the Church of Rome [he confided to his journal]. It seems to me nearer the truth, and the Church of England in greater peril. Our divisions seem to me fatal as a token, and as a disease . . . I am conscious of being less and less able to preach dogmatically. If I do so, I go beyond our formularies. Though not therefore Roman, I cease to be Anglican. . . . There seems to be about the Church of England a want of antiquity, system, fullness, intelligibleness, order, strength, unity; we have dogmas on paper; a ritual almost universally abandoned; no discipline, a divided episcopate, priesthood, and laity.[48]

Nor did this mood evaporate as the summer wore on. On 5 July he experienced 'strange thoughts' that took up twenty-five numbered paragraphs:

(1) I have felt that the Episcopate of the English Church is secularised, and bound down beyond hope. . . . (3) I have felt less desire for parliament and public station. . . . (7) Something keeps rising and saying, 'You will end in the Roman Church.' (8) And yet I do not feel at all as if my safety requires any change, and I do feel that a change might be a positive delusion. . . . (15) May not this be a feint of the tempter? I fearfully mistrust myself, especially when I see that those who stay seem humbler than those who have left us. . . . (19) Is the English Church enough to alter the whole case? (20) I think so. (21) Yet I am conscious that I am further from the English Church and nearer Rome than ever I was. (22) How do I know where I may be two years hence? Where was Newman five years ago? May I not be in an analogous place? (23) Yet I have no positive doubts about the Church of England. I

have difficultires – but the chief thing is the *drawing* of Rome. It satisfies the WHOLE of my intellect, sympathy, sentiment, and nature, in a way proper, and solely belonging to itself. The English Church is an approximate.[49]

The second day of August found him musing on infallibility: 'Now I see that St. Peter has a Primacy among the Apostles. That the Church of Rome inherits what St Peter had among Apostles. That the Church of Rome is therefore heir of infallibility.'[50] Two days later, it was once more the shortcomings of Anglicanism that preoccupied him: 'The Church of England, after 300 years, has failed – 1. In the unity of doctrine; 2. In the enforcement of discipline; 3. In the training of the higher life.'[51] On 16 August, when a dying parishioner looked eagerly over his shoulder and demanded, 'Who is she? Who is she?' Manning 'felt a thrill, and expected to see something break out on my sight'.[52] On 28 August he risked communicating some of his doubts about the Church of England to Gladstone. 'I have a fear amounting to a belief that the Church of England must split asunder, the *diversa et adversa continentes* must be absorbed by a higher unity or parted.'[53] This confession was a mistake. Gladstone could not understand his difficulties at all. If the Church of England was divided, then so was that of Rome with its Jansenist and anti-Jansenist wings. Puritan and Catholic prnciples were at odds within as well as without the Roman Church. Gladstone saw 'a *great* providential destiny' before the Anglican Church. He did not believe that they could possibly differ on a matter of such magnitude.[54] It was several months before Manning wrote again. But when he did, in December, he once more expressed his doubts. 'Our Ecclesiastical and Social Church system has duration in it but our theological and spiritual activities . . . are disengaging themselves rapidly.'[55]

Gladstone acknowledged that the English Church had its weaknesses, but he never experienced any insuperable problems about claiming to be both Anglican and Catholic. Indeed he refused to admit that a serious alternative existed for any right-thinking man. His obtuseness was based on a visceral anti-papistry that put the claims of Rome entirely out of court. 'The temptation towards the Church of Rome', he told another correspondent in June 1847, 'has never been before my mind in any other sense than as other plain and flagrant sins have been before it.'[56] The following year he gave readers of the *Quarterly Review* a fuller statement of his views, which is worth quoting as an example of the virulence that informed even the more intellectual variety of anti-Catholic prejudice.

She [Rome] offers us a sealed Bible; a mutilated Eucharist; an arbitrarily expanded modern creed; a casuistry that 'sews pillows to all armholes', and is still open to the reproach of Pascal, that while it aspires to the service of virtue it does not disdain that of vice; a scheme of worship involving constant peril of polytheistic idolatry; a doctrinal system disparaging Scripture, and driving her acutest champions upon the most dangerous and desperate theories; and a rule of individual discipline which offends against duty even more than against liberty, by placing the reins of the inward and outward life, given by God to conscience, in the hands of an extraneous person under the name of a Director.[57]

What was an archdeacon to do who found himself guilty of sympathy with so detestable a creed? He could declare straightway for Rome and resign his office. But how could he be sure that his drawing towards Rome was not, as he himself hazarded it might be, some passing fancy. ('I fearfully mistrust myself.')[58] A change which would mean the end of his career, and fellowship with a despised and ostracized minority, was not to be lightly undertaken. For the present, then, he would remain an archdeacon. He had accepted the brief and like a good trouper he would fulfil the role. But his position involved fearful difficulties. Early in 1846, for instance, he was obliged to accept a Roman convert back into the English Church.[59] On another occasion a woman broke off her engagement on Manning's advice because her fiancé joined the Roman Church. The archdeacon was obliged to hold his penitents back from Rome. One of them, who ventured to ignore his counsel, taxed him straight: 'But, Mr Archdeacon, are you quite sure of the validity of Anglican orders?' 'Am I sure of the existence of God?'[60] returned the ecclesiastic who had once dreamed of a political career.

The ability to cope with awkward questions should not be taken as a token of a mind at ease. In some respects Manning's situation was similar to that of the Soviet spies in the Foreign Office during this century. Of course he had not accepted his archdeaconry in bad faith, nor did he secretly aid the enemy. He did, however, most ardently sympathize with what his position demanded he should most ardently condemn. The strain was terrible, and the worse because increasing numbers were now looking to him as a leader of Anglican Catholicism.[61] His health perceptibly deteriorated.[62] A facial tic appeared,[63] disturbing the stern authority of his countenance. Save to one or two intimates, his reserve became impenetrable. F. D. Maurice, whose high praise of Manning was recorded in the last chapter, had despaired by 1849 of ever making a breakthrough. 'I knew Manning at Oxford,' he wrote, 'and suppose I ought to know him better than I do; but something has ailed us – and with a very fervent respect for him on my side – I have always fancied that there was a little contempt, or else suspicion, on his, and I have never got along with him half so well as with his brother-in-law the bishop, with whom indeed it is not very difficult to get on.'[64] Even Keble, the least malicious of men, found that there was something in the archdeacon's manner that provoked ill-nature. 'I am afraid I have been indulging in a subtle sort of spleen towards him,'[65] he confided in 1850.

The more Manning was compelled to present a mask to the world, the more dependent he became on those few who shared or sensed his secret. The letters which he wrote at this period to Robert Wilberforce, and to Henry's wife Mary Wilberforce, are strewn with expressions of the deepest affection. Though outwardly self-sufficient, he badly needed sympathy in this hour of trial. It appears that he showed little mercy to himself. In a sermon published in 1847 – 'Halting between God and the World' – he heaped obloquy on the spiritually indecisive. The voice of God, he declared, speaks clearly enough: to hesitate before following its bidding 'is not only a very miserable, but a very dangerous state; for such people grow to be morally impotent. To know truth, and to disobey it, weakens the whole character.'[66] That was certainly a consequence which Manning would have wished to avoid.

Early in 1847 his health broke down completely. On 7 February, while visiting his mother at Reigate, he noticed a faint thread of blood in his mouth, probably, he concluded, from the membrane of the throat. This symptom he somewhat over-hastily diagnosed as an omen of approaching death: 'If nothing come, what loss? If anything, all well.'[67] Later in life the Cardinal described this illness, rather less dramatically, as 'bronchitis'.[68] In June 1847, when he was convalescing, medical opinion pronounced that there were 'no tubercles, but great weakness . . . heart and pulse are young but the rest old'.[69] Medical opinion was patently at something of a loss. It is tempting to advance psychosomatic cause, but that would be to emulate the doctor in specious wisdom. All that can be said with certainty is that Manning was confined to his house for three months, during which period the fear of death, real or imagined, concentrated his mind with more than usual assiduity on the state of his own soul. There was, as he himself had remarked in a sermon, nothing like a season of suffering for nourishing the religious temper. 'When pain searches into the body or the spirit, we feel as though we had awoke up to know that we had learned nothing really until then.'[70] What Manning now learned heightened his propensity for self-reproach. In his own illness he remembered how 'coldly and heartlessly' he had visited the sick, and how inadequately he had previously apprehended the plight of those starving in the Irish famine.[71] He was, he considered, 'put to sport for my intoxications about perfection': it only needed a servant knocking at the door to bring a surge of impatience into his reveries of sanctity.[72] In sum, 'the sloth and unprofitableness of my life are only equalled by my vanity and self-complacency. I have talked like a saint; dreamed of myself as a saint; and flattered myself as if I did the work of a saint; and now I find that I am not worthy to be called a penitent.'[73]

That last phrase referred to Manning's formal confession, perhaps his first, that had been received by his curate Laprimaudaye on 18 March. After such remorseless self-accusation the relief was heady. 'What a help to reality,' he noted, 'what a safeguard to hypocrisy in receiving confessions.' A week later he described his penance as 'the greatest conscious act of my life'.[74] It was unfortunate, therefore, that Gladstone should have chosen this precise moment to send Manning another epistolary polemic against Rome, with special reference to 'the deadly blow at man in his freedom' represented by confession.[75] Manning wrote back that for himself it was the absence of auricular confession that made the Church of England's claim to be part of the Catholic Church so debatable,[76] a reply which, rather oddly, convinced Gladstone that 'our real meanings were not far apart'.[77]

Meanwhile Manning had passed on to consider the manifold blessings which 'God's special mercies' had bestowed upon him. These began early with '(1) My creation.' There followed '(2) My regeneration, elect from mankind' and '(3) My pure and loving home, and parents.' Number (5) embraced 'the preservation of my life six times to my knowledge –

(1) In illness at the age of nine.
(2) In the water.
(3) By a runaway horse at Oxford.
(4) By the same.
(5) By nearly falling through the ceiling of a Church.
(6) Again, by fall of a horse. And I know not how often in shooting, riding etc.'[78]

It comes as a surprise, in the light of this list, to learn that Manning was accounted an excellent horseman.[79] The Lord, however, had chastened as well as blessed his servant. Manning's wife's death had brought him more exclusively to religion, a reflection that appeared as '(8) By afflicting me, 1837' in this catalogue. Lytton Strachey seized gleefully on this fact. Eschewing any mention of the word 'afflicting', he contrived to suggest, by reference to the heading 'God's special mercies', that Manning had come to regard Caroline's death with complacency.[80] In fact, Manning intended, and conveyed, precisely the opposite. If Strachey found the compulsion to sneer at the marriage irresistible, there was more legitimate, if less sensational, material to hand in a further list of 'God's special mercies', where Manning alluded to 'sixteen lonely years',[81] a phrase which presumably comprehended his whole Lavington existence. The charge of indifference to Caroline's memory, though, simply will not stick. That summer of 1847, as in every summer, he recalled the onset of Caroline's fatal illness. 'This time ten years ago the end was in its beginning. It opened on the 22nd, and then I said from my soul what I say now, "Thy will be done." '[82] There is a clear distinction between acquiescence in God's will and indifference.

As the Lent of Manning's sickness drew to its close – 'what a Lent it has been to me'[83] – he once more became conscious that his nature was steeped in sin. Some tactless person complimented his curate Laprimaudaye within his hearing on having brought so many souls to God during Lent. Instantly the demon of jealousy leapt up. 'I could not bear to hear Laprimaudaye commended even in a matter which ought to make me give thanks. I abhorred myself on the spot, and looked upward for help.' The experience provoked another bout of self-recrimination. 'I fear to be again absorbed even in thought by the activities of life. I should again grow ambitious, conscious, and bold in speech. For I am *capable of all evil*, nothing but the hand of God has kept me from being the vilest of creatures, and nothing can. I feel now that if I were within the sphere of temptation I should sin by a perpetual backsliding.'

The matter was soon put to the test. The excellent Laprimaudaye appeared to have attracted more Easter communicants than the rector had in previous years. Again the green-eyed monster attacked. This time, though, Manning's defence was better prepared. 'I do not think that I have actively or voluntarily consented; but I have felt a sort of poisonous, feverish, impatient sensation, partly lest it be true, but chiefly that it should be thought true. . . . I have prayed that all pride, vanity, envy, jealousy, rivalry and ambition may be crucified in me; and I accept this as a nail driven into me, and desire to be more wholly crucified.' And so on Easter Monday Manning prayed that where he had gathered one of the Lavington flock, Laprimaudaye might gather ten. Alas, though, that very evening 'I was drawn by his showing me the list of Easter communicants into saying things which I know embodied and vented feelings of evil. In satisfaction for this, I desire now to give him this copy of the Breviary, and to say how sincerely I feel that my flock have been better in his hands than in mine.'[84]

It is easy to smile at Manning's spiritual writhings over such matters; easy, too, to miss the point that in this particular contest, as in so many others, he scored at least a partial victory over himself. Whatever may be made of his present of a Breviary (and Laprimaudaye, who later became a Catholic, probably made a great deal of it), this act of self-mortification is surely more estimable than a long, sullen and freely-indulged course of jealousy. All that makes Manning's struggles risible is the utter absence of any sense of humour from his self-analysis; and whether humour will count for much in the heavenly scheme of things remains to be discovered. Meanwhile Manning is not to be scorned because he waged merciless war on infirmities that most people are disposed to accept as an inexpugnable part of human nature. He was no moral equivocator; he saw distinctly that the New

Testament proposed an other-worldly ethic that could not be followed
without suffering; he saw also that since this standard had been set by Christ
Himself it must be seriously attempted, no matter what the cost, by all who
wished to consider themselves more than nominal Christians. Few are brave
enough to take up this challenge, least of all among those with First Class
degrees from Oxford. Of course he failed to meet the test, failed again and
again, as all must do who are not saints. But did that make his struggles
profitless? Manning possessed an urge to dominate, great capacity and
formidable will, a combination liable to result in something considerably
more unpleasant than a few humourless diary entries.

In reading them it is important to remember that he was the harshest
possible judge of himself, capable of finding sins where others might not
even have searched. The outwardly formidable archdeacon survived
spiritually through self-castigation. Even his mother's death in May 1847
appeared chiefly important for the light it shed upon his own iniquity. He
remembered 'how estranged, distant, loveless, thankless, irritable, selfish'
he had been on the occasion of their last meeting. 'I did nothing to cheer her
or make her happy. My whole conduct was hateful and guilty beyond
words.' One might wish for more about the dead mother and less about the
errant son, but there is no denying that self-accusation is a more Christian
response than self-justification. The excuses were there if he had cared to
use them. Those last days which he had spent with his mother had been the
first days of his own illness. Assuredly many consciences would have
quietened themselves without undue difficulty. Manning prescribed 'some
lifelong penance' for his filial shortcomings.[85]

Despite Manning's morbid fancies, recovery from his illness proved at
length to be unavoidable. 'How can I ever bless God for this sickness?
Without it I should have died eternally,'[86] he recorded in his diary at
Whitsun. As health returned his relentless critique of the Church of England
was resumed in a letter to Robert Wilberforce. 'If we look towards our
rulers, who is there that affirms Catholic dogmas or Catholic tradition?'[87]
Yet Manning still felt no immediate need for a decision. The first priority
was convalescence, and he meant to go to Italy, notwithstanding his
confessor's doubts about such a choice in his parlous religious state. He did
not depart, however, before experiencing some resurgence of faith in his
native Church.

27 June – I have just come down from Lavington Church, having given thanks for the
mercies of God in the last five months. . . . The Church seemed very beautiful; it had
lost its familiar look and seemed strange and new to me, as I remember school used to
after holidays. . . . I had, I think, a more real sight of the unseen world and the
object of worship; but my mind wandered on both sides. I felt moved and thankful.

But I asked myself today what I was getting well for? At longest, to be sick again soon and for the last time. And between now and then what?

On 5 July, the day before he set off for Italy, the service in Lavington church brought heartfelt joy. 'I never felt the power of love more: nor so much bound to my flock. It is the strongest bond I have. I believe it to be of the reality of the Catholic Church. And yet it will bear no theological argument except a denial of visible unity altogether – which is self-evidently false.' Native emotion appeared painfully well matched with unpatriotic intellect, and who could tell the outcome? 'Tomorrow by the will of God I go forth, it may be for a year, it may be for ever. I feel to be in His hands. I know not what is good for myself.'[88]

Five days later, in Malines, the experience of Roman Catholic worship clarified his mind on this last point. The evening of his arrival, a Saturday, he attended Exposition and Benediction of the Blessed Sacrament in the cathedral: 'the procession gave me a strong feeling of the reality of the Incarnation and of their way of witnessing to it.' On Sunday he was still more impressed by High Mass, and, best of all, 'the church very full all the morning, many thousands'. Next day he saw the relics possessed by the Frères de la Miséricorde, an order which devoted itself to prison work. 'I could not but feel that the effect of such objects is to awaken and keep alive a high standard of personal devotion. A theory at least which we have not. Also the whole objective worship gives a reality we have nothing to equal.'[89]

At Aix-la-Chapelle Manning looked upon the grave of Charlemagne, and mused with awe upon the power and influence of the Holy Roman Empire. The power and influence of his own background, however, were evident in his habit of describing whatsoever scenery the continent offered in terms of some English equivalent, a technique which he would sometimes elaborate to an extraordinary degree. The country round Aix, for instance, was 'a mixture of North Wales, the South Downs, Stroud, and Dove Dale'. In the town he was again struck by the huge congregations that thronged the cathedral and by the devotion they showed. The proportion of men was particularly gratifying, young men too, even well-dressed young men who used their rosaries with as much piety as the poor. Such outward marks of reverence – parents crossing their children with holy water, children crossing themselves, people dropping to their knees on their way in and out – were surely evidence that Catholic principles had laid a secure hold upon the mind and the will. 'It seemed strange that here on the moral site of the Western Empire and the Mediaeval Europe, there should be still an energy beyond anything I have seen elsewhere. Is there not a moral reason to explain this?' How different, how horribly different, was the experience of Protestant worship at Basle. 'Cathedral not so full; many hats on. The effect of

Protestant worship is dreary; want of object, aim, intelligibleness; cold, dark, abstract.' What a relief to go on the river to Little Basle. 'The R.C. Church; a queue of people at each door, and a knot against the wall opposite; hats off; crossing, joining in worship. Went in; thronged aisles, passages and all, with looks – visible – and great attention.'[90]

At Lucerne Manning's progress was interrupted by a recurrence of illness, serious enough to decide him to bolt back to England. Striking north to Strasbourg he travelled down the Rhine by steamer. The patient never missed a point in his own drama. 'I was so ill . . . that passengers made signs to each other as if they thought I was dying.'[91] Their alarm was premature. A fortnight in London, and Manning was off to Rome again, with his sister Caroline and her husband Colonel Austen, whose mind was perforce turned to theological discussion. They broke their journey for a few days at Nice, where Manning was on hand to bury H. F. Lyte, the author of 'Abide With Me',[92] and where he resumed his observations upon Roman Catholic worship. He made a round of the churches in the town. Notre-Dame: 'Full; and round the door a crowd bareheaded and kneeling on the stones.' Church of the Visitation: 'Full, with good plaintive chanting.' Church of the Holy Cross: 'Full, with a crowd on the plateau [sic] outside and below in the street; and all down the street, people kneeling at their thresholds.' Here, at last, was really effective, *successful*, religion. 'There was something very beautiful and awful in the lighted altar, with the incense seen from without the open door. A sad contrast to our [Anglican] Evensong, where everyone, so far as I saw, sat through their prayers.'[93]

Evidently the case between the two Churches had been settled in Manning's mind before he entered Rome again on the evening of 27 November 1847. On his last visit he had been a tourist; now he had come as a votary.

5 *The One True Fold*

It is Rome, or licence of thought and will.[1]

MANNING TO JAMES HOPE, 11 DECEMBER 1850

The first Englishman Manning ran across in Rome was Newman, who had been sent like any callow student to study at the Collegio di Propaganda, the Vatican department responsible for administering the Church in heathen lands such as that from which the former Oxford leader hailed. Newman was about to return home after fifteen months abroad, a prospect which afforded him considerable relief. He had never liked the Romans. 'One is struck at once with their horrible cruelty to animals,' he had written, 'also with their dishonesty, lying and stealing apparently without conscience.' These defects nevertheless went with 'a simple certainty in believing which to a Protestant or an Anglican is quite astounding . . . they show in a wonderful way how it is possible to disjoin religion and morality'.[2] The impression that Newman himself had made on Roman ecclesiastics was different, but hardly more favourable. The Pope, who had heralded his arrival by announcing that he would like to see Newman 'again and again', soon discovered that the press of business frustrated this intention.[3] Newman's fastidiousness, which prevented his pushing himself forward or making any claims, had no appeal for the Latin temperament, while his incapacity with Italian meant that no one took his true intellectual measure. It was still only two years after his conversion, but to Manning, who always, in spite of himself, possessed a keen sense of worldly status, he may already have appeared a diminished figure. The two men met on three successive days, with no recorded result save that Newman found Manning's appearance so changed by his illness that he failed at first to recognize him.[4]

Manning, who would always be at home in Rome, immediately perceived that a very different atmosphere prevailed as compared with his previous visit, a change that was attributable to the election, in 1846, of the Bishop of Imola, Mastai-Ferretti, as Pope Pius IX. The new Pope, who would be such a decisive figure in Manning's life, was warm-hearted, generous and humane. His political judgement, unfortunately, was not so well matched to his role.

Even if one rejects the prejudiced view of Metternich, the Austrian Chancellor, that the Pope was 'faible d'intelligence',[5] it cannot be denied that he came to his office with his head bursting with good intentions which had not been properly thought through to their likely consequences. Pius IX sprang from the provincial nobility of the Papal States, an environment in which liberal and nationalist ideas were continually being tossed around without doing any good or any harm to anyone. His own inclinations as a young man are probably better described as 'progressive' than 'liberal', which is to say that his enthusiasm was more likely to be aroused by new inventions like railways and gas lighting than by plans of constitutional reform.[6] But that is a distinction made with hindsight. To his contemporaries the new Pope was simply an Italian who loved his country and a saintly man who loved the poor. All classes responded joyfully in those first years to his charity, his humour, his accessibility, and his overflowing sympathy. He began his reign, moreover, with a series of measures that convinced liberals throughout Europe that their saviour had come. He gave an amnesty to more than a thousand political offenders held in prison, and to hundreds of others in exile; he introduced laymen for the first time into the government of the Papal States; he established an elected advisory assembly; he reformed the criminal law; he made the press more free; he allowed Rome its own municipal government. No wonder his subjects were ecstatic. Even Dr Jowett, the Master of Balliol, pronounced Pius to be 'a capital fellow'.[7]

If the programme could have been halted at this point, Pius might have remained secure. The liberal appetite, however, grows by what it feeds on. Pius's reforms were regarded by the hotheads as merely the preliminaries to the granting of a full democratic constitution. And another idea, still more exciting, was seizing the imagination of many both in and beyond the Papal States. Might not the Pope put himself at the head of the people and unite all Italians in an effort to throw off foreign domination? There were signs that Pius himself was susceptible to such a dream. He had been delighted by Vicenzio Gioberti's book *Il primato morale e civile degli Italiani* (1843), in which it was proposed that Italy should become a federal state bound together by the presidency of the Pope. As Bishop of Imola Mastai-Ferretti 'would often throw himself from one side to the other of his great armchair repeating Gioberti's words'.[8] Now it seemed that he might, as Pope, be preparing to act on them.

This hope appeared confirmed when Pius attempted to form a customs union between the various Italian States. The plan failed, ominously enough, owing to the opposition of Piedmont, the most powerful of the Italian kingdoms and one which nurtured its own ambitions of bringing the peninsula to nationhood. The Pope, however, seemed blithely unaware of any danger from Piedmont or of the need for effective allies if his temporal power were to be maintained. His misfortune was that the Austrians, who constituted the main obstacle in the way of Italian unity, were also the principal guarantors of the Papal States. For Pius, though, this dilemma apparently did not exist. When, in July 1847, the Austrians exercised their treaty right to garrison Ferrara in the Papal States, he protested with all the passion of an Italian who bitterly resented a foreign force on his native soil. In December Metternich ordered the Austrian troops to retire. Italian enthusiasm and expectation rose to fever pitch.

Nevertheless, Metternich was perfectly correct, in that annoying way reactionaries have of being correct, when he asserted that a liberal and nationalist pope was an impossibility. The liberals in the Papal States would not long rest content with a mere consultative assembly; and an elected legislative assembly would pose irresolvable problems. Supposing that it demanded secular education or passed a law sanctioning divorce, how could a pope accede without compromising the Catholic faith? Similar objections applied to a nationalist pope. A united Italy must entail expulsion of the Austrians from the north. Yet the Austrians were Catholic too. If the Church were to remain universal, it was unthinkable that political opposition to Italian ambitions should involve the enmity of its Sovereign Pontiff.

Too late these limitations upon his action began to reveal themselves to Pius. He had aroused radical hopes which he could not possibly fulfil and which he would now be obliged to deny. Metternich gave a gloomy and accurate prognosis of the Pope's situation: 'He has allowed himself to be taken and ensnared, since assuming the tiara, in a net from which he no longer knows how to disentangle himself, and if matters follow their natural course, he will be driven out of Rome.'[9]

Such was the interesting and dangerous prospect when Manning arrived in Rome. Always fascinated by politics, he spent time in the Circolo Romano, a political club where gathered the radicals who were determined to press the Pope into an extreme course. In particular he saw a lot of Father Ventura, a disciple of Lamennais, who had long since dreamt of an alliance between Church and people. Evidently Manning was impressed, because many of the ideas which Ventura was propagating were later incorporated into his 1848 Charge. 'Our work henceforward is not with the few,' Manning would write, 'with those whose hands hold the gifts and powers of the world, but with the poor of Christ, the multitude which have been this long time with us and now faint by the way; with the masses in mines and factories, herding in the desolation of crowded cities, or hurried onward in the train of deceivers and seducers.'[10] Ventura's influence is also evident in a letter Manning wrote to Gladstone from Rome in April 1848. 'It is wonderful to see the Catholic Church in America, France, and Italy distinctly of the progress and popular party – indeed, in many ways the head of it. It falls in with an old belief of mine in which I think you share. I mean that the Church of the last ages will be as the Church of the first, isolated and separate from the Civil Powers of this World.'[11] As Manning pointed out, this was hardly the state of the Church of England.

The Roman radicals also made Manning sharply aware of the strength of anti-English feeling over Ireland. Ventura told him flat that the Union must be repealed and Ireland given its own parliament.[12] As always the solution of this problem seemed a great deal simpler to foreign than to English eyes. Manning and Sidney Herbert, who was in Rome, arranged for the translation of a pamphlet by Charles Trevelyan that attempted to explain the English case. Manning never sold his country short abroad. Indeed, he moved resolutely into the attack, enquiring innocently of a radical friend in the Circolo Romano why it was that non-Catholic countries were invariably in material advance of Catholic ones. The answer, inevitable from such a source, was that the Pope had fraternized with princes instead of with the people, besides which the wicked Jesuits had pursued an educational policy of deliberately keeping their pupils ignorant.[13] Another diary entry shows Manning attempting to discuss the problem of clerical celibacy with a reluctant priest who considered that it was not right to speak a word where the Church had ruled. Manning was not so sure. He rejected the celibate ideal on grounds:

1 Of personal purity, (i) contradiction of instinct (said that it was very common), (ii) proximate occasions;
2. Of social example. Husband, wife, household, children.
Thought the ideal of priesthood abstract and mythical.[14]

It is not surprising, granted Manning's later exaltation both of the priesthood and of celibacy, that the rest of this entry has been excised.

In January 1848 Ventura explained to Manning that the Pope had already lost three-fifths of his popularity through his prevarication in the face of the people's revolutionary urge.[15] Events soon conspired to rob Pius of his remaining two-fifths, and some more. 1848 was the year of revolutions, in February at Naples, Florence and Paris; in March in Piedmont and, most dramatic of all, Vienna. Bowing to the prevailing wind Pius granted a constitution which gave substantial power to two assemblies, the lower of which was elective. But this concession passed almost unnoticed in the general excitement. With the departure of Metternich, Italy's moment of opportunity seemed to have arrived. Milan threw out the Austrians on 24 March and Charles Albert of Piedmont declared war. Pius sent the small papal army to defend the Romagna against possible Austrian attack, but made the mistake of putting this force under the command of a Piedmontese general who proceeded, quite unjustifiably, to claim papal sanction for all-out war. Pius was compelled to make his position unequivocally clear. On 29 April he issued an Allocution in which he categorically denied any sympathy with republican ideals or with schemes to unite Italy under his presidency. By this act he annihilated all the popularity in which he had basked over the two preceding years.

Manning's stay in Rome, therefore, coincided with a period of great stress for the Pope. Nevertheless, when Manning saw Pius give Benediction 'with a mixture of majesty, love, and supplication I never saw', he was quite lost in admiration. 'It was a sight beyond words,' he recalled. 'A man near me said *"Non é un uomo, é un angelo."* '[16] Manning essayed still higher praise. 'It is impossible not to love Pius IX. His is the most truly English countenance I have seen in Italy.'[17] Thenceforward, though he continued to listen to the fire-raising speeches in the Circolo Romano, he showed an acute sense of the Pope's difficulty. When news of the rising in Milan first reached Rome, wild rumours spread that the Pope would bless the standards of the papal army in the conflict with Austria that appeared imminent. But Manning was quick to observe the essential point by which Pius's hands were tied: 'This is not a religious war, but purely national against a Catholic Emperor.'[18] The only way out of the impasse, he reckoned, was a separation of the Pope's spiritual and temporal powers. 'It is plain that the civil institutions in Rome must be released from the ecclesiastical state,' whereas in England, Manning could not resist adding, 'the ecclesiastical must vindicate its divine liberty from the civil'.[19]

Of the divinity of the Roman Catholic Church Manning had long been convinced, and the impression only deepened at close range. In January he wrote to Robert Wilberforce about the effect of his Roman experience. 'Things seem to me clearer, plainer, shapelier, and more harmonious; things which were only in the head have gone down into the heart; hiatuses and gaps have bridged themselves over by obvious second thoughts, and I feel a sort of *processus* and expansion going on which consolidates all old convictions, and keeps throwing out the premisses of new ones.'[20] To another correspondent he was equally enthusiastic. 'The sacred beauty with which things are done here is, of course, beyond all places. I am very deeply impressed with what I see of the religious orders here, especially the Passionists.'[21] Nevertheless, Manning was careful to guard himself in his letter to Robert Wilberforce. 'I have never felt the fear of safety or pressure of conscience which alone justifies a change.'[22] And when writing to Mrs Laprimaudaye, the wife of his curate, he even castigated himself for the 'idle, empty and unseemly state into which my life abroad has led me',[23] and expressed nostalgia for Lavington. Evidently the inner struggle was not yet resolved.

Manning's newly conceived devotion to the Pope, however, weighed the balance more heavily on the Catholic side. Pius always remembered his first sight of the English archdeacon on his knees in the Piazza di Spagna as the papal carriage went by.[24] On 9 April Manning, along with some other English tourists, was presented to the Pope; on 11 May, the very day of his departure from Rome, he managed to obtain half an hour's audience. Manning delivered a copy of the translated pamphlet on Ireland and drew Pius's attention to certain passages. His Holiness, notwithstanding the manifold worries which were pressing upon him, appeared most interested in England. He had heard of Elizabeth Fry, the Quaker prison reformer, clearly an admirable woman. But the customs and practices of the Anglican Church were most mysterious to him. Was it really true that communion was received in both kinds? What, and the same chalice used by everyone? It was obvious that the Pope regarded this other branch of the Catholic Church as some kind of heathen sect, a sentiment most galling to a proud arch-deacon.[25] Come to that, the Pope also seemed astonished that there should be such things as Anglican archdeacons.

Meanwhile the Prime Minister, Lord John Russell, had been proving equally adept in drawing attention to the shortcomings of the English Church. Moved by some impish whim –

> He only does it to annoy,
> Because he knows it teases

– he appointed as Bishop of Hereford that same Hampden whom Newman had so violently opposed as Professor of Divinity in 1836. The gravity with which Manning received this news was not a whit diminished by his distance from England. Hampden, he told Robert Wilberforce, was a heretic, whose anti-dogmatic opinions opened the way to complete loss of faith. 'Can anyone doubt,' demanded Manning, unconsciously echoing Newman's question in the *Essay on Development*, 'can anyone doubt what judgement would be formed of him or his book here [Rome] or at Munich, or what would have been said of it by St Augustine or St Athanasius?'[26] Not that Manning was any longer content to trust his own interpretations of antiquity. 'What do I know of antiquity? At my next birthday, if I live, I shall be forty. I must rest on something which itself rests continuously on antiquity, whose consciousness is therefore continuous, running down from the Day of Pentecost to this hour.'[27]

Hampden's appointment provided yet one more sign that the Church of England was a puppet of the Government. Some of the bishops had protested, but to no avail. It seemed that Manning had finally come to the parting of the ways. 'Hampden's consecration', he wrote to Robert Wilberforce, 'declares the civil power to be *ultimate* and supreme, even in spiritual obligations. This overthrows the only defence I have ever been able to make of our position.'[28] Brave words came easily in Rome: to another acquaintance, George Moberly, the headmaster of Winchester, he expressed himself still more distinctly: 'The Church of England I left behind me, is not the Church I shall, if God so will, return to, unless by his blessing you and others shall have reversed those events.'[29] Manning professed also to Robert Wilberforce that he felt a clear duty to testify where he stood:

I cannot go on with any reserve. Truth is a trust to be laid out and accounted for, and time is spending fast. Moreover, people believe us to be what we are not, and are disbelieving truths we hold to be sacred, because we hold them in silence, which is a kind of unrighteousness. What I feel is, that a broad, open avowal of principle may probably suffice to clear us individually of responsibility, guide others the right way, make our position personally tenable, and begin a correction of the evil. This course would, I think, satisfy me. But I cannot rest in any fine distinctions, or theories unintelligible to the *pauperes Christi*, for whom we exist.[30]

At Milan, on his way back from Rome, Manning inspected the cadaver of St Charles Borromeo (died 1584) and was rewarded with what he took as an unmistakable call from that saint. 'I was thinking in prayer, if only I could know that St. Charles, who represents the Council of Trent, was right and we wrong. The Deacon was singing the Gospel, and the last words, *et erit unum ovile et unus pastor*, came upon me, as if I had never heard them before.'[31]

Yet no sooner was he back in England than certainty and confidence in the Roman Catholic claims evaporated. Gladstone, no doubt disquieted by the tone of Manning's letters from Rome, conducted an interrogation to discover whether Manning's faith still extended to the Church of England. He was well satisfied. Manning had shown a most pleasing disposition 'to dwell on her [the Church of England's] Catholic and positive character rather than on what is negative, or peculiar, or external viz. the Protestant and the national aspects'.[32] At some stage during that summer, when walking with Gladstone in St James's Park, Manning was rash enough to confess (or so Gladstone remembered) that during his illness in 1847 he had been visited with an absolute assurance that the Church of England was 'a living portion of the Church of Christ'.[33] This statement Gladstone would never allow him to forget. Meanwhile the happy news of Manning's apparent confidence spread. Keble heard that he had returned from Rome more Anglican than ever.[34] Those who, like George Moberly, had received letters from Manning in Rome were especially gratified, not to say stunned, by his 1848 Charge, in which he dealt extensively with the Hampden question. The archdeacon blithely pointed out that since Hampden had never been condemned by any Church tribunal he could not be called a heretic. Certainly the new Bishop of Hereford had written some regrettable passages in the past but, it now appeared, his public subscription to the 39 Articles served to close the entire question. Manning explained his volte-face with bare-faced candour in a letter to Moberly: 'My opinions are what they were when I wrote to you from Rome. My Charge is the case for the Church of England.'[35]

In fact, he was showing himself to be as timid in action as he had been bold in judgement. His private sympathies were unequivocally with Rome, but he seemed incapable of making the decisive and irrevocable break that would cut him off for ever (so it appeared) from a position in English life. He needed allies with whom he could share and perhaps mitigate his unease. Henry Wilberforce and his wife Mary were, he knew, themselves most deeply attracted to Rome. 'I feel that in the end nothing will part us three,' Manning wrote to Henry in October 1848. 'Either we shall all die where we are, or through much heartbreaking we shall all meet elsewhere.'[36] It proved to be Manning who stayed where he was the longest. His thoughts turned to Caroline: 'What would she have thought of what I am doing, feeling and believing? If it is a delusion perhaps she would have saved me.'[37]

The evidence against the Church of England continued to amass. In November 1848 the Dean and Chapter of Chichester contrived to lure back a clergyman who had forsaken his benefice to live in France by the simple device of making him a canon of the cathedral. This expedient, Manning correctly considered, belied all that he had ever hoped or said on behalf of the chapter. 'I am, as you may divine without any gifts of exorcism, in a profane state of mind,' he told Sidney Herbert. 'When I look for a remedy I see the Church of England divided and powerless.'[38] Yet he had by now nursed doubts about the Church of England for several years. Newman, looking on from the outside, judged that Manning would never convert.[39] He was exasperated when Henry Wilberforce, *his* former disciple, told him that the Church of England must be a safe resting place as it was good enough for the likes of Manning. 'What does Manning *mean* by telling *you* that there is a "deep gulf between him and me",' Newman expostulated to Henry in March 1848, 'while he tells all Catholics that he is already quite *one* with us. You are a clever fellow, but you will not reconcile these sayings.'[40]

Manning's 1849 Charge expressed surprise and, one feels, some disappointment that the European revolutions of the previous year had had no counterpart in England. 'It may be that our time is not yet to come. . . . They who know best our social state are least confident and sanguine. The elements and powers of popular convulsion lie deep and spread wide beneath our feet. We dwell upon a population in which every class has its galling sore: and the sway of our old political and spiritual order is weakening year by year.' The Church of England might save the country from the cataclysm, if only the Church of England possessed a more powerful influence. 'If, instead of jealousy and suspicions, statesmen had the boldness, energy, and breadth of soul to trust in the kingdom of our Redeemer . . . ; if they would but do it homage and service, not by money or statutes, but by giving range and freedom to its purely spiritual action, what might not England, what might not the world once more become!'[41]

Meanwhile, as a more prosaic instance of the principles at stake, the education issue was again to the fore. Did the Government's provision of funds give it the right to interfere with the management of Church schools? Manning's Charge was sure that it did not. Once more he urged his view that the State was incapable of conducting education properly since it lacked the Church's means of forming the character and curbing the will. Yet Manning always possessed a strong practical streak. In theory he feared any compromise with the Government. In practice he knew that compromise was unavoidable after the Maynooth grant had finally killed the ideal of the Anglican State. The Church of England could not now hope to receive grants for education without submitting to at least some of that inspection and control that other denominations were prepared to accept. Accommodation was necessary because victory was impossible. So Manning found himself trying to prevent the die-hard clergy from taking too intransigent a line against the Government at the National Society meeting of 1849. In public as in private affairs Manning preferred to avoid a clash. At his behest, an extremist resolution was softened and options for negotiation kept open. It was not glorious work, this undermining of his own convictions, but it showed the influence which he possessed. 'His power with the clergy is very great, greater certainly than that of any man living,'[42] commented F. D. Maurice, who was at the conference.

This very influence intensified his dilemma. Again and again the same pattern seemed to repeat itself. With a ruthless dissection of the Church of England's failings Manning would goad himself towards the brink, almost as if eager to place himself in a position from which there could be no honourable return. Then he would discover that, after all, the argument was not sufficiently overwhelming: perhaps he should await a heightened sense of certainty. Yet the recoil never quite matched the advance: the resurgence of doubt pulled him back from a decision, but never quite back to the same starting-point. His mind traversed vast distances in both directions, but inexorably he was edging closer to Rome.

His see-saw progress continued throughout 1849. At the start of the year Manning was scandalized to hear Goulburn, a former Chancellor of the Exchequer in Peel's Government, speak dismissively of Anglican bishops. 'He contended that money and a peerage are the chief social importance of a bishop: that it is his social not his spiritual character that impresses the people and serves the Church. I had thought the last specimen of this race had been some time in the British Museum. For some years I have never seen a live one.'[43] When Gladstone tried to cheer him by writing of the support that could be expected from the laity, Manning would have none of it. The upper classes were nine-tenths Erastian; the middle classes were equally lost; the only support to which Anglican Catholics might look consisted of one or two isolated individuals and the poor.[44] In February he was bemoaning the lack of religious. 'I have long felt that it is a sign of spiritual sterility, or of deep seated poverty in the life of the Church of England that it has never been able to perpetuate, hardly so much as to produce the higher forms of devotion. We are taunted, not unjustly, with our subscription lists and societies, while we cannot form one Sister of Mercy. The cause of this seems to me to be that the English public, or world, are too strong for the English Church, and that the world hates counsels of perfection, and lives which condemn its self-indulgence.'[45]

By Holy Week, however, his despondent mood had left him. To his 'dearest daughter in Christ' Mary Wilberforce he wrote: 'My deep belief is that He wills me to stay as I am; and all those whom He has submitted to me. . . . There are points in the R.C. which I could never do more than accept as from a Divine authority before which all my own belief must give place. I mean for instance the whole subject of invocations which I am persuaded is of purely human origin.' Neither he nor Mary Wilberforce, he was persuaded, would discover the solution to their problem in any outward observance. 'If with my heart, such as it is, I were before the Altar in any Church in Christendom, or at the foot of St. Peter himself in Rome or Antioch, I should be but what I am. The cure is within. External changes are but on the outside.'[46]

But this line, so totally at odds with Manning's usual bias towards firm dogma, did not last. There is little trace of ecumenicalism in a letter which he wrote to Mary Wilberforce at the end of the year:

You remember my promise that the day I feel my soul to demand anything for its safety you shall know. I have not forgotten it, and I have never yet felt this demand. But I have felt, and do feel, an overwhelming fear lest I should be under an illusion. . . . On St. Andrews Day I offered myself, as I have again and again, and never so often as in Rome, to follow on the spot if only I can have, not sign or token, but the conviction of a moral agent that it is the will of my Lord.[47]

These musings were the prelude to another fierce outburst against the Church of England. Robert Wilberforce was the recipient of this as of all Manning's most extreme utterances:

I have tried to hold my peace, to lose myself in work, to take in other subjects which I dearly love and delight in, but all in vain. My whole reason seems filled with one outline. The faith of the Holy Trinity and of the Incarnation subdues me into a belief of the indivisible unity and perpetual infallibility of the Body of Christ. Protestantism is not so much a rival system, which I reject, but no system, a chaos, a wreck of fragments, without idea, principle, or life. It is to me flesh, blood, unbelief, and the will of man. Anglicanism seems to me to be in essence the same, only elevated, constructed, and adorned by intellect, social and political order, and the fascinations of a national and domestic history. As theology, still more as the Church or the faith, it has so faded out of my mind that I cannot say I reject it, but I know it no more.[48]

Manning confessed that the burden of these feelings had grown to 'an almost intolerable weight'.[49] The next crisis might have been the last whatsoever it had involved. As it happened, the case of the Revd George Cornelius Gorham involved a great deal.

Gorham was a clever Evangelical clergyman of fairly advanced age (he was 63 in 1850) whose reservations regarding the doctrine of baptismal regeneration had first caused difficulties before his ordination in 1811. This doctrine was a touchstone of theological opinion. Since an infant could hardly experience that burning faith in Christ that Evangelicals regarded as the sole means of renewal, it followed that, for them, baptism could never be more than a sign or a token. High Churchmen, on the other hand, believing that the Church possessed power to convey grace whatever the state of the recipient, regarded infant baptism as a first lethal blow delivered against original sin. As the great majority of Anglicans held hazy views somewhere in between these two extremes, Gorham's uncompromising Evangelical view passed without comment for thirty-five years after his ordination. As Manning dispiritedly observed, a man might believe what he liked in the Church of England, as long as he kept quiet and upheld the Church.[50]

Whether Gorham kept quiet or not, there were no complaints about his teaching. It was tempting fate, though, when he moved to the Cornish parish of St Just in 1846. The village was in the diocese of Henry Phillpotts, Bishop of Exeter, a choleric High Churchman who was the most likely of all the prelates to enforce dogmatic rigour. For those who, like Manning, happened to share Phillpotts's opinions, he was a man of strong principle;

for those, like Charles Greville, who did not, he was a quarrelsome old tyrant with 'a desperate and a dreadful countenance'.[51] Phillpotts had installed Gorham at St Just without difficulty, but soon afterwards he unluckily caught sight of Gorham's advertisement for a curate 'free from Tractarian error'. From that moment the vicar of St Just was a marked man. And when after only a few months, Gorham, finding that he could not educate his children properly at the extremity of Cornwall, negotiated with the Lord Chancellor a transfer to the village of Brampford Speke, near Exeter, Phillpotts struck, refusing to install him without an examination to establish his orthodoxy.

Gorham duly sustained a total of fifty-two hours of hostile questioning, during which he exhibited a remarkable knowledge and formidable powers of defence. Of course it made no odds. Phillpotts declared himself unsatisfied with the candidate's view of baptism, and refused to install him. Gorham, who was a fighter, appealed to the higher instance of the Court of Arches, only to lose again, after interminable delays, in August 1849. Nothing daunted, he proceeded to take the case to the final court of appeal, which was the Judicial Committee of the Privy Council. Whichever way the judgement went, there looked like being a split in the Church, probably more serious if Gorham lost than if he won, because he enjoyed strong Evangelical support. The Archbishops of Canterbury and York, therefore, went out of their way to signify that they considered Gorham's opinions legitimate. The High Churchmen, however, were no longer mainly concerned with the doctrinal issue. Of course Manning and his like supported Phillpotts; indeed Manning had written to Phillpotts bemoaning the 'slovenly unbelief'[52] that afflicted the Church. (Phillpotts, for his part, showed himself most uncharacteristically anxious to obtain Manning's good opinion.) The vital issue now, though, was that a court in which laymen easily predominated – six lawyers and Lord Lansdowne as against the two Archbishops and the Bishop of London – should have the last word on a matter of doctrine. Manning explained his position to Samuel Wilberforce (24 January 1850): '. . . it is indifferent which way the judgement may go. Indeed a decision in favour of the true doctrine of Baptism would mislead many. A judgement right in matter cannot heal a wrong in the principle of the Appeal. And the wrong is this: "The Appeal removes the final decision of a question involving both doctrine and discipline out of the Church to another centre and that a Civil Court." '[53]

This time Manning really did seem determined to trap himself into a definite decision. If the principle of civil jurisdiction over the Church in matters of doctrine were accepted, he told Robert Wilberforce, 'I should feel that the Church of England had given me my release.'[54] One feels, nevertheless, that James Hope, another intimate of Gladstone's who fully shared in the concern, was justified in his sharp comment to Manning that 'if you have not hitherto read Erastianism in the history of the Church of England since the Reformation, then I fear you and I have much to discuss before we can meet upon common ground'.[55] Robert Wilberforce, who held Manning in more awe, cast about desperately for some expedient that might satisfy their consciences without precipitating them into the Roman Church. Might they not get hold of a sympathetic colonial bishop and found a Free Church?[56] Manning would have none of it. 'No. Three hundred years ago we left a good ship for a boat; I am not going to leave the boat for a tub.'[57]

For all Manning's insistence that the actual decision in the Gorham appeal was not material to his position, the announcement of a judgement in Gorham's favour sent him into a flurry of activity. That same day, 9 March 1850, he met with a group of like-minded clerics in the vestry of St Paul's, Knightsbridge – 'they made me preside'[58] – to discuss tactics; and two days later they had decided to draft a Declaration repudiating the judgement. This document, signed by Manning, Robert and Henry Wilberforce, Keble, Pusey and eight others, appeared in *The Times* on 20 March: 'Inasmuch as the faith is one and rests upon one principle of authority, the conscious, deliberate, and wilful abandonment of the essential meaning of an article of the Creed destroys the divine foundation upon which alone the entire faith is propounded by the Church.' Any portion of the church, therefore, which abandons the doctrine of baptismal regeneration becomes 'formally separate from the Catholic body, and can no longer assure to its members the grace of sacraments and the remission of sins'. The Anglican Church must make an authoritative statement of the doctrine of Holy Baptism that the recent sentence had impugned.[59]

A notable absentee among the signatories was Gladstone. His abhorrence of the Gorham decision was all that Manning might have required, but then he professed himself 'placed between a variety of distinct obligations, the harmony of which is not easy to discern at certain given points'.[60] The dilemma which this phrasing covered was that the preservation of the Catholic element within the Anglican Church seemed now to demand a complete separation of Church and State, while the advocacy of this solution would have involved an end to Gladstone's political career. This was a sacrifice which he often considered, but never made. Manning told him that the time for doing anything for the Church in Parliament had passed, but Gladstone prevaricated: perhaps the bishops would act to repudiate the Gorham judgement. In the mean time Gladstone proposed a pact whereby the opponents of that judgement should bind themselves to take no decisive act without giving two months' prior warning to the others. This proposal

Manning flatly rejected. As for the bishops, on whom Gladstone rested his hopes, his Lordship of Exeter threatened to excommunicate His Grace of Canterbury for supporting Gorham.[61] The Bishop of London, more constructively, introduced a bill into the House of Lords designed to make the Episcopal bench, rather than the Privy Council, the final judge in matters of doctrine. But Manning pronounced this bill 'a total and vital failure'[62] even before the Lords had rejected it.

Gladstone remained adamant that Manning would never secede. Even Samuel Wilberforce, who did not understand how anyone could be 'ensnared by such a painted hag as that Roman Jezebel',[63] now realized that his dearest brother was likely to go, but when he raised this prospect with Gladstone in April 1850 the idea was dismissed. Perhaps Gladstone's conscience was troubling him; in any case he could not bring himself to contemplate the likelihood of Manning's desertion, which he considered would be 'a step more ruinous (in my mind) than any other, except one, namely the abandonment of an article of the Christian faith'.[64] To avert such a disaster Gladstone thought it wise, on 23 June, to inform Manning that Roman Catholicism 'never can be the instrument of God among us; the faults and virtues of England are alike against it'.[65] This information, so kindly conveyed, finally inspired Manning to reply, albeit with a double negative, that his conversion was a distinct possibility. 'I dare not say that my conscience will not submit itself to the Church which has its circuits throughout the world and its centre by accident in Rome.'[66] This tortuous confession by no means served to destroy Gladstone's trust in the steadfastness of his friend's Anglicanism, although to other intimates it must have seemed that Manning's course was irremediably set. The archdeacon wondered whether his wife was guiding him from another world. 'For some years', he told Robert Wilberforce, 'I have thought, even half-believed, that intercessions within the veil have been drawing me whither they now see the One Light to shine. But this is a daydream, perhaps.'[67]

Yet there were still signs, during the spring and summer of 1850, that Manning's familiar habit of drawing back at the last might be reasserting itself. He seemed so extraordinarily anxious to explore every conceivable means of getting the Gorham judgement reversed; so eager to take steps, so dilatory in taking action. Immediately after the judgement he convened the Chichester clergy and elicited from them a near unanimous protest against the decision. In the summer he organized a circular inviting every clergyman in the country to sign a Declaration against the application of the Royal Supremacy in matters of doctrine. In July he published a letter to his bishop on the same subject. 'I have written myself fairly over the border – or Tiber rather,'[68] he daringly reported to Robert Wilberforce.

But had he? These public acts were accompanied by private statements that seemed to tell the other way. In May he wrote to Mary Wilberforce, who was on the point of converting, giving her 'the reasons which make me strive to subdue both haste and fear in the great probation which is upon me'. The Church of England seemed more in harmony with Scripture than the Church of Rome; many more holy and more intelligent people than himself had lived content within its ranks. The Gorham judgement *might* be intended as a revelation, but then he could not be absolutely sure. 'I have not yet heard Him in my conscience saying "Flee for thy life." Till then, I will die rather than run the risk of crossing His Will.'[69] This mood of uncertainty was on him again when he wrote (18 June) to his sister Caroline. 'The world has sent me long ago to Pius IX, but I am still here; and if I could lay my bones under the sod in Lavington Churchyard with a soul clear before God, all the world could not move me.' He added, however, that the difficulties in the way of this happy outcome were considerable. 'I am compelled to acknowledge that the laws which I believe to be divine are violated, and that the Church of England is in many points indefensible.'[70] Even as late as July, however, the archdeacon was still conscientiously restraining his penitents from too hasty a passage to Rome. Late events, he admitted, had taxed his faith in the Church of England, 'but it seems to me too soon yet to pass sentence upon it'.[71] Gladstone, who saw Manning on 21 July, reported to his wife that 'as to Church matters I am not less well pleased with his present frame than I was'.[72]

This time Manning's hesitation did not last. By September his mind was finally made up. Early in that month Samuel Wilberforce visited Lavington, and afterwards he strove to make Gladstone see that the die was cast.[73] The truth, if Gladstone had cared to acknowledge it, was that Manning had been moving towards Rome ever since Newman's conversion. The tide on which he was borne had risen inexorably against the barriers of Englishry until finally, almost involuntarily, he found himself swept over into the faith of his soul's desire. Being Manning, he liked to believe that he had been in conscious control; and in his letters to Robert Wilberforce he again and again went over the case for Rome and against the Church of England. The constant ratiocination served to quiet his terror at the step which he now foresaw, but it did not really take the argument any further than the point he had reached several years before. The Gorham case did not bring any new insights; it simply brought matters to a head, as the conversion of Mary Wilberforce in June and Henry Wilberforce in September 1850 demonstrated. Gorham was finally instituted at Brampford Speke in August, an event that could be taken as the moment when the battle for Catholic doctrine in the Church of England was finally lost. For Manning, where there was no dogma there could be no faith. 'If I stay I shall end a simple mystic,'[74] he told Robert Wilberforce. The most depressing part was that the whole Gorham case, which seemed like life and death to Manning – 'all Divine authority in England is at stake'[75] – left the mass of clergymen completely unmoved. Less than 10% of them bothered to sign the circular which he had sent out.

He spoke now of his suffering, no longer of his perplexity. The appeals of his friends became more hectoring and more tiresome as his certainty grew. At the beginning of October there were two 'jarring and useless'[76] meetings with Gladstone, who then removed to Italy without in any way allaying his persecution. Had Manning really, he demanded, unlearnt the lesson of 1847, when, under fear of death, he had been convinced of the Catholic credentials of the Church of England?[77] Manning was quite content to admit the inconsistency. 'I have the deepest anxiety to clear my integrity before God and man, but to square myself by myself is of no high importance to me.' He was also, now, quite content to sting his assailant. 'Will you allow me to appeal to you for such a re-examination of your theological conclusions as you have given to your political opinions? To you I seem what you seem to others.'[78] Likewise, when Samuel Wilberforce unguardedly used the word 'dishonesty' in his analysis of the errors that led to Rome, Manning discovered a killing charity: 'My very dear Brother, the word dishonesty shall be laid up for judgement at that day when our common Lord will take account of His servants. I thank you for it with all sincere affection.'[79] The charge was still rankling when Manning wrote to Robert Wilberforce two days later, on 22 October. 'Multitudes, very well worth thinking of, think me all but dishonest.' But now that slur only provided another reason for proceeding. 'Public honour is essential to character and usefulness; and I feel that my work in the Church of England is over. I hinder more than I help.'[80]

At this critical moment his fellow countrymen were suddenly goaded into their last really ferocious bout of anti-papal fury. No one could accuse Manning of seeking a popular cause. He had become devoted to Pius IX while the Pope was being denounced as a traitor on all sides; he embraced Roman Catholicism in England while the English were demented with Protestant prejudice. The occasion of this outburst was the restoration of the Catholic episcopacy in England on a traditional basis, with twelve new sees taking the place of the eight Apostolic Districts into which the country had previously been divided. The change involved nothing more sinister than the creation of a diocesan organization to deal with the sudden increase in Catholics consequent upon the Irish immigration. Almost certainly it would have passed without comment had not Wiseman, now designated Cardinal

Archbishop of Westminster and Metropolitan, taken it into his head to issue a flamboyant and hugely tactless Pastoral to herald the new system. This production, grandiosely delivered 'from out the Flaminian gate' in Rome, succeeded in striking just that note of Catholic triumphalism guaranteed to make English hackles rise. 'We govern' – so Wiseman described his own role in the hierarchy – 'the counties of Middlesex, Hertford and Essex, as ordinary thereof, and those of Surrey, Sussex, Berkshire and Hampshire, with the islands annexed, as administrator with ordinary jurisdiction.'[81] Queen Victoria, for one, was not a little surprised by the words. 'Am I Queen of England or am I not?'[82] she is supposed to have asked. The Bishop of Durham, that same Maltby who had ordained Manning seventeen years before, wrote to Lord John Russell calling Wiseman's Pastoral an 'insolent and insidious' aggression, a phrase on which the Prime Minister set his own imprimatur. Lord John did not, however, despair. 'I rely with confidence on the people of England . . . a nation which looks with contempt on the mummeries of superstition, and with scorn at the laborious endeavours which are now making to confine the intellect and enslave the soul.'[83] The people of England duly responded in their usual unsuperstitious way by burning the Pope in effigy, burning Cardinal Wiseman in effigy, hooting at Roman Catholic priests, breaking the windows of Catholic churches, and otherwise conveying their high sense of the value of Protestant freedom.[84]

Manning was requested to convene the Chichester clergy that they too might express their horror at Roman Catholic presumption. He agreed, under pressure from his bishop, to fulfil his duty and call a meeting, but only on the understanding that he would resign immediately afterwards. When the clergy had passed their resolutions, Manning made a decorous little speech bidding them all farewell. 'My dear old friend the Dean was crying, and many others. So we ended and parted. It was our last meeting and the end of my work in the Church of England.'[85]

'I feel my foot is in the river,' he wrote to Robert Wilberforce, 'it is cold and my heart is sad.'[86] Sadder still was his departure from Lavington on 3 December, only six days after the village church, which he had rebuilt, had been reconsecrated.

There followed a short breathing-space. Notwithstanding the end of five years' inner struggle, Manning felt it would be unfitting to rush too precipitately from Anglican to Catholic altars. At first he thought of joining Gladstone in Italy, but the tone of his friend's letters, which became ever more hectoring as the cataclysm they sought to avert moved nearer, was not encouraging. In the end Manning stayed in London with his sister, and Gladstone was favoured (6 December) with a remarkably prescient letter on his political future:

Let me say what I believe. Parties will from this time form round two centres: the one will be the Protestantism of England protecting or trying to protect itself by legislation; the other, political government, maintaining a powerful neutrality and arbitration among all religious communities. If you retain your seat for Oxford and accept the leadership, which is approaching you through the old Conservative parties, you must take the former centre as your standing point. Which God forbid! If you take the latter centre you know the cost. But I believe that it is the path of Truth, peace and Christian civilisation to this great Empire.[87]

This interim period was not a happy time for Manning. He had lost the solace of work and activity without yet enjoying the support of his new faith. He filled his hours reiterating for the hundredth time to the unfortunate Robert Wilberforce the convictions that were now impelling him to join the Catholic Church. Still he needed to hold himself up to the mark. Memories of Lavington kept pressing in on him. There would be no doubts where the One True Church was, he assured himself as much as Wilberforce, if they had not been born into the Church of England.[88] Manning, in fact, was suffering from the common affliction of pre-conversion nerves. Knowing that James Hope was also on the point of becoming a Catholic, Manning looked to him for support. He even confessed, a most uncharacteristic admission, that he was experiencing some shrinking from the final act of will. 'It would be to me a very great happiness', he told Hope, 'if we could act together, and our names go together in the first publication of the fact.'[89] Hope, who had married Sir Walter Scott's granddaughter, invited Manning to spend Christmas at Abbotsford. This important intelligence instantly found its way to the nerve centre of Catholic gossip, the Oratory in Birmingham, where Newman presided as Father Superior. 'Manning is with Hope at Abbotsford,' Newman wrote to a friend. 'What does this mean?'[90]

One of the reasons for Manning's delay in taking the final step was that he needed time to prepare his family for the shock. 'They are all most kind,' he told Robert Wilberforce, 'except my elder brother, who has a way of his own.'[91] Frederick, always conscious of his position as head of the family, was determined that Henry should not proceed to Rome without being made to feel the awfulness of his act. He poured forth strictures upon his errant brother, and when argument failed, as it inevitably did with so marked a disparity in intellect, he appealed to the duty that was owed to him by virtue of his seniority. Such a brother would have tested the charity of a saint: Manning did not fail the ordeal. He replied to Frederick's diatribes with patience and forbearance, and managed to maintain affection in quite the manner prescribed.[92] 'My brother Frederick', he recalled later, 'was like a Spanish hidalgo in his high sense of honour and in his loyalty and allegiance to the Church of his Baptism. He looked at my leaving that Church as an act of dishonour which he never forgave.' When the blow finally fell, Frederick's principles would allow him no further intercourse with his tainted charge. Many years later the two brothers did find themselves together on Rugby station, but neither word nor gesture of acknowledgement passed between them. 'It was Frederick's great love for the Cardinal that would have made the meeting so painful,' their sister Caroline helpfully explained.[93]

Even in these difficult pre-conversion days, though, Manning's spirits occasionally rose. The political situation afforded him some brief satisfaction. Lord John Russell lost his support in the House of Commons and resigned. There were those who pointed to the fluid state of the parties as the fundamental cause of this event, but Manning, mindful of Russell's shameless truckling to anti-Catholic prejudice, took another view. 'Let those deny it who will, he has fallen before the Church of God.'[94] A few more days, and the Church of God apparently reversed its sentence, because Russell was back once more in office. By then, however, Manning had other things to worry about. Gladstone had returned from Italy. Manning asked for a meeting, to which Gladstone agreed, though once more confessing himself morally and intellectually unequal to the encounter. This was generally the signal for a particularly savage onslaught. Gladstone's diary for 9 March 1851 records three hours of discussion with Manning, 'in which I found him unsatisfactory in his grounds as well as apparently fixed in his conclusions'.[95]

There were two more meetings on the succeeding Sundays, but all to no avail. On 25 March Manning went into the City and legally resigned his archdeaconry. Afterwards he returned over Blackfriars Bridge to Southwark, where he entered the Catholic Cathedral, knelt before the Blessed Sacrament, and said his first 'Hail Mary'. The following Sunday, 30 March, Gladstone confessed that 'Manning smote me to the ground by answering with suppressed emotion that he is now upon the *brink*. . . . Such terrible blows not only overset and oppress but I fear also demoralise me.'[96] In old age Manning left a more dramatic impression of this encounter:

Shall I tell you where I performed my last act of worship in the Church of England? It was in that little chapel off the Buckingham Palace Road. I was kneeling by the side of Mr. Gladstone. Just before the Communion Service commenced, I said to him, 'I can no longer take the Communion in the Church of England.' I rose up – 'St. Paul is standing by his side' – and laying my hand on Mr. Gladstone's shoulder, said, 'Come.' It was the parting of the ways. Mr. Gladstone remained; and I went my way. Mr. Gladstone still remains where I left him.[97]

In fact Mr Gladstone made further attempts at dissuasion. 'Oh look well whither you are going and what work you are marring,' he wrote on April Fool's Day, 'but most of all for God's sake look whether you are dispassionately using the means given you of holding fast or reaching the truth.'[98] On 2 April they had another three-hour meeting, in which Manning 'never got to the subject',[99] an evasion that Gladstone quite correctly considered ominous. Manning's message that Saturday – 'Bear me in mind in your prayers tomorrow'[100] – indicated that the hour had come.

On 6 April, Passion Sunday, in company with Hope, Manning was received into the Roman Catholic Church by Father Brownbill in the Jesuit Church in Farm Street. Father Brownbill, it was gloatingly related by the almost excessively Catholic Lady Georgiana Fullerton, taught the distinguished converts by his manner 'that they could bring to the Church nothing, and were to receive from her everything'.[101] One sees Lady Georgiana's point, but it cannot be said that the Church did too badly by the bargain. Later that day Manning sent the joyful tidings to Robert Wilberforce: 'We have sought admission into what we alike believe to be the one true fold and Church of God on earth.'[102] The phrasing was curiously similar to that in the letter which Manning had received from Newman in October 1845.

Newman now conveyed his 'inexpressible joy'.[103] Poor Robert Wilberforce was tempted to follow Manning, but cringed before his ultra-Protestant wife. Samuel Wilberforce sent a curious note, begging that Manning and he should not act in opposition in their native country. 'If we must be parted,' he suggested fraternally, 'cannot you found a Church in some distant land?'[104] Old Mrs Sargent, Manning's mother-in-law, who had now lost two daughters and three sons-in-law to Rome, bemoaned that 'beloved H.E.M. is gone from me quite'.[105] Sidney Herbert wrote to say that in the circumstances it would be better if he and Manning did not meet: 'As politics part men, how much more that to which politics are nothing!'[106] Gladstone registered shock, dismay and pain. 'I felt as if he had murdered my mother by mistake,' he told a friend.[107] On the morrow he wondered whether these conversions 'may be a sign that my work is gone with them.'[108] That, at least, proved a false alarm, but he had suffered a bitter personal blow. 'I do indeed feel the loss of Manning, if and as far as I am capable of feeling anything. It comes to me cumulated, and doubled with that of James Hope. Nothing like it can happen to me again. Arrived now at middle life, I never *can* form I suppose with any other two men the habits of communication, counsel, and dependence, in which I have now for from fifteen to eighteen years lived with them both.'[109] Many years later Gladstone could take a more detached, even a chilly, view. 'Our common bond was interest in the Anglican cause. It was the breath in the nostrils of our friendship. We had nothing else in common. Manning never spoke to me of his friends. When he became a Catholic our friendship died a natural death.'[110] At the time, however, Gladstone passed through an acute emotional trauma. For a while he even lost the will to go on flogging himself for his impure thoughts.[111]

And what of the object of all this concern? 'Now my career is ended,'[112] Manning remarked to Hope as they walked together on the day before their reception. It was indeed a full fourteen years before the new convert became Archbishop of Westminster and Metropolitan of all the Catholics in England.

6 A Forward Piece?

An amount of pugnacity exists among Roman Catholics, which
by no means finds a sufficient vent in onslaughts on Protestantism.[1]

Saturday Review, 1863

Within a few days of his conversion Manning was declaring to Robert
Wilberforce that he was 'much impressed by the *hard work* that is going on in
the Catholic church . . . the hold it has on people of all degrees is beyond all I
thought'.[2] Having sacrificed his Anglican career to his belief in the One True
Church, Manning was not the type to look for faults in his ideal:
commitment and action were ever the mainstays of his faith. Nevertheless,
the sense which he conveyed from the very beginning of his Catholic
existence, of belonging to an institution which was playing a vital role in
English life, did not correspond to reality. The truth, as it emerges from the
tedious Protestant science of statistics, is that the English Catholics were an
insignificant sect. Although they still occasionally served, on remote
historical grounds, as convenient butts of popular fury, they had not
constituted any threat to Protestant establishment since the Glorious
Revolution of 1688. In the 1780s Edmund Burke reckoned the number of
English Catholics at only 60,000. Perhaps he underestimated, but it is
unlikely that they then made up so much as 1 per cent of the population.
Later, in the 1820s, Whigs like Sydney Smith who supported Catholic
Emancipation would insist that it was ridiculous to persecute a religion that
had been so patently discredited.[3] The penal laws, though relaxed in 1791,
had virtually extirpated the old religion from the country. If, by 1851, there
were suddenly close on 700,000 Catholics in England and Wales, or nearly
4% of the population, that was not due to any religious renascence, nor to
the tiny trickle of converts from the Oxford Movement.[4] It was simply and
solely the consequence of Irish immigration.

In 1851 there were some 521,000 Irish-born inhabitants of England and
Wales, the vast majority of whom were Catholics. To these might be added
others who, though English-born, were the children of first-generation Irish

immigrants. *The Times*, then, may not have been far wrong in judging that only some 150,000 of the country's Catholics were what it described as '*bona fide* English papists'. If so, this select group had grown no faster than the population as a whole since Burke's 1780 estimate.

It would have been surprising if they had done. The old Catholics, though intensely loyal to the faith for which their families had suffered so much, felt no compulsion whatever to offer its consolations to a wider public. The penal laws had forced them to treat their religion as a wholly private matter, and even though most of those laws had now gone, old habits die hard. As Wiseman put it, the 'shackles had been removed, but not the numbness and cramp which they had produced'.[5] No sooner had Catholic Emancipation been passed than Bishop Brampton, Vicar Apostolic of the London District, warned his flock against the perils of taking too active a part in public life. The advice was superfluous: few English Catholics had either the inclination or (being still barred from Oxford and Cambridge) the education to suceed in politics. Only twelve Catholic peers were qualified to sit in the House of Lords. For the most part Catholic leaders belonged to the squirearchy rather than to the aristocracy; and the squirearchy was quite content with local rather than national influence. Dotted here and there about the country Catholic landowners formed with their tenantry and underlings odd little knots attached to the old faith. Only in the north, in Northumberland, Durham, the North Riding and Lancashire, were their numbers at all concentrated. Elsewhere there were whole counties with scarcely a Catholic within them. In the south families like the Arundells of Wardour and the Welds of Lulworth, who possessed enough land to make their religion a force in the area, were quite exceptional. The highest ambition of most Catholic gentry was to merge unprovocatively into the English country scene. As if to cast off any imputation of disloyalty, they often became more John Bullish than John Bull, involved with agriculture, dedicated to sport, scorning any suggestion of intellectual interests.

One aspect of this Englishry was their attitude of indifference, even sometimes of hostility, towards extreme papal claims. It was not forgotten that Pius v had excommunicated Queen Elizabeth I from the security of Rome, leaving his spiritual subjects trapped helplessly in the heretic pen. In the eighteenth century some of the Catholic gentry had been prepared to compromise the authority of the Pope in order to gain emancipation. Sir John Throckmorton, backed by a Catholic Committee, had advocated that English Catholics should separate themselves from Rome in matters of discipline, and that they should possess the right to elect their own bishops.[6] A sell-out to the Government on these lines had been avoided by the stern opposition of Bishop Milner, Vicar Apostolic of the Midlands District from

1803 to 1826, in many ways a forerunner of Manning in his refusal to yield Catholic essentials for the sake of political expediency.[7] Milner was strong, determined and immovable, qualities which he needed to get his way. As a caste, the Catholic gentry were too accustomed to treating the clergy as some species of superior servant to be much impressed even by bishops. In the absence of a proper diocesan system, priests had often been dependants of a country house rather than subordinates of the Vicars Apostolic; and the 'prelates of the squirearchy' did not hesitate to direct the activities of the clergy under their care. 'My father is head of the Protestant Church,' remarked the Prince Regent, 'and Lord Petre is head of the Catholic Church.' So Milner faced a severe struggle to enforce his episcopal authority, although he did find some support among the humbler Catholic laity, who no doubt resented the landowners' hegemony. The hostility of English society in general never in the least deterred Catholics from prosecuting fierce antagonisms in their own ranks.

Another feature of the old Catholic families was that they had remained largely ignorant of the new devotions that Rome had developed since the Counter-Reformation. In the eighteenth century there had even been a Catholic Bible Society in England, a practice which caused great distress to Pope Pius VII. 'We have been truly shocked at this crafty device', he remonstrated, 'by which the very foundations of religion are undermined.'[8] But how were the unfortunate English Catholics to know better when the Church's teaching reached them so spasmodically? All too often a priest was unavailable on a Sunday, so that the laity were thrown back upon their own resources. They might gather to read prayers or simply concentrate upon books of devotion like Challoner's *Garden of the Soul*. There was never a hint of emotion or display: worship was austere, reserved, even cold.

Of all English sects the Catholics had been the least affected by the Evangelical movement. Families which had clung to their faith through centuries of persecution, and whose piety was further attested by the numbers entering religious orders from their ranks, felt no call to make any parade of their convictions. It was the depth and not the tumult of their souls that they considered the fittest offering in prayer. Communion was received rarely, perhaps no more than three times a year, but each occasion demanded a week of conscientious preparation. In the Mass itself there was a minimum of ceremonial, while music would have been exceptional. The rite which Manning had so much admired upon the continent, Exposition of the Blessed Sacrament, had no place among English Catholics.[9] Disciplines, hair shirts and rosaries were unknown to them; invocations to the saints aroused their suspicion; devotions to the Virgin Mary were dismissed as 'Continental' and quite unsuited to England.[10] When, early in the century, a statue of the Virgin was introduced into the chapel at Prior Park, near Bath, there had been an outcry: 'Let us have no Romanizing here. Take it away!'[11] As for sermons, no one looked for uplift from that source. Wilfrid Ward tells a story of one priest who made do by translating French Court sermons. 'Hear this, you butterflies of fashion,' he would address the astonished rustics in his congregation, 'hear this, you that love to haunt the antechambers of the great.'[12] The anecdote conveys the same sense of faded grandeur, of time stood still, that Manning observed. 'When I came from the broad stream of the English Commonwealth into the narrow community of the English Catholics, I felt as if I had got into St. James's Palace in 1687. It was as stately as the House of Lords and as unlike the English Commonwealth as my father's mulberry velvet court-dress was to his common-day blue coat and brass buttons.'[13]

However staunch and admirable the old English Catholics might be on their own terms, Cardinal Wiseman, the head of the newly restored hierarchy, was undoubtedly right in believing that they were not material from which any Catholic revival in England might be fashioned. Wiseman had spent many years in Rome, where he had become Rector of the English College; his instinctive policy was to present Roman ways and Roman claims in their most challenging and confident guise. Many English Catholics, by contrast, were appalled by the bold and tactless manner in which he announced the new hierarchy. Among the Catholic aristocracy indignation may have been fuelled by the realization that the advent of diocesan bishops must mean the end of lay dominance over Catholic life in England. Two Catholic peers, the Duke of Norfolk and Lord Beaumont, denounced Wiseman's pretensions in the House of Lords, the Duke of Norfolk even carrying resistance to the extreme of becoming an Anglican. 'I should think that many must feel as we do,' he wrote to Lord Beaumont, 'that ultramontane opinions are totally incompatible with allegiance to our Sovereign and with our Constitution.'[14]

It was not just Wiseman's Romanism that aroused antagonism among his flock; there was also his partiality for converts. In his last years Manning would recall how English priests of the old school used to dislike receiving converts. 'They supposed us [Anglicans] to be impostors, or to have worldly motives, as we did when Jews came to be received.'[15] Manning even remembered one priest who boasted of his innocency of bringing any newcomers into the Church. It must be said, though, that sometimes the converts had only themselves to blame for the suspicions they incurred. They could be infuriatingly arrogant. There was W. G. Ward, for example, who delighted to use his formidable logical powers to justify the kind of complete mental abandonment to Roman authority that the old English

Catholics instinctively rejected. 'My great intellect is no more important than my great leg,'[16] Ward would say, and no one denied that his leg was indeed abominably swollen. Having registered his contempt for his own remarkable mental attainments, Ward failed to understand how his co-religionists could take it amiss if he said what he thought of theirs. An English Catholic meeting a Protestant in controversy, he remarked, was 'like a barbarian meeting a civilised man'.[17]

All too frequently the Oxford converts failed to disguise their sense of intellectual superiority to those who had merely imbibed their faith with their mothers' milk. In other respects, too, the newcomers could be easy to dislike. They were so ostentatiously keen and enthusiastic, so irritating alike in their credulity and their scepticism, so eager to prostrate themselves before the Pope, so bent on provoking solid Victorian opinion, as though the courting of Protestant hostility might redeem their own former heresy. Where old English priests had eschewed even black coats, convert priests gloried in sporting Roman collars and in parading in cassocks and birettas. When they were hooted in the street many old Catholics thought, like Dr Lingard,[18] that it served them right. Even at Mass, convert affectation was inescapable, whether in their slavish imitation of Roman ceremonial or in their adoption of the Roman pronunciation of Latin. Worst of all, they would talk wildly of the prospects of converting England back to the faith. Cardinal Wiseman was sufficiently ignorant of English life to be impressed; he spoke of saying Mass in Westminster Abbey.[19] The old English Catholics knew that this was a perfectly ridiculous notion.

Still, both old Catholics and converts could agree that the Irish constituted a problem. In her *Recollections of a Northumberland Lady*, Mrs Charlton left an artlessly frank sample of old Catholic attitudes on this subject. She had been dining with the Westminsters at Eaton Hall, and the conversation turned to the number of Irish Catholic prisoners at the local assizes. The Marquess of Westminster intervened to forestall any embarrassment: 'Gentlemen, a Roman Catholic lady is sitting on my right!' Mrs Charlton was proud to recall how she had risen to the occasion. ' "Yes," I said at this, "but an English Catholic, not an Irish one, which is all the difference in the world. English Catholics are responsible beings who are taught right from wrong, whereas Irish Catholics, belonging to a yet savage nation, know no better and are perhaps excusable on that account." ' It is only fair to add that the Charltons, like many of their kind, contributed generously to schools and church building in their area, though Mrs Charlton was of the opinion that rather more gratitude might have been forthcoming from the local priest, whose father, after all, had been nothing more than an Irish commercial traveller.[20] As for the Oxford converts, even those who recognized the obligations of charity could not always conceal that the Irish were an embarrassment. Faber complained that at the London oratory the poor were introducing 'immovable *belts* of stink' which were chasing away Catholics from the washing classes. Moreover, 'we are so plentiful in bugs that they walk about our surplices and take possession of gentlemen's hats'.[21] No wonder Gladstone's convert sister declared that she could bear it no longer.

London, though, was one of the few places where the appalling living conditions of the Irish forced themselves on the attention of the ordinary English Catholic. Outside the capital the immigrants congregated in squalid new industrial towns, with which native Catholics had no contact other than the dedicated and self-sacrificing service given by a few devoted priests. The Irish were so isolated that many of them never learnt to speak English. In their foreign and degraded environment the local Catholic church was the one potential source of aid and comfort. The trouble was that all too often the local Catholic church did not exist. 586 churches and chapels in the whole of the country were nowhere near sufficient for a Catholic population of 700,000. On the Sunday of the 1851 census only 252,000 attended Mass, and a quarter of that number did not find seats. Sheer lack of amenities meant that the Irish were being lost to the Church in their thousands even as Cardinal Wiseman rejoiced over each new convert from Oxford. At the same time the manner in which the Irish gave their precious pennies to create and sustain their own churches represented an infinitely more moving demonstration of faith than any of the English Catholics, old or new, were able to provide. It occurred to very few, however, that the despised Irish were the best hope of reviving Catholicism in England. The event has proved that this was so. In areas like East Anglia, where the Irish never penetrated, Catholicism is still almost extinct today.

To be fair, Wiseman felt strongly for the poor;[22] he simply lacked the administrative capacity to be very effective. Manning, who possessed both the feeling and the capacity, would one day seize the opportunity, but for the moment, as a new convert, he was in no position to follow his own lights. He meant to become a priest, but beyond that he knew that his best hope of performing useful service for the Church was to act as Cardinal Wiseman directed. The Cardinal was delighted with his new capture. His policy had been to attract distinguished Anglicans into the Church, and as the *Tablet* commented,[23] Manning was in some ways the most distinguished of them all. Wiseman did not mean to let this talent run to waste. The sooner the convert became a priest the better. Manning's diary for 13 April 1851, just one week after his conversion, records his scramble through the lower echelons of the Church. 'Palm Sunday. Confirmation. Tonsure. First

Communion. Minor Orders. Sub-deacon. Retreat. Deacon.'[24] Many English Catholics felt that such haste was indecent. But Wiseman was determined, and he had the support of the Pope, who sent the new convert a cameo of Christ's profile. Evidently Manning had made a good impression in Rome. The Cardinal ordained him on Trinity Sunday, 14 June 1851, embellishing the occasion with a typical flourish. 'I look upon you as one of the first fruits of the restoration of the hierarchy by our Holy Father Pius IX. Go forth, my son, and bring your brethren and fellow countrymen by thousands and tens of thousands into the one true fold of Christ.'[25] The *Tablet* was less impressed, making the caustic comment that the new priest was being sent to Rome 'for the purpose of commencing his ecclesiastical studies'.[26]

Manning later confessed to Robert Wilberforce that the prospect of becoming a student again, twenty-four years after he had left Balliol, did not fill him with unalloyed delight.[27] Nevertheless, Wiseman's decision that he should go to Rome set the course of Manning's Catholic career. Certainly the Cardinal could have wished no more ardent disciple of his Roman ideals. Manning had not become a Catholic in order to be a member of some insignificant minority sect. What he had sought, what he had submitted to, was the infallible authority of Christ's Church on Earth. That such authority must, by its very nature, be indivisible was the principle that had brought Manning into the Church; and by the same logic the decrees of that Church had to emanate from one source alone. The primacy of Rome was not just the source but actually the condition of infallibility. Manning did not become a devotee of the Holy See because, as has so often been suggested, he was ambitious or calculating, any more than he had left the Church of England because he was careless of worldly fortune. He looked to Rome because it was the ultimate stronghold of his faith.

How desperately that stronghold was now required. When Manning met Döllinger, the celebrated German theologian, in the spring of 1851, they agreed that the battle lines were now clearly drawn between Rome and infidelity: no intermediate position could hold.[28] Manning did not under-estimate the strength of the enemy forces. It was, in fact, precisely because, like Newman, he apprehended both the power and the destructive potential of scepticism that he sought out such a well-prepared bastion. Give the mind free rein, he believed, and not just the Christian faith but all principles and all standards would ultimately be insecure. The intellect, no less than the appetites, must be set upon a leash. The acceptance of certain limits for thought was the necessary means of attaining the ability to act with unswerving purpose. In submitting to Rome Manning for ever put behind him profitless and paralysing internal debate. He called his conversion his last act of reason and his first act of faith; he meant, not that he had ceased to use his reason, but that reason would henceforth be the servant of dogma received through faith. There need be no more questions; the answers were all determined in Rome. Manning was perfectly adapted to maintain such a position. His mind was efficient to the point of genius, and he never showed any disposition to pursue speculative problems into labyrinths of ambiguity. What he demanded from theology was a clearing of the decks for action; once in the fight his capacity and dispatch were unrivalled.

The liberating effect of his conversion was immediately evident. 'I seem to have entered into the substance and reality of all my long visions of many years and nothing now remains,'[29] he wrote to Robert Wilberforce in August 1851. After five years of mental tension, the relief of having taken the plunge was palpable. That summer, before going to Rome, Manning almost seemed to enjoy himself. It was certainly the last extended period in his life when he had time on his hands. He stayed at his brother Charles's house in Surrey, exhibiting both his riding skills and (some thought) a newly acquired liveliness of manner.[30] He also snapped up his sister-in-law into the Church; his brother Charles, who had always been, according to one unfriendly witness, 'rather a bore than otherwise but NOTHING to what he is now',[31] succumbed a few months later in Rome. In April and again at the end of June Manning paid visits to Newman at the Birmingham Oratory. Evidently these meetings went off well because in October Newman, recently appointed Rector of the new Catholic University in Dublin, asked Manning to be his Vice-Rector. He needed, he explained to a third party, 'a resident *locum tenens* with whom I was most familiar and confidential'. What a shame that Manning was bound for Rome. Still, Newman quite agreed (or so Manning remembered) as to this course: 'It will be well for you to go to Rome, for if the Cardinal's life dropped you would not be known.'[32]

Manning undertook the journey in company with the boring Charles, the admiring Aubrey de Vere, whom he received into the Church at Avignon, and a convert priest called George Talbot, who was destined to play a vital part in his history. Talbot, fifth son of Baron Talbot de Malahide, was eight years younger than Manning, but already in a position of considerable power. Educated at Eton and Oxford, he had taken Anglican Orders before being received into the Catholic Church by Wiseman, whom he worshipped. Not surprisingly he was one of those who raised an eyebrow at Manning's speedy elevation to the priesthood[33], for he himself had been obliged to spend three years at Oscott seminary[34] before being ordained in 1846. But the claims of breeding were not to be for ever denied. After Talbot had worked for a few years in London, Wiseman sent him to Rome as his personal representative. There Talbot immediately became both a papal chamberlain and a close friend of the Pope, so close that '*mio buono Giorgio*'[35] would invariably be given the task of breaking bad news, of which there was plenty, to the hard-pressed pontiff. Talbot's secret was to combine the deepest reverence for the Pope's office with the most familiar manners towards his person. This attitude was perfectly expressed in a remark which Talbot once made about papal encyclicals: 'As the Pope is no great theologian himself, I feel convinced that when he writes them he is inspired by God.'[36]

Talbot soon established himself as the intermediary through whom Pius received news about the Church in England, a position which gave him considerable importance, as he himself was the first to recognize. He claimed to exercise a hundredfold more influence than he could have done in the College of Cardinals.[37] There was nothing, he declared upon another occasion, which he could not carry through if he choose to be underhand.[38] He chose frequently to be underhand. Talbot was a man of violent prejudice and limited understanding, defects partially disguised by genuine good-nature. In other circumstances he would have been a faintly ludicrous but fundamentally harmless figure. As papal chamberlain he was by no means harmless. In all controversies that rent the Church in England he took Wiseman's part. Perhaps his influence was not quite so decisive as he himself liked to imagine. Pius may not always have taken him very seriously. Nevertheless many times in the 1850s and 1860s English bishops, and others who were at odds with Wiseman, would complain about backstairs intrigues.

In 1851 Talbot was only beginning his Roman career, but already it was clear that he was potentially a valuable contact, offering lines of communication to both Wiseman and the Pope. Although there is no evidence that Manning deliberately befriended Talbot at this stage, the journey to Rome offered opportunities of fellowship which it would have been perverse to ignore. Manning did not consciously scheme; what was far more effective, the instinct for useful people was bred into him. He believed in his friendship for the influential rather as a Don Juan believes in his undying passion for the present object of his desire. The illusion is essential to the achievement.

But this is to run ahead. On the way out to Rome the travellers stopped at Avignon, where there occurred an incident which shows Manning in quite another light. The following account is taken from Aubrey de Vere's *Recollections*.

A few minutes after our diligence entered the courtyard of our hotel, a small black bag belonging to him [Manning] was missed. It had been stolen, and all our enquiries, whether instituted by the police or the clergy, failed to recover it. He declared that whoever had it in his possession might keep what else it contained, which included £100 in money, if only he restored the letters in it. At the first moment after the discovery of his loss the expression of grief in his face and voice was such as I have seldom witnessed. He spoke little; and when I was beginning to speak, he laid his hand upon my arm, and said, 'Say nothing! I can just endure it when I keep perfectly silent.' The loss probably was that of his most precious memorials; but it did not even at that time make him negligent of the 'casual stranger'. After he had given his directions we entered the dining room and he sat down apart. Not long afterwards he observed that at a small table not far distant there sat a maid-servant, alone and neglected. The future Cardinal rose and did for her all that her master and mistress had forgotten to do. He brought a waiter to her, became her interpreter, and took care from time to time that nothing should be wanting to her dinner. When all efforts to recover the lost treasure had failed he went to Rome by sea, and I went to Florence. We met again at Rome. He met my enquiries with a brief reply. 'No; the loss was probably necessary – necessary to sever all bonds to earth.'[39]

It was his wife Caroline's letters that had disappeared. Her memory was still uppermost in his mind on 12 December, the day that he began his studies in Rome. 'Natal. C. d.ssimae' (birthday of Caroline dearly loved), he noted in his diary.[40] She had been dead for fourteen years.

The situation in which he now found himself naturally evoked mixed feelings. The life of a student was far removed from that of an archdeacon who had been accustomed to hob-nob on equal terms with Cabinet Ministers. 'It was a time of great peace but of great trial,' he later recalled. 'I found myself at forty-two among youths; and a stranger among foreigners – I had broken almost every old relation in the world, and was beginning life over again.'[41] Sometimes, when he was lonely, his mind would drift nostalgically. 'What memories of Lavington,' he recorded on 14 December, 'and Sunday night, and of Advent. . . . I have felt much human sorrow today. My softness shames me.'[42] Memories of Lavington would recur throughout his Catholic life. Now his inner moods fluctuated wildly between spiritual elation and self-disgust. '28 March 1852. Monday night after general confession in Retreat I could hardly sleep for joy. I had the feelings I remembered in 1832–3 down to the summer of that year. . . . Wonderful grace carrying me through all. If after this I perish, I perish indeed. God be merciful to me a sinner.' A week later, though, all was despair. 'Said rosary with a hard, absent heart; carried a taper to the altar, and felt as if I had seven devils – Judas – and a hypocrite, and as I went forward, as if I might fall dead. It was a profound humiliation.'[43]

At least his worldly fortunes appeared to be set consistently fair. He had not been in Rome more than a few days before the Pope sent for him. No doubt Wiseman had written a glowing account of the new convert; perhaps Talbot had added his word. Pius IX had been through many tribulations since his last meeting with Manning. In November 1848 mob rule had triumphed in Rome. The Prime Minister had been murdered in full public view, and Pius himself forced to flee to Gaeta in the Kingdom of Naples – 'I doubt if he even had time to take Trevelyan's pamphlet,'[44] Manning had observed to Sidney Herbert. Rome had been left to Mazzini and his Republic, until French arms once more created the possibility of the Pope's return, which took place in April 1850. Pius now presided again over his benevolent theocracy, while Piedmont plotted the absorption of the Papal States into a united Italy.

Whatever problems pressed, however, the Pope regularly found time to see Manning. Evidently he drew comfort from this most devoted Englishman, who took such an exalted view of the papal office and showed so sympathetic an understanding of its difficulties. One would not have predicted that two such disparate characters would hit it off so well: the Pope, garrulous, impulsive, overflowing with good spirits; Manning, reserved, guarded, always dignified. Pius's humour did not always appeal to the Victorians. A party of Anglican clergymen had been not a whit amused to be greeted by the pope with the blessing usually reserved for incense: 'Ab illo benedicaris in cuius honore cremaberis'[45] – Mayest thou be blessed by him in whose honour thou shalt be burnt. It was just the sort of joke that would not have amused Archdeacon Manning. Nevertheless, the two men became fast friends. 'I had free access at any moment to the Pope,' Manning told Robert Wilberforce in 1854, 'who treated me as a father treats a son, with an affection and playfulness of kindness, as well as with a confidence greater than I ever had from an Anglican bishop.'[46] Again, playfulness was not a quality that Manning encouraged in the generality. Before his first year in Rome was out, however, he was tactfully refusing the title of Monsignor.[47]

The base for his studies was the Accademia Ecclesiastica, entry to which was itself a sign of his privileged status. The Accademia, he told Robert Wilberforce, was 'the college of the Pope for his public service'. In more vulgar parlance it was known as 'the nursery of cardinals'. 'It gives me an apartment, refectory and chapel, and is like our old life at Oriel and Merton again. . . . There is a good library and I am enjoying my reading greatly, feeling that it is the will of God that I should be where I am, and employed as I am.'[48] The will of God also permitted some valuable social contacts. In later years Manning looked back upon this period as the seed-time of his subsequent career. 'I came to know intimately a large number of men, Roman and others, filling public offices, and also the men who are now in chief places of responsibility were my companions and friends.'[49] It seems, though, that Manning soon tired of the 'bib-and-tucker, pap and high stool'[50] approach demanded of the Accademia students. At any rate he deserted the public lectures and put himself under the direction of the celebrated Jesuit teachers Perrone and Passaglia at the Collegio Romano. It was gratifying to discover that these men represented a theological tradition that squared very well with what he had worked out for himself in his Lavington study.

During the summer Manning returned to England in order to avoid the Roman heat. In London he became associated with the Jesuits at Farm Street, not actually living in the community but having a confessional and saying Mass daily in the church. He was much in demand as a preacher and always ready to meet every request. A course of sermons delivered at Southwark resulted in another book, *The Grounds of Faith*. Yet being a Catholic priest in Mayfair did not come easily to the former archdeacon. 'God knows what it cost me', he wrote in 1856, 'to be a priest, and to do the work of a priest, and to bear the name of a priest, here in the midst of kindred and old friends, and the world in which I had lived before. No one I believe had more sensitive shrinking from this peculiar stage of trials.'[51] As he chose many years later to describe his predicament at this time: 'In all the world where Samuel Wilberforce lived, I was as a dead man out of mind.'[52] He looked on as Walter Hamilton, who had obtained a First in the same Oxford class list, and who had teetered on the edge of conversion, accepted the bishopric of Salisbury in 1854. A member of the Cabinet, meeting Manning, told him that he would have had the see if he had remained an Anglican. 'What an escape my poor soul did have'[53] was Manning's very proper reaction.

A further consolation was the number of converts whom he received into the Church. When he returned to Rome to resume his studies in the autumn of 1852 his tally had already reached seventeen. Their names were entered in a special book, which would receive 343 entries by 1865.[54] These were the years when Manning was known as the Apostle of the Genteels[55] on account of the impeccable social credentials of some of those whom he gathered into the Church. Female genteels, indeed women of all varieties, always proved especially amenable to his persuasions. The Duchesses of Argyll and Buccleuch, and Lady Herbert, widow of Sidney, were among those who felt the force of his arguments. Rome and Cardinal Wiseman loved to crow over such successes; the power of the Spirit was measured by numbers and quarterings. Newman, by contrast, would make entries in his journal about the dangers of over-hasty conversions.[56] There was nothing over-hasty, though, about the conversion which gave Manning most satisfaction, that of his old friend Robert Wilberforce, whom he landed after a titanic struggle against the combined forces of Keble, Gladstone and Samuel Wilberforce. Samuel never forgave Manning for luring his much loved brother into the harlot's toils. Manning, for his part, reflected upon the attraction which the

Catholic church possessed for the sons of the great Evangelicals. 'I look on this as the blessing of God upon the children for their father's sake.'[57]

In July 1852 Manning received a high honour for a convert of one year's standing when he was invited to preach to the English bishops at the Synod of Oscott. His address, however, was eclipsed by Newman's sermon on the 'Second Spring' of Roman Catholicism in England, a remarkable *tour de force* of sustained rhetoric, although its note of visionary promise has scarcely been fulfilled. Afterwards the enthusiasm of the congregation threatened to overwhelm the preacher, but there was Manning ready to intervene and conduct his old friend quietly back to his room.[58] 'Long years have passed since I heard anything which touched me more,' he told Newman in August. 'And I had a delight which no one else there present could know – for no one there could look back over two or three and twenty years of kindness from you, and of memories such as we have.'[59] Five years later Newman would dedicate the volume in which the 'Second Spring' sermon was published to 'My Dear Dr Manning' 'as some sort of memorial of the friendship which there has been between us for nearly thirty years'.[60] The book, he told Manning privately, was 'not worthy of its Dedication'.[61] The friendship between the two men appeared at its zenith in 1857–8. Newman was even 'yours most affectionately'.[62] When he came to London he stayed with Manning at Bayswater.[63] Manning, on his side, sent a graceful acknowledgement of the dedication. 'Few things would be more grateful to me than to be owned by you *in facie ecclesiae* as a friend of thirty years. It is with me as with you. Old memories are sweet beyond words, and I do not readily form new friendships. The old is better. And ours, if not always close, has never had a jar.'[64]

Cardinal Wiseman had been reduced to helpless blubbing by Newman's 'Second Spring' sermon, but he was already discovering that in workaday affairs Manning appeared decidedly the more useful of the two most renowned converts. Wiseman had far more need of practical than of intellectual assistance. The range and sweep of his mind were matched by his facility: there seemed no aspect of the arts or sciences upon which he could not deliver a brilliant address at a moment's notice. If a Latin epigram was required the Cardinal could toss one off without pausing for thought. But this remarkable brainpower went with the character of a child. He picked up subjects like toys, played with them a moment, and cast them away. Application to the mundane routine of business was beyond him; he was, as Newman discovered to his cost, full of resource and suggestion but too busy to be strenuous about anything.[65] There was but one exception to Wiseman's eclectic dilettantism: he was a stickler for strict liturgical observance. Woe betide any priest who failed in some point of ceremony.

Manning, who was himself careless about such matters, confessed to his chief: 'I am never afraid of you – except when you are in vestments.'[66] In the secular sphere also Wiseman adored the trappings of his position as a Prince of the Church, the gorgeous equipage, the train of servants. When first a Cardinal he would insist on being greeted in the Roman fashion by a procession of torchbearers when he dined out.[67] Dining, and – more endearingly – entertaining children, were his principal worldly enjoyments. 'The Cardinal has a lobster salad side as well as a spiritual side,' one of the converts observed.[68] In Lent he would serve four full fish courses; he owed as much to the grandeur of his office. Certainly his sense of position did not diminish the grandeur of his person.

No more than the Pope did Wiseman appear to be the kind of character to attract the austere Manning, but here, once again, appearances proved deceptive. Manning was captivated by the Cardinal's wisdom, privileged to share his trials. What a comfort for Wiseman to discover this supremely able administrator as his eager servant. In his first two years as archbishop he had proved quite unable to organize any adequate response to the appalling hardship that many of his Irish flock faced in the capital. He had introduced five religious orders into his diocese, but when it was suggested that they might work among the poor they tended to discover, with the best will in the world, that their rules contained limitations that made this impossible. Some, so Wiseman complained to Propaganda in 1860, replied that their institute was for the inhabitants of the mountains, which hardly existed in England, and not for cities.[69] In the face of these refusals Wiseman began to think of creating a body of priests banded together in community, which would act as a kind of task force directly under his command. 'Mr. Manning, I think, understands my wishes and feelings, and is ready to assist me,' Wiseman wrote in October 1852.[70]

So the shape of Manning's Catholic career began to emerge. The future was also foreshadowed by an excursion which he made to Ireland in August and September 1852, a visit which he repeated the following year. Ireland's unwavering loyalty to the Catholic faith greatly impressed him. 'In the supernatural order, for more than fourteen centuries', he told a congregation in Dublin, 'she has shone more resplendent in glory, in grace, and suffering than any other people.'[71] In September 1852 Manning again anticipated his destiny by visiting Poplar, at the heart of London's dockland.

But it was in Rome, whither he returned in the autumn, that his present fortune was cast. This was the first experience that the Romans had had of a First Class Balliol mind serving the church and golden opinions multiplied. In contrast to Newman, Manning's confident demeanour and his fluent Italian gave no opportunity for underestimating his abilities. Whereas

Newman had achieved the remarkable feat of offending the Pope by preaching a sermon that took too harsh a line with worldly-minded (but important) Protestant visitors – 'Rome is no place for them but the very place in the whole world where Michael and the Dragon may almost be seen in battle'[72] – Manning enchanted both indigenous Catholics and touring Protestants with his perfectly judged addresses. 'It is not only an eminent preacher but a great orator that the Church has acquired in him,' judged the Roman correspondent of the ultramontane French journal *Univers*.[73]

Manning's growing reputation stamped him as a candidate for early promotion. The only snag was that the Pope was loth to let him go at all. Early in 1853 Wiseman was agitating for his return that he might set about founding the community of priests which had been envisaged, but since Pius, in taking leave of his protégé, insisted that he should return the next winter,[74] this plan had to be postponed. Manning's journal reveals him as less than delighted by this turn of events. 'Because He would have some praise of me which I do not like, I am dreary and sad – My Lord, I accept all, and with a ready heart. Only do not let me go dreaming and deceiving myself, lest I be disappointed of my hope and lose my soul.'[75]

The old difficulty of his Anglican days, how to respond to the prickings of ambition, was back with a vengeance. A diary entry in the spring of 1854 confronted the problem:

I am conscious of a desire to be in such a position (1) as I had in time past, (2) as my present circumstances imply by the act of others, (3) as my friends think me fit for, (4) as I feel my own faculties tend to. But, God being my helper, I will not seek it by the lifting of a finger or the speaking of a word. If it is ever to be, it shall be (1) either by the invitation of superiors, or (2) by the choice of others; and then I desire to remove the final determination from my own will to that of others, according to the resolution of last year.[76]

There were those, actuated by jealousy no doubt, who took a less lofty view of his proceedings. Mgr Talbot, not yet a reliable friend, spoke of one of the converts at the Accademia who was 'already manoeuvring for a mitre'.[77] Yet in September 1854 Talbot found himself assessing Manning's claims. It was clear that Wiseman needed an auxiliary bishop if the administration of the Westminster diocese was not to grind to a halt, and Manning was considered a possible candidate:

The great objection felt to him [wrote Talbot] is that he is yet a neophyte, but still it is a difficulty which I think might be got over if the Cardinal wished to have him as an Auxiliary. He certainly would be useful as a means of gaining converts, who are growing in number and power every day. The only objection I have heard to him is that he retains a good deal of the Oxford and Puseyite way of viewing things, and that some people do not think he is yet heart and soul a Catholic, but I think this is more manner than else, and that he will get over it in the course of time.[78]

This was high praise from Mgr Talbot, who was rarely disposed to be convinced that any convert save himself was 'heart and soul a Catholic'. The proposal that a convert of only three years' standing should be a bishop was still more exceptional. The old English Catholics would have been outraged, which is probably why the idea was shelved.

The outbreak of the Crimean War in 1854 gave Manning the chance to demonstrate the administrative talents that qualified him so admirably for episcopal office. Using his former contacts with the English governing class he worked with Bishop Grant of Southwark to arrange that Catholic chaplains who went to the Crimea should be independent under the Commander-in-Chief and not, as had originally been projected, subject to the Protestant Chaplain-General. Manning also saw in the war a marvellous opportunity for the Roman Catholic Church in England to identify itself with the national cause. What if Catholic nuns were to go as nursing sisters to the Crimea? He had explored the idea even before Florence Nightingale had been put in charge of the expedition of nurses; with her appointment he gained another contact to be exploited. He had first encountered Miss Nightingale during his 1847–8 visit to Rome. Since then they had kept up a correspondence, with Miss Nightingale constantly coquetting with Catholicism. The Germans knew why they were Protestants, she had written to him; 'I never knew an Englishman who did, and if he enquires he becomes a Catholic.'[79] She herself, nevertheless, always held back just short of surrender. Manning did not underestimate her. Collecting ten nursing sisters from convents in Bermondsey and Norwood was only the start of his problems. He knew Florence Nightingale too well to suppose that she would brook any nurses outside her control; he knew Roman Catholic bishops too well to imagine that they would easily accept the idea of nuns under Protestant command.

The situation was made for the exercise of his political skill. The government was informed that the nuns were to be subject to Miss Nightingale; the Catholic authorities were assured (which was true) that they were being sent by their ecclesiastical and religious superiors. The sisters did wonderful work in the Crimea. 'A few such things', thought Manning, 'will do more for us than all the books of controversy in the world.'[80] Greatly encouraged, he organized a second, mainly Irish, group of nuns to join the party that was being sent out to help the original band of nurses. Miss Nightingale received these additions, for which she had not asked, with cold fury. For a while it seemed that the Irish nuns might be sent straight back, which would have been, as Manning remarked, 'a most mischievous and serious event',[81] not least for the man who had dispatched them. Fortunately, a compromise was arranged; and the Irish sisters stayed to work as valiantly as their predecessors from Bermondsey and Norwood. To the mother superior of the Bermondsey nuns Florence Nightingale wrote: 'I would be glad that the bishop of Southwark should know, and Dr. M.,. . . that you were valued here as you deserved, and that the gratitude of the army is yours.'[82]

Doctor Manning, be it noted. The title had been awarded to him at the end of his Roman studies. The Pope tempted Manning to stay permanently in Rome by offering a position as papal chamberlain with full prelatial rank,[83] a post similar to that occupied by Mgr Talbot. Considering how much greater Manning's abilities were than Talbot's, it is clear that, had he chosen, he could have become a formidable influence at Rome. He preferred, however, the prospect of working in London as a simple priest. 'I desire to live for nothing but to save my own soul and others by plain unbending truth.'[84]

Early in 1856 his connection with the Jesuits at Farm Street ended. Manning's account of this parting is odd, to say the least. He continued at Farm Street, he explained,

till the number of people who came to me, penitents and converts, made some inconvenience in the church: and F. Waterworth told me that objection had been raised. Some one in stupid ill-will the other day said 'that I took this ill'. Far from it. F. Waterworth was my confessor and friend, and nothing could have been more friendly on both sides. I said at once I will go as soon as possible, very grateful for the long spiritual hospitality, in which I hope I did them no harm; for I left many people behind me.[85]

It may have been so, but somehow the notion of the Jesuits worried about the number of penitents and converts crowding their church does not carry conviction.

At all events, Manning was now free to found the order of priests that Wiseman wanted. This work, he would recall, came 'unsought and undesired',[86] and it is certainly true that in 1857 he wrote to Wiseman of his 'dread of leaving the quiet and retirement which after many years of trial I have had in the last six'.[87] He also remembered that he was 'slow in taking up the work, not from unwillingness or disobedience, but from doubt of myself'.[88] One can only report that this latter difficulty was marvellously overcome.

In 1856 he drew up a first outline for his community, which Wiseman envisaged as a sort of 'Oratory with external action',[89] under direct control of the bishop. The model was the community of Oblates which had been established in Milan two hundred and fifty years previously by that same St Charles whose corpse Manning had inspected on his way back from Rome in 1848. The Milanese Oblates were still in existence, and at the end of 1856 Manning went to investigate their work, discovering the order well adapted to Wiseman's London requirements. He also sought relics. 'There was no portion of the body to be obtained,' he reported regretfully back to Wiseman, but 'the Archbishop received us very kindly, and has given us two relics of the blood of St. Charles'.[90] Thus provisioned, Manning continued to Rome, where details of the rule were finalized in consultation with Vatican theologians and the Pope bestowed his blessing upon the project.

At the beginning of 1856 Manning had bought some houses off Buckingham Palace Road which were being converted into a church and a school, but for the new community Wiseman offered a less central site, in Bayswater. The area was being developed in the 1850s, and Westbourne Grove was in the process of becoming a busy shopping centre. At its western end, though, this thoroughfare still bore traces of its former status of country lane. Here, some years earlier, two Catholic women had begun to build a Neo-Gothic church; curiously enough there had been some talk in the late 1840s of Newman's Oratorians establishing themselves there. That came to nothing; the fount of charity ran dry; and the church was left for several years unfinished, standing without a roof among fields that were being steadily surrendered to the developers. To the north, the district was becoming a refuge for Irish immigrants, many of them non-English-speakers from Galway, who lived there in conditions of the utmost squalor.

Such was the area to which Manning was sent to establish the Oblates. The architecture of the church caused him aesthetic anguish since the Lavington enthusiast for Gothic had now been translated into a devotee of the classical Italian style, as befitted one with such marked Roman sympathies. (His attempts at the Italian pronunciation of Latin were unhappily defeated by his ineradicable English accent.) To alleviate his embarrassment he draped over the tracery of the Gothic windows, and introduced oil paintings on walls that had been intended to reflect the light of stained glass. At least, thanks to Manning's dynamism, the church was ready for the opening ceremony on 18 July 1857, attended by an impressive collection of Catholic ecclesiastics and aristocrats.

Few of them repeated this venture into the wilds. Looking back on his time in Bayswater Manning remarked that he had been as much out of sight as if he had been in Australia.[91] He called those years the happiest of his life,[92] an astonishing judgement in view of the savage antagonism he would arouse. Yet there was no question of the success of the Oblates. Once again Manning proved his ability in practical action. He started with just seven other priests; within three years the community had grown to twenty. (In 1867 the Pope was surprised and disappointed to learn that Newman's Oratory at Birmingham was down to nine priests, including novices.)[93] By 1860 the number of weekly communicants at Bayswater had multiplied tenfold from a hundred to more than a thousand.[94] By 1865 three more churches had been built, and eight schools accommodating 790 children, including a reformatory and a choir school. Manning also introduced four convents into Bayswater.[95] The area became such a hotbed of papistry that a defensive associaton, the West London Protestant Institute, was set up to counter the alarming Romish advance. But whom could the Protestants put up against Dr Manning, whose energy was unquenchable, whose ability was unmatched, whose eloquence was unrivalled, and whose moral authority, over priests and congregation alike, was unquestioned? The father of a would-be convert who angrily confronted Manning as he was disrobing in the sacristy was soon made aware of the blasphemy of addressing the Lord's anointed in his own house.[96] With the Oblates themselves, though, the Father Superior gallantly attempted fellowship, to the point of demonstrating the sparring skills that he had learnt at Oxford. There were also jokes.[97] The impression he left, nevertheless, was of stern religious endeavour. It was a privilege, one of the Oblates remarked, to have had 'so holy a power upon our lives'.[98]

There were many who took another view. The old Catholics sneered at the Oblates' Institute as 'Widowers' House', an allusion to the number of convert parsons who had buried their wives before joining the Catholic priesthood. In fact two of the widowers, and those the closest to Manning, had died before the order ever began work. Robert Wilberforce had followed Manning into the Accademia, but did not survive to complete his studies. Laprimaudaye, his Lavington curate, who had also converted, succumbed to smallpox. Of the Oblates who worked in Bayswater it might have been kinder to observe that, widowers or no, they contributed huge sums out of their own pockets towards the task in hand.[99] But the old Catholics were not minded to judge converts kindly; and least of all were they concerned to be fair towards Manning. There was something about him that never failed to get on their nerves, and which neither his obvious merits nor (still less) the favour that he enjoyed in high places did anything to dispel.

Even some converts could find his manner repellent. His fellow Harrovian Robert Coffin, for example, who had entered the Church in 1845 and subsequently become a Redemptorist, met Manning on some business and considered the ex-archdeacon 'stuck-up' and 'cold'.[100] Lady Herbert, Sidney Herbert's widow, found him similarly reserved when she converted in 1865. 'He had written to me that "one of his greatest joys was to think that I was one of his new children". Yet he thought it right to assume a coldness and hardness of manner, which was utterly unnatural, as if he feared any affectionate intimacy with a woman.'[101] If former Anglicans received that kind of impression, it is no surprise that old Catholics simply could not stomach Manning. Herbert Vaughan, a young priest from an old Catholic family who travelled out to Rome with Manning in 1852, actually fled from the horror of the man. 'I was a raw and restless youth of twenty, and no doubt very trying to the grave and solemn convert parson, as I then called him, who gently, and, I fear, unsuccessfully sought to keep me in order. So at Lyons I said to Father Whitty, "I can stand this old parson no longer; let us go straight on and leave him to follow as long after as he likes." '[102]

The most interesting point about these three adverse judgements, however, is that they were all reversed upon better knowledge of their butt. Father Coffin's opinion was abruptly changed when he boldly told Manning that he still had too much of the convert parson about him, and (a common complaint) that he received converts far too quickly, without any proper instruction. Manning received this criticism with becoming submission. 'You must promise me one thing,' he urged upon Coffin, taking his hand, 'it is that for the glory of God, you will always speak out to me thus the truth.'[103] This most Christian behaviour instantly converted Coffin into a wholehearted admirer; subsequently he would play a vital part in securing Manning's accession to Westminster. Lady Herbert, for her part, discovered that as the years wore on Manning lost much of his constraint, or was it (a point she did not consider) that the attraction which he so much feared dimmed with the passage of time? As for Herbert Vaughan, having arrived in Rome a few days ahead of Manning, he became within a few weeks his most ardent disciple, rising every morning at six in order to serve his Mass.[104]

Vaughan was exceptional among old English Catholics at this time in appreciating Manning's qualities, but then he was not quite a typical member of the breed; his mother had been a convert from an Evangelical Anglican background, which gave him some affinity with William Manning's son. For a true dyed-in-the-wool old Catholic it would be difficult to find a better sample than George Errington, Archbishop of Trebizond (a title granted in virtue of his position as Wiseman's Coadjutor and appointed successor at Westminster). It would be difficult also to find anyone who regarded Manning with more determined hostility.

Errington came from a family well supplied with martyrs, and he himself was a formidable representative of this ancient, uncompromising strain. There was no argument either about his virtues or his defects: he was upright, honourable, determined, conscientious and courageous; he was also narrow, inflexible and wholly lacking in imagination or vision. His theology he took from St Thomas Aquinas, regarding anyone who dared question an argument in the *Summa* as a practical heretic.[105] He was expert in canon law, the principles of which he applied with rigour to all the day-to-day problems of the Church. Mgr Talbot, who was not a friend, considered that Errington was perfectly satisfied that souls should go to hell provided they went there by the book. Margaret Hallahan, foundress of the English Dominican nuns, told the Archbishop after one brush that he must have been hewn out of rock: 'I am sure you never had a mother.'[106] There were rumours that in private life he could be gentle and affectionate, but this view did not readily occur to those who came under his hawk-like gaze, the more alarming for being filtered through blue spectacles, during diocesan visitations. Least of all did it occur to converts submitted to his scrutiny. And if there was one kind of convert whom Dr Errington disliked more than another, it was those who, with Wiseman's encouragement, imported extravagant – Errington would have said 'exhibitionist' – Italian devotions. 'The best form of meditation is to look at a dead body,' he said; 'and it is a very old form.'[107] Errington was not wise, however, to pick a quarrel with the one English Catholic whose will was as strong as his own, and whose abilities were much superior.

In origin Errington's difficulties were with Wiseman, not Manning. It had been an inept decision on the Cardinal's part to choose him as Coadjutor. The two men had been educated together and were thus officially designated friends; in fact, their background was the only thing they had in common. The strain had shown in the early 1840s when Errington had served as prefect of studies under Wiseman's presidency at Oscott seminary. With the restitution of the English hierarchy Errington at first became Bishop of Plymouth until Wiseman, in 1855, insisted that 'old George' should join him at Westminster. Several people, including old George, realized that the Cardinal's Roman ways and relaxed approach to business were ill matched to the stern English style of the man he had chosen as his Coadjutor; and Errington only agreed to accept the post on condition that he was given a completely free hand in diocesan administration. Unfortunately Wiseman proved incapable of keeping his promise on that score. When priests complained to him about Errington's over-rigorous approach, he would good-naturedly reverse his decisions. In particular, the two bishops wrangled about the position of W. G. Ward at St Edmund's seminary, Ware. Errington found it scandalous that a convert and a married man should be instructing and moulding candidates for the priesthood. He wrote a critical report and Ward promptly resigned. But then Ward took his case to

Wiseman and was equally promptly reinstated.[108]

Within six months of his appointment Errington was writing to Rome asking to be relieved of the coadjutorship. Being anxious to avoid a scandal the Roman authorities did not grant his request, but tried to defuse the situation by sending Errington to take temporary charge of the diocese of Clifton, pending the appointment of a bishop to that see. This arrangement meant that Errington was out of London from 1855–7, the time when Manning was beginning to establish himself as a force to be reckoned with in the Westminster diocese.

It was still a surprise when, early in 1857, the Pope suddenly appointed Manning Provost, or head, of the Westminster Chapter. Manning himself could not believe this elevation, and wrote to Wiseman implying that there might have been some mistake.[109] The truth was that Wiseman had recommended that Manning be made a canon, but had not dared to suggest he should be Provost for fear of the opposition such a promotion would arouse. His apprehensions were fully justified. Manning was unknown to many of the Westminster clergy; his ways did not ingratiate; he was rumoured to owe his rise to influential friends; he was a convert thrust into office over the heads of long-serving Catholics who had been born to the faith. This combination of circumstances provided a test of Christian charity that few English Catholics were capable of passing. 'I hate that man; he is such a forward piece,' declared the president of Ushaw seminary.[110] Some kind friend passed on the remark to Manning, who did not appear a whit discomforted. 'Poor man, what is he made of;. does he suppose in his foolishness, after working day and night for nigh on twenty years in heresy and schism, that on becoming a Catholic I should sit in an easy chair and fold my hands for the rest of my life?'[111]

Nevertheless, Manning's position was now delicate. As Father Superior of the Oblates he was, with Wiseman's blessing and favour, pursuing the Cardinal's Romanizing aims. As Provost of Westminster he was set over a Chapter which had become the centre of the old English Catholic opposition to this policy. One canon especially, Mgr Searle, Wiseman's secretary, regarded Manning with all the venom of a former favourite who finds himself being displaced. A weaker man than the Provost would have found it intolerable to encounter such loathing (the word is not too strong) at every meeting of the chapter. Manning appeared quite unmoved. He knew, though he was never so vulgar as to say, that in an organization where all power flows from the top there is only one kind of support which counts. While at the Roman Accademia he had warned himself in his diary against 'particular friendships', and he could certainly claim, a few years later, that this peril had been safely negotiated. In fact his particular friends were now reduced to three. They were the Pope, Cardinal Wiseman and Mgr Talbot. Pius IX, Manning found, gave him a clearer idea of the supernatural than any other man whom he had met.[112] Cardinal Wiseman inspired such ideals of service that, so the newly appointed Provost told him, but 'one thing gives me comfort, which is the hope that I may be of more use to you, and better able to relieve you of some, among your many, lesser employments.'[113] As for Mgr Talbot, he was the very person on whom Manning could unload all his worries about the condition of the Church in England.

With such allies he was well placed to meet any attack. Although he could hardly have foreseen the virulence and persistence with which Errington would assail the Oblates, it was clear from the start that he had an implacable opponent. The two men had been in Rome together early in 1857, when Manning had tried to win Errington's support for his new order. The only consequence was that Errington reported to the Prefect of Propaganda that Manning was nursing a plan to keep control of the Oblates in his own hands, independently of the bishop.[114] Since the essence of Manning's idea was that the Oblates should serve the Cardinal, this did not seem a promising line of attack. Errington, however, continued to press the point on his return to England; and his minute study of the Oblates' rule revealed that Manning did indeed possess some rights to recall members into the community even against the wish of the bishop, rights that were not to be found in the original Milanese rule. The matter was reported to Wiseman, who, though not greatly interested, agreed for the sake of peace that the rule should be modified to meet Errington's criticism. It need hardly be said that Manning accepted Wiseman's alterations with the best of grace.[115] Nevertheless, the first round had gone to the Archbishop of Trebizond.

Encouraged but by no means appeased, Errington turned his attention to trying to prove that Wiseman, in giving the Bayswater church to the Oblates, had perverted the intention of the trust under which the original funds had been provided. In this instance, however, legal opinion supported the Cardinal. The preliminary sparring was inconclusive.

The main contest now commenced. It was ironic, though, that one of Errington's principal objections to the Oblates, that their presence in the diocese undermined the prestige of the ordinary parish clergy, touched on an issue where the two men were actually in full agreement. Nobody was ever more determined than Manning to exalt the parish priest. He utterly rejected Errington's charge that the Oblates constituted a threat to this aim; indeed, he intended that they should serve it. His difference with Errington was not over how priests should be considered, but over how they should be trained. So the quarrel between the two men came to centre upon the control and direction of the diocesan seminary at St Edmund's, Ware.

Wiseman and Manning were determined that English seminaries should be reformed to mould priests according to Roman ideals. The English Catholics were no less determined to preserve their own traditions, which were as much gentlemanly as theological. Newman instinctively sympathized with them when he visited St Edmund's soon after his conversion. 'Everything I saw impressed me with the one idea you get elsewhere, of *simplicity* . . . Dr Cox [the president] is mild and taking in his deportment. I liked him very much.'[116] Newman was bound to admit, however, that 'there is little learning or cultivation there – they are behindhand'. This was something Wiseman meant to rectify. One of his first moves on becoming Archbishop was to remove the 'mild and taking' Dr Cox. The new mood was further signalled by the appointment of W. G. Ward as lecturer; and then in 1855 Herbert Vaughan, still only twenty-five, was made vice-president. To fit himself for this position Vaughan undertook a special study of continental seminaries. Then in 1857 he became a founder member of the Oblates, while two other Oblates joined the St Edmund's staff. It was apparent that Wiseman meant to use Manning's order as the instrument through which Roman ways were to be introduced into the college. The direction of seminaries had been a feature of the work of the original Milanese Oblates, as Manning had pointed out to Wiseman. Indeed, at one stage, Manning envisaged that his order would eventually be run from St Edmund's, with Bayswater as only an outlying house.[117]

The old type of clergy, Manning believed, did well enough to give the sacrament to Irish immigrants and to the inhabitants of isolated country houses.[118] If, however, the Church were to become a force in English national life, a far better educated and disciplined body would be necessary. Manning observed with dismay that the educated laity were going not to secular priests but to the religious orders for the satisfaction of their intellectual and spiritual needs.[119] The remedy was to improve the training which the priests received in their seminaries, and Manning was quite clear how that should be achieved. 'I do not believe that seminaries will ever be what they ought to be in England,' he wrote, 'unless they are directed by secular priests who have learned to live by rule, and can act with unity of mind and purpose.' That meant, of course, that they should be directed by his Oblates. 'I do not think anyone has a fuller sense than I have of the imperfections of our Congregation; but I only say, "Let somebody do better and we will gladly give place." '[120]

Manning's actions were not designed to give anyone else the chance to do better. From 1858, with Wiseman's backing, he assumed direction of St Edmund's in characteristically high-handed manner. Without reference to the president of the college, he instructed Vaughan to undertake a review of the seminary's work and 'to set forth the only way in which you believe the College can be raised in its studies, discipline and ecclesiastical spirit'. Lest Vaughan should be in doubt as to what this only way might be, Manning specified in advance that it would be through a higher standard of ascetical teaching and practice. Vaughan was further instructed to make it known that he had joined the Oblates because his work in the college would be the more efficient for his being under their rule. 'This, I think, will make all concerned see that it is a question, not of a chip, but of a block.'[121] Assuredly, Manning did not mean anyone to be in doubt of his determination that the Oblates should rule the seminary.

The old Catholics were furious at this presumption on the part of a bumptious convert. They feared and despised the practice of continental seminaries, which they thought would be introduced, particularly the system of encouraging pupils to spy on each other and to report misdemeanours to the authorities. Sneaking, it was called in England. As natural leader of the old Catholics, Dr Errington was soon made aware of what was happening at St Edmund's. He appraised the situation and came to a swift, simple and irrevocable decision. The Oblates must leave the seminary forthwith.

It was never Manning's way to downplay the dire prospects involved in the defeat of his own cause:

We are in a crisis [he informed Mgr Talbot] in which, if the spirit represented by Dr. Errington, Dr. Grant, and Searle prevail, the work of the Church in England will be done by the Religious, and the secular clergy will, for a generation to come, lose ground in all the points most essential for their action upon the people in England. They will continue to administer the Sacraments to the almost exclusively Irish population now in England, but the work and mission of the Church as contemplated by the Holy Father in the Hierarchy, and demanded by the state of England, and I will say by the manifest will of God, shown in His providential acts, will be thrown back for a whole generation.[122]

Manning's view of the old English Catholics was extreme enough to satisfy Mgr Talbot's most demanding moods: 'I look upon them as one of the greatest evils in England.'[123] To Wiseman, who scarcely needed instruction on this matter, Manning summarized the position as follows: 'The question [is] whether England shall be organised and assimilated to the living devotions and spirit of Rome, or perpetuate itself under its own insular centre.'[124]

It is as well to have established that there were genuine principles at stake, because in the conduct of the quarrel which ensued both sides exhibited a petulant small-mindedness that would have brought discredit to squabbling schoolboys. The battle was fought in the Westminster Chapter, with

Errington's role behind the opposition to Manning becoming increasingly evident.

The Chapter opened its campaign to eject the Oblates from St Edmund's by demanding that Manning should bring a copy of his order's rule to be examined at the next meeting. The Provost refused to commit himself, and consulted the Cardinal. Wiseman was outraged that the canons should presume to make such a request: it was an invasion of episcopal privilege; the Chapter's function was purely advisory. Thus fortified, Manning declined to allow the canons to inspect the rule.[125]

Unfortunately Wiseman had forgotten how he himself, in earlier and happier days, had specifically deputed two canons to supervise St Edmund's, in accordance with the duties laid upon chapters in respect of diocesan seminaries by the Council of Trent. The Westminster Chapter drew his attention to this oversight. Wiseman, never at a loss, blandly maintained that the Trent decree was irrelevant because St Edmund's, which educated lay boys as well as clerics, was not properly a seminary.

Perhaps Wiseman and Manning felt some unease about this contention, although it was later upheld at the Synod of Oscott (1859). Anyhow, in July 1858 Manning suddenly announced that he would 'most willingly'[126] bring the rule for inspection. His rider was that the canons should examine it privately, and not in official capitular session. The Chapter pressed its right to scrutinize the document as a formal body. Manning remained adamant. The Chapter continued to press. Manning continued adamant. Eventually, 'after long resistance I entered a protest into the Capitular book and was silent'.[127] The Chapter, sensing victory, demanded that Manning should leave the room while the rule was examined. Manning would not budge. In the end it was the Chapter that withdrew. 'I can well go through anything this can excite,' Manning informed the Cardinal.[128]

As a result of their consideration of the rule the canons drew up an address to Wiseman requesting the exclusion of the Oblates from St Edmund's. Wiseman riposted by asking to see the Chapter's minute book, in order to show that its discussions had been outside its competence. The Chapter sent not the minute, but the resolution book. Wiseman reiterated his order for the full minute book, and on 1 December 1858 annulled the Chapter's proceedings. All this time Errington, the instigator of the Chapter's campaign, had been living in Wiseman's house and sleeping in his dressing-room. On 2 December he was closeted with Mgr Searle. Wiseman, coming into his dressing-room, was aware of someone hurriedly leaving by another door.[129] Clearly there was a plot afoot. Animus against the Provost was extreme. It was said that the Archbishop of Trebizond used the words 'hypocrite' and 'traitor' when speaking of him.[130]

The moment had come for a heartfelt declaration of loyalty:

All my affairs are of little importance to me compared to the trial in which your Eminence stands for a moment [Manning wrote to Wiseman on 3 December before the critical chapter meeting]. I say for a moment, because I believe it to be a crisis permitted to put an end for ever to an unsound state, full of future dangers of a graver kind. The last three Masses I have said, I may say, for you. And I am calmly and firmly convinced that all this is for the solid good of the Diocese and of the Seminary, for the final rooting of the Congregation [of the Oblates], and the ascendancy of a Roman over every other kind of spirit, as I can be of anything which rests on the acts of men. I go to this Chapter with a light heart and with a feeling that nothing can give me pain, for I have felt that all the pain has come upon your Eminence. I wish I knew how I could lighten it.[131]

Having delivered himself of these lofty sentiments, Manning went to the Chapter meeting and took up once more the nit-picking contest. The canons produced an appeal to the Pope in which they asserted their rights at St Edmund's. Manning refused to sign it. Once more he was invited to leave the room. Once more he declined to do so. In the end the senior canon was obliged to sign the document, adding '*renitente praeposito*', with the Provost demurring.[132]

Such was the manner in which the One True Church conducted its affairs amidst the lost masses of heretic England. 'Thank God,' Manning wrote to Talbot in 1860, 'the Protestants do not know that half our time and strength is wasted in contests *inter domesticos fidei*. We have two great antagonists: the Protestant Association of Bayswater and the Chapter of Westminster. This is very grievous and must displease God.'[133]

It certainly displeased Cardinal Wiseman, who complained bitterly that 'my Coadjutor has been acting as solicitor against me in a law suit'.[134] He was now clear that Errington could not continue as his Coadjutor, a momentous decision since the right of succession to Westminster went with this office. It was the opinion of Father Morris, a lifelong friend of Wiseman's, that the Cardinal had decided as early as 1859 that Manning should be his successor.[135] The following letter, which Manning addressed to Wiseman on 6 March 1858, suggests that some form of promotion had been suggested even at that early date. 'I have tried to think of the subject of last night, but I fear I can do nothing but place myself in your Eminence's hands. The weighing of the two sides places me in a position from which I shrink; I am afraid of inclining to that which, if I know myself, I ought to avoid, and I am afraid also of crossing what may be the Will of God.' And Manning went on to assure Wiseman that the Oblates were now sufficiently well established to carry on without him.[136] Whatever Wiseman had said to

Manning, it is clear that, whereas after the disagreements of 1855 he had been anxious to patch things up with Errington, by 1859 he had decided that there was no choice but to procure his dismissal. Furthermore, he stuck to this purpose with a tenacity and consistency that he did not often show.

Nevertheless, the campaign to end Errington's coadjutorship was ultimately of Wiseman's own making. Manning was involved as a sympathetic friend and counsellor who strengthened the Cardinal's resolve, but he was not at the root of the quarrel. The other dispute, concerning the Oblates' position at St Edmund's, touched him more closely. The antagonism which he attracted in this cause was a measure of the fear which he inspired. 'He is . . . personally very unpopular', one of the canons would write to Mgr Talbot, 'and suspected (very much owing to his reserved and diplomatic manner) of disguised intentions and objects. Hence he speedily lost all influence with the Chapter.'[137] Manning knew, however, that there was powerful support available elsewhere. When the Chapter drew up a petition to Rome against the Oblates, he rushed out there in order to ward off the attack. Surely Pius IX would never allow his 'sempre docile' Manning (a description the Chapter might have had some difficulty in recognizing) to be destroyed by 'quello benedetto Errington', that blessed Errington.[138] On the other hand, Manning could not predetermine the outcome of the St Edmund's dispute. There might be some measure of personal security in the Pope's favour, but this did not mean that Pius meant to become involved in the details of the argument; indeed he showed every sign of wanting to distance himself from the wrangles of the quarrelsome inglesi. The final ruling on the rights of the Oblates at St Edmund's would come from Propaganda, over which neither Wiseman nor Manning exercised decisive influence. If anything, it seemed that Cardinal Barnabo, the Prefect of Propaganda, preferred Errington.[139]

Wiseman, meanwhile, began to develop an overpowering concern for Errington's health. He wrote to Talbot in March 1859 that Errington's medical condition was so bad that 'it would be better and in his own interest if he assumed Archiepiscopal charges elsewhere and more proportionate to his strength.'[140] (Errington would live until 1886.) Mgr Talbot was full of ideas for meeting this crisis. Trinidad or Calcutta were the sees that sprang to his mind as likely to benefit Errington's health;[141] or perhaps Goa – 'he would be a fit person to remove the bad Portuguese priests'. An English bishop visiting Rome at this time thought it likely that 'they will send Dr Errington on a mission to Hayti'.[142] There was something about the Archbishop of Trebizond that readily inspired thoughts of the Church Universal.

The trouble was that Dr Errington refused to be sent anywhere. For this obduracy Mgr Talbot's tactlessness was much to blame. He had written to Searle that Errington was 'radically anti-Roman' and 'retrograde'[143] in his policy, a judgement that Searle immediately passed on to Errington. Talbot compounded this gaffe by informing Errington that 'the Holy Father desires to arrange this affair as quietly as possible, and to prevent the scandal of having recourse to more vigorous measures'.[144] Errington was not a man to give in to threats; he bitterly resented aspersions being cast on his loyalty to Rome merely because he happened to be against Manning's Oblates. Thenceforth he considered that a voluntary resignation would be tantamount to admitting himself guilty of the unjust charges that Talbot had made against him. There was no escape from the scandal of public dismissal now. By April 1859 Wiseman had written directly to the Pope begging for Errington's removal. That summer Errington underscored the implacable nature of his opposition by acting against Wiseman in the debate over the government of seminaries at the Synod of Oscott. The situation gained an extra touch of drama from Wiseman's suffering a heart attack in September 1859. Thereafter the Cardinal's health never gave any grounds for confidence. Suppose he should die while Errington was still his designated successor? In that case, as Manning discreetly put the matter to Mgr Talbot, some of the best men would have to leave the diocese.[145]

Provided the Cardinal's health held, though, there was no cause for alarm. 'You need not be anxious about the result of your visit to Rome,' Mgr Talbot told Wiseman in the autumn of 1859. 'You may be certain that the Pope will grant you all you want, and that he will desire your Coadjutor to retire.'[146]

Manning continued to take steps to rebut the charges which Errington was bringing against him. He addressed a long letter to Wiseman, who was in Rome and well placed to make his lieutenant's defence known in the appropriate quarters:

I am accused of a love of power [Manning wrote]. I would ask to know what there is in my past or present acts to show that I have enriched myself or acted in rivalry with anyone, or crossed any man's path, or deprived him of any due, or sought honours, titles or promotions, or indulged in the arts of ambition, or made the elevation of myself the end of my actions. At least those who know me best will hardly think this of me. If by love of power any of those things are meant, then I leave myself in your Eminence's hands, and in the judgement of the Holy See, and of Him who I hope will give to my actions a better name, and in my life will read a better intention. But I will make a free and frank confession. There is a power I earnestly desire, strive, and pray for. It is the power to make a reparation for years spent in ignorance, which I trust I can say before God was not voluntary; to spread in England the knowledge of the one only faith; to make others partake of the grace I have myself received; to win back as many souls as I can to the unity of the Church, and to promote in every way, with greater devotion of life and efficacy of labour, the salvation of souls and the submission of England to the Holy See.[147]

That was the kind of freedom and frankness that went down well in Rome. Wiseman, for his part, penned a long letter descriptive of Manning's excellences to Cardinal Barnabò. He related the achievements of the Oblates, and how the Father Superior had yet found time to labour in the cause of a reformatory for juvenile offenders at Hammersmith, and how he had striven to rescue Catholic children from Protestant workhouses. Dr Manning had such excellent contacts with the English Government: when he went to see Mr Villiers, the Minister in charge of the workhouses, he had been most courteously received, three times. (Manning's connections with the Palmerston Government were indeed impressive, at least in potential. He knew the Duke of Newcastle, Sir Charles Wood, Edward Cardwell and, through the convert duchess, the Duke of Argyll. Fortunately none of these Ministers had ever been such close friends as the Chancellor, Gladstone, with whom he was still [1860] incomunicado. Sidney Herbert, who died in 1861, was another Minister with whom relations were inhibited by depth of affection.)

Wiseman then dealt with the accusation that Manning 'governs my diocese, and that I see everything through his eyes'. 'I answer . . . that a Bishop who possessed a man gifted with so many excellent qualities, prudence, learning, disinterestedness, gravity and piety, and who has done so much for God, and [who] should repel him and keep him at a distance, make little account of him, and even persecute him and seek to drive him away, instead of rejoicing in his good fortune in possessing him, would have indeed to give an account to God.' The facts spoke for themselves. 'I do not hesitate to say that in all England there is not a priest who in double the time, has done what Dr Manning has for the advantage of the Catholic Church.'[148]

As if these encomia were not sufficient, Wiseman ordered the paragon to present himself once more in Rome. Manning duly arrived at the end of February 1860. His energy was astonishing. He ran the Oblates, writing regularly to members of the community when abroad. He produced a profusion of books, sermons and articles. He kept abreast of every shift in politics, ecclesiastical and otherwise. Now Errington's accusations involved him in continual epistolary defence and regular attendance at Rome. 'It has been two years of hard trial upon hard work,' he wrote later in 1860. 'Either alone would have been enough, and both together have been nearly too much.'[149] Once in Rome he produced yet another essay in self-justification, this time addressed directly to the Pope. 'I am thankful that Mgr. the Archbishop of Trebizond has at length brought the whole subject before your Holiness, and that I may now place myself with an entire submission, as I did in 1857, at your sacred feet.' This edifying humility was sustained right to the end of the letter:

Finally, Holy Father, if in the anxious and laborious work of the last three years, undertaken, as I have shown, not at my own pleasure, but in obedience to my Bishop, and with the full cognisance and benediction of the Holy See, I have in any way erred, I pray for the correction of your Holiness. . . . I hereby submit myself entirely to your judgement and your will. As I have not been the sower of these disastrous and afflicting events, so neither will I be the cause of their continuance. One word or sign of your Holiness's good pleasure will release me from one of the most painful duties I have ever had to discharge. But if I shall have the consolation to know that in the judgement of your Holiness I have not failed in my duties to my Bishop, to the diocese, and to the Church, all the sufferings and crosses of the last two years will be abundantly rewarded.[150]

Errington was not nearly so well versed in the language of deference. It would have made little difference if he had been. The issue of the coadjutorship (as opposed to that of the Oblates at St Edmund's) was, as Mgr Talbot had indicated, prejudged. The Church could not possibly tolerate a situation in which two bishops were constantly intriguing against each other in the same diocese; and it was not likely that the Cardinal Archbishop of Westminster would be removed. In two audiences, in March and July 1860, the Pope begged Errington to resign. Neither cajolery nor scolding, however, would induce Errington to budge. Indeed, he provoked Pius to fury by calmly taking out his pocket book to note down the precise words that His Holiness had used.[151] St Peter himself could not have shifted this subject from his principles. Errington would obey a command to go, but he would not inculpate himself by voluntary resignation, not even to become Archbishop of Trinidad. Pius was left with no choice. On 22 July 1860 a special decree deprived Errington of his post of coadjutor, together with all rights of succession to the Westminster archbishopric. The Pope referred to this process as 'il colpo di stato di Dominiddio', the coup d'état of the Lord.[152] Manning considered it to be 'certainly un-English, but eminently Catholic'.[153]

He had now become convinced that Dr Errington had gone out of his mind, a proposition that did not preclude the comforting reflection that 'the contest has been not of persons but principles, and I believe the full effect of it will not be seen until we are gone to our rest'.[154] Some of the lesser effects, however, would be evident before that. To begin with, Manning became Protonotary Apostolic, though this was a title that he claimed to despise. Mgr Talbot hailed a new hero. 'Mgr. Manning has come out wonderfully in this affair, and has gained the approbation of all the Sacred College, and many other officials in Rome. He was warmly greeted on being made Protonotary Apostolic, and I think this promotion will be of great service to him.'[155]

Mgr Talbot was aware that the new protonotary attracted less flattering references in his own land. James Patterson, another convert priest, wrote to him of 'a great and growing mistrust of Manning . . . founded on the belief that he is a schemer – a man fond of influence and power'. Patterson, who was a friend of Wiseman's, further thought that in the St Edmund's dispute Manning had 'driven the Cardinal further in his defence than perhaps he originally meant to go'.[156] Certainly, since the mass of the English clergy supported Errington against the jumped-up convert, Wiseman found himself increasingly isolated from his flock. The worst of it was that this unpopularity did not even produce the results that had been sought. Ironically enough, despite the air of triumph that attended the dismissal of Errington, Manning was totally defeated in his own cause. In 1861 Rome decided that he must withdraw the Oblates from St Edmund's.[157]

Typically, Manning scarcely seemed to notice that this was a setback. Having previously declared that the very future of the Church of England hung upon the Oblates being at St Edmund's, he now discovered that their withdrawal was simply a step backwards for the diocese that might very well be followed by two steps forward. 'If the seminary were offered to us now,' he told Mgr Talbot, 'we would not take it, and that because we hope to do it someday and to do it as it should be done. To try too soon would be to fail.'[158] For the Oblates themselves, he went on, the decision was 'a great advantage. We now have all our men together under one roof, and I believe we shall be far more efficient in any future work.'[159]

What would Errington have made of this letter, Errington whose efforts to secure this 'great advantage' had so compromised his position with Pope and Cardinal, Errington who now found himself stripped of his coadjutorship and the Westminster succession?

7 *The Unnamed Coadjutor*

I suppose Manning has been in London some time. He is very much admired here, and the Cardinals say he ought to be a Bishop. More than one wish him to be your successor in the See of Westminster.[1]

MGR TALBOT (IN ROME) TO CARDINAL WISEMAN, 11 MAY 1863

It was not remarkable that Pius IX had little time for the burning question of the Oblates' position at St Edmund's. While the Church in England was being riven by internal squabbles, the Church in Rome was being threatened with the loss of all its Italian possessions. This was the period (1858–60) during which Napoleon III of France, by means of a deal quite perfidious enough to be worthy of Albion, received his thirty pieces of silver in the form of Savoy and Nice, and left Piedmont free, as a *quid pro quo*, to pursue unmolested its designs upon the Papal States. From 1859 the Pope's possessions in the Romagna, Umbria and the Marches were all under threat. If Pius had been a politician he might have salvaged something through a timely concession of part of his territories, but, as Mgr Talbot was ever on hand to point out, the Vicar of Christ was not in a position to barter the dominion that had been laid upon him by God. So in September 1860 the unfortunate papal volunteers were massacred by the Piedmontese at Castelfidardo, and two months later all the Papal States save Rome and its surrounding patrimony had been incorporated into the new Italian kingdom.

These material losses did not inspire Pius IX to any caution in his claims of spiritual authority. On the contrary, his tone became more and more uncompromising, culminating in the issue of the *Syllabus Errorum* (1864). This document summarized the Church's previous condemnations of the errors that afflict the modern world, including, most notoriously, the error that 'the Church can and ought to reconcile itself with Progress, Liberalism and Modern Civilization'. Today, no doubt, such an anathema would find many supporters. It would, however, have been difficult to conceive a reactionary stance better calculated to evoke shock and horror among

Victorian intellectuals. Not to believe in progress was the ultimate blasphemy. And in many English circles, including the Cabinet, not to believe in Italian unity was only marginally less heretical.

Manning cast himself against this intellectual fashion with the reckless courage of one who delights to be pilloried for his faith. He would describe the *Syllabus Errorum* as 'among the greatest acts of the Pontificate'.[2] It was the Pope's temporal power, however, that attracted his most fervent advocacy. The Pope's earthly kingdom was an indispensable guarantee that his heavenly authority should be freely exercised. Sermons, articles and books poured out of Manning in defence of this view. Their tone was not just unyielding; it was downright fanatical. Though the machinations of Piedmont might appear for the moment to be crowned with success, Manning insisted that local temporal power would be found at the Second Coming: 'No human hand founded it, and no human hand can overthrow it.' He looked to the possibility of the Pope's defining his temporal sovereignty as an article of faith,[3] a proposition that even Pius was obliged to deny. 'Perhaps before we are in our graves', Manning warned, the Pope's enemies would be scourged by wars and revolution beside which the French Revolution and the wars of Napoleon would appear as faint anticipations. Manning judged his own country particularly ripe for chastisement. Palmerston's foreign policy 'gives England the melancholy and bad pre-eminence of the most anti-Catholic, and therefore the most anti-Christian, power in the world.'[4] Yet the continental Catholic powers were almost as bad. 'They see the commerce, the manufacturers, the agriculture, the capital, the practical science, the irresistible armies, the fleets which cover the sea, and they come flocking to admire, and say "Nothing is so great as this great country of Protestant England." '[5] It all looked alarmingly like 'the prelude to Anti-Christ'.

As to the identity of this gentleman Manning was conspicuously well informed. He considered that, in view of the 'deadly and changeless antagonism' that existed between the Jews and the Church, the racial background of Anti-Christ was a foregone conclusion:

There is nothing out of the context or proportion, or *ethos*, as we are wont to say of the nineteenth century, that a person should arise of Jewish blood, naturalised in some of the peoples of Europe, a protector of the Jews, the purse-bearers, and journalists, and telegraph wires, of the revolutions of Europe, hailed by them as their saviour from the social and political dominion of the Christians, surrounded by the phenomena of anti-christian and anti-Catholic spiritualism, an arch-medium himself, and professing to be more than either Moses or Mahomet, that is, more than of human stature and proportions.[6]

Manning's normally pellucid style quite broke down under the horror of this approaching event. Whatever temporary sway the Anti-Christ might obtain, however, his long-term prospects were bleak. 'There is One Power which will destroy all antagonists; there is One Person who will break down and smite small as the dust of the summer threshing-floor all the enemies of the Church, for it is He who will consume his enemies "with the Spirit of His mouth", and destroy them "with the brightness of His coming".'[7]

Errington, remember, was the English Catholic who had supposedly gone out of his mind. The language which Manning used on the temporal power was so unrestrained that it is tempting to speculate that he must have been treading hard upon some writhing serpent of doubt. Such an interpretation does not fit the man. The explanation for Manning's immoderate statements is simply that the intransigent mood of the Vatican perfectly matched his own temperament. Had he not dreamed when at Oxford of championing some great cause against the world?

He even thought it worthwhile to send Gladstone one of his publications upon the temporal power. The two men had met again in the street in 1861 and resumed their relations after the ten-year gap with a two-hour argument on papal sovereignty. Thereafter they corresponded copiously and met occasionally, but the plight of the Pope always lay athwart any resumption of true intimacy. 'The gulf between us is indeed wide,' Gladstone informed Manning on receipt of his polemic, 'so wide that I must forbear attempting to tell you what I think.'[8] There was, however, one telling point that Manning repeatedly urged. Was it not dangerous hypocrisy for the British Government to encourage nationalist revolutionary movements in Italy even while stamping ruthlessly on every manifestation of the same phenomenon in Ireland?[9] Gladstone denied the parallel,[10] but no doubt the contradiction continued to nag him. In particular, Manning objected to the way in which the English Establishment fawned upon Garibaldi, the self-confessed foe alike of popes and kings, when he visited England in 1864.[11] Gladstone received some severe epistolary lectures upon the subject, and it was with obvious relief that he was able to tell Manning in February 1865 that Garibaldi would not be coming to England again. 'Am I not now a good boy?'[12] the Chancellor of the Exchequer demanded of the Provost of Westminster.

The Provost was not to be cajoled. 'I have just seen Gladstone,' he told Lady Herbert in April 1865, '. . . his obstinate narrowness of mind is phenomenal.'[13] Gladstone may perhaps be forgiven his obtuseness. As a consequence of Manning's letters he would come to fear that Catholic leaders would go to any lengths to regain the Pope his possessions[14] or, as Manning put it, to maintain 'the great providential order of Christian

Europe'.[15] Nevertheless, Gladstone did offer his old friend one favour, promising in 1864 that if ever he was in a position to assure the Pope's personal safety he would do so.[16] This pledge was redeemed in 1870, when he ordered a frigate to stand by off Civita Vecchia.

Manning attracted criticism for the apocalyptic zeal with which he defended the temporal power even in Rome, a truly remarkable achievement in the reign of Pius IX. But then he had made a most incautious remark. 'Mgr Capalti', warned Talbot, 'expressed regret at the prophecy which you had introduced that the City of the Popes would relapse into paganism and become the city of Anti-Christ. This statement Mgr Capalti held to be inopportune.'[17] Manning was amazed – 'It never crossed my mind that I was in danger of saying anything capable of misinterpretation on the subject of the Holy See'[18] – but he knew how a good Catholic responds to criticism from headquarters. 'If anything I have written needs correction or suppression it should be done with the greatest promptness. I should rejoice, not in the need, but in the opportunity of giving an example of docility in opinion at a time when we are in danger from a contrary spirit, and in England where we have neither censorship nor even counsel.'[19] In the event Mgr Talbot, or so he claimed, smoothed out this difficulty for Manning without any need for such an exemplary act of docility. Talbot was inclined to attribute the whole affair to personal motives. 'You have enemies in every quarter,' he assured Manning, 'not merely amongst the old Catholics, but also amongst many converts, who are jealous of you because you have gained for yourself such an European reputation, and got ahead of them. Your study, therefore, should be to stand well with the Holy See, and this you will do by showing yourself every year in Rome.'[20]

Mgr Talbot's advice was redundant. The troublesome province of England continued to throw up problems, and as Wiseman ailed, Manning consolidated his position as the Cardinal's representative both at Rome and Westminster. His rise to influence only strengthened his Roman predilections, in matters of the spirit no less than that of the temporal power. He found it fatally easy to dismiss those who held more moderate views than his own as bad Catholics when they were really only different Catholics. In particular, he gradually came to be suspicious of Newman, whose friendship he had always professed to value so deeply. And since Newman on his side possessed a formidable capacity for nursing a sense of grievance, relations between the two men were destined to enter a steep decline.

Already their fortunes in the Catholic Church had proved widely different. Whereas Manning's eager deference to authority and his outstanding administrative ability had quickly secured him a position of considerable power, Newman's Catholic career had been a prolonged course of worldly failure. His Oxford friends had warned him that his qualities would be unappreciated in the Catholic Church, and around 1860 it seemed that they had been right, at least in the rather narrow sense in which the prediction had been offered. Spiritually Newman found in Catholicism everything he had sought, and more; externally he was scarcely recognizable as the former leader of the Oxford Movement. 'As a Protestant,' he wrote, 'I felt my religion dreary, but not my life – but, as a Catholic, my life is dreary, not my religion.'[21]

Manning's work prospered; Newman's appeared to be under some fatal jinx. 'What I wrote as a Protestant', he recognized, 'has had far greater power, force, meaning and success than my Catholic works.'[22] The attempt to build up a Catholic university in Dublin, to which he devoted five years in the prime of his life, proved to be a hopeless enterprise. 'You cannot have a University till the gentlemen take it up,'[23] he observed; and unfortunately the gentlemen would not oblige, even after Newman's provision of a billiards table and cricket pitch. That was not Newman's fault, any more than he was to blame that a subsequent scheme to translate the Bible petered out. Nevertheless, his diary shows him gnawed by a consciousness of wasted powers and buried talent. All he had to show for fifteen years as a Catholic was the Oratory and its school. In 1860 the Oratory contained only six priests, while the school, intended as a kind of Catholic Eton, did not profit from its location at Birmingham.

These achievements were an insignificant tally to set beside the vast hopes that had been indulged when Newman joined the Catholic Church in 1845. To Cardinal Wiseman and the Pope, who measured success by numbers, they seemed derisory. There was a story that Wiseman had said that he would gladly surrender all the converts but one.[24] Newman would not have been at a loss to know whom Wiseman intended. Of course he could discover religious consolation for his plight. At the beginning of his Catholic career he had urged the need 'to despise the whole world, to despise no member of it, to despise oneself, to despise being despised';[25] and as an old man he would tell Lord Braye that 'it is a rule of God's providence that we succeed by failure'.[26] In 1860, however, such reflections could not always assuage the ache of his discontent.

At the best of times Newman had never been an easy friend. It was as natural to him to be touchy as it was for Manning to ingratiate himself with his superiors. Disappointment sharpened the edges of his sensitivity, so that the first half of his Catholic career was littered with petty rows and with broken or diminished friendships. Even within his own Oratory he would retreat into stony silences: there is a story that one of the fathers was not favoured with a remark for twenty years.[27] The hagiographers, a species with which Newman has always been well supplied, have been eager to attribute the abundance of personal ruptures in his life to the inability of ordinary human clay to take the true measure of his saintliness. Anyone who wants to believe that is welcome to his point of view. The sheer number of those who fell foul of Newman, however, suggests that the truth may have been rather more complex. Cardinal Wiseman, Father Faber, officials at Rome, fellow Oratorians, the entire staff of the Oratory school: no doubt these men were tiresome and made mistakes; perhaps they deserved the unfavourable opinion that Newman formed. But did he really have to treat them with such an implacable sense of his own wrongs? Is the injunction to forgive and forget an unrealistic counsel, born of worldly hypocrisy? Newman sometimes acted as though he thought so. Once he had decided that a man was against him, and it was a feeling that came to him easily, there was rarely any hope of reconciliation.

For years Manning was notably successful in maintaining affectionate relations with Newman. The continuation of their friendship is surprising, because from 1857 Newman was in evident sympathy with Lord Acton's attempts to bring a more open mind to Catholicism, a policy which was anathema to Manning. It is interesting, though, that as late as 1858 Acton could suggest that Manning should be on the committee of his liberal Catholic journal the *Rambler*.[28] Clearly he had failed to take Manning's measure, and perhaps Newman was similarly ill-informed. With Manning far too busy with his practical work to maintain close contacts with the Birmingham Oratory, the essential foundation of distance and ignorance upon which the friendship of the two men rested was not threatened. In June 1859 Manning, writing to Mgr Talbot, was generous in acknowledging Newman's special mission to deal with problems of faith among the more intelligent laity. 'They could be easily directed by anyone they thought fair and friendly, especially if, in the way Dr Newman has done, he grapples with their intellectual difficulties.'[29] The very next month, however, Newman was to take this grappling rather too far for Manning's taste.

The *Rambler* had soon got into trouble with the bishops for its free-ranging articles on Catholic history and doctrine. In 1859, in the hope of saving the periodical from censure without wholly compromising its principles, Newman was appointed editor. He was keenly aware of the delicate situation in which he found himself. 'When faults were objected to in my first number I said to Mgr. Manning, with a reference to the *Great Eastern* which was then attempting to get down the river, that I too was striving to steer an unmanageable vessel through the shallows and narrows of the Thames, and that Catholic readers must be patient with me and give me time if I was to succeed in my undertaking.'[30]

In fact, after one more issue Newman's bishop conveyed to him a wish that he should resign as editor. Newman obeyed. In the last, July, number under his aegis, however, Newman had written an article 'On Consulting the Faithful', in which he illustrated the part that the laity had played in the evolution of doctrine. He pointed out that in the fourth century the laity had actually upheld the true doctrine of the Church against erring bishops. This may have been, as Newman believed, an indisputable historical fact, but it did not for that reason find any favour in high places. Dr Brown, the Bishop of Newport, was particularly upset by Newman's remark that there had been, in the fourth century, 'a temporary suspension of the functions of the *Ecclesia docens*'. He cast around for a suitable person to expostulate with Newman. Who would be more likely to carry influence than Dr Manning, one of his oldest Catholic friends?

The appearance of Manning at the Oratory in the role (however tactfully disguised) of emissary from authority was not a promising development in the relations between the two men. Nor was his immediate aim achieved. The most that Newman would concede was that he had not *meant* to imply that the Church had fallen into error. Dr Brown required a better recantation than that. Manning tried his hand at a letter. 'I wish you would write and print a sermon on the Office of the Holy Ghost in the Church, in which you could bring out *in ordine theologico* what *in ordine historico* as in the *Rambler* is confusing to common readers.'[31] Manning helpfully enclosed a pamphlet of his own in order to show how the thing might be done. It was one of his rants about the temporal power. Newman remained unconvinced. He did not see how his position could be assailed. He did not see either that Dr Brown would delate him to Rome for heresy.

Newman sent off an aggrieved letter to Wiseman, offering to elucidate his remarks for the Roman authorities. His tone was by no means contrite:

I marvel, but I do not complain, that after many years of patient and self-denying labour in the cause of Catholicity, the one appropriate acknowledgement in my old age [Newman had thirty more years to live] should be considered to consist in taking advantage against me of what is at worst a slip of the pen in an anonymous, un-theological paper. But I suppose it is a law of the world that those who toil much and say little, are little thought of.[32]

It is instructive to compare Manning's letters to Talbot when *his* writing came under criticism in Rome. Whether one prefers Newman's whingeing or Manning's cringing, that is, whether one estimates the higher Newman's integrity or Manning's obedience, is a matter of taste. There was no question, however, which attitude found more favour at the Vatican. Newman had his answer to that, too: 'I suppose saints have been more roughly treated at Rome than anyone else.' It was his contention that the ultramontane excesses of Pius IX's pontificate were a departure from, not an expression of, the true spirit of the Church.[33]

Wiseman professed sympathy with Newman over the heresy charge, but did absolutely nothing to clear his name, although he was in Rome for the Errington affair. Manning, also in Rome, was detailed to write to Newman (April 1860) explaining that his case was in hand and that Wiseman hoped for an acceptable conclusion. Newman's letter to Wiseman offering to elucidate his article, however, was never passed on to the Roman authorities, and undoubtedly his reputation suffered from what was construed as his disaffected silence. His supporters, ever eager to sniff a plot, subsequently suggested that Manning, if not actually guilty of deliberately withholding Newman's letter, was at least content that his rival's name should be under a cloud.[34] The two men were not even antagonists at that time. What could be more likely, given Wiseman's business incompetence, than that he told Manning he would take up Newman's case with Propaganda and then forgot to do so?

As for Manning, the Newmanites constantly forget that he had a great many other things to preoccupy him besides the fate of their hero. He could not possibly be responsible for Wiseman's every word. When he did think of Newman, he was still well-disposed. At Easter 1861 he dedicated his book, *The Present Crisis of the Holy See tested by Prophecy*, to Newman in lavish terms. 'To you I owe a debt of gratitude for intellectual help and light, greater than to any one man of our time; and 'it gives me a sincere gratification now publicly to acknowledge, though I can in no way repay it.' Whether Newman much liked the work, which contained some of Manning's wilder statements on the Pope's temporal power, may be doubted. He did, however, feel obliged, in June 1861, to put up some defence of Manning against the sneers of Lord Acton. 'People who don't know him well, seem to misunderstand him. He is most sensitively alive to the enormous difficulties, political, social, and intellectual in which we are.'[35] Manning had been invited to preach at the Oratory in the previous month. Clearly he had been as diplomatic a guest as ever.

Nevertheless, Manning's extremist views on the Pope's temporal power did prove to be the critical dividing line in the history of the two men's relations. Certainly Newman's cooler approach to the subject was more prescient and realistic. While he regretted the loss of the Papal States and fulminated against the intrigues which had brought about this outcome, he feared the consequences of the Church's pinning its colours too flamboyantly and irrevocably to an issue of worldly politics. This was not, Newman considered, a field where the Almighty's intervention could be relied upon.

Suppose the Papal States were not returned, and the Anti-Christ did not conform to Manning's prognostications, how would apocalyptic prophecies have served the cause of Roman Catholicism? Manning's own faith, being born of the will, might be adapted by the will to meet any new circumstance. He failed to understand that others might be less ruggedly constituted.

Yet Newman's more guarded position also held difficulties in those days of ultramontane rigour under Pius IX. A man who joins the Roman Catholic Church because he believes it to be the divinely appointed means of salvation must walk on a logical tightrope if he finds himself out of sympathy with the policy of Rome. The rise to power of Manning, who was hard put to conceive any circumstances in which God might allow his Vicar to err, was not going to make this delicate balancing act any easier. Manning, moreover, was at this time much under the influence of W. G. Ward, who was determined to see Newman's more liberal tendencies suppressed. Ward flinched at no dogmatic excess: 'I should like a new papal Bull every morning with my *Times* at breakfast,' he once declared.[36] So convinced was he of the beneficial effects of Roman authority that he allowed his great intellect to dwell with some favour upon the persecutions of the mediaeval Church. The highest ideal, after all, was not a universal liberty to differ, but the union of society in one true religious belief. 'Independence of intellect', he considered, 'just like independence of will, is not man's healthy state but his disease and calamity.'

Manning showed himself as committed to ultramontanism in action as Ward was committed in theory. He brought pressure on Lord Acton to stop supporting Palmerston's Government in Parliament and to defend the Pope's temporal power, warning him that a censure upon the *Rambler* from Rome was impending.[37] Manning was most agreeable, said Acton, but courtesy never mitigated the ruthlessness of his purpose. It might be said that he was merely carrying out orders from Rome, but whence came Rome's concern with the *Rambler* save through information provided by Ward, Talbot and himself? Such tactics irritated Newman, who did not appreciate Roman intervention in the details of English affairs. 'How is Propaganda to know anything about an English controversy,' Newman demanded, 'since it talks Italian? By extemporary translation (I do not speak at random) or the *ex parte* assertion of some narrow-minded Bishop, though he may be saintly too? And who is Propaganda? Virtually, one sharp man of business, who works day and night, and despatches his work quick off, to the East and the West; a high dignitary indeed, perhaps an Archbishop, but after all little more than a clerk.'[38] Newman even extended such criticism to the Pope: 'I was a poor innocent as regards the actual state of things in Ireland when I went there, and did not care to think about it, for I relied on the word of the Pope, but from the event I am led to think it not rash to say that I knew as much about Ireland as he did.'[39]

No one capable of such a sentiment about Pius IX could be a true friend of Manning's, least of all in the 1860s. The first rift with Newman, however, appeared in unlikely circumstances. Cardinal Wiseman was bent on founding an Academy of the Catholic Religion to provide English Catholics with intellectual defences against the hostile age. Manning became the driving force behind the institution, and he later outlined its aims in a way that might have been designed to appeal to Newman. 'There is no zone of calms for us,' he wrote. 'We are in the modern world – in the trade winds of the nineteenth century, and we must brace ourselves to lay hold of the world as it grapples with us and to meet it intellect to intellect, culture to culture, science to science.'[40] Newman, however, decided that the Academy would be used to disseminate extreme ultramontane propaganda on the temporal power. In June 1861 he sent an abrupt and ungracious letter to Manning announcing that he would withdraw his name if Wiseman raised the dreaded subject in his inaugural address. Manning replied politely with the excellent advice that it would be better not to join the Academy at all than to incur the odium of resignation,[41] but he was shaken by Newman's sudden display of claws. 'From that day', he would later write, 'a divergence began between us.'[42]

For the moment Newman appeared to be unaware of the fact. As the pressure upon the *Rambler* increased, he continued, albeit somewhat equivocally, to defend Manning to Acton. On the one hand, 'What Manning aims at, I suppose, is the suppression of the *Rambler*';[43] on the other, 'Manning is of all men most desirous to keep all Catholics together', and Acton would profit from his 'tolerant nature'.[44] Manning's nature was rendered distinctly less tolerant by an article in the November 1861 *Rambler* which poured scorn on his excessive zeal for the temporal power.[45] He believed, on the strength of Catholic gossip, that Newman was the author, or at least the inspirer, of the piece.[46] Catholic gossip, not for the first or the last time, had erred, but it was years before Manning established that. In the mean time Newman became an object of suspicion and, that being the case, it was only a question of time before he would also be revealed, like Dr Errington, as disloyal to the Holy See. Manning always had a perfect conviction that Catholics who disagreed with him were betraying the Lord's purpose for his Church.

Yet civilities still flowed between Newman and Manning in 1862; they were even communicated to third parties. Early in the year Newman wrote to his Bishop, who was locked in combat with Manning in Rome (of which more in a moment), expressing his 'great sorrow . . . that one of my dearest

friends, Dr. Manning, should be on the side opposite to your Lordship'.[47]
And when Newman in October 1862 finally lost patience with the *Rambler*
and supported an episcopal condemnation of the journal, Manning was
warm in his appreciation – 'not that I doubted what he would say, but I
feared that he would not say it. He has a sort of sensitiveness about standing
by his friends even when in the wrong, which is very honourable to his
generosity.'[48] Acton was less impressed by Newman's desertion; his feelings
would mature into a 'deep aversion' for the Oratorian. At the end of his life
he would maintain that Newman had always been an ultramontane at heart
and that he had only espoused liberal positions out of personal animosity
towards the English representatives of the Pope's claims.[49]

This judgement was certainly misconceived if Acton had Newman's
relations with Manning in mind. Indeed Manning, calling at the Oratory on 6
August 1862, and 'very kind as always', succeeded in putting his host almost
too much at ease, as Newman's diary records:

In course of conversation I said to him that I had lately in print said that the Church
was the land of Canaan; that I felt [quite] as strongly that, looking at it in a temporal
earthly point of view, it was just the contrary. I had found very little but desert and
desolateness ever since I had been in it – that I had nothing pleasant to look back on –
that all my human affections were with those whom I had left. He responded, yes, no
friends, none to sympathise with you, etc., etc. I think he quite took my meaning and
he seemed to be deterred in consequence from speaking of the Cardinal, Talbot,
Barnabo etc et id genus omne.[50]

No doubt Manning's agreement was quite sincere; he was himself still
suffering from attacks of nostalgia for Lavington.[51] It was not his way,
however, to speak such thoughts, and his contempt for Newman's plaints is
easy to imagine. To what purpose did a man submit to the Church of God if
he grumbled about the worldly consequences? Newman, for his part, came
to think himself mistaken in having spoken so openly to Manning. Thirteen
years later he appended a note to the above diary entry. 'This was one of the
last times that Manning wormed things out of me. Our Bishop put me on my
guard.' The Bishop's opinion was that 'Manning never went anywhere, but
in order to find something out'.[52] By 1865 Newman had deeply imbibed that
lesson. 'Be on your guard against Manning's getting any thing out of you,' he
wrote to a friend in February of that year. 'He is a desperate hand at
pumping. And avoid all confidential and candid talks with him. And have no
confidants, except such as Manning cannot pump.'[53]

The Bishop who effected this remarkable change in Newman's estimate of
Manning was Bernard Ullathorne, the outstanding character among the
English hierarchy, and the only English Catholic, apart from Newman, who

possessed both the ability and the will-power to cross swords with Manning on equal terms. Ullathorne represented the old Catholic tradition at its finest, as befitted a direct descendant of Sir Thomas More. A Yorkshireman and a Benedictine, he derived his qualities from both these vocations. His blunt determination and his fearless integrity were akin to Errington's, but his adventurous past, which included a period as a cabin-boy and a spell as missioner among Australian convicts, gave him a breadth of outlook that Errington entirely lacked. Ullathorne's robust common sense was always effective, whether applied to recondite theological problems or to routine business affairs. He even contrived to avoid any serious row with Newman, although as Bishop of Birmingham he was his ecclesiastical superior for forty years. (Once, under pressure, Newman called him a coward,[54] but the Bishop never got to hear of this opinion.) Ullathorne's relations with Manning, by contrast, were born in conflict. In the early 1860s the English bishops were continually at odds with Wiseman, and Ullathorne was as natural a representative of one side at Rome, as Manning was of the other.

The subject-matter of these disputes was tedious and technical. There was the continuing argument over the control of seminaries; there was the question of whether Catholic trusts should be registered with the heretic English State which might declare them illegal; there were rows over the division of property between dioceses. To some extent the differences were an inevitable concomitant of the restored hierarchy, in which all parties needed to discover their rights. The fundamental point at stake was whether the Archbishop of Westminster should rule as dictator or as *primus inter pares*. Wiseman, who favoured the former system, was outraged by the pretensions of his suffragans. 'The policy now is to carry by majorities not by weight of argument,' he wrote in dudgeon after one bishops' meeting. 'Eight against one or two, such is our mode of carrying on our affairs.'[55] Did it mean nothing to be a Cardinal?

Wiseman was now afflicted with diabetes in addition to his frequent heart attacks, and no doubt his irritability was connected with his declining health. But whereas the bishops might have overlooked the crotchetiness of the Cardinal, whom they admired, and whose sheer inefficiency, even in the best of health, militated in practice against his absolutist theories, they were not prepared to stomach being governed by Manning, who was not in the least inefficient, and who increasingly appeared to be the real ruler of the Westminster diocese. Vaughan told Talbot that the English bishops regarded Manning as 'extreme, exaggerated, contentious'.[56] Manning was not conciliatory. 'It is as necessary for the bishops in England to feel the weight of Rome as it was ten years ago for the priests in England to feel the weight of the hierarchy,'[57] he told Talbot. The quarrel became so violent that the Roman authorities began to fear schism among the English Catholics. Eventually the Pope felt it necessary to intervene personally with the request that both sides should put the highest and largest mountain in the Alps upon their differences.[58]

These quarrels were a tragedy for Wiseman, who had been genial and magnanimous in his prime, only to find himself in his declining years starved of the affection he craved. His dependence on Manning grew all the time. 'If God gives me strength to undertake a great wrestling match with infidelity, I shall owe it to him,' he wrote in 1858.[59] But his surrender to this influence condemned him to isolation from former friends who saw the good angel in quite another light. Mgr Searle, who had once been Wiseman's familiar, accused Manning to his face of underhand intrigue. Manning was unruffled: 'I answered that I owed him no relations; that I had a duty to the Cardinal and none to him.'[60] It was Wiseman and not he who suffered from Searle's estrangement. 'If Searle were to leave me (as he did for some months in the winter),' the Cardinal wrote pathetically to Talbot in 1863, 'I should almost be obliged to live alone . . . I know *no one* who would suit me as a *companion*.'[61] Manning did his best to provide comfort, but he was too busy to be always on hand, and he really had little but Romanism in common with his chief. 'It was to me sometimes a pain and sometimes a source of amusement', remembered Father Morris, 'to observe the effects of the good Cardinal's entirely artless manifestation of his enjoyment of good things and of the simplest pleasures in the presence of one so entirely remote from all sympathy with such satisfactions as was Manning.'[62]

Wiseman's association with Manning, which cost him so dear in human terms, did not even have the countervailing merit of enabling him to enforce his claims of authority over other English bishops. Manning had encouraged him to take an overbearing line with his suffragans, and had sustained the will to keep it up, but he could not avoid defeat when the bishops took their case to Rome. At first it had seemed that Manning's influence at the Vatican might prove irresistible. Ullathorne, however, was not lightly to be pushed aside. Sensing that his case was being lost by default, he drew attention to the injustice by dramatically petitioning the Pope for permission to resign his bishopric. 'This is policy,' considered Manning,[63] but it was remarkably successful policy. Thereafter Ullathorne was guaranteed a better hearing and, since his brief was a strong one which he deployed with skill, nearly all the issues were decided in his favour. Cardinal Barnabò, the Prefect of Propaganda, never showed the same enthusiasm as the Pope either for Manning or for Manning's claims.

Also, Manning underestimated Ullathorne. This is clear from a report which Vaughan, Manning's lieutenant, sent to Wiseman in February 1862, near the beginning of the Roman contest:

Dr. Manning has . . . told me of his late interviews with Mgr. *Ego Solus*, the Bishop of Birmingham, as someone has named him. He has come out in his true colours, Anglican and Gallican in the strongest way. He has tripped himself up and dropt again and again into the power of the Protonotary, who, though exceeding courteous and amiable, does not in the least object to cutting his legs off, and that operation seems to be in the course of being satisfactorily done.[64]

Vaughan's account does not leave a pleasant impression. The smearing of opponents as 'Anglican and Gallican' was a stock tactic of the ultramontanes at Rome, employed especially by Manning, who always found the greatest difficulty, when engaged in controversy, in discerning any shade between his own white and his antagonist's black. Even the saintly Bishop Grant of Southwark was dismissed as 'disproportionately mischievous'[65] in a letter to Talbot.

When Manning fought, the enemy was invariably a dragon defending some iniquitous cause; after the battle was lost his moral definition instantly became less sharply focused. It had happened when the Oblates were withdrawn from St Edmund's; it happened again over the Cardinal's right to retain exclusive control of seminaries within his diocese. In August 1862 Manning considered this question 'the greatest next after the Hierarchy'.[66] When, next year, the decision went against Wiseman, Manning simply informed the Cardinal that 'the winnowing of principles' had been 'a vast gain'.[67] Conversely, Ullathorne ceased in his judgement to be merely Anglican and Gallican, and became a man to be reckoned with. The two of them established what Ullathorne's biographer has called 'a sort of growly friendship' at Rome without either rancour or illusion. During their walks beside the Tiber, Ullathorne was 'very malicious against Protonotaries',[68] whom Manning styled 'Bishop-takers'[69] in riposte. Nevertheless, the Protonotary gave a good account of the Bishop to the Pope.[70]

Wiseman's case against his fellow bishops had been so weak that Manning's reputation in Rome suffered not a jot in defeat. It seems a pity, with hindsight, that he had not curbed the Cardinal's litigious spirit, but no such reflection tarnished the golden opinions which he was now winning. In 1863 Mgr Talbot was beside himself with enthusiasm at the success of his protégé:

Mgr. Manning has come out nobly this year in Rome. He has gained immensely in the opinion of the Pope and I may say of all the Cardinals. They are open-mouthed about him. He is looked upon as a first-rate man, especially since his discourse at the *Trinità*. He is certainly immensely improved and as different from what he was ten years ago as possible. He is more *sciolto* and open. Everyone sees that he is called to do great things in England.[71]

There was but one potential blight over this exciting prospect. It was rumoured in Wiseman's camp that Archbishop Errington was not disposed to take his exclusion from the Westminster succession in the spirit of a loyal Catholic or even of an English gentleman. In January 1862 Vaughan wrote in alarm to Wiseman that Errington was in Dublin, 'and the reports which have reached me more than once are that he intends to remain there till Westminster is vacant, and then by the help of the Chapter to return'.[72] Sheer nerves made Wiseman's party credulous of such rumours. As Mgr Talbot observed to Manning with his accustomed finesse, if Dr Errington were to return to Westminster, '*povere voi* and the Oblates of St Charles'.[73] Anxiety was increased by the fact that the English bishops felt much sympathy for Errington on account of the way in which he had been treated, and were pressing Rome for his rehabilitation. Even so, it does seem extraordinary that Errington was still perceived as a threat. There was really no possibility that the Pope would ever reappoint him to Westminster; indeed Pius said as much in November 1861.[74] Errington, though he was not prepared to declare himself actually ineligible for that see, acknowledged, as Ullathorne reported in February 1864, 'that he had never entertained the notion, after what had passed, he could claim the succession'.[75]

Talbot and Manning still felt the need to make assurance doubly sure: it was, after all, a question of securing Cardinal Wiseman's romanizing work against a reactionary backlash on the part of the old Catholics. Manning was clear that Errington must be banned not merely from Westminster but, for the moment at least, from all other English sees. It was a pity that the awkward fellow had once more declined the offer of Trinidad. The Pope, unfortunately, had shown himself inclined towards generosity regarding another English see: the idea must be squashed.

As to Dr. Errington [Manning wrote to Wiseman on 13 December 1861], I wish to see him treated with all respect due to a man who is personally good and upright; and if hereafter, where no danger would result, he were replaced in some position, I should see it with satisfaction; but at this time when the whole conflict is still under arms, and everything gained still precarious and at stake, and your work not consolidated, and in many ways already affected by reaction, and the old party not only biding their time, but exulting in the hope of chance, and the bishops sending a *procura* to Rome avowedly against your Eminence, I should look on any replacing of Dr. Errington not as the restoration of a person but as the reversal of a whole line of action, and the consolidation of its opposite.[76]

To put the issue beyond all doubt Talbot and Manning decided that a new

Coadjutor and successor to Wiseman should be appointed forthwith. In February 1862 the idea that Manning himself should fill the post was floated in Rome, though apparently without Manning's knowledge.[77] Canon Oakeley had given the reasoning behind this proposal in the previous year. 'The ascendancy of Manning's policy in the Diocese . . . would undoubtedly render it impracticable for any future Archbishop to govern it, unless he were himself an Oblate,'[78] he wrote to Talbot. The loyal Vaughan urged the same point with more enthusiasm in June 1863. 'Everybody naturally expects him, and if it is done it will cause little surprise.'[79] Wiseman, however, thought otherwise. He had had more than enough rows already and he simply could not face the storm of protest that such an appointment would bring in England. Even Talbot was obliged to admit that the bishops would be aggrieved, although Ullathorne had assured him that they would willingly see Manning in another see.[80]

Once Manning had been discounted for Westminster Ullathorne was the logical candidate:

He has many faults [Talbot wrote condescendingly to Wiseman], but with them all he is a good Bishop and will not undo your work. The plan would be to name him Coadjutor with orders to remain as Bishop of Birmingham as long as you live. The second part of the plan, *not matured yet*, would be to make Mgr. Manning a Bishop *in partibus* to help you in London. It has also been suggested that he should succeed to Birmingham.[81]

It is an intriguing thought that Manning might have become Newman's bishop in Birmingham. Although that part of the scheme was soon forgotten, Manning took up with energy and determination the task of persuading Wiseman to accept Ullathorne as his Coadjutor and successor. It was uphill work because Wiseman regarded Ullathorne as leader of the opposition, yet Manning persisted in a way that makes nonsense of any suggestion that he was covertly intriguing on his own behalf. 'I trust and believe that we shall have you many years among and over us,' he tactfully began a letter to Wiseman from Rome on 4 December 1863, 'and I always feel that it does not shorten our life to make our will.'[82] At this stage he avoided the dreaded name of Ullathorne, although he made it clear that one bishop had figured prominently in his discussions with Propaganda. A few days later Manning revealed the identity of this bishop as 'Dr. U.',[83] and by January 1864 he was pressing Dr U.'s claims without any reserve. 'I know all you feel about him,' Manning told Wiseman, 'but there seem many reasons why that nomination would ensure union among the bishops and peace for yourself.'[84] There followed, in Manning's usual style, nine numbered paragraphs setting forth the merits of Ullathorne. This objective analysis of his qualifications came on top of the more subjective enthusiasm of an earlier letter. 'I have a very high sense of his goodness both as a man and a bishop; and I think him beyond all compare the fittest man to come after you.'[85]

Wiseman, however, remained adamant in his refusal to countenance Ullathorne as his Coadjutor, and resisted all Manning's attempts to get him to come to Rome, where the pressure might have proved irresistible. He even roused himself sufficiently to protest against Manning's harassment, though Manning passed off the incident lightly enough in a letter to Talbot. 'I told him that I knew he wished to scold me for urging Dr. U. upon him, and that he had better begin at once. So he had his say, and I think he is satisfied.'[86] It would seem that Manning was no longer under his old compulsion to express deep reverence for the Cardinal's qualities. What Wiseman actually said in this interview, according to a later note of Manning's, was that he felt as though his last friend had deserted him.[87]

It was an ironical situation. Manning was widely suspected, by the English bishops and many others, of taking advantage of Wiseman's ill health to further his own ends. Dr Neve, President of the English College at Rome, expressed the general feeling. 'There will be no peace as long as Manning is here. He is always scheming.'[88] In fact, Manning was annoying the Cardinal by pressing upon him a plan that would, if accepted, have meant the extinction of his own chance of succeeding to Westminster. 'The only *altiora* before me', he told Ullathorne, 'are, I hope, St Benedict's twelve steps and the rest which remains for us.'[89] If Manning was suggesting that he wanted to become a monk, he was undoubtedly deceiving himself. The fact remains, however, that he would become Archbishop not because, as Lytton Strachey deduced from Purcell's biography, he was an ecclesiastical Machiavelli meticulously plotting each step in his progress, but because his virtuous intentions of installing another candidate were thwarted.

Manning always remained deferential to Wiseman personally, but when writing to Talbot he did not disguise the impatience he felt over the Cardinal's refusal to accept Ullathorne as Coadjutor: 'He is timid and wishes to end his days without any more troubles.'[90] It was an additional irony attaching to Manning's subsequent elevation that this rejection of Ullathorne was the last important issue over which Wiseman's independence asserted itself. With his life ebbing away the Cardinal had neither inclination nor capacity again to overrule his indefatigable lieutenant. 'Ask Mgr Manning' became his stock response to all enquiries.[91] So in 1864, when the question whether Catholics should be allowed to attend Oxford came to the fore, it was Manning who took control.

Oxford had removed the obligation for undergraduates to subscribe to the

Thirty-Nine Articles in 1854, and a trickle of Catholics had attended the university in the ensuing decade. Wiseman, who had always welcomed the involvement of Catholics in the mainstream of English life, appeared at first to be in favour of this development, even to contemplate the establishment of a Catholic college at Oxford or Cambridge.[92] As the number of Catholics at Oxford grew, however, sterner counsels began to make themselves heard, to the effect that education at a Protestant university must constitute a grave danger to the faith. Manning was strongly of this view, although he showed himself sensible of both sides of the argument in an article that he published in the *Dublin Review* (July 1863).

He fairly outlined the case for integrating Catholics into such an important national institution, and he set forth the possibility that a Catholic college at Oxford might enable them to draw benefit from the university without putting faith to the hazard. The counter arguments, however, were more fully developed. Manning was always the first to acknowledge the need to provide higher education for Catholics, but he wanted it to be provided in an entirely separate Catholic university, not in a Catholic college at a Protestant university. The truckling with Oxford seemed to his sensitive social conscience to be pandering to the wealthy. In London he had worked to withdraw Catholic children from the workhouses into Catholic schools; 'How shall we refuse a common secular education for our poor children if we court and catch at it for the children of the rich?'

As to faith, Manning had remarkably little confidence in the ability of Catholics to resist the infection of Protestant thought. He had rejected any idea of union with Anglicanism on the grounds that the Church could not compromise divine truth; now he trembled for the security of that truth in the corrupting Oxford atmosphere, which had indeed become noticeably more liberal since Newman's departure. An approach to study which a don might see as embodying academic detachment, Manning deemed to be bias against the unchallengeable facts of religion. 'Count de Maistre has said that history since the Reformation has been in conspiracy against the Catholic Church. We may say that philosophy since Descartes has to a wider extent than is suspected joined in the conspiracy.'[93]

Manning had loved Oxford himself, which only led him to treat the university as a temptation that had to be resisted all the more violently for its very seductiveness. The attitude of his opponents must have helped to fortify his resolve:

There is no doubt [a convert urged] that Catholic young men make a bad show in London society; at the best clubs they are pretty sure to be blackballed, and why? Not on religious grounds. What does the Travellers' Club care for a man's religious opinions? Nothing, – but it knows that Catholics are exclusively educated, have little in common with its other members, and would be a *bore*, and so they are rejected, and rightly. London ladies say the same: 'Excellent young man, but a bore; we don't know what to say to him, nor he to us.'[94]

The tragedy of this predicament would have cut little ice with Manning. Indeed, his suspicion of Catholics who wanted to have their sons educated at Oxford derived from his conviction, drawn from the very best authority, that faith should be held against the world not with it. 'Worldly Catholicism' became one of his stock terms of opprobrium. Those who regard with pious liberal horror his efforts to secure a ban upon Catholics going to Oxford should first assure themselves that there have been no deleterious effects upon the faith of Catholic undergraduates since the Church lifted the prohibition after his death, for that is the sole criterion which Manning applied.

Moreover his anti-Oxford line was not a personal idiosyncrasy but standard Catholic policy of the period. The Pope had a horror of liberal universities on the continent, and recoiled in shock from any suggestion that Catholic higher education should be conducted outside a seminary. The *Syllabus* of 1864 explicitly condemned the proposition that 'Catholics can approve of that manner of educating youth which is separate from the Catholic faith and the authority of the Church, and which looks only or primarily to the knowledge of natural things and the ends of earthly social life'. Unlike Newman,[95] Manning treated the *Syllabus* as an infallible pronouncement, and this ruling on education he embraced with particular relish. So clear-cut was the Vatican's view that for once even the English bishops found themselves sharing Manning's opinion. As for Wiseman, whatever he may have thought in his prime, he was unyieldingly hostile to an Oxford scheme in his dotage. Manning had been formidable enough with the entire English episcopacy arrayed against him; with their support he could hardly fail to get his way.

There was much else on his mind at this time. In 1864 he entered the controversy over *Essays and Reviews*. In this collection of essays, first published in 1860, various Anglican writers had allowed themselves some scepticism about traditional doctrines. Manning profited from the occasion to produce three lengthy open letters expressing of his deep sorrow (which reads more like unbounded delight) that the Church of England should have fallen to such depths. The last of these letters, addressed to Dr Pusey, partially inspired that worthy to write his *Eirenicon* (1865), purportedly a plea for unity but actually, as Newman remarked, an olive branch discharged 'as if from a catapult',[96] with Manning frequently in the line of fire. Beside these excitements the universities issue was merely an internal

Catholic affair involving the application of certain well-defined principles. Unfortunately for Manning's reputation, though, his part in this process would establish him as the demon figure in that powerful and insinuating Newmanite lore which has dominated the history of nineteenth-century English Catholicism.

Newman's interest in Oxford was the consequence of a sudden and unexpected recovery in his prospects and morale. In the early 1860s, as we have seen, he had been cast down into an apparently unconquerable depression. 'Oh how forlorn and dreary has been my course since I became a Catholic . . . as a Catholic I seem to have had nothing but failure personally.'[97] He had now come to identify Manning unequivocally as an enemy, a most successful enemy, moreover, whom he deemed chiefly responsible for the suspicion with which he was regarded in Rome. The incident that finally broke his trust in Manning was trivial enough: Manning failed to include the Oratory in a list of Catholic colleges.[98] Newman began to fear that the school would be closed. He knew that there were reports abroad, not unfounded ones either, that the Oratory had been preparing boys for Oxford.[99] Every such piece of Catholic tittle-tattle came back to Newman. In 1866 Bishop Grant of Southwark would warn Manning 'how intimately he [Newman] is acquainted with everything said or even thought about him in London'.[100] This active Oratory intelligence system did nothing for its Father Superior's peace of mind. To live in seclusion and receive accounts of hostile manoeuvring in the outside world is not conducive to a sense of proportion. By 1863 Newman appeared to believe that his antagonist was irresistible. 'Manning will decide, I think, both Pope and Cardinal';[101] 'the dull tyranny of Manning and Ward'[102] carried all before it.

Yet Newman must have been aware that his own Bishop, Ullathorne, had emerged successfully from his struggles against Manning in Rome. He dwelt on Manning's underhand advantages because it salved his pride. He knew the kind of invidious comparisons that were being made. 'Why, he has made no converts, like Manning and Faber,'[103] a former Oratory master blurted out in Brighton, a remark that was instantly conveyed to Birmingham, where it provoked some bitter reflections in Newman's journal. 'Manning then and the others are great,' he wrote, 'who live in London and by their position and their influence convert Lords and Ladies.'[104] What riled Newman was the knowledge that this was precisely the kind of influence the Pope had expected from him in sending the Oratory fathers 'especially to the educated classes, and what would be called the class of gentlemen'.[105] Something, at least, must have caused his delusion that Manning's work in the slums of Bayswater was confined to the aristocracy.

Newman, however, was more easily offended than destroyed. It was invariably on the rebound that he was at his most effective. Early in 1864 Charles Kingsley, unable to resist a passing glance, accused him in the course of a review article of teaching that 'truth, for its own sake, had never been a virtue with the Roman clergy'. Newman turned the jibe into an occasion for a masterpiece. In six weeks he wrote *Apologia Pro Vita Sua*, an account of the religious odyssey which led him to the Catholic Church, and in its latter part an examination of the nature of Catholic authority, which he upheld even against the discouragements of 'a violent ultra party which exalts opinions into dogmas, and has it principally at heart to destroy every school of thought but its own'.[106] The victory over Kingsley, though full of controversial spice, was of small account; in fact there were some who felt that Newman had shown an unseemly glee in trampling his opponent into the dust, as well as too fine a sense of what was due to his own feelings.[107] The most important point about the *Apologia* was its reception by the English public. John Bull found himself conceding, for the first time in three hundred years, that an intelligent man might become a Catholic without either losing his mind or donning the hypocrite's mask. The *Apologia*, Shane Leslie observed, marked the ebb of the Reformation in the English mind. Thenceforward anti-papal prejudice gradually ceased to be an indispensable passport to intellectual respectability.

The old English Catholics were overflowing with gratitude to their deliverer. That Newman had been a victim of ultramontane rigour only added to his popularity; that he brought his worshippers no social message by no means diminished his appeal. Messages of support and congratulation flowed in, including one from the Westminster clergy which Newman modestly attributed to the opposition to Manning in the diocese. 'For three or four months past the Westminster clergy have been in a state of extreme anxiety, lest Manning should be made Coadjutor to the Cardinal.'[108] Wiseman, Talbot and Manning declined to share in the general applause for the *Apologia*. 'He had ceased writing, and good riddance,' remarked Mgr Talbot, 'why did he ever begin again?'[109] Manning made the same point in more circumspect fashion. Reading the *Apologia*, he said, was 'like listening to the voice of one from the dead'.[110] His acolytes exercised themselves over 'literary vanity', Vaughan generously concluding that the egotism displayed by Newman 'may be disgusting, but it is venial'.[111] Henceforth Manning became disposed to reflect upon his own uncluttered sense of vocation: 'I am not, like Newman, a poet, or a writer of autobiography, but a priest, and a priest only.'[112]

It was after his triumph with the *Apologia* that Newman's thoughts turned towards Oxford. Manning, meanwhile, had been examining the possibility of sending Catholics to Rome for their higher education, pending the establishment of a university in England. 'The young men would have the entrée into all the best houses there,' he somewhat uncharacteristically remarked, at least according to Newmanite report.[113] Newman himself dismissed this scheme with contempt: 'I think the progenitors of it must be mad.'[114] So they may have been, but the point, in this context, is that Manning's anti-Oxford convictions were widely known well before Newman considered any plan of his own in connection with the university. Manning was quite innocent of any personal vendetta towards Newman in the matter, though Newman and his entourage, in their more paranoiac moments, sometimes seemed to doubt it. 'Bellasis told me that, from what he saw at Rome, he felt that Manning was more set against *my* going to Oxford, than merely against Catholic youths going there.'[115]

Yet Newman had still been labouring at the *Apologia* when, in the spring of 1864, Manning brought the universities issue before the bishops, who duly condemned the idea of a Catholic college at Oxford or Cambridge, and pronounced that Catholic parents should be discouraged by all means from sending their children to such dangerous places.[116] After that, Newman was sticking his neck out when, that autumn, he bought five acres in Oxford between St Giles and Walton Street. At first he toyed with the idea of a Catholic college or hall, to be set up 'without a word to anyone',[117] although this plan was quickly dropped as he gauged the strength of the opposition. Nevertheless Manning was certainly right in his suspicion that neither Newman nor Ullathorne was opposed in principle to a Catholic college.[118] Publicly, of course, Newman spoke only of establishing a branch of the Oratory at Oxford, with the aim of ministering to the spiritual needs of Catholic undergraduates.

That was still sufficient to arouse Manning, who recognized that Newman's presence in Oxford, in whatever capacity, would certainly encourage parents to defy the bishops' ruling against universities. A list of questions was speedily dispatched to the Oxford converts, but not to Newman, who aptly described the tenor of the enquiries as 'Are you, or are you not, one of those wicked men who advocate Oxford education?'[119] In December another, specially convened, meeting of the bishops reiterated their earlier decisions, and applied to Propaganda for ratification. Yet neither Manning nor anyone else prevented Newman from founding an Oratory in Oxford; it was just that, as soon as Newman realized that the bishops were implacable in their determination to discourage Catholics from sending their sons to Oxford, he no longer saw any point in pursuing his plan. The town of Oxford needed an Oratory as much as the university, but that was not work to which Newman felt himself called. He sold the land and abandoned the project without even waiting for the decision of Propaganda, which he insisted on regarding as ineluctably bound to Manning.[120] It was true, at least, that Cardinal Barnabò appeared to regard Newman with a distaste equal to that which he felt for Manning. Conversing with Newman, he remarked, always induced a heavy weight upon the stomach.[121] To Newman's disciple Ambrose St John, however, Barnabò expressed himself more diplomatically: 'I know Manning best, but I love Newman.'[122]

Manning was certainly not so sure of his ground that he took victory in the Oxford affair for granted. In January 1865 he posted out to Rome once more in order to guard against the possibility of any hitch. In fact, the decree which Propaganda eventually produced on the universities question fell short of the absolute prohibition that he himself would have wanted.[123] But then he had only spent a few days in Rome before news came that Cardinal Wiseman was dying. The Pope tried to persuade Manning to stay, believing that he would not get back to London in time to see Wiseman alive.[124] But Manning travelled day and night, 'sixty-eight hours without lying down',[125] and witnessed the Cardinal's last three days. Wiseman recognized him once, he thought.[126] In any case, it had been necessary to return. There must be no suspicion, Manning told Ward, that he was intriguing in Rome over the succession.[127]

8 Archbishop of Westminster

Your appointment has been a severe blow given to the club theory, I mean the view that the Catholic body, as it is called in England, is a kind of club, and that the dignities in it ought to be the property of the Cliffords and other Catholic families.[1]

MGR TALBOT TO MANNING, 10 JULY 1865

The question of who was to be Wiseman's successor remained unresolved for ten weeks after his death. This period was naturally filled with feverish speculation, not always conducive to that state of internal resignation becoming to ecclesiastics who are awaiting the decision of the Holy Spirit. 'I have seen Manning this morning,' W. G. Ward wrote to his wife in March 1865. 'He is a good deal out of spirits. Dr. Clifford has been telegraphed to Rome.'[2] This was indeed alarming news. Dr Clifford, Bishop of Clifton, was the candidate that Manning dreaded above all others. 'I hardly deprecate any appointment,' he had written to Mgr Talbot on 24 February, 'except Dr. Errington and Dr. Clifford – and the latter even more than the former.' Clifford was a member of an ancient Catholic family; he was lukewarm about the Pope's temporal power and unexcited about his infallibility; he was unsound on the universities issue; he was a friend of Newman's; he was young. Manning could not conceive of a worse archbishop: 'We should be overrun with worldly Catholics and a worldly policy without his meaning or knowing it.'[3] Fortunately Clifford's summons to Rome turned out to be a false alarm.

Yet Ward, who desperately hoped that Manning would succeed, could find no cause for rejoicing. He believed that the decision would rest with Propaganda rather than the Pope; and Cardinal Barnabò's lack of enthusiasm for Manning was well known. 'I have therefore given up almost all hopes of Manning's appointment. He says himself that there is not the remotest chance of it nor again of Clifford.'[4]

That was undoubtedly a correct assessment under the procedure designed to produce the new Archbishop. On 14 March the Westminster Chapter would meet and draw up a list of three names which would be sent on to

Rome after ratification by the bishops. To Manning it seemed outrageous that the Chapter which, time and again, had shown its contumacious spirit should possess the power of choosing the Metropolitan of the entire English province. 'I wish the Holy Father would reserve the Archbishop in perpetuity to the Holy See,' he told Talbot.[5] 'I care less who the next Archbishop may be than to see six or eight incompetent men, who have crossed the Cardinal's great work, caressed and encouraged.'[6] When Manning preached Wiseman's panegyric he must have feared that he was also pronouncing the obsequies of ultramontanism in England. There was even a danger that the Chapter might put forward Newman, for some of the canons had been 'literally playing the fool about him in this Kingsley affair'.[7]

Since, however, the Pope could always override the Chapter's choice, Manning found it worthwhile to make his opinions known to Mgr Talbot. On the whole he still reckoned that Ullathorne would be a satisfactory choice, although the Bishop of Birmingham's apparent collusion with Newman in the Oxford affair had rather lessened his appeal. Still, Manning now had a new bugbear which required a strong controlling hand:

I have reason to know that the Jesuits are working about the See of Westminster. Dr. Clifford's name, I am persuaded, has been put forward by them. . . . The sectional personal influence of Farm Street has grown in the last five years. If this be not checked, the work of the Diocese will be dangerously impoverished and impeded. . . . One man who could check it and also quiet the Bishops would be Dr. Ullathorne. . . . A second would be Dr. Cornthwaite, who would be more personally liked. Urge the one or the other with all your power.[8]

If Manning did not go quite to the length of Vaughan, his successor, who would write to Rome insisting on his lack of suitability for the position, it can at least be said that he promoted the claims of his rivals.

As things turned out, it was the despised Chapter which unwittingly set in motion the chain of events that led to a solution Manning found acceptable. In spite of warnings from Rome, the six or eight incompetent men fixed upon the candidate favoured by the great body of English Catholics – Errington! The two others on their list were Clifford and Grant, but as these withdrew their candidature, Errington was left as the only name presented to Rome. Manning must have recognized that this state of affairs, which the Pope was bound to resent (His Holiness had not forgotten the note-taking incident), threw the whole succession wide open. He had promised Talbot to telegraph the Chapter's choice as soon as it was made, but now he suddenly discovered that his conscience did not permit him to convey information that ought to reach Rome through the English bishops.[9] Clearly it had become important not to attract any accusations of behind-the-scenes dealing.

Mgr Talbot, left in ignorance of how matters were developing, now took it upon himself to prepare Manning for disappointment. He therefore wrote to Canon Morris asking him to let Manning know that there was no chance of his being appointed. Manning replied on 31 March:

I thank you sincerely for your kind thought about me, and your fear of giving me pain. It gave me none. If I were to say that the subject of it has not been before my mind, I should go beyond the truth; for in the last year, both in England and abroad, people have, out of kind but inconsiderate talk, introduced the subject. But if I say that I have never for a moment believed the thing to be probable, reasonable or imaginable I should speak the strict truth. I have therefore never, as you once said people thought, 'aimed at it', or desired it. God knows, I have never so much as breathed a wish to Him about it. And all this time I have been as indifferent as if nothing were pending. . . . If I had wished for my reward in this world, I should not have spoken out to the last syllable what I believe to be true. I have consciously offended Protestants, Anglicans, Gallican Catholics, national Catholics, and worldly Catholics, and the Government and public opinion in England, which is running down the Church and the Holy See in all ways and all day long.[10]

The Pope's reception of the news that Errington was the name submitted by the Westminster Chapter proved to be all that might have been expected. 'The moment the Pope saw Your Grace's name at the head of the list,' Errington was informed, 'he struck his breast three times and exclaimed, *"Questa è un offensa."* ' The English bishops were gravely rebuked for permitting this *'insulto al Papa'.*[11] Pius declared that he would take the matter into his own hands, and ordered a month of Masses and prayers in order to ensure the guidance of the Holy Spirit.[12] The question at issue, to take a secular view, was not whom the Pope wanted – there was little doubt about that – but whether he would dare to enforce his choice in the knowledge that he would be appointing a man who had consistently incurred the suspicion and enmity of almost the entire English hierarchy. Alternative counsel pressed in upon Pius. The English laity and the Irish hierarchy bravely continued to urge Errington. Propaganda finally decided to recommend Ullathorne.[13] Lord Palmerston, the Prime Minister, let it be known that the choice of either Clifford or Grant would be satisfactory.[14] Cardinal Antonelli, the papal Secretary of State, influenced by this diplomatic pressure, also adopted the cause of Clifford.[15]

It was not surprising that the Pope hesitated. There was one glorious moment when, still uncertain how to act, he suggested to Mgr Talbot that perhaps he should be the man. Mgr Talbot, quite impervious to the joke, quickly wrote to give Manning the joyful tidings. Manning, as always, was equal to the occasion. 'Your letter of the 3rd and 4th April came yesterday. I thank God for what it tells me. And trust you will be sent to us. It will be my happiness to work with you and for you; for I believe that the love of souls and the love of Rome are your two motives.' Manning added, doubtless for Talbot's comfort, that all the rumours of division in England were grossly exaggerated. The Westminster Chapter, not the English church, was rebellious. 'Do not let anyone alarm you or any one else with notions of dissension and schism and the like. It is all absurd: I would answer for the union and peace of the future, if only the Holy See acts for itself.' It was wicked, Manning thought, the way some people were trying 'to mislead the decision of Rome'.[16]

Happily Father Coffin, the Vice-Provincial of the Redemptorists in England, was in Rome to offer the authorities more correct representations, possibly the only occasion on which one old Harrovian has been able to do a good turn for another at the Vatican. At the end of April the Pope received the instruction for which he had been waiting: '*Mi sono trovato propriamente ispirato a nominar lei: E io crederò sempre di sentire una voca dicendo, "Mettetelo lì, Mettetelo lì."* '[17] – 'I shall always believe that I heard a voice saying, "Put him there, put him there." ' And so there he was duly put.

It is interesting that although the Pope's decision was not officially made until 30 April, Manning received a letter of congratulation, from a canon of Westminster, dated 25 April.[18] Evidently the news that the Pope had reserved the decision to himself sufficed to spark off well-grounded speculation about the eventual outcome of his deliberations. Cardinal Barnabò, always a straw in the wind, began during April to feel a compelling desire, decidedly at variance with his former opinion, that Manning should be appointed.[19] Manning would claim that the official letter from Propaganda, which reached him in Bayswater on 8 May, came as a surprise,[20] but the surprise was less than total. Nevertheless, this official confirmation did cause an emotional upheaval: Manning's nephew William, also an Oblate, found him in tears before the Blessed Sacrament.[21]

The prediction that the English Catholics would rally round the choice of Rome proved abundantly justified. Such sectional spirit as was shown came from the small band of Manning's own supporters. The temptation to crow was all the greater because the event confounded all expectation. Vaughan, who was fund-raising in South America, wrote to Manning on 24 May, still in ignorance of the appointment, with words of consolation for the difficult time he must be going through. 'I hope you are not at all sharp or severe with those who are against you, or rather I should say *coldly* reserved and *ominously* civil.'[22] Vaughan was so much aware of the rebarbative effect that Manning could produce that he would deem it a sign of spiritual growth in Mrs Ward when she stopped hating the man.[23] Yet Vaughan's admiration for Manning was wholehearted. His enthusiasm at Rome's choice was conveyed in a letter which gloried in the discomfiture of the opposition. 'I suppose by this time more than half of those who used to bite their lip on seeing you have humbly bent their knee, and forgotten their former thoughts. . . . Poor Searle! . . . I am sure you will be magnanimous to him, and a hundred other poor devils who will think *you are come to torment them before the time.*'[24] Indeed Manning was generous to Searle, and as for Maguire, the former vicar general whom Wiseman had sacked in the course of the row with the Chapter, he would soon claim that the sound of Manning's step on his stair was music to his ears.[25]

Mgr Talbot, of course, was quite beside himself with joy, though he found himself in some difficulty over whether the appointment should be attributed to himself or to a higher power:

My policy throughout was never to propose you *directly* to the Pope, but to make the others do so; so that both you and I always can say that it was not I who induced the Holy Father to name you, which would lessen the weight of your appointment. This I say, because many have said that your being named was all my doing. I do not say that the Pope did not know that I thought you the only man eligible, as I took care to tell him over and over again what was against all the other candidates; and in consequence he was almost driven into naming you. After he had named you the Holy Father said to me 'What a diplomatist you are to make what you wished come to pass'. Nevertheless I believe your appointment was specially directed by the Holy Ghost. . . . I did not think the Holy Father would have had the moral courage which it required to name you against so much opposition.[26]

Talbot was equally excited about the future. It would be necessary to make some arrangement about their correspondence in order not to arouse the susceptibilities of Propaganda. Barnabò and other officials were very jealous of those who enjoyed direct contact with the Pope.[27]

The old Catholics, so consistently traduced by Manning and Talbot, were generous in their welcome for the new Metropolitan. Manning found his reception as Archbishop so satisfactory that it could admit of but one explanation. 'I can ascribe all this', he told Talbot, 'only to the act of the Holy Father and the prayers that went with it.'[28] What did not, apparently, occur to him was that he might previously have underestimated the religion of those Catholics who happened to disagree with his particular views. On the contrary, his grateful wonder was all the more joyous because he felt himself to be the beneficiary of a miracle. Even the canons of Westminster, poor men, now came forward with their declarations of delight. Manning triumphantly registered, for Mgr Talbot's benefit, the long succession of civility. Religious orders, diocesan priests, professors at St Edmund's, Catholic aristocrats – 'Lord Herries, Lord Petre, Mr. Langdale, and many more' – all, through the ardour of their welcome, earned themselves favourable reference in Manning's letters to Rome.[29]

The bishops, too, hastened to make their peace. Ullathorne wrote in especially generous terms and gladly put his episcopal experience at Manning's disposal.[30] His friendship with Manning would have its ups and downs in the ensuing years, for he was ultra-sensitive about any attempt to interfere with the affairs of his Birmingham diocese, and never afraid to express his dislike of backstairs influence at Rome. There was, moreover, one kind of seniority that could never be reversed. 'My dear Sir,' Ullathorne would remind the Archbishop of Westminster, 'allow me to say that I taught the catechism with the mitre on my 'ead when you were still an 'eretic.'[31] Manning endured both Ullathorne's independence and his jocularity, because he realized that his hopes of maintaining harmony with the English hierarchy depended on their good relations. From the start he was determined to avoid the rifts which had plagued Wiseman's rule. He even asked Ullathorne whether it would be 'prudent, delicate and free from false interpretation if I were to write to Dr. Errington to say that in the event of his ever coming to London, I hope he would feel the assurance that my house would be his home'. Ullathorne thought this would be 'a little too much'.[32] In general, though, he was thoroughly appreciative of the efficient dispatch which the new Archbishop brought to business, a welcome change after the chaos of Wiseman's methods.

Manning was not so carried away by the euphoria attending his appointment that he failed to notice the occasional missing letter. All the Catholic lawyers and physicians had written, he observed, *with only one exception*. Again, though 'five Jesuits had written to me most warmly', he noted that the Jesuits of Farm Street had maintained an eloquent silence.[33] 'If only you saw the Farm Street faces . . .',[34] one of Newman's female devotees wrote to the Birmingham Oratory. Newman himself remained sternly conscious that Manning's assumption of archiepiscopal responsibilities could scarcely be a matter for congratulation. He did, however, allow himself some comment in a letter:

As to the new Archbishop, the appointment at least has the effect of making Protestants see, to their surprise, that Rome is not distrustful of converts, as such. On the other hand, it must be a great trial to our old Priesthood – to have a neophyte set over them all. Some will bear it very well – I think our Bishop will – but I cannot prophesy what turn things will take on the whole. He has a great power of winning men, where he chooses – witness the fact of his appointment – but whether he will care to win inferiors, or whether his talent extends to the case of inferiors as well as superiors, I do not know.[35]

Manning certainly did not succeed in winning Newman. Conscious of the need to unify English Catholics, he realized, with the help of a little prodding from Ullathorne,[36] that his elevation provided an opportunity to mend his fences with Newman. As early as 1854 Wiseman had informed Newman that he was about to become a bishop, a proposal no sooner explicitly made than tacitly dropped, to Newman's understandable distress. Manning had for some time wanted to rectify this *faux pas*, and he now reopened the possibility of creating Newman a bishop *in partibus infidelium*, that is, of giving him episcopal rank without tying him down to the administrative duties of a see. There is no reason to suppose that Manning was actuated by any sinister motives, but Newman's virtue appeared as outraged by this new proposal as it had formerly been by Wiseman's maladresse. The whole idea was obviously a plot: 'He wants to put me in the House of Lords and muzzle me.'[37]

So, when Manning sent an invitation to his consecration as Archbishop ('no one will know better than you how much I need your prayers'),[38] Newman seized the occasion to emphasize *his* aversion even to the thought of becoming a bishop.

I will readily attend your consecration – on one condition. . . . A year or two back I heard you were doing your best to get me made a Bishop in partibus. I heard this from several quarters, and I don't see how I can be mistaken. If so, your feeling towards me is not unlikely to make you attempt the same thing now. I risk the chance of your telling me that you have no such intention, to entreat you not to entertain it. If such an honour were offered to me, I should persistently decline it, very persistently; and I do not wish to pain the Holy Father, who has always been so kind to me, if such pain can be avoided. Your allowing me then to come to your consecration I shall take as a pledge, that you will have nothing to do with any such attempt.[39]

Manning could only reply that he would not force anyone to become a bishop against his will, a message which he sent on 4 June.[40] That same day he reflected that 'it is on second thoughts that I dislike anyone'. He was on retreat with the Passionists at Highgate, taking advantage of the opportunity both to look back on his life and to prepare himself for the tasks that lay ahead. The journal he kept during this retreat is of the highest interest.[41] His starting-point, as with any good Evangelical, was still a torturing consciousness of his own sinfulness: 'I have always had a great fear of death. . . . But I fear still more the first meeting with God. I cannot conceive my standing before Him and being saved. This comes from my not knowing whether I be worthy of love or of hatred. It seems impossible that in a life like mine there should not be an accumulation of sin which I do not see. When I to begin to analyse any one action of my life, I am self-condemned and I hide myself from myself.' His faults, he realized, were all too evident in his outer manner. 'By nature I am very irascible, and till the Grace of God converted me I was proud, cold and repulsive. Since then, I hope less so, but I have always been cold and distant except to those whom I personally loved.'

Yet alongside his consciousness of his failings, and alongside his fear of the Last Judgement, Manning also possessed, contradictorily enough, something of the Evangelical confidence that he would be saved. 'It has impressed itself vividly upon me that God has predestinated me to Eternal Life.' This came close to the Calvinist's belief in assured salvation, but Manning's hope was never unconditional. It had been purchased, it must continue to be purchased, at a heavy price. 'The way is by conformity to His Son. . . . His Image is the *Volto Sagro* which hangs over my bed at St. Mary's, the Sacred Countenance wounded and darkened by sorrow and suffering.' The loneliness which Manning endured and the enmity which he encountered were tokens that he was on the path to heaven:

When I entered the Church I had much to suffer, less from Protestants than from Catholics, less from old Catholics than from converts, excepting only the Chapter affair. In these fourteen years I have been, with all my strength put out, sometimes warding off blows, sometimes rowing at the oar, and I know that both in word and in will my character has changed from the passive state under the Fig Tree to an attitude of hard toil, sometimes also of warfare. In one sense I have become less charitable, and I know I have become, or at least have been accused of, imperiousness, presumptiveness, sharpness, suddenness and the like. But this has been, I believe, inevitable. When I was in a system of compromise I tried to mediate, reconcile and unite together those who differed. When I entered a system which, being divine, is definite and uncompromising, I threw myself with my whole soul and strength into its mind, will and action. So it must be to the end. Less definite, positive, un-compromising, aggressive, I can never be. God forbid!

That his harsh, unloved life-style was justified had been made abundantly clear. 'He has suffered me to try to convert souls to Him, which seems to imply that He has first converted my own.' And now his elevation came as a glorious confirmation that he was still upon his predestinate path. How could he ignore so many and obvious links between cause and effect? For instance, he had long kept a special devotion to the Holy Ghost. Every day he had addressed the Third Person of the Trinity in prayer. 'I searched for books upon it. I made notes to write about it. I began twice a book about it.' And what happens? The Holy Father, God's own vicar on earth, 'for a month asks the light of the Holy Spirit, and then overpassing all usages and precedents, says, "I am inspired to name M".' Manning believed in the Holy Ghost rather as Churchill and Napoleon believed in their sense of destiny.

He also found it significant that he had been raised by Pius IX, 'the most supernatural person I have ever seen'. Mgr Talbot ventured to assert that the Pope was not a saint, but Manning disagreed with him.[42]

Even with these assurances that his life had won favour, however, Manning knew that he could never drop his guard. 'I feel very deeply the danger of losing my soul by this elevation. If I am to be lifted up by it, it were better for me not only to have never been called out of a low state but to have been taken away from the evil that is to come. . . . I shall be in danger of vain glory, self-worship, forgetfulness of God, usurpation upon His rights, hardness towards the troublesome and repulsive.' It would be specially necessary to guard against intellectual and spiritual inflation 'because I know I am prone to it. I have seen it and the tarnish it leaves on a great mind and a great Christian' (perhaps a reference to Newman). Manning worried about his own lack of spirituality: his practical activity seemed only a cover for spiritual sloth. 'I am conscious how much more readily I turn to work than to prayer, how much more willingly I turn from prayer than from work.'

Yet if his past was acceptable to God, so might his future be, on the same terms of endeavour and suffering. 'My dear Lord, I willingly give myself to the Cross and the Work Thou hast laid upon me. I bless Thee for having called me to it. I count the work and the toil, the suffering and the Sorrow which may be before me as the highest crown I could receive on earth. Only let me save my own poor soul, and not stand empty before Thee at Thy coming.' To accomplish this prayer there could be no easy options, no currying favour with the powers of this world. Only one authority counted: 'It is by the mind and voice of the Holy Father that the mind and voice of the Spirit is made definite and known to me. . . . I desire always to derive my guidance and counsel immediately from Rome. This I learned in the case of N. Card. Wiseman in 1859, 1860. I desire to hold inviolate the doctrines and laws of the Church without compromise and I resolve by the Pallium of St Thomas so to do!' To emphasize this resolve Manning's first instinct had been to post out to Rome to receive consecration from the Pope in person, but it had been pointed out to him that the more tactful course would be to be consecrated by an English bishop in the midst of English bishops.

The determination that Manning took from his retreat, then, was that the Archbishop should continue in the same way as the priest, striving still harder against the faults which he so frankly acknowledged in himself.

In my relations with the Bishops, I desire to proceed with the utmost measure of humility, respect, forbearance. Next, with the Priests, endeavouring to treat them as Fathers and Brethren and Friends in the fullest sense. With this view to live among them as much as I can, inviting them to me, going to them, making them feel that they can say anything to me, come to confession to me, as all my dear Fathers and

Brethren at St. Mary's have done. . . . Next, for the Laity. . . . I wish that the
poorest may feel confident of a welcome as the richest. Now I resolve by God's help
to guard against coldness, haste, haughtiness and distance of manner. To be most of
all on guard when dealing with the poor or the humbled or the unhappy. To treat
priests as *alter Christus* with great respect both in word and bearing. To bear
contradiction without answering. To let time elapse before answering if I must. To
make others read over all letters in contentious correspondence. To indulge no
partialities in friendship and to watch against the formation of a clique or coterie
around me.

Of course these were counsels of perfection. No one knew better than
Manning 'the long interval between what I have written and what I am'. He
cited St Gregory: '*pulchrum hominem pinxi pictor foedus*'. Yet Manning
certainly struggled to bring his imperious nature into conformity with the
gospel of humility. The strain showed in his face, every nerve of which, as
one observer delicately phrased it, was alive to some vivid feeling. As he
emerged from his Highgate retreat the transparent pallor of his countenance
seemed barely to cover the skull beneath. 'Why have they given us an
Archbishop with one foot in the grave?'[43] demanded one witness of his
consecration. Another wrote that 'he looked like Lazarus coming out of the
tomb in cope and mitre, – a richly vested corpse, but very dignified and
placid'.[44] Appearances were deceptive. Earlier in the 1860s he had
effortlessly vaulted a five-bar gate at Ushaw,[45] and his athleticism proved a
better guide than his asceticism to the life span that lay before him. He
himself reckoned he still had a dozen years' work in him.[46] Within a few
months Canon Morris was hoping he would not kill himself with overwork.
'The amount of good he does is wonderful; I have never seen a sign of the
least weariness about him, and however pressed he may be, his readiness to
listen to everyone and to help everyone, and to take part in every good work,
I never saw in anyone in my life.'[47]

The direction which his work would take had been made clear even before
the consecration. In May 1865 a meeting had been called to approve and
ratify a scheme to build a metropolitan cathedral at Westminster as a
memorial to Cardinal Wiseman. Manning declared that the project was one
after his own heart; he would gladly take upon himself the labour of carrying
it out. On the other hand, there was a work which must come first, and that
was the building of the *spiritual* Church within the diocese. More
specifically, he must provide for the thousands of poor children who were
being lost to the Church for want of any proper Catholic education. The old
Catholics at the meeting quickly directed the discussion back to its original
purpose: £16,000 was raised on the spot to institute the fund for the new
cathedral. But Manning's priorities remained clear. 'Could I leave 20,000

children without education, and drain my friends and my flock to pile up stones and bricks?'[48] As far as the cathedral was concerned he would content himself with buying up the land. He purchased two sites on either side of Carlisle Place in 1868 and 1869, and later (1883) exchanged this ground for a better position which became available when the Middlesex county prison in Tothill Fields was abandoned. It is the former prison site that Westminster cathedral now occupies. The building was not begun until after Manning's death, but thanks to his policies there were thousands more Catholics to fill it than there might otherwise have been.*

Within a year of his consecration Manning had issued three important pastorals on the education question. His basic philosophy was still the same as it had been in his sermon on National Education in 1838: education without religion was no education at all. The difference was that 'religion' now meant Roman Catholicism. The theory might be simple; the practical problems were daunting. Manning was faced with the task of providing sufficient primary school places for the poor of his diocese, of establishing orphanages and reformatories for destitute Irish children, and of rescuing hundreds of Catholic children who were losing contact with their religion in the aggressively Protestant atmosphere of the workhouses.

His great Pastoral of 8 June 1866 proposed the establishment of a diocesan education fund. That in itself was not an especially original proposal; what was new was the force of his appeal, which surely derived as much from the Evangelical background of his youth as from his Catholic present. He challenged the wealthier members of his flock to make atonement for the sterility of their lives:

Reckon up what you spend on yourselves, upon your houses and costly ornaments, upon your feasting and profusion of luxury, upon your jewels and baubles, upon your softness, refinement, self-indulgence in clothing and apparel, upon the pleasures of the senses, the excitement of an hour, the caprice of imagination, on nothings, each of which cost [sic] the maintenance of an orphan, upon waste and squandering which would save whole families from perversion.[49]

These thrusts had been preceded by an anonymous article which *The Month* published in March and April 1866 under Manning's auspices, and which may well have been written by him. The subject matter, the plight of Catholic orphans, answered well to the title, '*De Profundis*', but the style was satirical and sharply pointed against worldly Catholics. The author introduced Sir Phelim, a Catholic MP who never troubled to defend his

---

* Manning's and Wiseman's coffins were moved from Kensal Green to the cathedral crypt in January 1907.

religion in the House of Commons. There was also Lady O'Toole, who complained of having to put up with horror stories about orphans every Sunday; really, if the music were not so excellent she would be inclined to give up her place in the Belgravia chapel which she patronized.[50]

This was not the style in which Wiseman had addressed the Catholic aristocracy, yet whether as a consequence or in spite of Manning's methods his appeals were answered. Immediately after the meeting called on 14 June 1865 to set up the diocesan education fund, Manning wrote delightedly to Talbot: 'The support given me surpasses all my hopes. Before we went to the meeting every post brought in contributions. Donations about £2,200; subscriptions £2,300 a year. In the meeting we had £1,200 more, making nearly £6,000. . . . Lord Petre, Lord Edward Howard, Lord Stafford, Sir R. Gerard, Hope Scott and many more have helped me very largely.'[51] By the spring of 1867 twenty more Catholic schools had been opened and 1,100 more places made available.[52] This was only the beginning. Manning kept up the impetus in the years ahead, devoting every Lenten Pastoral, and many others besides, to the needs of poor children.

It was never his idea, however, that the wealthy might buy themselves into heaven with regular cash payments. To give money was the coldest form of charity, often indulged simply to avoid the trouble of becoming involved with the problems of one's neighbour. 'Personal care of the sick or the sorrowful or the sinful', he would write in his book *The Eternal Priesthood* (1883), 'is more precious in God's sight than all gold and silver.'[53] On that principle Manning always deprecated bazaars and lotteries as a means of raising money. 'Even our amusements have taken a pious turn,' he wrote scornfully in 1863: 'we have concerts, theatricals, balls, excursions and the like, for religious ends. The world itself, it seems, is becoming pious.' Ultimately, he believed, such charitable forms would be of no avail. 'Concerts will not move mountains and the Church in England has mountains in its path. . . . Catholics have taught the world to sell all and follow Christ; that His words are to be taken to the letter now as in the beginning, in England as in Palestine.'[54]

Certainly some Catholics had taught that. Many English Catholics, however, were aware that less demanding interpretations of the New Testament were available than those which now issued forth from Westminster. Newman, for instance, in electing to become an Oratorian rather than to espouse a more rigorous rule, had remarked: 'I must own I feel the notion of giving up property [to] try my faith very much.'[55] His faith, then, was not likely to solicit any heroic sacrifice from his disciples, and his restraint in this regard did nothing to diminish the old Catholic opinion of his wisdom and holiness. In contrast, Manning's fundamentalist approach appeared to them dangerously like Methodist enthusiasm. Indeed, Manning never tired of expressing admiration for Wesley, a figure whom Newman detested.[56] 'If it had not been for the teaching of John Wesley,' Manning wrote, 'no man can tell how deep in degradation England would have sunk.'[57] Wesley had touched men's hearts, and that, for Manning, was the first condition of all charitable activity. Manning insisted that rich Catholics should not leave their charity in collecting boxes (though they should certainly keep them replenished); they should get to know the poor, and seek to share their lives. To this end he even suggested in 1866 that they should take up working with their hands and sell the results of their labour for the benefit of the less fortunate.[58] That was utopian indeed.

Manning's efforts to goad Catholic consciences into active involvement with the plight of their co-religionists sprang from policy as well as from conviction. When he remonstrated about Catholic children trapped in Protestant workhouses *The Times* made the not unjustified sneer that his complaints simply amounted to an admission that 'there are good Protestant philanthropists ready to take in hand young Catholic vagrants and delinquents unable to find a shelter in their own communion'.[59] Manning laboured hard and successfully to nullify this criticism by developing orphanages and reformatories, as well as the so-called 'industrial schools' in which neglected children were boarded. The government inspector would judge that the industrial school established at Ilford under the managership of the repentant Searle was the best institution of its type in the country.[60]

It was one thing to provide places in these and ordinary schools, another to extricate Catholic children from the workhouses. A series of Acts had theoretically permitted their transfer, but no legislation had conferred powers strong enough to overcome the obstinacy of the Poor Law guardians, who were often not at all the types to imagine that they were doing a child a favour by delivering him into the hands of the papists. The ethos which the Guardians inflicted was militantly Protestant, with Catholic children liable to be informed that their co-religionists would be sent to hell with copies of the Bible in their hands. Between 1859 and 1867 the workhouses in London surrendered only four of the thousands of Catholic children in their care.[61] Manning had been in contact with the Government from the 1850s in search of a means of thwarting the Guardians' recalcitrance, and finally in 1866 and 1868 amendments to the Poor Law were passed under which the Guardians could be compelled to give up children. Manning's influence with Gladstone, who was now

Leader of the House of Commons, proved useful in this connection. It was a case of Gladstone's feelings for natural justice overcoming his antipathy towards Roman Catholicism. Both in Government and Opposition he urged Manning's cause over the workhouse children. Manning was duly grateful. 'I write one word to thank you for your kindness in watching and supporting the Poor Law Bill,' he wrote in September 1868. 'It is a great act of justice for which we have worked, waited and prayed. I am very glad that you took part in its completion.'[62]

Some Poor Law Guardians fought to the last ditch against surrendering Catholic children, and it was 1884 before Manning could declare that not a single Catholic child remained in the care of the workhouses. Already by 1869, though, the *Tablet* could boast of 'a second chapter in the history of Catholic emancipation', a victory won this time not against the Government but with the Government against the Poor Law Guardians, those 'petty potentates who love to feel their power and make the weak feel it long after rulers have learned fairness and laws have been framed justly'.[63]

Manning's determination to ensure that poor children should not be lost to the Faith shows him at his best, his concern for the unfortunate and his pastoral zeal combining with his great administrative ability to secure effective action. If only his work could always have been directed towards such practical objectives, from which no Catholic could reasonably dissent, there would never have been any shadow upon his reputation. He would be remembered for what he was, easily the most accomplished and beneficent man of affairs that the Church has possessed in England since the Reformation. An archbishop, however, is responsible for more than the rescue of souls; he must maintain them in the way of apostolic truth, a task that begged many difficult questions which Manning found rather too easy to answer.

One of his early problems was that posed by the Association for the Promotion of the Unity of Christendom. This organization, founded in 1857, boasted 8,000 members by 1865: 6,700 Anglicans, 300 Greek Orthodox, and 1,000 Roman Catholics. Manning was certainly right to judge that its proclaimed ideal was quite unrealizable, and that the Anglicans involved were a wholly unrepresentative minority. In any case, since there was but one true Church, this talk of union with other Churches was self-contradictory nonsense, dangerous nonsense too, because it might prevent those without the fold from stepping inside. 'Our mission', he grandly insisted, 'is not only to a section or to a fraction who may be approaching nearer to us, but to the whole mass of the English people.' In this connection he made it clear that his sympathies extended as much to Non-Conformists as to Anglicans, perhaps more. 'They [the Non-Conformists] are marked by a multitude of high qualities of zeal, devotion to duty, conscientious fidelity to what they believe.'[64] There was hope that such earnest seekers might find the truth, but a pastoral letter summarily dismissed any tendency towards accommodation. 'Compromise, concession, conditions, transactions, explanations which soften Divine decrees and evade the precision of infallible declarations of the Church, are not inspirations of the Holy Ghost.'[65] Secure in that knowledge he had persuaded the Holy Office in Rome to issue a harsh letter (September 1864) condemning the delusive dreams of the APUC enthusiasts.[66]

In the autumn of 1865 there appeared Dr Pusey's *Eirenicon*, which maintained the counter view (once espoused by Manning) that the Church of England was 'a portion of Christ's Holy Catholic Church, and a means of restoring visible unity'. The great obstacle to attaining this end, Dr Pusey considered, was the extreme ultramontane opinions voiced by the likes of Manning and Ward, and the extravagant devotions to the Virgin indulged in by rabid converts. These animadversions elicited an open letter from Newman, who seized the opportunity to make some feline thrusts at his Catholic opponents under the cover of defending the Catholic religion. Of course there were excesses among the converts, he admitted, but surely Dr Pusey did not imagine that the outpourings of extremists like Faber and Ward represented the true spirit of the Church? 'They are in no sense spokesmen for English Catholics, and they would not stand in the place of those who have a real title to such an office.' Whether the Archbishop of Westminster possessed such a title was left deliberately obscure: 'I put him aside because of his office.'[67] Newman had contrived to make his point without exposing his own flank.

Rage and frustration were extreme in the ultramontane camp. 'Dr. Newman is more English than the English,' complained Mgr Talbot in a letter to Manning; 'his spirit must be crushed.'[68] W. G. Ward had not required Newman's 'Letter to Pusey' to reach the same conclusion. He was fearful of Manning's conciliatory instincts. 'Is it not dangerous to speak of J. H. N. with *simple* sympathy?' he had demanded on the day of the new Archbishop's consecration. 'If it is true (and I for one have no doubt at all) that he is exercising a most powerful influence in favour of what is *in fact* (though he doesn't think so) (1) Disloyalty to the Vicar of Christ, and (2) Worldliness – is not harm done by conveying the impression that there is no cause for distrust?'[69] The odd thing about Ward was the way in which he accompanied his campaign against Newman with protestations of deep affection and reverence for the hero of his youth. Newman not unnaturally came to take a cynical view of this manner of proceeding. 'Ward says he loves me so, that he should like to pass an eternity with me but that whenever he sees Manning he makes him creep – (I have not his exact words) – yet that Manning has the truth and I have not.'[70]

In pursuit of that truth Ward now wrote a reply to Newman's 'Letter to Pusey', to be published in the *Dublin Review*. Manning, however, meant to avoid a row. Having established that Newman had some support for his opinions among the bishops, he prevented the publication of Ward's article even though it defended his own point of view. 'Any internal variance', he explained, 'would be sure to be seized and used by the public of this country and the Protestants as a division in the Church. This ought to be averted at any personal cost. And I am most anxious that Dr Newman should be spared all pain.'[71] Manning even brought himself to write a friendly letter to Newman about his answer to Pusey: 'I thank you for doing, so much more fully, that which I am going to attempt.'[72] Newman acknowledged this gesture, Manning told Ullathorne, in 'the driest possible'[73] way. If he suspected the Archbishop of insincerity he was not far wrong, for Manning had written in a very different tone to Talbot.

This letter, dated 25 February 1866, is the frankest written exposition which he ever gave of his antipathy to Newman:

What you write about Dr. Newman is true. Whether he knows it or not, he has become the centre of those who hold low views about the Holy See, are anti-Roman, cold and silent, to say no more, about the Temporal Power, national, English, critical of Catholic devotions, and always on the lower side. I see no danger of a Cisalpine Club rising again, but I see much danger in an English Catholicism of which Newman is the highest type. It is the old Anglican, patristic, literary, Oxford tone transplanted into the Church. It takes the line of deprecating exaggerations, foreign devotions, Ultramontanism, anti-national sympathies. In one word, it is worldly Catholicism, and it will have the worldly on its side, and will deceive many.[74]

Holding such views Manning was bound to be concerned when, in 1866, the question of Newman's establishing a branch of the Oratory in Oxford once more materialized. Newman tended to imply that the whole idea was being forced upon him by Ullathorne, who was still conscious of the need to expand Catholic representation in the town. There was much hand-wringing. 'The very seeing Oxford again,' Newman wrote to a friend, 'since I am not one with it, would be a cruel thing – it is like the dead coming to the dead. Oh dear, dear, how I dread it – but it seems to be the will of God, and I do not know how to draw back.'[75] Well, not buying land in Oxford would have been a start. Although Newman had sold his original site off St Giles early in 1865, he acquired a fresh plot in St Aldgate's Street at the end of that year, to which he added in 1866.

Whatever Ullathorne may have envisaged, Newman stated quite openly that he meant to be associated with the university. 'Cardinal Barnabò should clearly apprehend that I feel no calling to go to Oxford, except it be in order to take care of Catholic undergraduates or to convert graduates.'[76] He conceded one of Manning's main objections, that his presence in the university would encourage Catholic parents to send their children there. He agreed, too, that Oxford was a very dangerous place for faith and morals . . . 'but then I say that *all places are dangerous*, – the world is dangerous. I do not believe that Oxford is more dangerous than Woolwich, than the army, than London, – and I think you cannot keep young men under glass cases.'[77] The only evidence that Newman could find for the contention that Oxford undermined faith was that 'Weld-Blundell ducked a Puseyite in Mercury, and Redington has been talking loosely about the Temporal Power in Rome'.[78]

All the same, Newman must have known that he was crossing the Church's declared principles in his willingness to be associated with Oxford undergraduates, and he must have known also that Manning, as the chief representative of the Church in England, would be bound to try to thwart him. 'I think this of him,' Newman told a friend in January 1867, 'he wishes me no ill, but he is determined to bend or break all opposition. He has an iron will, and resolves to have his own way. . . . He wanted to gain me over; now, he will break me, if he can.'[79]

That was more than a little melodramatic. Yet it was certainly true that Manning meant to prevent Newman's becoming involved with the *university* of Oxford. Both men set about capturing support in Rome, but of course Manning's contacts were infinitely better placed. Mgr Talbot was alerted. 'I think Propaganda can hardly know the effects of Dr. Newman going to Oxford,' Manning wrote to him in the hope of rectifying this ignorance. 'The English national spirit is spreading amongst Catholics and we shall have dangers.'[80] Manning knew that Propaganda could hardly refuse what it was somewhat speciously being asked to grant, namely the opening of an Oratory in the *town* of Oxford, but Rome was not to be duped. The permission for an Oratory in Oxford which Ullathorne received at the end of 1866 was given on the condition that young Catholics should not be attracted to the university.[81] There was also a secret injunction that Newman himself should not reside in Oxford, a prohibition that came from the Pope himself.[82] Manning later claimed he had been ignorant of this ban,[83] but he was certainly not ignorant of how His Holiness had come to concern himself with such a trivial matter.

Manning wanted Rome to make a definitive pronouncement against Oxford. Vaughan was at headquarters, proving in every way a loyal disciple. One should not scruple, he wrote back to Manning, at removing Newman from Oxford 'with a pitchfork',[84] if he still harboured any ambitions of opening a college there. In an interview with the Pope Vaughan emphasized that Newman was not a person who could be relied upon, with his 'liberal' and 'national' views. These were terms that never failed to arouse Pius's fears, and Vaughan was able to render a most satisfactory report to Manning: 'The Holy Father was very attentive, but said little; only this, that N. was very vain, that he had expressed his readiness to obey the Pope.' Further, whatever Manning's difficulties with Propaganda in the past, Vaughan was able to assure him that nothing would be denied to the Archbishop of Westminster. 'You are all powerful at Propaganda. Talbot says that whatever you distinctly ask for will be granted, even though the Bishops be opposed to it. So also with the Pope, who trusts his Archbishop but not much his Bishops.'[85]

In the summer of 1867 Propaganda declared that 'a youth can scarcely, or not scarcely even, go to Oxford without throwing himself into a proximate occasion of mortal sin'.[86] It was still open to the Birmingham Oratory to establish a branch in Oxford, but Newman could hardly pursue his declared aim of ministering to Catholics in the university in direct defiance of Rome's pronouncement. He therefore threw up the whole scheme, not without some expressions of relief. 'All along I have professed and felt indifference, reluctance, to go to Oxford'.[87] He did not, however, seem at all disposed to thank Manning for his deliverance. And so the legend was allowed to grow, assiduously fostered by Newman's acolytes, that the harsh Archbishop had come between a dear old man and his most heartfelt desire. Feeling ran high on both sides. When one of Manning's supporters suggested to a Newmanite that Newman's conversion was 'the greatest calamity to the Church in England', the reply came pat: 'No, the greatest calamity was the death of a woman' – Caroline Manning.[88]

The animosity between the two men was exacerbated by an article which appeared in the April 1867 number of the *Weekly Register*. The Roman correspondent had seen fit to imply that it was Newman's questionable orthodoxy that lay at the root of Rome's objection to his meddling with Oxford. 'Only an Ultramontane without a taint in his fidelity could enter such an arena as that of Oxford life with results to the advantage of the faith in England.'[89] Manning had nothing to do with this slur, which he regretted as much as anyone, the more so when the Catholic laity, who appreciated a martyr to ultramontanism, rallied to Newman's side. A petition signed by over two hundred distinguished Catholics, with the old recusant families to the fore, informed Newman of their conviction that 'every blow that touches you inflicts a wound upon the Catholic Church in this country'.[90] The Westminster Chapter also planned a petition of the clergy in Newman's favour, which the Archbishop only narrowly managed to thwart.[91] Manning, in fact, suddenly found himself confronted with just the kind of split in English Catholicism that he had striven to avert.

To make matters worse, the laity's address to Newman induced a brainstorm in Mgr Talbot, who was now but three years removed from the lunatic asylum where he was destined to pass his final years:

What is the province of the laity? [he furiously demanded of Manning]. To hunt, to shoot, to entertain? These matters they understand, but to meddle with ecclesiastical matters they have no right at all, and this affair of Newman is a matter purely ecclesiastical. . . . Dr. Newman is the most dangerous man in England, and you will see that he will make use of the laity against your Grace. You must not be afraid of him.

There followed an ill-disguised threat. 'It will require much prudence, but you must be firm, as the Holy Father still places his confidence in you; but if you yield and do not fight the battle of the Holy See against the detestable spirit growing up in England, he will begin to regret Cardinal Wiseman, who knew how to keep the laity in order.'[92] Assuredly Newman had been correct when he had written to Pusey in 1865: 'Manning is under the lash as well as others. There are men who would remonstrate with him, and complain of him at Rome, if he did not go to all lengths – and in his position he can't afford to get into hot water, even tho' he were sure to get out of it.'[93]

Manning's difficulty was that maintaining his position at Rome and keeping English Catholics together were objectives that it was not always easy to reconcile. In 1867, for instance, Manning ruffled several feathers at home when, apparently at Talbot's behest, he replaced Neve, the Rector of the English College at Rome, who was known to be sympathetic to Newman. Neve asked Talbot why he had been dismissed. 'He replied that I was so fresh from Eton and Oxford that I did not understand Catholic young men. I remarked that he was fresher from both places.'[94] Neve's successor was one of Manning's Oblates, name of O'Callaghan. The bishops were furious. 'Unless we take due notice of these doings, we may as well have Talbot Pope,' complained Bishop Brown. 'Surely no one of us except the Archbishop will employ O'Callaghan as agent.'[95] Soon Ullathorne was complaining of 'a mischievous camarilla' at Rome, which sought to 'pull down the bishops and clergy of their country'.[96]

Manning was sharply aware of the danger that Newman might become the central figure around whom the opposition to his rule would cluster. He patiently explained some facts of life to Mgr Talbot. He had not been influenced by fear or neutrality in failing to slap down the laity for their address to Newman, but by the necessity of holding the English bishops together. 'A word or act of mine towards Dr. Newman might divide the bishops and throw some on his side. . . . The chief aim of the Anglicans has been to set Dr. Newman and myself in conflict.' So Manning professed himself delighted that Cardinal Barnabò, in writing of the permission given by Propaganda for an Oratory in the town of Oxford, had described it as a favour which the Archbishop of Westminster had secured 'to serve an old friend'. It was true enough that Manning had not objected to this limited permission: there were no grounds on which he could possibly have done so. But it was surely disingenuous, granted all the circumstances, to accept credit for this fact. Barnabò's statement, he blandly informed Talbot, 'has given me untold strength here at this time'.[97]

It was precisely that mode of operation that Newman found so antipathetic in Manning. He had already, earlier in 1867, given vent to his feelings in a letter to Ullathorne written after he had heard of Manning's desire to come and see him at the Oratory. 'I will say to your Lordship frankly, that I cannot trust the Archbishop. It seems to me that he never wishes to see a man except for his own ends.'[98] Doubtless Ullathorne was not displeased to discover that his warning against Manning had been so closely heeded.

Manning continued to work for the restoration of good relations. In August 1867 he wrote to Newman inviting a frank examination of their differences. What he sought, most certainly, was rather the unity of English Catholicism than the recovery of an old friendship. This was not an ignoble aim, however, nor did Manning make a generous response difficult:

It would give me a great consolation [he wrote] to know from you anything in which you have thought me wanting towards you. I have seen that something has come between us, and that representations contrary to truth have been made to you – perhaps to both of us; and I sensibly felt that the separation of an old friendship was both painful and evil, and that the use made of our supposed variance, both by Catholics and by Protestants, was adverse to that which we count more precious than any private friendship. It would, therefore, give me a real happiness to enter with you into the openest and fullest explanation of all my acts and thoughts towards you. I shall be ready to do so by letter if you will, but it would be far easier to both of us, overfull as our time is, to do so by word.[99]

Newman's rejoinder was marked by a devastating frankness – by an uncompromising honesty as his admirers would insist – that immediately cut out any hope of reconciliation. He freely admitted the difficulty that lay between them:

You must kindly bear with me, though I seem rude to you, while I give you the real interpretation of it [i.e., his feeling towards Manning]. I say frankly, then, and as a duty to friendship, that it is a distressing mistrust, which now for four years past I have been unable in prudence to dismiss from my mind, and which is but my own share of a general feeling (though men are slow to express it, especially to your immediate friends) that you are difficult to understand. I wish I could get myself to believe that the fault was my own, and that your words, your bearing, and your implications, ought, though they have not served, to prepare me for your acts.[100]

This exhibition of cold-blooded self-righteousness was every bit as repellent as Manning's political sleight of hand. After this preliminary interchange nothing remained for these two great Catholics but to wrangle copiously and unprofitably about who had first wronged whom, until the correspondence petered out in a mutual intention to say Masses for one another.[101]

This remedy seemed to produce little effect. In 1869 a theological controversialist named Ffoulkes provoked another row when he published a pamphlet in which he accused Manning of having deliberately suppressed the letter that Newman had written to Rome in 1860 offering to explain his 'Consulting the Faithful' article. (Propaganda had finally become aware of the existence of this letter in 1867.) Manning was, not unnaturally, furious, though it was Ullathorne and not Newman whom he accused of originating this slander.[102] Newman he merely requested to provide a copy of a pamphlet to which Ffoulkes had referred. This demand sufficed, however, to convince Newman that he was suspected of complicity with Ffoulkes. 'My dear Archbishop,' he wrote, 'I can only repeat what I said when you last heard from me. I do not know whether I am on my head or my heels, when I have active relations with you. In spite of my friendly feelings, this is the judgement of my intellect. Yours affectionately in Christ, John H. Newman.'[103] The only merit of this performance was that it relieved Manning for some years of the necessity to waste time corresponding with Newman.

He had, in all conscience, many more important matters to engross his attention. Manning never made the mistake of imagining that the prosperity of the Catholic faith in England depended upon the caprices of intellectual Oxford converts. On the contrary, he told Talbot in 1866, 'The thing which will save us from low views about the Mother of God and the Vicar of our Lord is the million Irish in England, and the sympathy of the Catholics in

Ireland. . . . I am thankful to know that they have no sympathy for the watered, literary, worldly Catholicism of certain Englishmen.'[104] Even the Irish, though, had faults. In particular, they were rarely as sober as Manning could have wished them. Their behaviour at Christmas led him to ban Midnight Mass at that festival;[105] their celebration of St Patrick's Day usually degenerated into drunken rout.

Manning understood the pressures which the Irish in England were under, and that their drunkenness was a symptom of radically wretched lives. 'If I were an Irish hodman I should be a drunkard,' he once remarked.[106] He found the vinous excesses of English Catholics infinitely more culpable.[107] But drink did not imprison the rich in a state of material as well as moral degradation, nor did it earn them the contempt of their fellow citizens. Manning wanted to make the Irish working class respectable, to integrate it fully into English life. He remembered how, when he had been at Bayswater, he had left some petition to the House of Commons out for signature, only to discover that a young Irishman had upset an ink-bottle over it as a protest against the English Parliament.[108] Manning would have preferred a dissident to be in a rage to get *into* Parliament. If the Irish were ever to be taken seriously by the English, if they were ever to deliver themselves from their appalling plight, they must first become sober.

Such were the considerations that drew Manning towards the temperance movement, a campaign for which he soon discovered great natural affinity. Self-denial had ever been one of his cardinal principles: the rejection of immediate gratification for some greater, more distant advantage was the root of his entire religious outlook. The English Catholics never felt the same enthusiasm for this principle, and least of all when it was applied to drink. Fortunately temperance societies were often run by militant Protestants, which gave the conscientious papist a wonderful excuse to recoil with horror. Catholics also remembered, conveniently enough, that it was heresy to impute to drink itself the evils that were more properly attributable to the individuals who misused it. Their conclusion was that the temperance crusade was not, somehow, one in which any gentleman should involve himself. Newman expressed this attitude when he remarked airily that he could not make up his mind whether there were too many or too few pubs in London.[109] Manning, who had taken the trouble to visit the squalid tenements where whole families lived in single rooms, was never in doubt upon that point. He knew that in such conditions a drunken father or mother not only destroyed their own lives but involved the next generation also in total degradation.

Even so, he proceeded at first with caution as well as with determination in his battle against drink. He did not himself rush to take the pledge of total abstinence. In fact he told a meeting of Catholic teetotallers (a rare tribe) at Spitalfields in 1866 that his doctor would not allow him to change his habit of drinking half a glass of wine twice daily. 'Change your doctor,' came the ribald response.[110] Yet Manning soon achieved a real success in tackling the St Patrick's Day embarrassment. Under the Truce of St Patrick, instituted in 1867, any Catholic who abstained upon the feast day and the days before and after received a forty-day indulgence.[111] Perhaps it was this offer which induced the country's main temperance organization, the United Kingdom Alliance, to send a deputation to Manning, and to ply him with literature in support of their cause. He was especially impressed by the 1853–4 report of the House of Commons Select Committee on Public Houses. 'When I read it I felt to enter a new world, so horrible and very sad, so repulsive . . . that it seemed to me for the first time opened to know the real condition of our people . . . it seemed to me as if I were going from chamber to chamber, from abomination to abomination in the prophets' vision in Jerusalem.'[112]

The United Kingdom Alliance, notwithstanding its Non-Conformist associations, appeared to Manning to be the only organization powerful enough to combat this vast evil, which was strongly sustained in parliament by the political interest of the drink trade. In 1867 he attended the UK Alliance's Annual General Meeting, the first time since the Reformation that a Catholic bishop had allowed his name to be linked with a purely social, non-religious cause in England. Two years later Manning appeared as a witness before a Commons committee set up to investigate the possibility of Sunday closing. When, to his disgust, this committee recommended against any further legislation, he came out in open support of the UK Alliance plan to put local ratepayers in control of licensing within their own areas. Meanwhile, he tried the unlikely expedient of trying to influence Catholic publicans in his diocese to close on Saturday nights and Sundays.[113] Within a few years of his becoming Archbishop the campaign against drink had emerged as one of the great causes of his life.

His predominantly Irish flock also stimulated another of his later crusades, his determination to persuade English Governments to do justice to Ireland. The Archbishop of Westminster was a natural intermediary between the Irish bishops, who were the most important influence in that unhappy country, and the Government. Manning found this role of go-between, which involved him in important negotiations with the Cabinet, most congenial. He established the closest possible contact with Archbishop Cullen of Dublin, and kept himself *au fait* politically by inviting Irish MPs to his Tuesday evening receptions. As it happened, Manning's appointment as Archbishop coincided with the return of the Irish Question to the forefront of English politics. In the mid-1860s the activities of the Fenians, first as instigators of armed rebellion, then as terrorists in England, forced English politicians to turn their attention to the dreaded subject, which they had determinedly ignored so long as circumstances permitted.

Manning's attitude to Ireland was compounded of oddly opposed elements in his character. One side of his imagination was captivated by the idea of England's imperial mission. 'As the Greeks and Latins of old,' he wrote, 'so the Saxon blood and speech are now spread throughout the earth, prelude now as then, of some profound design of God.' He liked to claim that 'without ceasing to be an Englishman I have got nationalism out of my soul',[114] but that only held as regards his choice of Church. He described himself as 'one who next after that which is not of this world desires earnestly to see maintained the unity, solidity, and prosperity of the British Empire'.[115] In his later years radical allies would be astonished by his sudden swoops into chauvinism. 'He combines the spirit of a Palmerston with the philanthropy of a Shaftesbury,' wrote W. T. Stead.[116] And Dilke found him 'a ferocious Jingo'.[117]

On the other hand, his intense feeling for the underdog and his natural love of justice, as well as his position as Metropolitan to a million Irish, made him bitterly conscious of the ills which England had inflicted upon her neighbour. England as an abstract idea might work upon his deepest instincts; England as a fact incurred his fiercest criticism. He never had any illusions about the nature of English rule in Ireland. 'I am convinced that we hold Ireland by force,' he told Gladstone in February 1865, 'not only against the will of the majority, but in violation of all rights, natural and supernatural – that is of political justice and religious conscience.'[118] For a clear-sighted, compassionate blimp there was but one course – to insist upon the satisfaction of Irish grievances, not only as a necessary act of restitution, but also as a means of restoring the honour of the English race and of maintaining the integrity of the Empire. Manning saw how Ireland looked across the Atlantic, 'with her back turned to England and her face to the west',[119] and was fearful that American republicanism would end by crushing the imperial ideal.

He wanted Ireland to be placed on the same footing as Australia or Canada, where there was complete religious equality between religious denominations. This might seem to imply that Manning was already an advocate of some measure of Home Rule. Yet his continued insistence on the parallel between Italy and Ireland militated against Irish autonomy. 'I have warned those who have praised, flattered, fostered, abetted, justified, glorified the Italian revolution that the same principles would recoil upon themselves . . . the Church condemns them both in Italy and Ireland.'[120] Presumably then the Church also condemned Irish self-government. The great thing about being Archbishop of Westminster as opposed to Prime Minister was that one was not necessarily called upon to resolve potential inconsistencies in clear-cut policy statements. It was far easier for Manning to lecture Gladstone upon what ought to be done in Ireland than it was for Gladstone to put these no doubt excellent ideas into practice. In fact Gladstone was growing a little tired of Manning's homilies. When he lost his Oxford University seat in July 1865, Manning had deemed the moment fit, in sending his commiseration, to issue a warning against extremism in politics. Gladstone wrote back politely enough, but he communicated his real feelings to Bishop Wilberforce: 'The man is gone out . . . and has left nothing but the priest. No shirt collar ever took such a quantity of starch.'[121]

The poet Spenser anatomized the intractable nature of the Irish problem as early as 1599. 'There have been divers good plots and wise counsels cast about the reformation of that realm, but they say it is the fatal destiny of that land that no purposes whatsoever which are meant for her good, will prosper and take effect.'[122] Or is the fatal destiny not rather that, with the exception of Gladstone, no great English politician has conceived a plan for her welfare that has not been tainted by narrow calculations of party advantage? Manning, who possessed a keen political sense, was also guilty in this respect. For all his professions of love for the Irish, he tended to see the Irish problem too exclusively in the Catholic context. He realized immediately, for example, that the Fenian outrages provided an excellent opportunity to demonstrate the importance of the Church's influence to the English Government: 'I have never known a more propitious moment', he told Archbisop Cullen of Dublin in 1866, 'for making the Government feel that they cannot do without us.'[123]

It was a time, then, for stressing the civic virtues of Catholicism. England should not undermine the faith of Ireland because that faith was the only principle of loyalty or submission in the country. 'Show me an Irishman who has lost the Faith,' Manning told a Birmingham meeting in 1867, 'and I will show you a Fenian.'[124] But when Ullathorne reversed the argument – 'Show me a Fenian and I will show you a bad Catholic'[125] – Manning would have none of it. Irishmen who joined the movement were not so much evil as misguided. 'My heart bleeds for those who are deceived by their higher and nobler affections. They believe themselves to be serving in a sacred and holy war for their country and religion.'[126] If they hated England the reason was obvious enough. 'Has that animosity nothing to do with the three confiscations of almost every acre in Ireland, and the folly of striving for more than three hundred years to force the Reformation upon a Catholic people?'[127] Give the Irish justice, abolish the Protestant supremacy, and the violence would cease.

Manning vigorously urged this line in his 1867 Lenten pastoral, copies of which were dispatched to both Gladstone and Disraeli. A month later, in May 1867, Gladstone announced in the House of Commons that the time was nigh when the position of the Anglican Church in Ireland would have to be looked fully and fairly in the face. It would be too much to claim that the Liberal leader had acted according to the dictates of the Archbishop of Westminster. A politician must consider Commons majorities as well as the merits of the case. Nevertheless, throughout the 1860s Manning had kept the Irish cause constantly before Gladstone's mind, surely contributing to the process of fermentation, if not to the ultimate issue therefrom.

In 1867–8 there was a minority Conservative Government, Disraeli succeeding the Earl of Derby as Prime Minister in February 1868. Disraeli was partial to talking about creating religious equality in Ireland by 'levelling up', i.e. by endowing the Presbyterians and the Roman Catholics as well as the Church of England. In practice, however, the only gesture that he dared to attempt was the creation of a Roman Catholic university in Dublin, with a charter but no money. This measure was initially well received, and Manning confidently took on himself the hazardous task of interpreting to the Prime Minister (Disraeli) exactly what the Leader of the Opposition (Gladstone) felt about the matter. 'I am able to say of my own knowledge', he wrote to Disraeli, 'that any favourable proposal from the Government on the subject of the Catholic university would not only encounter no opposition, but would be assisted.'[128] He also left Disraeli with the impression that the Irish bishops would be in favour of the scheme. In both cases his advice proved over-sanguine, with fatal consequences for the Conservative Government.

Disraeli felt that he had been stabbed in the back.[129] Once out of office he took his revenge by novel writing, sketching Manning in *Lothair* (1870) as Cardinal Grandison, the Machiavellian prelate who plots to secure the wealth and influence of the hero for the Catholic church. Disraeli reflected the ignorance and indifference of English society concerning Catholic affairs when he has Grandison advise that his ward should go to Oxford. It was also unlikely that by this stage in his career Manning would have emulated Grandison by preaching at a Jesuit church. Nevertheless, Disraeli well caught Manning's peculiar combination of worldly aplomb and religious fanaticism, of credulity expressed in lapidary phrases such as Disraeli himself delighted to fashion. 'Perplexed churches are churches made by Act of Parliament not by God.' 'A Christian estranged; a Christian without the consolations of Christianity.' And the description of the Cardinal's person left the *cognoscenti* in no doubt that Manning, even though not yet a prince of the Church, was intended: 'Above the middle height, his stature seemed magnified by the attenuation of his form. It seemed that the soul never had so frail and fragile a tenement. . . . His countenance was naturally of an extreme pallor, though at this moment slightly flushed with the animation of a deeply interesting conference. His cheeks were hollow, and his grey eyes seemed sunk into his clear and noble brow, but they flashed with irresistible penetration.'[130] (In fact Manning's eyes were dark brown.) There was a curious sequel to the publication of this novel. Lothair had been based on the Marquess of Bute, who had converted to Roman Catholicism in 1868. Four years later Bute was married at the Brompton Oratory. The ceremony was performed by Manning. Mass was said by Mgr Capel, a socializing priest who had appeared as Mgr Catesby in the novel. And Disraeli was one of the five witnesses to the marriage.[131]

Despite the questionable usefulness of Manning's first interference in the politics of the Irish question, the human misery of Ireland evoked from him in that same year of 1868 the most forceful and effective pamphlet that he ever wrote. The 'Letter to Earl Grey' was a passionate denunciation of the wrongs which England had committed against Ireland. Manning began in characteristic style by asserting that the gravity of the present crisis could not be overrated as to either depth or danger. 'To our own hurt, we have made the English name hateful in the past, and we must bear the penalty until we have repaired the wrong. . . . We English can be cool and calm in the matter, but we must not forget that the accumulated animosity of the past is born in the blood of Irishmen. My surprise is not that they control it so little, but that they control it so much.' Manning poured scorn and contempt upon the smug exculpations that sought to impute the blame to the Irish themselves. 'It has been the pleasure of Ireland to pass upon itself a sentence of perpetual poverty,' the *Quarterly Review* had recently announced. That kind of wilful blindness stirred all Manning's indignation. 'Did Ireland suicidally strip itself of all its lands, reduce itself to mud-cabins, potato diet, and evictions, fever, and famine? . . . Who checked its agriculture, its cattle-trade, its fisheries, and its manufactures by Acts of Parliament? If poverty was ever inflicted by one nation on another, it has been inflicted on Ireland by England.'

In a particularly effective passage Manning imaginarily transferred Irish events to England and demanded whether Parliament would have remained inactive in the circumstances:

If any sensible proportion of the people of the English counties were to be seen moving down the Thames for embarkation to America, and dropping by the roadside from hunger and fever, and it had been heard by the wayside that they were 'tenants at will', evicted for any cause whatsoever, the public opinion of the country would have risen to render impossible the repetition of such absolute and irresponsible exercise of legal rights. . . . If five millions, that is a fourth of the English people, had either emigrated in a mass, by reason of discontent, misery, or eviction, or had died by fever or famine since the year 1848, the whole land system of England would have been modified so as to render the return of such a national danger impossible for ever.

As always, Manning refused to be taken in by the cant of those with a vested interest in the *status quo*, whether political economists parroting heartless jargon, or landlords regretfully deploring the immutable nature of the laws of property. Private property was indeed, in Catholic theology no less than in the laws of England, a right to be upheld, but there was another, anterior, consideration that took priority, 'by which every people has a right to live off the fruits of the soil on which they are born'. Taking this principle to its logical conclusion, as was Manning's wont with principles, he developed his argument into a heresy against the ethics of Victorian capitalism: 'A starving man commits no theft if he saves his life by eating of his neighbour's bread so much as is necessary for the support of his existence.' Manning's determination that human beings should not be sacrificed to any abstract theory repeatedly appears in his writings. In the religious context he found reality malleable enough to be forced into the most rigid Catholic mould; in the social context reality was not to be cast into any form save that which would serve the people at large. Manning possessed an admirable capacity for calling a spade a spade:

The 'Land Question', as we call it, by a somewhat heartless euphemism, means hunger, thirst, nakedness, notice to quit, labour spent in vain, the toil of years seized upon, the breaking up of homes, the miseries, sicknesses, deaths of parents, children, wives; the despair and wildness which spring up in the hearts of the poor when legal force, like a sharp harrow, goes over the most sensitive and vital rights of mankind.[132]

This was superb polemic. Whether it achieved anything is another matter. As with his 1867 Lenten pastoral there was a remarkable coincidence of events: four days after receiving a copy of Manning's pamphlet, Gladstone announced in the House of Commons that the time for disestablishing the Irish Church had ceased to be nigh (as in 1867) and was now actually upon the nation. Again, though, it would be unwise to claim too much for Manning's influence. The Duke of Argyll, one of Gladstone's closest friends, explained the kind of ideals that move politicians: 'There was really no other way of getting Dizzy out of office.'[133]

By the end of 1868 Gladstone had become Prime Minister. The occasion naturally called for some recognition on the part of an old friend, but Manning did not lapse into anything so superficial as mere congratulation.

'And so you are at the end men live for, but not, I believe, the end for which you have lived. It is strange so to salute you, but very pleasant. I take much consolation from the fact that what has made you so is a cause in which my whole heart can go with you.' Why should Manning have required consolation? Perhaps the answer lay in Gladstone's Non-Conformist support: 'I fully recognise', Manning wrote, 'the prudence of our not meeting now.'[134]

Many English Catholics, conversely, did not share their Archbishop's enthusiasm for the new Prime Minister. Even disestablishment of the Anglican Church in Ireland, which so delighted the Pope and the Irish bishops, appeared to some of the old Catholics to confer a doubtful benefit. In the House of Lords a Catholic peer named Gormanston, conscious of implications adverse to landowners, strove with his Anglican colleagues to preserve as much as possible of the heretic Church's endowments. In the Commons, by contrast, there were Irish MPs who held that the disestablished Irish Church should be allowed to retain no endowments at all. Gladstone asked Manning to apply 'a little confirmation' to these dissidents and, when the Irish Church Bill finally passed, he acknowledged the help which he had received: 'I am much indebted to you on behalf of the Government for the firm, constant and discriminating support which you have afforded to our Bill during the arduous conflict, now happily concluded.'[135] Manning's reply was very much in character: 'My joy in the event is not only as a Catholic, though that must be, as it ought to be, my highest motive, but as an Englishman to whom, as I remember you once saying, the old English monarchy is dear next after the Catholic Church.'[136]

Next year Gladstone's Land Bill also elicited Manning's approval, although when the Archbishop, under pressure from the Irish hierarchy, lobbied for a bolder measure, the Prime Minister gave him a lesson in political realities: 'we might as well propose the repeal of the Union'.[137] Nevertheless, Manning appeared so closely involved in the nation's affairs that in 1869 the *Spectator* recommended he be made a peer. Evidently Catholic integration was proceeding apace.

In 1870, however, Manning stood forth ostentatiously as the champion of a principle which separated him alike from Gladstone and the English nation. It is often said that the English as a race have never cared much for ideas, whether for or against. One idea, though, never fails to provoke their righteous horror and to stimulate their uncomprehending mockery – that of the infallibility of the Pope. 'How sad for us both considering our personal relations', wrote Gladstone just before Manning set out for the Vatican Council in Rome, 'that we should now be in this predicament, that the things which the one looks to as the salvation of faith and Church, the other regards as their destruction.'[138]

9 Infallibility at Rome and Westminster

A leader of this conspiracy [against the Church] said the other day, 'The net is now drawn so close about the Church of Rome that if it escape this time I will believe it to be divine.' If God grant him life, I have hope of his conversion.

MANNING, *The Vatican Decrees in their Bearing on Civil Allegiance* (1875)[1]

Granted the premise that God established the Roman Catholic Church on earth as the voice of revelation that should endure to the end of the world, the doctrine of infallibility is neither extreme nor illogical, but simply unavoidable. It would certainly be perverse to postulate that the Almighty should have created this mighty organization to proclaim his ordinances to mankind, and then allowed it to err in its fundamental principles. Infallibility, therefore, had been inherent in the Church's claims from the moment of Christ's declaration to St Peter, and recognized as such by generation after generation of Catholics. As Manning put it, 'If the Church were not infallible, obedience to it might be the worst of bondage.'[2] The only questions to be settled were, first, whether that power was vested in a General Council or in the Pope himself; second, the limits within which the doctrine might legitimately be applied; and third, the recognition of the occasions on which the power had been exercised.

There was never any doubt of the direction of Manning's sympathies on these contentious topics. He had become a Catholic because he had discovered in the one infallible Church the authority which he needed as a sure grounding for his faith, and he was not inclined to imagine that a prescription which had worked so well for himself would fail for the world at large. He believed that 'an internecine conflict is at hand between the army of dogma and the united hosts of heresy, indifferentism and atheism'. The more aggressively infallibility was asserted, and the more widely spread its reach, the better protected the faithful would be against the rationalist infection of the modern world. W. G. Ward even considered that the doctrine should be extended to cover the Pope's private correspondence. Manning never committed himself to that extent in writing, but he was certainly with Ward in spirit. Clearly it was preferable, in a world where events moved increasingly fast, that the Pope should not be encumbered by the necessity of calling a General Council before he could speak with the voice of Peter. And with Manning subjective necessity and objective truth were ever closely knit.

He easily persuaded himself that the Pope's claims were incontestably proved by the history of the Church, although history was never a witness upon which he ultimately relied. 'History must be tested by faith, not faith by history,' he proclaimed.[3] (Döllinger paraphrased the point: 'The faith that moves mountains will be equally ready to make away with the facts of history.') For Manning, one of the glories of the doctrine of infallibility was that it provided such a magnificent counterblast to the pride of intellectuals, whether historians, scientists or theologians. Unlike Newman, he was not at all impressed by Darwinian theory. The religion of science, he complained, 'traces mankind to a progenitor among the least graceful and most grotesque of creatures, and affirms that thought is phosphorous, the soul a name for the complex of nerves, and, if I rightly understand its mysteries, that our moral sense is a secretion of sugar.'[4] Since God was the fountain of both science and revelation, and since the Church had been divinely empowered to determine the meaning of that revelation, it followed that if science set the doctrine of the Church at risk, science must be in error.

Infallibility also conferred the benefit of serving as a bulwark against that 'exaggerated spirit of national independence'[5] which now presumed to assail the Pope's temporal power. Undoubtedly the devotion which Manning felt for Pius IX contributed to his zeal for the doctrine of infallibility. Pope worship, however, was not an individual phenomenon. Manning was a moderate beside some of the continental ultramontanes. 'When he [the Pope] thinks,' announced *La Civiltà Catholica*, organ of the Roman Jesuits, 'it is God who is thinking in him.' In France *Univers*, the extreme ultramontane paper edited by Louis Veuillot, went so far as to substitute the word *Pius* for *Deus* in one Catholic hymn. The *Univers* remained confident that the new Italian God was every bit as much of a French nationalist as the old *Deus*: '*A Pie IX, qui représente mon Dieu sur la terre: Iste Deus meus et glorificabo eum, Deus patris mei et exaltabo eum.*'[6]

The Pope himself, although not personally in need of any General Council to confirm his confidence in his own infallible powers, quite saw the advantages of having these powers officially defined for the benefit of the faithless world. He does seem, however, to have laboured under some inhibitions about bringing forward the subject himself. The earliest plans for the Council, which was first mooted in 1864–65, scarcely mentioned infallibility. Rumour asserted that the Archbishop of Westminster had been secretly charged with ensuring that the matter came before the Council.[7] Manning denied this, and indeed any such instruction would have been quite superfluous: his natural disposition was to urge infallibility with all his might. Perhaps it was he who suggested to the Pope that he should fill the role of leading advocate.

In any case, Pius kept his close and loyal disciple well informed of developments from the very beginning of preparations for the Council. Although Manning was not then even aware that he was about to become a bishop, he was one of thirty-four prelates privileged, in April 1865, to be sent a secret letter which unfolded the Pope's intention of summoning a General Council and which called upon the recipients to consider what subjects should come under discussion. The news of the Pope's intention did not become generally known until 1867, when a great number of bishops was assembled in Rome for the centenary of St Peter and St Paul. Manning recalled how, after assisting at Vespers on the evening of the Feast Day, he made a joint vow with Bishop Senestrey of Ratisbon (Regensburg) that neither of them would rest until they had secured the definition of papal infallibility.[8] Both men remained true to their oath. Manning devoted two lengthy pastorals to the propagation of the great cause, hundreds of pages dedicated to investigating and drawing out this one absorbing truth.

In Rome, Manning advocated a fighting manifesto for the Council, 'wounding in order to strike home'. To more moderate spirits he seemed to be predeciding the Council definition which he desired: thus the word 'infallible' was excluded from the final document. But Manning insisted, in a heated debate, that the doctrine should be stated in substance if not in name. 'We fully accept,' ran the final version, 'that the Roman pontiff is the Vicar of Christ and Head of the whole Church, and Father and Teacher of all Christians, and to him in Blessed Peter has been given by Jesus Christ full power of feeding, ruling and governing the universal Church.' Manning's intransigent approach to the drawing up of this address won him enemies. 'Ce n'est pas le temps de casser les vitraux,'[9] the Bishop of Grenoble angrily exclaimed to Ullathorne.

It would have required more than a few resentful bishops to stay Manning's hand where, as he believed, the foundations of his faith were at stake. He urged infallibility with all his power in his 1869 Pastoral, though he did guard himself by seeking expert theological sanction. 'You should have seen the former production,' commented Ullathorne of this Pastoral, 'before it was revised and several pages cut out of it – it would have put France into a fury.'[10] Manning humbly submitted to correction, as he so often did in the case of his written works. At the last moment, though, he dashed off an appendix which was not submitted to scrutiny before publication. If it hardly stirred the entire French nation, it did at least rouse the controversial spirit of Dupanloup, the Bishop of Orleans.

For France, where, in defiance of synthesis, thesis and antithesis perpetually thrive, provided not only the main emotional thrust for the definition of infallibility, but also the main intellectual opposition. Dupanloup was the leader of the latter group. He did not, could not, deny the doctrine, for that would have been to undermine the whole basis of the Catholic faith. In fact Dupanloup had written a long screed in defence of infallibility for his doctoral thesis. His attitude to the prospect of the doctrine's being formally defined, however, was essentially that of the Bishop of Grenoble cited above: the moment was not opportune. There appeared to be no pressing necessity for a definition. Dupanloup believed that to erect infallibility into a dogma would heighten the barriers which kept Protestants and the Eastern Church out of the one true fold, a proposition in direct contrast to Manning's eagerness to throw down the gauntlet before the modern world. Dupanloup worried about the reaction of governments to such a strong assertion of universal spiritual sovereignty; Manning gloried in their expressions of alarm. Dupanloup foresaw difficulties in defining the limits and conditions of infallible power; Manning was not sure that he wanted any limits or conditions at all. At least, though, Dupanloup shared Manning's confidence in the guidance of the Holy Spirit upon the forthcoming Council; he undertook in advance to submit to whatever decisions might be reached 'from the very bottom of my heart and soul'.[11]

Newman adopted a position similar to Dupanloup's; he was especially critical of the timing of the definition. 'I certainly think this agitation of the Pope's Infallibility most unfortunate and ill-advised,' he would write in June 1870, 'and I shall think so even if the Council decrees it, unless I am obliged to believe that the Holy Ghost protects the Fathers from all inexpedient acts, (which I do not see is any where promised) as well as guides them into all the truth, as He certainly does. There are truths which are inexpedient.'[12] As always Newman manages to discover a logical way of holding what might seem, at first sight, to be illogical opinions for a Catholic. Yet with all his refinements and qualifications and reservations, he hardly leaves an impression of blazing faith. On the whole, he told W. G. Ward, he thought the doctrine of infallibility 'likely to be true'.[13] Ward duly passed on this letter to Manning, who would have been surprised neither by the views which it contained, nor by the preference which the English public showed for Newman's line rather than his own. 'If a Catholic be found out of touch with authority by half a note,' he observed with some bitterness in his 1869 pastoral, 'he is at once extolled for unequalled learning and irrefragable logic.' No doubt Manning felt, with some reason, that his own stand on infallibility was more straightforwardly consistent with the grounds upon which they had both become Catholic. What Newman felt about Manning's position appears to his private correspondence. 'I cannot help thinking he holds that the world is soon coming to an end – and that he is in consequence carless about the souls of the future generations which will never be brought into being.'[14]

In fact Manning held that the Vatican Council would distinguish the nineteenth century to future generations as the Councils of Nicaea and Trent had marked the fourth and the sixteenth centuries. How gratifying to play a prominent part in such a gathering. His role was well described by Purcell as 'chief whip' of the infallibilist party. His performance stimulates the reflection that it was as well for parliamentary democracy that he never achieved his political ambitions. Those who are doing the Lord's work are not over-sensitive about consulting the interests of the opposition, even when it consists of bishops of the Roman Catholic Church. Manning's tactics were ruthless. Heretics, he held, came to general councils to be condemned,[15] not listened to, and he never paused to reflect that opposition to an as yet undefined doctrine could hardly be deemed heretical.

The issues which came before the Council were considered in their first and last stages by a congregation of all the bishops, but between these sessions the difficulties which arose were thrashed out in one of four committees, where the real work, of producing formulas upon which the full assembly would vote, was done. Each of these committees contained twenty-four members, elected by secret ballot. The infallibility definition was entrusted to the important Deputatio de Fide. Manning was at the centre of a powerful infallibilist lobby which, aware that few of the seven hundred bishops knew anything about one another, helpfully drew up a printed list of twenty-four names before any voting on the personnel of this committee took place. The principles upon which this list was concocted were: first, that the candidate should be in favour of the definition; second, that various nationalities should be represented; and, third, that the names should be transmitted to the Archbishop of Westminster. Needless to say, Manning's own name appeared on this unofficial list, which, through a mixture of ignorance among the electors and extensive lobbying by the infallibilists, was carried without any change of a single name. It was irritating that the other English bishops, all but two of them inopportunists and (Errington among them) unresponsive to Manning's tactics, should have met separately and elected Grant as their candidate for the Deputatio de Fide. Ullathorne recorded how this decision was made 'to the Archbishop's surprise, evinced by sundry snortings and extra politeness'. Nevertheless, Manning could not see his way to allowing a purely English vote to upset the larger scheme of things, either as to his own membership or Grant's exclusion from this key committee.[16]

With the Deputatio de Fide solid behind the definition of infallibility, the decision of the Holy Ghost appeared to be manifesting itself at an early stage in the Council. It was shameful, Manning thought, how the inopportunists intrigued against such a clear manifestation of the divine will. For their part, members of the opposition like Lord Acton blamed Manning for the struggles that took place. The inopportunists' understandable sense of grievance at being wholly excluded from the Deputatio de Fide made their antagonism, doomed to failure as it was, more determined and longer drawn out. The Bishop of Poitiers, though he was for the definition, shared their outrage, describing the tactics employed in electing the committee as more appropriate to municipal government than to a Council of the Church.[17] Manning's activities earned him the soubriquet 'il diavolo del concilio'.[18] But did not the Pope himself say that a General Council always passed through three stages: first, that of the devil, then that of men, and finally that of God? Manning seemed eager to participate in all of them, so that one observer wrote witheringly of the 'humble convert' who carried all before him.[19]

Foreign views of Manning are interesting as they show that objections to his mode of procedure were not confined to Anglo-Saxons of questionable faith. Emile Ollivier, Prime Minister of France in 1870, was a French Protestant who wrote an excellent book about the Council, so scrupulously fair that it won the approval of Pope Leo XIII. Ollivier was struck by the blend of asceticism and power-lust in Manning's appearance:

The love of domination emanates from every pore, and when his thin lips allow a smile to hover, one feels it is from pure condescension. Certainly he is pious, sincere, utterly wrapped up in God; nevertheless, do not mistake him for those emaciated monks whom he resembles. Underneath his seraphic air of content there lurks a politician as insinuating and energetic as any of the kind. He has known how to keep in with English liberals even while siding with the party of absolute authority at Rome. His activity is prodigious; he is involved with everything; he speaks about everything and upon everything; he writes indefatigably, and he does not neglect the fashionable world in which he is so pampered and sought after.[20]

Gregorovius, a Roman gossip who sat near Manning at a reception, closely observed the English fanatic, a little grey man looking as if encompassed with cobwebs'. Actually Manning was tallish, but Gregorovius was concerned with the general impression not the petty detail. 'He

[Manning] extended his hand to be kissed by new arrivals in the manner of an elderly courtesan accustomed to such acts of homage.'[21]

Canon Moufang, theologian to the Bishop of Mainz, an inopportunist, described Manning's lobbying technique:

Archbishop Manning, by his vehement and vivid forecasts of the evils which threatened us, made my hair stand on end. But there was a great deal of force in his arguments. Our opposition to the opportuneness of the definition was confined more or less to historical or theoretical objections; we gave little or no practical view of things which Manning insisted upon, to the coming events in the political order, wars and revolutions which he predicted with such terrible earnestness.

In the circumstances Moufang's conclusion was generous: 'We were, perhaps, more of theologians; he more of an ecclesiastical statesman.'[22]

At first the Council applied itself to the task of bringing dogmatic precision to Catholic teaching on the nature of God and His revelation. This might be reckoned a considerable task for any assembly, but the certitudes of Catholic tradition gave short shrift to the errors of rationalism, materialism and atheism. There was one heated debate in which Strossmayer, the Bishop of Diakovo in Bosnia, was rash enough to suggest that there were many Protestants who loved Christ and who erred in good faith. This assertion led to an ugly scene. 'He is Lucifer, anathema, anathema, let him be cast out,'[23] shouted the horrified audience. At least, though, the bishops did not actually come to blows as had occurred at the Council of Trent.

Clearly the atmosphere was favourable for a definition of infallibility, which, even before it was brought forward, was recognized as *the* great business of the Council. Far away in Protestant England, where Anglicans and Non-Conformists alike thrilled themselves with horror at the Council's doings, the issue seemed certain as early as January 1870. 'Now I don't see how they can help passing the personal infallibility,' commented the shrewd Richard Church, an old friend of Newman's, in his remote Somerset rectory. 'Not to do it, or to evade it, would simply be to show themselves beaten by internal disunion. They had better risk schism, which I don't expect, however, than that. It may cost them a great deal in the next generation, but I doubt whether they care for that.' Church felt that the definition would be 'almost the crowning event of the age, and one which no one could have imagined possible. And I suppose it really would not have happened but for Manning and Ward.'[24] There, no doubt, Church exaggerated, but his remark reflects the astonishment among Anglican intellectuals that the former Archdeacon of Chichester should be playing a leading part in such a scene. 'How strange the contrast between the outward lot of Manning and dear JHN,' Pusey wrote to Newman's former curate at Littlemore at this time, 'but you, I, and dear JK [eble] would have no doubt which and where we would rather be. Manning's is an awful gain in this world.'[25]

Really the only hope for the inopportunists was delay. If the debate could be extended, perhaps some exterior event might intervene to break up the Council before the definition could be made. Meanwhile, Newman was becoming more and more alarmed. He sent a letter to Ullathorne, who kept him informed of all developments at the Council, complaining of the 'aggressive and insolent faction', which sought with cause to disturb the peace of the faithful by its relentless determination to press for a definition:

I look with anxiety at the prospect of having to defend decisions, which may not be difficult to my private judgement, but may be most difficult to maintain logically in the face of historical facts. . . . If it is God's will that the Pope's infallibility should be defined, then it is His Blessed Will to throw back 'the times and the moments' of that triumph He has destined for His kingdom; and I shall feel I have but to bow my head to His adorable, inscrutable Providence.[26]

By some mysterious process this private letter found its way into a newspaper. The aggressive and insolent faction, however, in no wise repented of its ways. Manning, its master tactician, now involved himself in some diplomatic shuffling in defence of the sacred cause. His fear was that the Powers might act to foreclose the Council with the definition still unmade. No one knew better than he of Gladstone's hostility. 'Of the Council I will say nothing,' the Prime Minister had written to him in January, 'except to express my earnest desire that it may end well: the only thing it is within my power to say without the fear of giving you pain.'[27] Manning was concerned that Gladstone was receiving inopportunist propaganda from Lord Acton, so he obtained the Pope's permission to break the oath of secrecy in order to keep Odo Russell, the British diplomatic resident at the Vatican, informed of his own view of events. He also wrote directly to Gladstone on 6 April 1870, warning him against any intervention with the Council. 'For the sake of us all, for your own sake, for your future, for the peace of our country, do not allow yourself to be warped, or impelled into words and acts hostile to the Council.'[28]

The Powers did not intervene, but that had little to do either with Manning's talks with Russell or his letters to Gladstone. Russell took his line from Acton, however diplomatically he concealed the fact from the Archbishop. He can only have been alarmed by Manning's fanatical zeal. Was there no way in which the definition could be prevented? he asked 'Certainly,' Manning replied, 'cut our throats.'[29] As for Gladstone, he was left gasping at the change of character in his old friend. 'When he was archdeacon with us, all his strength was thought to lie in a governing faculty, and in its wise moderation. Now he is ever quoted as the *ultra* of ultras, and he seemed greatly to have overshot his mark.'[30] Manning, of course, knew that this change simply reflected his graduation from the service of a muddled human institution to that of a divinely inspired Church. This, however, was not a point that Gladstone would ever grasp. The Prime Minister warned darkly that 'for the first time in my life, I shall now be obliged to talk about popery; for it would be a scandal to call the religion they are manufacturing at Rome by the same name as that of Pascal, or of Bossuet'.[31] Gladstone believed that the Catholic Church was destroying itself. The minority bishops, he wrote to Manning on 16 April, were 'contending for the religious and civil interests of mankind against influence highly disastrous and menacing to both'.[32]

It was upon the Council itself, not upon the English Government, that Manning's influence proved critical. He was to the fore in organizing petitions for bringing the subject of infallibility before the Council (granted by the Pope on 6 March), and then in urging the necessity of advancing the timing of its discussion (Pius was duly persuaded by 20 April). As a member of the Deputatio de Fide Manning helped to prepare the 'schema' for debate by the General Congregation of bishops, in which he himself spoke on 25 May. His speech, like all the others, in Latin, lasted nearly two hours. 'Before I got up I was nervous; but once up perfectly calm. I saw dear old Cardinal de Angelis look in despair at the Cardinals next to him, as if he thought I should never end.'[33] In fact, the speech was a great success. Manning emphasized that he was the only convert at the Council; as such he knew that the doctrine of infallibility, so far from scaring Protestants away from the Church, would be a powerful attraction for all who wished to escape from confusion and chaos. In any case, infallibility was already a fact, accepted by all Catholics: 'To hold back from defining it would be a sign and source of weakness in the Catholic position.'[34]

The general debate was ended by closure, applied on 3 June. It was now high summer, and several bishops were flagging in the Roman heat. Ten of their number had died in the first two months of the Council, and that had been in winter.[35] Now the English bishops began to suffer. Bishop Grant of Southwark died on 1 June; Clifford, Bishop of Clifton, was getting distressingly thin. The Archbishop of Westminster solicitously enquired whether Clifford and his colleague of Nottingham had not better return home;[36] they were both inopportunists. Manning himself remained indefatigable. On the Deputatio de Fide he pressed for an extreme statement of the definition, urging his case with such importunity that he received a magisterial rebuke from the chairman: '*non ita sunt tractendae res Ecclesiae*'

– It is not thus that the affairs of the Church should be conducted.[37] Once more Manning's zeal miscarried: the formula that was finally agreed* was a more limited and more precisely qualified doctrine than that which he had been advocating. Indeed, some leaders of the inopportunist cause saw the possibility of voting in its favour if only the Pope could be prevailed upon to make some concession that would bring out the share which the body of bishops might claim in the Church's infallible power. Bishop Ketteler of Mainz threw himself upon his knees before Pius: 'Good Father, save us, and save the Church of God.'[38] But Manning and Senestrey, faithful to their vow to the last, were on hand to guard against the unlikely possibility of any weakening in Pius's resolve. 'I had access by private passage into the Pope's apartments,' Manning would later recall. 'On one occasion, I remember the surprise shown by Cardinals and Ambassadors – they had not seem me go in – as I passed out into the Antechamber where they were awaiting an audience of his Holiness.'[39]

The inopportunist bishops, all but two Americans, left Rome. On 18 July the definition was voted and promulgated at a great ceremony in St Peter's. A fierce thunderstorm raged outside, and brought a pane of glass down in smithereens beside the papal chair. A superstitious mortal might have trembled at this portent. The infallible pontiff merely issued a Latin instruction: '*Non in commotione Dominus.*'[40] Manning also was undisturbed. 'Critics saw this thunderstorm an articulate voice of divine indignation against the definition,' he wrote. 'They forgot Sinai and the Ten Commandments.'[41]

Manning never allowed the relatively restricted nature of the definition to moderate his joy in its accomplishment. He hastened to write a two-hundred-page pastoral (October 1870), in which he gave the decree the largest possible interpretation. Against more prudent Catholic theologians he described infallibility as being applicable to a whole corpus of issues, including dogmatic facts, papal censures, the canonization of saints and the approbation of religious orders. The word 'define', he added, was not to be understood in any narrow legal sense, but simply as indicating the final decision given in any doctrinal judgement of faith and morals.

---

* 'We teach and define that it is a dogma divinely revealed: that the Roman Pontiff, when he speaks *ex cathedra*, that is, when in discharge of the office of Pastor and Doctor of all Christians, by virtue of his supreme Apostolic authority he defines a doctrine regarding faith or morals to be held by the Universal Church, by the divine assistance promised to him in blessed Peter, is possessed of that infallibility with which the divine Redeemer willed that His Church should be endowed for defining doctrine regarding faith and morals: and that such definitions of the Roman Pontiff are irreformable of themselves, and not from the consent of the Church.

'But if anyone – which may God avert – presume to contradict this our definition; let him be anathema.'

Newman, on the contrary, was thrown into a depression. 'It looks as if our Great Lord were in some way displeased at us,' he reflected on hearing the news from Rome.[42] Having told one correspondent that he refused to believe the definition could be carried until it became a *fait accompli*,[43] he was so disappointed by the event that he failed, initially, to find comfort in the moderate wording of the new dogma. His mind remained preoccupied with the heedless impetuosity of the extremists. 'There are too many high ecclesiastics in Italy and England,' he reflected, 'who think that to believe is as easy as to obey – that is, they talk as if they did not know what an act of faith is.'[44] In August 1870 Newman privately clung to the notion that since the Council had never been formally dissolved, the infallibility definition was not yet absolute. 'No one is bound to believe it at this moment, certainly not till the end of the Council. This I hold in spite of Dr. Manning.'[45] Newman wisely refrained from confronting Dr Manning directly with this view. Judging by the manner in which the Archbishop of Westminster pressed Lord Acton for a statement of submission,[46] he would certainly have deemed Newman's prevarication to be tantamount to heresy.

Newman's idea that the Council might possibly be reconvened was always far-fetched. As things turned out, Manning had been well-advised to urge that the definition be pushed through as quickly as possible. Even while the Council was sitting, the international situation sharply deteriorated, and the day after the definition was promulgated the French declaration of war against Prussia was delivered in Berlin. Within weeks the collapse of the French armies necessitated the withdrawal of the troops which had been guarding Rome against Italian designs. In September Victor Emmanuel's army entered Rome, and subsequently a plebiscite showed a large majority in favour of the city's being removed from papal control and united with Italy. The Italian Government moved there in the following year, and Pius IX, refusing to compromise or make terms, became the 'Prisoner of the Vatican'.

The Council was the apotheosis of Manning's Roman career. The evidence of his power and influence in such a quarter, however, merely increased the suspicion with which he was regarded by the Victorian establishment. Samuel Wilberforce, the 'dear brother' of Lavington days, conceived a rage that found vent in the pages of his diary. The following entry, dated 13 June 1868, records a conversation with Odo Russell, who told him:

Manning's influence at Rome absolutely a personal influence with the Pope. The Pope, a man of strong will, though of intense vanity, cannot bear the slightest contradiction, but very fond of all who take his absolute dicta as law. This Manning has played upon, and got on. He is more Papal than the Pope – repeats to the Pope all his own ideas, which pleases him exceedingly. Clifford had resisted the Pope, which was why he passed him by as Archbishop. Manning's appointment protested against by all the old Roman families in England, but the Pope would not listen. Manning most obsequious: creeps on hands and knees to kiss his toe, and, even when bidden to get up, remains prostrate in awe. This delights Pio Nono.[47]

Poor Samuel Wilberforce: the bishopric of Winchester proved to be the utmost mark of his high-ranging ambition. His animus against his brother-in-law was retained to the bitter end. Riding with Lord Granville, the Foreign Secretary, on the Surrey Downs in July 1873 he regaled him with accounts of the insinuating power of Roman Catholicism, with particular reference to the character and influence of Manning.[48] Whether in the midst or at the conclusion of these interesting remarks, he was thrown from his horse and instantly killed. Some years later, when his biography appeared, his estimate of Manning became public knowledge. Manning recorded that he kept silent 'from old affection, true sorrow, and the law of charity'. Yet was it not sad, his journal continued, that Samuel Wilberforce, so talented and delightful, should have been corrupted by the world? How different had been his own course. 'In all the world where Samuel Wilberforce lived, I was as a dead man out of mind. No doubt my Good Master saw that I should have lost myself and my soul. He has kept me out of the contagions of the English public and private life, with its refinements, fascinations, and subtle transforming power. I have been as dead to this as I have been to the world of politics in which Gladstone has lived.'[49]

It was not evident in 1870 that Manning was making any desperate efforts to avoid Gladstone and the world of politics. In fact, as soon as he returned from Rome, he wrote to the Prime Minister requesting an interview. It was granted with a chilly warning: 'Forgive me if I suggest that perhaps we had better not talk of what has been going on at Rome. Our opinions on the matter are strong on both sides, and are wide as the poles asunder: I am not vain enough to think I can act upon you, and for you to act upon me would tear up the very roots of my being.'[50] Gladstone was too busy just at the moment to settle scores with the Pope's infallibility. He had, however, told Manning even while the Council was in progress that 'the impression here of what is going on at Rome' was creating an atmosphere in which it was becoming harder to do justice to Catholics, whether as regards the Irish Land Bill or the Education Bill.[51]

It has been said that Manning might have been able to achieve a better deal for Catholic education if he had not been in Rome at the time when the Bill which aimed at establishing universal primary education was under discussion. Ullathorne reported (23 February 1870) that when the English bishops met in Rome to discuss the Bill, the Archbishop of Westminster most uncharacteristically confessed that he knew nothing about it.[52] But really that was not surprising considering that Forster, the Minister in charge, had only introduced the measure into the House of Commons on 17 February. Manning lost no time in writing to Gladstone for details, and Gladstone sent a copy of the Bill out to him. Moreover, whatever Manning said to the bishops, he had been neither ignorant nor indifferent about the nature of the threat that faced Catholic schools.

The world had come a long way since the days when Manning and Gladstone had dreamed that the Anglican Church should take responsibility for the nation's education. It was now clear that the State must fulfil this role, and more specifically that local education boards would be elected to levy a rate to finance the provision of primary schools for those children who had escaped the educational net. To many liberals, this plan seemed to imply not merely that the Government should be neutral between the different religions, but also that it should not countenance any distinctive religious teaching. As Forster put the matter, it would be unfair to tax Roman Catholics to teach Methodism, but it would not be unfair to levy a rate upon Roman Catholics for the *secular* education of Methodists.[53] In the board schools, therefore, religious instruction should be confined to uncontentious biblical study, the kind of religion without dogma that Manning regarded as no religion at all.

But what would become of the denominational schools? From 1847–62 Catholic schools had received over £200,000 from the Privy Council, had even achieved recognition of the principle that the government inspection, which was an inevitable concomitant of government funds, should be carried out by a Catholic. Now, though, the more aggressive secularists wanted to cut off all government aid to denominational schools, which it was presumed, and in some quarters positively hoped, would gradually wither away for lack of funds. Manning was determined to prevent this danger. Before he left for Rome at the end of 1869 he lobbied Gladstone on three points: that denominational schools should continue to receive grants, that these grants should still be paid by the Privy Council, and that Catholic schools should not in any respect or under any conditions be subjected to control by the local boards. Manning regarded the prospective boards with lofty Harrovian disdain: they would consist of middle-class bigots of the same variety as the Poor Law Guardians who made the business of extracting Catholic children from the workhouses so difficult.[54] Manning was even prepared, in order to avoid board control, to give up the right to have Catholic inspectors for Catholic schools.[55]

Unfortunately, however peremptorily Manning addressed the Prime

Minister, he had no real pressure to exert upon a Liberal Government that was ultimately dependent on Protestant Non-Conformist support. Far more important than Manning's advocacy in saving denominational schools was the fact that Gladstone himself, though he had long since abandoned his youthful ideal of the Anglican State, yet remained an Anglican High Churchman, anxious to safeguard what the Church of England had achieved in education. Forster's Act therefore compromised by setting up a dual system. Denominational schools were given six months to provide education where nòne had previously existed; thereafter the situation in each areaˆ would be assessed by the local boards, which would build their own non-denominational schools where necessary. Manning tried hard to win a longer period in which to prove that Catholic schools were making adequate provision. 'In the past three years we have opened in London 30 new schools,' he told Gladstone on 25 March 1870, 'and have gathered out of the streets 3,000 children. Give me time and just proportionate help, and there will not be one of our children without a school.'[56] This plea was to no avail. Really the only satisfactory thing about the Act from Manning's point of view was that the denominational schools would still receive grants from the Privy Council. Yet, though these grants were increased, they were meagre compared to those which the boards could bestow upon their schools from the local rate. In the aftermath of the Act the eventual extinction of government-aided denominational schools seemed all too likely.

In the affairs of this world Manning was always a pragmatist. It is interesting to note how his attitude to the local education boards changed as soon as the Act had been passed. They immediately ceased in his mind to be a danger to be avoided at all costs, and became instead a reality that had to be coped with. Whereas Ullathorne was initially inclined to keep his conscience pure by refusing all government aid for Catholic schools, even from the Privy Council, Manning urged him to co-operate in working the Act. 'The Boards may destroy our lesser schools by reporting them to be insufficient or inefficient. The effect of this in London would be to destroy one half of our schools. By opening negotiations with the Board, as I have with the Privy Council, I hope to save these. By standing aloof from the Boards we should be exposed to the danger of their hostility.'[57]

There were Catholics who bitterly resented Manning's policy of accommodation to the Act. The Archbishop of Westminster, so inclined himself to judge that his opponents were the enemies of God's purpose, now found some of the more intransigent members of his flock reaching the same conclusion about him. 'Anything more simply anti-Christian I have never read,' wrote a priest of one of his conciliatory articles. 'His first act is to open the gate of the citadel and to let the enemy have free ingress.'[58] Manning did more than that. He diverted towards schools which had made their peace with the boards a £40,000 fund that had been specifically raised for the opposite purpose, that of keeping Catholic education independent of government assistance.[59]

Manning's pragmatism did not mean that he liked the Act. The quest for a fairer deal for the denominational schools now became another of his crusades. It was a cause which he embraced with particular fervour not only for its own sake but also because it was an action in which Catholics could associate themselves with a considerable proportion of the people at large. 'It is the field on which I would most like to fight a general action,' he wrote in 1873. 'A large part of the English public would be with us or would not fight against us.'[60] Manning was always careful to insist that he was fighting for *all* denominational schools, not just Catholic ones.

On the schools issue Manning's policy brought him closer to the Tory Party than to the Liberals. In his temperance campaigns, by contrast, he became an ally of Protestant Non-Conformity in its most anti-establishment vein. Here again, though, his instinctive theoretical extremism was tempered as occasion demanded by his no less instinctive sense of the possible. He was appalled by the manner in which the UK Alliance zealots, determined to achieve everything they wanted at one fell swoop, helped to wreck the 1871 Licensing Bill with their intransigent demands. Manning took the sensible view that any progress was better than none: 'I am for promoting any step,' he said in 1868, 'though it be the slow step of the tortoise.'[61] It was both rare and invaluable for the UK Alliance to be able to claim the support of a natural member of the ruling class, especially one so well connected as Manning, who did not hesitate to press the Prime Minister to 'do something to control the terrific domination of Brewers, Distillers and publicans'.[62]

Manning's advocacy was not confined to the respectability of backstairs influence. After the failure of the 1871 Licensing Bill, he trounced the parliamentary interest of the drink trade as roundly as any UK Alliance supporter might have wished. The working men of England, he somewhat over-confidently pronounced, would deliver the country from the monopolistic power of the drink capitalists. Prohibition itself appeared in at least one of his speeches as a likely instrument of vengeance. When an Anglican bishop let it be known that he would prefer that 'England should be completely free than that England should be completely sober', Manning was the only religious leader to indicate dissent: 'I am no believer in drunken freedom; I believe such freedom is not liberty.'[63]

Manning fearlessly bearded the rowdiest audiences to preach temperance. Once at Cambridge a drunken horde of undergraduates and publicans stormed the platform, smashed the furniture and yelled abuse. The Archbishop never flinched for an instant, appearing as the embodiment of the Chuch Militant in a world given over to the enemy.[64] He led now by example, having taken the pledge himself in 1872. The Catholic upper classes scorned him as a bigot, but Manning drew comfort from a higher authority. 'One of my own kinsmen, in an audience of the Holy Father, asked the Pope to lay a command on me to abstain no longer; and he only laughed in their faces.'[65] Manning's campaign grew ever more effective. About the time that he forswore drink, and when he was despairing of any action by Parliament, he founded a Catholic temperance society called the League of the Cross. Two qualifications were required for membership: regular attendance at Mass and total abstention from drink. Manning had originally thought in terms of two kinds of oath, one for teetotalism and another for temperance, but characteristically he decided that only the absolute measure would serve. The apostles had been teetotalers,[66] it now appeared; and mere temperance was the duty of all Christians, with or without an oath.

The organization of the League of the Cross was on military lines, as much in anticipation as in imitation of William Booth's Salvation Army, which was then developing out of the Christian Mission. There were sections, cadres, officers, banners and colours, all showing how Manning had grasped the importance of appealing to the imagination as well as the intellect. Four times a year the members took part in a great public parade at which Manning would preside, occasions perhaps even further removed in spirit from Harrow and Oxford than the Vatican Council. In his addresses to these gatherings he would deploy a waggish humour which he deemed, correctly it seems, to be well tailored to his audience. There was, for instance, the story of the Irishman to whom he had suggested teetotalism. 'No,' the man had returned, 'my confessor says that I don't need to take the pledge.' 'Well, I have taken it,' Manning urged. 'Maybe you needed it,' came the ready response.[67] Quite a card, the Archbishop of Westminster. Joviality, however, was not the leading characteristic of the League. The more dedicated members, bedecked and beribboned as became so great an honour, formed Manning's special guard of honour on public occasions. They also, in the 1870s, met Manning every week in private, when they reported on progress and did not fail to mention those priests whose commitment to the great principle of the League was less than absolute. Naturally priests who did not share their bishop's opinion of the drink evil bitterly resented the airs which the League fanatics gave themselves on the strength of their association with Manning.[68] Still, the success of the League spoke for itself: more than 58,000 had taken the pledge by 1876. And it is not altogether surprising to read that 170 priests in the Westminster diocese petitioned Parliament in support of Bruce's 1872 Licensing Bill.

Manning's crusade against drink was conducted with ever fiercer, ever more blinkered zeal, but it by no means exhausted his capacity for moral indignation. He was living now in the high age of Victorianism, with Britain at the summit of its power and prosperity *vis-à-vis* the rest of the world. The role he adopted was that of an English Amos sent to castigate the nation which he loved back into the ways of righteousness:

If there be any one sin more evident than another on the face of England [he thundered in 1871], it is what St. John called 'the pride of life'. There are, indeed, a multitude of dark stains upon us; they are, however, common to other people. But is there any nation in the world that exhibits such self-consciousness, such self-gratulation, such depreciation of other people, such self-trust, such self-contemplation? Our insular security, our tradition of success, our exceptional prosperity, delude us into a belief that they are for ever. Kingdoms may be dissolved, empires may pass away; the fishermen may dry their nets before the stones of Tyre, and Babylon the Great may be buried in the sands; but the Empire of Britain shall never be moved.[69]

Manning insisted on the folly of such presumption. Apart from any question of moral decline, he was one of the first to notice how lamentably England was slipping behind Germany in technical education; and even as an Anglican he had drawn particular attention to the deficiencies of Oxford in this respect.[70]

Looking around him he found the country in the grip of 'terrific social evils . . . more terrific than in any people except it be in those who are descended from ourselves'.[71] The upper classes were becoming wholly corrupt. He saw 'amusement followed as a trade, and the pampering of the body studied as a science'. He had been shocked to see an article in the *Saturday Review*, 'misnamed, we think, by an unseasonable jocularity, "Frisky Matrons" '. *The Times* was as bad, with its pieces on 'Pretty Horsebreakers' and on the growing infrequency of marriage among young men of the higher classes. 'This is not the atmosphere to which we desire our Catholic women to be acclimatised, or in which we wish their daughters to be reared.'[72] Yet his reprobation of such things came rather from the Evangelical than from the Catholic tradition. And it was the stock Evangelical panacea of family prayers that he recommended as the best means of keeping Catholic families pure amid all the surrounding filth.[73] His disgust with social conditions might be traced to the same source. He became increasingly convinced that if the capitalist system did not reform itself there would be some terrible revolutionary cataclysm. A fairer society was not just due in justice to the poor; it was a condition of survival for the rich.

So Manning was prepared to lend the authority of his office to such causes as the newly founded Agricultural Labourers' Union. His old Lavington sympathies for the country labourers were now translated into action on a national scale. The work found no favour in Rome: 'This man goes with swaddlers'[74] (Methodists), cried those who had died the death of orthodoxy. The Agricultural Labourers' Union evoked panic stricken hostility among landowners, but the sacrifices which Manning had made in his own life had long since cut him free from any narrow class interest. *Laissez-faire* theory, that magic talisman by which the Establishment transformed its selfish indifference to suffering into a point of economic principle, was always anathema to Manning. 'My belief is that some energetic and sympathetic act on the part of Government would avert great dangers,' he told Gladstone apropos the agricultural workers.[75] Further instruction followed. 'Prohibit the labour of children under a certain age. Compel payment of wages in money. Regulate the number of dwellings according to the population of parishes. Establish tribunals of arbitration in counties for questions between labour and land.'[76] By temperament Manning was a thoroughgoing *dirigiste*. Misery and suffering called forth his sympathy, but then they call forth most people's sympathy. What was special and valuable about him was his need to express his feelings in practical action. Strong emotion went in harness with common sense and a forceful will. Pain and distress were evils to be assaulted, and he never doubted that he knew the most effective means of attack. Animals as well as humans benefited from this rare combination of compassion and effectiveness: he fought against vivisection[77] as determinedly as he assaulted the callousness of the rich.

His first political principle was that society existed for man, not man for society. His loathing of social dogmatism was as pronounced as his love of religious dogmatism. Perhaps his most eloquent statement of this disposition was made in 'The Dignity and Rights of Labour', an address which he delivered to the Mechanics' Institution at Leeds in 1874:

If the great end of life were to multiply yards of cloth and cotton twist, and if the glory of England consists or consisted in multiplying, without stint or limit, these articles and the like at the lowest possible price, so as to undersell all the nations of the world, well, then, let us go on. But if . . . the hours of labour resulting from the unregulated sale of a man's strength and skill shall lead to the destruction of domestic life, to the neglect of children, to turning wives and mothers into living machines, and of fathers and husbands into . . . creatures of burden . . . the domestic life of man exists no longer, and we dare not go on in this path. . . . The accumulation of wealth in the land, the piling up of wealth like mountains, in the possession of classes or of individuals, cannot go on, if these moral conditions of our people are not healed.[78]

Manning's social thought owed something to John Ruskin, whose *Unto This Last*, with its indictments of Victorian materialism and its advocacy of government regulation of the labour market, had been published in 1862. The later *Fors Clavigera*, a series of essays which Ruskin addressed to working men throughout the 1870s, also impressed Manning, who described it as 'like the beating of one's heart in a nightmare'.[79] No doubt Ruskin's contention therein that 'bishops cannot take, much less give, account of men's souls until they first take account of their bodies' struck a responsive chord. The two men forged enduring friendship out of enduring mutual admiration. Manning hoped for a conversion. Had not Ruskin told him that 'no educated man could be a Christian without also being a Catholic'? Alas, Ruskin discovered that Manning's interpretation of that word 'Catholic' was too narrow for his taste. 'You are a long way yet from being able to rejoice over your "piece which was lost",' he told the Archbishop in 1878. Besides, he fearlessly proceeded,

it seems to me that your Catholic Hierarchy is, to the Christian Church it governs now, precisely what the Hierarchy of Caiaphas was to the Jewish Church, and that you are, as a priestly order, leading it to its ruin – desirous, at heart, the main body of you, only of your own power or prevalence in doctrine, and regardless wholly of the infinite multitude of your flock, who are perishing because you do not separate yourselves heroically from the rich and powerful, and wicked of this world, but entangle yourself in their schemes, comply with their desires, and share with them in the spoils of the poor.[80]

Nobody could have held Manning guilty on the last count: indeed, he would have agreed with much of Ruskin's argument. It must be said, too, that Ruskin's animadversions against bishops did not prevent him from kneeling in his hall 'to receive Manning' when he went mad in 1881.[81]

The two men also encountered each other at meetings of the Metaphysical Society, where throughout the 1870s Victorian intellectuals of widely different mental casts (other members included Tennyson, Browning, Gladstone, W. G. Ward and Huxley) sought to enlighten one another with exchanges of views about the meaning of life. The cause of truth was not notably advanced, but there seem to have been some agreeable evenings, too agreeable in Huxley's opinion. 'We all expended so much charity that, had it been money, we should every one have been bankrupt . . . the society died of too much love.'[82] Manning probably extracted rather more charity than most, though his willingness to take on the Victorian heavyweights on subjects of such fundamental importance to his own peace of mind is evidence of his courage, confidence and conviction. Newman, by contrast, refused to join the society, and expressed pious shock that

Manning should be prepared to listen to Huxley's arguments against Christ's resurrection. Or was it all a ruse of Manning's, he jokingly wondered, 'to bring the professor into the clutches of the Inquisition?'[83] Manning gave as good as he got in the society; and the first at least of the five papers that he read – 'What is the relation of Will to Thought?' – covered a subject upon which none could doubt his expertise. His tendency to cite long passages from Aquinas in Latin placed some strain on his audience. Being a man of the world, however, he would season his intransigent opinions with good humour. When telling members about some miracle, he insisted that he had investigated the facts with especial care – 'You know that I am a person of a rather sceptical disposition.' 'At these words', it was reported, 'the society exhibited some signs of amusement in which the illustrious speaker heartily joined.'[84] But when Manning in 1872 produced a discourse entitled 'That Legitimate Authority is an Evidence of Truth', Gladstone, for one, cried off: 'My brain will not now stand that kind of exertion.'[85]

The Prime Minister's brain was taxed severely enough at that time by the need to find a solution to the dreaded Irish university question on which Disraeli's first Government had foundered. The problem was to find some formula whereby a Protestant parliament might be persuaded to establish a Catholic university, or at least a university for Catholics. Disraeli had offered Catholics some measure of control but no funds; Gladstone now offered some money (if no permanent endowment) and sought to sell the project to the Liberal House of Commons by creating a university that would be religiously neutral in constitution and teaching even if largely Catholic in personnel.

Manning failed to profit by his unhappy experience with Disraeli: he declared himself well pleased with Gladstone's scheme as he had previously expressed satisfaction with the Conservatives' plan. Gladstone was favoured with a note of congratulation on his carefully constructed project, while the Irish bishops were counselled to accept the Bill as the best that they were ever likely to get. Even when the bishops showed their hostililty Manning explained to the Prime Minister that there were tactical considerations involved: 'If it were thought that the Catholic bishops were not opposed to the bill, an anti-Catholic noise would be got up.'[86] By March 1873, however, it was clear that the Irish hierarchy was not bluffing, and that Irish MPs would be instructed to vote against the Bill. Disraeli saw his opportunity: a strangely assorted alliance of Irish and Tory MPs defeated the measure by three votes. Disraeli refused to take office immediately, but the morale of Gladstone's Government had suffered a serious blow.

The Prime Minister told Manning that he reproached him for nothing, a particularly gallant gesture, since the cheery optimism that issued forth from

Archbishop's House cannot have made magnanimity any easier. 'You will not, I hope, take to heart the opposition of the Bishops in Ireland,' Manning wrote. 'Treat it as an earthquake.' Who would not take an earthquake to heart? When the Bill failed in the Commons he sent consolation that may or may not have reached its mark: 'I cannot conceal from myself that there may be a providence of God in this check.'[87] The Prime Minister may equally have looked askance at the candid confession that Manning made in an open letter to the Archbishop of Armagh that summer. Manning admitted that, looking at the matter from his English viewpoint, he had initially been in favour of Gladstone's Bill, but he saluted 'the higher and nobler attitude'[88] adopted by the Irish bishops in refusing to countenance mixed education. His new stance was certainly more consistent with his position in the Oxford question although, oddly enough, the Irish bishops never showed the same determination to prevent their flock attending that den of iniquity. As for the Irish university, the continued failure of Parliament to find a solution to the problem impelled Manning further in his belief that some form of Home Rule was a prerequisite of justice for Irish Catholics.

Perhaps it was this conclusion that inspired Manning with the gift of prophecy when Gladstone lost the election of 1874 and announced his retirement from politics. 'You have exhausted the mission you undertook. Say what you will, you will have another.'[89] Meanwhile, though, Manning fired off squibs at the Liberal Coalition which Gladstone had led. 'I do not confide in the ethical character of Non-Conformists. They have each swallowed a Pope, and I have no chance with legions of infallibilists. And I like still less the Philosophical Radicals and Oriental Despots of the Pall Mall type, and still less the strong-minded women.' Nevertheless, the former chief of this unprepossessing band should not despair. 'Do not be sharpened or soured or saddened,' Manning counselled, before being visited with a rare understanding that his lectures to Gladstone might be going too far: 'If I go on you will burn me.'[90]

The conflagration which Manning helped to provoke, however, was in Gladstone's mind. Ever since the Vatican Council the sparks had been flashing in that combustible chamber, and every time Manning referred to the claims of the infallible Church some massive explosion seemed imminent. Manning was certainly compassionate about the sufferings of the unfortunate, but he was never at all sensitive about the effect of his views on his peers. He went blithely on with his sermons to Gladstone, sending him at the beginning of 1874 a pamphlet in which he identified 'perfect Christianity' with ultramontanism.[91] Gladstone,' in the throes of an election defeat, strove nobly to maintain his calm. 'My rudimentary perception seems to differ from yours,' he told Manning in January 1874. 'Nature has made a mistake in one or other of us. My only comfort is that a time will come when, if I am a tenth part as good as you are, we shall both of us know how a higher power solves all these problems for us.' Unfortunately Manning, who could not even consider the possibility of error in the fundamentals of his faith, was incapable of responding to, even of recognizing, Gladstone's appeal for restraint. In reply to Gladstone's exposure of the unbridgeable gulf between them he had nothing but chaff to offer. Would that the Prime Minister trusted as fervently in ultramontanism as he the Archbishop trusted in his old friend's economics.[92] When the great statesman, now out of office, came up to London in March 1874, Manning hastened to visit him. 'It is kind of him to come, but most of it is rather hollow work, limited as we are,'[93] Gladstone ominously recorded.

Perhaps no amount of tact could have prevented Gladstone from letting loose a tirade upon the Vatican Council once he was free from the cares of government. Yet the venom of his attack, published in his pamphlet 'The Vatican Decrees in their Bearing upon Civil Allegiance' (November 1874), was surely distilled in part from his long-repressed frustration at the insufferable self-assurance which Manning showed on the subject of papal infallibility. The effects of their arguments over the Pope's temporal power were also in evidence. Gladstone told Lord Granville of his satisfaction at having dealt a blow 'to the pestilent opinions which have so grievously gained the upper hand in that Church, and to the party that *means* to have a war in Europe for the restoration of the temporal power'.[94] This fear might seem ludicrously far-fetched with the benefit of hindsight: it was understandable enough in one who had imbibed the spirit of Manning's pamphlets. In like manner the doctrine of infallibility became, for Gladstone, the sinister prelude to a wider and still more sinister design, that of winning back the Papal States through practising upon the civil loyalties of Catholics. In every country Rome could count upon the support of organized and devoted followers, whose allegiance to the Pope might transcend their duty to their own States. Gladstone was not short of immoderate language with which to describe these prospective horrors. His pamphlet became the sensation of the hour: 145,000 copies were printed before the end of 1874. As the leader of English Catholics Manning was bound to produce a reply.

He began with a letter (7 November 1874) to *The Times*, in which he asserted that the infallibility definition had not by a jot or a tittle changed either the obligations or the conditions of civil allegiance; that Catholics, like other Christians, must owe their first duty to God, but that this limitation did not prevent them from holding 'a Civil allegiance as pure, as true, and as loyal as is rendered by the distinguished author of the pamphlet, or by any subject of the British Empire'.[95] But in another letter, to the *New York Herald*, Manning was rash enough to refer to the dispute with Gladstone as 'the first event that has overcast a friendship of forty-five years'.[96] Gladstone, in his follow-up pamphlet, professed himself astonished that Manning should be labouring under such a vast misapprehension. In sending a copy of this second pamphlet to Manning he was at pains to ensure that no such error should occur again. 'I offer no apology. Apologies in such cases only seem to mock. There is no remedy on this side of the grave.' And then Gladstone proceeded to turn the knife with consummate skill. 'Vaticanism', as he called it, was an unmitigated evil, yet 'If we had Dr Newman for Pope we should be tolerably safe, so merciful and genial would be his rule!'[97]

This piece of malice had been suggested by Newman's 'Letter to the Duke of Norfolk', a brilliant reply to Gladstone's diatribe, of which Gladstone himself admitted the effectiveness. The great statesman wrote peaceably to Newman thanking him for his 'genial and gentle manner' and for the 'golden glow' with which he had invested the controversy.[98] In fact, Gladstone's pamphlet had not been unwelcome to Newman, who discerned another chance to settle accounts with Manning. 'Gladstone's excuse is, I suppose, the extravagance of Archibishop Manning', Newman told an Anglican friend, 'and he will do us a service if he gives us an opportunity of speaking.'[99] His 'Letter to the Duke of Norfolk' followed the pattern of that to Dr Pusey in denying that the maximizing tendencies of the ultramontanes represented the true spirit of Catholicism. 'The Rock of St. Peter on its summit', Newman wrote, 'enjoys a pure and serene atmosphere, but there is a great deal of Roman *malaria* at the foot of it.' Again, 'there are partisans of Rome that have not the sanctity and wisdom of Rome herself'.[100]

These sentiments aroused the utmost indignation among those who felt themselves attacked, the Roman malaria passage in particular being adjudged '*troppo irreverente*'.[101] The Prefect of Propaganda wrote to Manning that parts of Newman's 'Letter' were likely to do great harm to the faithful; should he be censured? Manning had at first avoided reading Newman's work as he wanted to keep hs own answer to Gladstone 'clear of any seeming divergence, which, I hope, is not likely'.[102] Now he rallied to Newman's side with a generosity that was both admirable and politic. 'The heart of the revered Father Newman,' he informed Propaganda, 'is as right and as Catholic as it is possible to be.' Such blemishes as his 'Letter' possessed would be evident only to 'the more clearsighted among Catholics', upon whom, of course, 'they have no influence at all'. Censure would be not only superfluous but dangerous. 'It would occasion the appearance, perhaps even more than the appearance, of division among Catholics in the presence of our enemies and of our non-Catholic friends. It would arouse a domestic controversy such as aforetime blazed amongst us, but is now by the grace of God extinguished. It would introduce among us the evil spirits of hates and jealousies and personal bitterness.'[103]

The breach between Manning and Gladstone, however, could not now be avoided. In answer to Gladstone's amazed dismissal of the claim that their friendship had never previously been overcast, Manning admitted that there had indeed been an interim of 'some twelve years'[104] after his conversion, but he sought, rather lamely, to distinguish between the friendship which he had continued to feel and its expression, which had undeniably been interrupted. 'Our friendship has indeed been strained to any degree you will fix, by public opposition for conscience' sake, but never by private acts or words unworthy of either you or myself.'[105] To Ullathorne, however, Manning had written in somewhat less lofty a vein, attributing Gladstone's outburst to lowly political motives. 'I know that his party are seeking a new base. . . . My expectation is to see Gladstone at the head of a Puritan anti-Catholic party.'[106]

His public reply to Gladstone, issued that February, ended with a lengthy and magisterial rebuke of Gladstone's action in having instigated Catholics to rise against the divine authority of their Church. 'I must tell him that if he would incline the Catholics of the Empire to accept the ministries of his compassion, he must first purify his style both of writing and of thinking.'[107] Unbelievably, this pamphlet was considered in some Roman quarters to savour of conciliation.[108] Gladstone, at least, was not conciliated, nor was he impressed. 'Manning in his two hundred pages has not, I venture to say, made a single point against me,' he complacently remarked.[109] What Manning *had* achieved, though, was the complete cessation of all his relations with Gladstone. For ten years the two men did not correspond; if they met, it was only on formal occasions. Manning keenly felt the loss of this friendship; still more, perhaps, he felt the removal of his best contact with the circles of influence in English government, for Gladstone remained a power in the land even in opposition, even in retirement. What the Archbishop had forfeited, moreover, none of his underlings were permitted to enjoy. When Oakeley was invited to breakfast with Gladstone, Manning informed him that he would consider it a personal affront if any of his priests should visit the great man's house. Oakeley relayed this remark and noticed that Gladstone became 'visibly affected – for a moment there was almost a vindictive gleam in his eye'.[110] It did not take Manning long to decide that the break had been inevitable, 'for Mr. Gladstone is a substantive, and likes to be attended by adjectives. And I am not exactly an adjective.'[111]

Many Catholics in his diocese would have agreed on that score. In theory

Archbishop's House was open four days a week to receive priests and laymen on business; Manning had resolved as much on his 1865 retreat at Highgate, and he noted with satisfaction eighteen years later that in fact he had given every day for this purpose.[112] But how many of his flock cared voluntarily and uninvited to encounter his formidable presence in the bleak and intimidating surroundings in which he lived? Manning had snapped up his cavernous and gloomy habitation, which still stands on the corner of Carlisle Place and Francis Street, that is, on the edge of his original cathedral site, in 1872. The building had served as a club for privates in the Guards, and Shane Leslie memorably described it under Manning's care as being like 'a Dissenting chapel doing duty as a railway waiting room'.[113] Manning divided the top floor into many rooms, reserving one of the meanest as his own bedroom. He spent the day in one of the large rooms on the floor below, sitting behind a screen, the floor scattered with envelopes which were the daily harvest of his astoundingly copious correspondence. 'Since 1838 I have never had curtains or carpets except what you see in my rooms,' he told a friend. 'There is no affectation or mortification in it, but I like it. It does me good. In furnished rooms I am not quiet.'[114] No wonder, despite the coal fire that blazed at all seasons in Manning's room, people spoke of the gloomy house as a wonderful place for catching colds, or that they referred to the Marble Archbishop[115] who dwelt within. The manservant, incidentally, was called Newman.

From this gaunt stronghold Manning ruled the English Catholic community. He was not quite an absolute monarch because the bishops retained independence in their own sees and he himself was subject to the higher authority of Rome; but Rome chose new bishops upon his instructions and resolved religious controversy in England at his direction. At Westminster he could indulge whatever fad he pleased, even in a field such as music where his own expertise was, to say the least, questionable. Like many a philistine he knew his own mind. He detested what he called 'flash-singing in churches'[116] and considered Gregorian chant the only really religious mode. 'I can make a better act of faith when I hear the Credo sung to Gregorian music,'[117] he said, and what was true for himself he naturally assumed must be true for everyone else. It was a point of principle that women should be altogether excluded from choirs. Even male choirs, however, were suspect: Manning wanted full congregational singing.[118] When someone reminded him that operatic music was popular in Roman churches, he was not a bit put out. 'Too true, and what is the consequence? Victor Emmanuel is in the Quirinal.'[119] And the remark was punctuated with the sniff that invariably accompanied his more ludicrous argumentative scores.

There was one Catholic body, the Jesuits, over whom the tyrannous old man knew that he could exert no ultimate control. As a new convert he had been, by his own account, 'strongly drawn'[120] to the Society: it will be recalled that he had spent his summer breaks from Rome attached to their church in Farm Street. Whatever the true history of his departure therefrom, he had by 1860 turned decisively against Farm Street. Although he could still speak in 1863 of the great contribution that the Jesuits might make towards the establishment of a Catholic university,[121] by the time he became Archbishop his animus against Farm Street had spread to cover the entire Society. Rightly or wrongly, he saw the Jesuits as aristocratic, élitist, absolutist and arbitrary; it was a shrewd thrust of Ullathorne's, then, that Manning's distrust was the recoil of like from like.[122] Other religious orders never attracted his hostility in the same measure: indeed, he imported foreign orders into the diocese to found schools and help with reformatories. He knew, though, that he could never bend the Jesuits to his will; hence he tended to regard the Jesuits as undesirables. History was commandeered to support his case. He read Tierney's edition of Dodd's *History of the English Catholics* and discovered therefrom that the Jesuits were the source of many of the ills that attended the Church in England. The activities of the Society from the time of James I down to 'good Father Lythgoe whom I just remember' appeared to Manning as 'the continual thwarting of the English clergy'. The whole story, he concluded, seemed 'a mysterious permission of God for the chastisement of England'.[123]

It should not be imagined, though, that Manning's suspicions of the Jesuits were the fruit of pure wilfulness. His antagonism was also the reverse side of an essentially noble aim, to raise the status of the secular priesthood, which he considered suffered from the assumption that life as a religious represented a higher calling. In his last years he would describe this endeavour as 'the one chief aim of my whole life since I became a priest'.[124] And when he became Archbishop, 'my first thought was that no Provincial or Father General had any obligation to multiply and perfect his Order greater or more absolute than I had to multiply and to perfect the priesthood of the Diocese of Westminster'.[125] He was furious when Father Gallwey, the Provincial General of the Jesuits, in an 'unseemly speech' called the *Sincere Christian* and the *Catechismus ad Parochos* 'books for the secular clergy'. 'He did not say, but this means, that all that is higher is not for them.'[126]

Manning abhorred the very term 'secular clergy' as a thirteenth-century aberration. There should be nothing secular about *his* clergy. The priesthood was 'the highest state of perfection in the world' and should appear as such. The pastoral office, he urged, could be traced back through the apostles to Christ himself, whereas the religious orders were mere ecclesiastical foundations. Even the episcopate was only the *sacerdotium supremum et absolutum*.[127] Manning therefore insisted on the outward forms of clerical dignity: priests should always be addressed as 'Father' instead of the 'Mister' that had previously been used in England, and they should at all times give evidence of their sacred office by wearing a clerical collar.

In order to nurture his ideal of the priesthood he encouraged the foundation of a seminary in each diocese. This was a hopelessly ambitious plan for the moderate requirements and resources of English Catholicism. Even the Westminster seminary which Manning established at Hammersmith in 1869, moving those training for the priesthood from St Edmund's, Ware, proved a costly failure and was abandoned after his death. Yet he had seen the seminary as a declaration of principle. 'I saw that the pastoral clergy were at a disadvantage, depressed, and lightly esteemed; but I saw that they were our Lord's own Order. I came to see that the chief need of the Church everywhere is that they should be what our Lord intended, and that all religious Orders united cannot fill their place or do their work. This has made me work for them.'[128]

As early as 1860 he had criticized the Jesuits at Farm Street for attracting wealth and influence away from the ambit of parish priests, whose needs were desperate. 'I cannot overstate the comparative disadvantages of the missions round Farm Street, and the way in which the educated laity are passing from the secular clergy.'[129] Manning determined that the Jesuits should never enjoy any favours from him. He would never allow the Society to have a school in the Westminster diocese, though no one was more conscious than he of the need for Catholic secondary education for the middle classes. No Catholic parent with the fear of God before their eyes, he considered, could possibly entrust a son to one of the Anglican public schools.[130] But whatever the solution of this problem might be, Manning was quite sure that it did not lie with the Jesuits. They had acquired land on the present site of Victoria Station around 1860, and it was Manning's doing that Wiseman forbade them to found a grammar school there.[131]

When Manning became Archbishop he maintained this absolute refusal to countenance a Jesuit school in the diocese against all the persuasion and politics that the Society could muster. Partly, no doubt, he wished to protect St Charles's College, which his nephew William Manning had founded in Notting Hill. Yet he allowed several other private secondary schools for Catholics in London, whereas the Jesuits were not even permitted to establish a non-teaching house in Chelsea. Father Gallwey begged in vain: 'Will your Grace allow us to open a grammar school at a safe distance from St Charles's College, say not nearer than three miles?'[132] No, his Grace would not. He feared that if the Jesuits had a London school they would cream off for their own Order the most talented boys who wished to become priests. Nor did the support which the Society enjoyed among the old Catholic families do anything to endear its cause with Manning. As if another reason were required, he disliked the Jesuit emphasis on classical education instead of the technical studies which he saw as the country's crying need. Rather than tolerate Jesuit schools, he tried in 1880 to persuade the French De La Salle brothers, whose particular vocation was the education of the poor, to undertake a grammar school.[133] Conversely, the nuns of the Sacred Heart, being in Manning's mind closely associated with the Jesuits, were forbidden to take charge of a poor school within the diocese, or even to occupy a house which they had bought in Dorset Street.[134]

As Manning waged war upon the Jesuits, some of those under his immediate care found themselves, they knew not why, irresistibly drawn towards the proscribed order. Canon Morris, who acted as Manning's private secretary when he first became Archbishop, was the first to experience this calling. Manning reluctantly gave his permission, for which Morris, sensible of what it must have cost his master, expressed the most grovelling gratitude. 'You had better complete your work and make Newman, my faithful attendant, a Jesuit lay-brother,' Manning harshly jested.[135] Father Humphreys, one of the Oblates of St Charles, was the next associate to enter the Society. Worst of all, William Anderdon, son of that John who had laboured to force the brash young Manning into the paths of righteousness, gave up his post in the Archbishop's household for the same purpose.

Anderdon junior much resembled his uncle in looks and in happier days he had strongly supported Manning against Newman, with whom he had worked in Dublin during the 1850s. Newman had described him then as 'a petted and spoilt fellow, and he is now in his element, for the ladies are all about him, filling him with sympathy and mutton chops'.[136] Anderdon certainly seems to have possessed his measure of self-importance, for no sooner had he entered his Jesuit noviciate than he began to express to his uncle his sense of grievance at the unkind treatment which the Jesuits had received in the Westminster diocese. The presumptuous nephew did not quite dare to make a direct attack, but he was not without resource in finding a way of making his point. 'If you came to see me upon my deathbed,' he wrote to Manning, 'or if I sent you my intended death letter, what I would wish to say would be couched somewhat thus.' His message lived up to this promising introduction. Have you, he asked his uncle, 'sufficiently considered it as the great misfortune of your life that you have never practically had a superior? that you have always been in the way of making your own views and opinions. . . . I ask myself, why is anyone to be tempted to look forward to the termination of a few years as marking the dawn of a more wholesome state of things in God's Church here in England?'[137]

The whirligig of time was bringing in his revenges for the days when the adolescent Manning had lashed Anderdon's father with his impertinences. The venerable Archbishop now behaved in exemplary fashion. 'I have carefully read your letter, and thank you with all my heart for the motive which prompted it. Your object in writing is so full of charity that I refrain from any thought or word but one. . . . I wish. . . . that I may derive from your letter all the good you desire.'[138] To this end he placed Anderdon's communication in the hands of two priests, who presumably chastised the Archbishop as they saw fit. The whole incident would have been decorous in the extreme had not Anderdon pushed his luck by writing again in the following year:

My affection for you [he informed his uncle], even with all the radical differences which sever us, makes me at times burn with indignation to see the line and the view which you have – unhappily, if I may say it – adopted, travestied and vulgarised by other minds, to the diminution of God's glory and the detriment, if not the loss, of souls. I wish we could ask St. Chrysostom whether he only referred to temporal rulers in saying, I wonder if any ruler is saved?[139]

Manning, seeing that Anderdon had not profited from his former display of archiepiscopal meekness, decided this time to answer (24 July 1876) in another style:

When you entered the Society I foresaw that certain faults of your mind would be intensified. I mean a conscious criticism of other men and an unconsciousness of your own state. . . . You say that you 'burn with indignation'. These words have no sense if they are not a censure pronounced by you upon me in the office I bear and other Bishops of the Catholic Church in England. If I were to lay them before the General of the Society, I think he would read you better than you know yourself. If I were to lay them before the Holy See, one more light would be cast upon the dissensions which at this moment are afflicting the Church in England.[140]

It is a wonderful thing to be able to combine meekness of person with so keen a sense of the duty to maintain the dignity of office. Manning, in fact, was no longer a mere Archbishop. In 1875 he had been made a Cardinal. This promotion came surprisingly late; it had been expected almost from the moment when Manning first became an Archbishop. But his high-handed conduct at the Vatican Council – 'troppo fanatico' was the verdict in Rome[141] – had left him enemies among the Cardinals, and Pius IX may have been wary of immediately overruling this opposition by conferring a favour that might seem like a *quid pro quo* for the infallibility definition. When the honour finally came to Manning, he expressed a seemly concern that it might adversely affect the Church in England. 'Anyone who in the world's eyes rises high is thought to seek it, and love it; and that hinders his work for souls.'[142] There was, however, another thought that instantly banished such worries. 'I ought not to fear when the Vicar of Our Lord acts. It was He that willed it, as I know.'[143] The elevation had the excellent effect of making Manning more willing to delegate some of his work in the Westminster diocese. Thenceforth his activity was merely stupendous.

As it happened, the cardinalate came at a time when his career was a little in the shadow of unfavourable circumstance. He had no such close contact with Disraeli's Government as he had once enjoyed with Gladstone's. Ireland, which might have provided him with another opportunity to mediate between the Cabinet and the Catholic Church, was comparatively quiescent, unlike the Irish MPs, who were developing the tactic of obstructing the business of the House of Commons with interminable speechifying. This behaviour aroused all Manning's conservative disgust, and a decade later he would quite approve of the introduction of a device for forcibly closing debates: had not the Vatican Council done likewise? Nevertheless, out of touch though he was with Disraeli's administration, Manning could not forgo his habit of keeping the Prime Minister informed of his close concern with events. He professed himself a particular admirer of the Government's imperialist policies. 'I am no politician,' he modestly told Disraeli in December 1879, 'but it is clear to me that, having an Empire, we must either give it up or keep it up. To give it up would be our extinction as a power in the world; to keep it up seems to me to demand, and even to dictate, the policy you have pursued. And Englishmen must give up trembling at dangers and puling about taxes.' The cynical Prime Minister returned an appropriate reply – 'the voice of patriotism from one so eminent as yourself will animate the faltering and add courage even to the brave'[144] – but kept his distance.

Manning discovered that he had a better chance of holding the Prime Minister's interest with gossip about Gladstone than with state affairs. He contrasted the young Gladstone *sans peur et sans reproche* with the fierce old man whose enmity they had both incurred. 'You surprise me,' said Disraeli, 'I thought he had always been an Italian in the custody of a Scotsman.'[145] After the Conservative defeat in the 1880 election, Disraeli finished another novel, *Endymion*, in which he again portrayed Manning, this time as Nigel Penruddock, 'the prophet who had been ordained in Mayfair', who 'might have been a Dean if he had been a practical man', but who joined the Roman

Church instead and ended as 'Archbishop of Tyre'. (The implication that preferment came easily to well-connected Roman converts was a stock Anglican jibe. There was a story that Samuel Wilberforce once encountered Manning with some priests in attendance. 'And is that gentleman also an Archbishop?' he enquired, pointing to one of the acolytes.)[146] Yet Penruddock, for all Disraeli's sneers, is a friendlier portrait than Grandison: Manning certainly preferred it. Perhaps, as Robert Blake suggests, Disraeli was appreciative of Manning's description of Gladstone as 'the most revengeful man he ever knew'.[147]

More disappointing to Manning than his exclusion from the counsels of government were failures within the English Catholic community over which he presided, in particular the failure of his attempt to found a Catholic university. The creation of such an institution had always been implicit in his stand against Oxford and Cambridge. The old Catholic families hoped that the Jesuits would assume the task, a possibility that made Manning even keener to tackle the work himself. He can only have regarded it as a sinister development that the Jesuits established a mission at Oxford in 1871. The danger to Manning's policy on universities became clearer still in the following year when a committee which the bishops had appointed to consider higher education recommended that the question of Catholics being allowed to go to Oxford should be reconsidered. Manning used a meeting of the bishops to quash this proposal, but the voting was only seven to five.[148] Under some pressure, he undertook to write to Propaganda setting forth once more the pros and the cons of the case. This he did in predictable terms, as an opponent recorded. 'I have never read a document that so disgusted me, from its palpable injustice and even occasional falsehood . . . it goes very far in my mind towards justifying the hardest things that Newman has ever said of its author. I suppose it arises from sheer inability to take in any view of the subject which differs from his own.'[149] The consequence of Manning's report, however, was that Rome reiterated its hostile views on Protestant universities and instructed the Provincial Synod of 1873 to bend its deliberations towards the creation of a Catholic university in England.

Acting with his usual energy and resource, Manning soon collected an impressive staff of professors. His plan was that the university should be affiliated to London University for examination purposes but should otherwise be entirely independent. 'We refuse Oxford and Cambridge as mixed and Godless,' Manning explained to Gladstone (with whom he had not yet, in 1873, broken); 'we accept the London University because we have no contact with it but for examination.'[150] That contact, however, sufficed to give Newman a pretext for boycotting the university when

Manning politely asked him to assist in the enterprise. 'I could not without a great inconsistency', the fastidious intellectual replied to this invitation, 'take part in an institution which formally and "especially" recognises the London University; a body which has been the beginning, and source, and symbol of all the Liberalism existing in the educated classes for the last forty years.'[151] It must have been satisfying to lecture Manning on the horrors of Liberalism.

In fact, as Newman well knew, it was Manning's illiberalism which made him quite unsuited to run a university. From the beginning he determined that the college should be under the control of the episcopacy, which, for this purpose at least, meant himself. In order to involve the other bishops financially he was obliged to create a governing body, called the Senate, upon which other dioceses and even the laity were represented. But when at the first meeting a Mr Hardman presumed to suggest that the subject proposed might be better discussed in the absence of the bishops, Manning, in his own words, 'saw at once that the effect would be to surrender the whole treatment and guidance of the question to laymen, priests and regulars. I made up my mind that our scheme would not work, and that it was necessary to let it die.'[152] The Senate never reconvened. And so jealously did Manning guard his college against any contact with the religious orders that Father Bernard Vaughan, as a young Jesuit, was refused permission even to attend chemistry lectures.[153]

It was not as though there was ever a superfluity of students. The college was established in Wright's Lane, Kensington; and in its first year (1872) it attracted sixteen undergraduates. As Newman had found in Dublin, no Catholic university could hope to survive without the support of the upper classes, and these were just the people whom Manning had antagonized with his line on higher education. Thwarted of their desire for Oxford and Cambridge, they were not inclined to patronize an alternative offered by the man who had imposed this prohibition. Manning compounded his difficulties by the appointment of Mgr Capel as Rector, or head of the university. It was an extraordinary mistake for him to make, as Mgr Capel, a priest given to soliciting aristocratic souls in drawing-rooms, was the last person whom Manning might have been expected to consider. The choice proved in every way unsatisfactory. The college staggered on for four years; at one time it boasted as many as forty-four students; in 1878 the number was down to twelve.[154] By that time the venture, always in debt, was hopelessly bankrupt; and it did not help either that Mgr Capel had failed to keep accounts, or that he demanded the repayment of considerable sums which he claimed to have paid out of his own pocket. The total debts were in excess of £10,000, and the other bishops, who had never been allowed a say in the running of the university, now had to stump up to save Manning from a scandal. 'In all this trial our Lord has helped me almost palpably,' the fortunate beneficiary would later conclude.[155]

His fellow bishops, and all others, judged the university an expensive farce. Manning did not give up easily, though. Rather than admit defeat by abandoning the project altogether, he kept on three or four of the staff to run what he described as 'a private diocesan work in the Cromwell Road'. Eventually, in 1882, the 'Catholic University College' was united with St Charles's College. 'A new wing to contain the library and museum is building,'[156] Manning defiantly announced. By this time the students were virtually non-existent. No matter; the university had 'struck spurs into all our flanks, and we are straining upward in our studies'.[157]

So Manning had decided by 1887. During the mid-1870s he found solace harder to come by, even in Rome. Although by sheer experience and force of personality he could still carry his point on English affairs at head-quarters, there were signs in the Holy See as elsewhere of some recoil from the methods of this most dedicated and ruthless of Roman disciples. Augustus Paget, accredited by the British Government at the Vatican, retailed gossip of Manning's being under criticism for the 'violent and aggressive manner in which he conducts his Archiepiscopal duties in England'.[158] There was probably substance in this report because the French Ambassador told a similar tale in 1876. 'Manning's opinions are his, and his alone – frequently in sharp contrast to those of the rest of the Curia. He is regarded here as one of the staunchest supporters of the Papal authority as defined at the 1870 Vatican Council; but at the same time as a Utopian individualist, who takes too great a part in politics.'[159]

Manning was aware, when he visited Rome in 1876, that he was not quite so much in his element as usual. 'I was really ill, which always does me good,' he noted characteristically.[160] But there was more to it than that. He saw the Vatican being run by old men who did not always put off their offices with the onset of senility. Astonishingly, his criticism extended even to the Pope, whom he described (or so Purcell related) as 'growing old and garrulous, and not to be trusted with a secret'.[161] Perhaps the root of this disenchantment was that he now, through a strange moderation of his opinions, found himself at odds with the prevailing Vatican sentiment over the temporal power.

When Rome had been seized in 1870, Manning had thundered defiance in his usual extreme style. 'The Italians have forced their way into Rome; and as I believe that there is a God that judgeth the earth, so sure I am that their doom will not tarry.'[162] When their doom did tarry, though, Manning did not beat his breast in impotent rage. He retained his conviction that the seizure of Rome had been legalized robbery, but he ceased to hope for thunderbolts, or even for some spontaneous rising by the powers of this world, that should right the evil. As his pragmatism asserted itself he gradually came to believe, against the Pope and his advisers whose policy he publicly sustained, that it would be necessary to negotiate with the Italian Government. He scorned '*la politica d'inerzia*' favoured by the '*miracolisti*', who confidently awaited some divine intervention that would vindicate the Pope's territorial sovereignty; he knew better than any man that God helps those who help themselves. Besides, if it had previously been a providential ordinance for good that the Pope should hold an earthly kingdom, might it not now be equally a part of the divine plan that the Church should be stripped of its external possessions in order to fit it for the time of the peoples that was surely forthcoming? Was the loss of the papal territories not therefore a providential spoliation?[163] As a kingdom of this world the papacy might be subject to the tribulations of this world; as the unadorned expression of God's purpose, never. As early as 1870, notwithstanding his indignant protests at the Italian action, he agreed privately with Gladstone that 'a mathematical point would suffice' for the Pope's earthly domain 'if it be really secure'.[164]

'Manning's eloquent advocacy of a *modus vivendi* between Vatican and State obtains, as can be imagined, small support here,'[165] the French Ambassador in Rome noted in 1876. The former cynosure of Roman opinion now found himself regarded as an '*italianissimo*',[166] almost equivalent to a traitor at a time when the Italian Government was beginning to meet the Pope's intransigence with aggressive measures against religion. The days when he could be suspected of currying favour were well and truly past. Yet Manning's compromise proposals were almost as unrealistic as the Pope's refusal to negotiate. 'He proclaims that the Italian capital should be moved back to Florence – or on to Naples!' reported the French Ambassador.[167]

It was certainly not surrender that Manning counselled. All the same, it may be thought that he had previously supported the temporal power in such unguarded terms that he was unable now to retreat with honour. A man who has consistently identified his own views with those of the Holy Ghost, who has called down the wrath of heaven upon his opponents, who has cast aspersions on fellow Catholics unable to share his zeal, does not inspire confidence when he suddenly decides that circumstances necessitate the adoption of more moderate courses. That was not, of course, how Manning saw the matter. 'I am beginning to feel my feet in the Italian question,' he blithely announced at the end of his life.[168] By 1888, perhaps earlier, he was 'fully convinced that Rome can only return to the Pope *by the will of the*

Italian people, and that armed intervention or diplomatic pressure will only revive and harden the resolve of the Italian people. If it were restored by either of these interventions *ab extra*, it could only stand by support *ab extra* over again, from which may Heaven preserve us.'[169] Such sound and sensible judgement could not possibly be objectionable, unless in one who had formerly spoken of the loss of the Pope's territories as a sign of the coming of Anti-Christ, or in one who had appealed to the faithful in all countries to restore the Pope's independence. By 1889 Manning's apocalyptic impulses were running quite the other way. Perhaps the course of events had been permitted 'for the expiation of sin, and the purgation of Italy so as by fire'.[170]

But this is to run ahead. Despite his gloomy sojourn in Rome during 1876, an experience which 'made me understand the *tristis est anima mea usque ad mortem*',[171] Manning set off for more of the same treatment in the following autumn. This time it was in Paris that he became seriously ill. What started as a slight cold turned into bronchitis 'and, I believe, gout'. He was imprisoned in his rooms for five weeks. 'I do not think this is my last illness, but it is one of my last,' the patient reflected.[172] While he was convalescing, news came of another sick man, whose condition gave no grounds for optimism. Pius IX was dying. Manning rushed to Rome and spent much time in the ensuing weeks beside the Pope's bed. What a scene for a painter: the graceful, open-hearted, *simpatico* Pope on the edge of eternity, flanked by his impenetrable English protégé trying so hard, for once, to avoid all mention of business. 'I had the happiness of conversing with him only on such thoughts and things as were consoling and cheerful and free from all anxious thought.' Manning was satisfied with his efforts: 'More than once in those five weeks I was able, as I hope, to bring him some momentary solace; and I thank God that my lot was so ordered that I stood beside the Pontiff, whom we have so revered and loved, in the last days and in the last moments of his great and glorious life.'[173]

This was literally true. Popes who linger on their deathbeds must face the additional ordeal of an audience of cardinals. Manning arrived at the Vatican on the morning of 7 February 1878 to be told that Pius IX was struggling for breath. 'I went in at once. On reaching the Antecamera I found many of the Cardinals already there. It was at once evident that the end was near. I went into his bedroom and found him somewhat raised in his bed, breathing with difficulty. He was motionless, and his face calm and grand. I bent down and kissed his hand. He said "*Addio, carissimo.*" '[174] This parting gesture was not the least of the many rewards which Pius had lavished upon Manning. The emotionally remote and inaccessible Archbishop, who needed affection like every man, but who had long since forced out of himself those human foibles in which affection breeds, treasured Pius's dying remark as a vindication against those like Samuel Wilberforce who accused him of calculated sycophancy. It was, on the very worst construction, a sycophancy that stretched beyond the grave. 'To Rome and to the Churches', Manning wrote to an English Catholic, 'it is the loss of one of the greatest Pontiffs who ever reigned.'[175]

The obsequies of a pope, however, soon give way to fevered speculation about his successor. In the midst of his 1876 depression Manning had melodramatically speculated with himself on the possibility of a conclave taking place with Italy at war with the papacy, and Rome in the hands of a satanically inspired populace. He even considered the possibility of martyrdom at the hands of the rabid mob, 'but I hardly venture to think Our Lord would call such as I am to so great a grace. It would be, indeed, to say to a soul in the mire, come up hither!'[176] The circumstances of the 1878 conclave were considerably less alarming than Manning's perfervid imagination had envisaged. The cardinals met in unmolested knots beforehand and decided that Cardinal Pecci of Perugia, though he had been regarded by Pius IX as a dangerous liberal, was the prime candidate. Some gentlemanly haggling about who should be second choice ensued, with each cardinal in turn disclaiming his own qualifications. Cardinal Bilio deemed he had too weak a character; Cardinal Monaco commented on his shocking lack of self-control; and Cardinal Manning, when his claims were politely urged, pointed out the absolute necessity of having an Italian pope at this critical juncture in the papacy's affairs.[177] It does not appear that Manning was ever seriously considered, though his name might have gathered support if there had been a deadlock in the voting. The English newspapers, effortlessly shrugging off the boring constraints of fact, reported that Manning was energetically canvassing for himself, an account which caused some twitting among his fellow cardinals.[178] Still, he did achieve a vote or two in the conclave, the first Englishman to be so favoured since Nicholas Breakspeare was elected in 1154.

It remained to be seen whether Leo XIII would prove as amenable to Manning's influence as his predecessor had been. The signs were not altogether encouraging. As Cardinal Pecci the new Pope had been in favour of the infallibility definition but with no fanatical enthusiasm; at the Vatican Council he had tried to prevent the issue being brought forward in front of other business. Pecci was a cool, unemotional man of affairs. A pope can hardly avoid being ultramontane, but Leo XIII's understanding of his role was far removed, in practical though not of course in doctrinal terms, from the other-worldly spirit that informed the intransigence of the previous reign. Had Manning's ascendancy at Rome come to an end? The only matter on which the Archbishop of Westminster had shown himself flexible, the need to reach an accord with the Italian State, was the one issue on which Leo inclined to despair. The Pope would even consider leaving Rome, so oppressed did he become with the designs of his enemies.[179]

Leo XIII's goodwill was especially important because in 1875 Manning had embarked on one of the greatest struggles of his career, impelled by his desire to settle accounts with the Jesuits. The *casus belli* had arisen in the Salford diocese, where Herbert Vaughan was now bishop. Vaughan shared his mentor's determination that the Jesuits should start no schools in his diocese; he, too, wished to protect vocations to the secular priesthood against the rival attractions of an élite order. The Jesuits, aware of Vaughan's opposition, but apparently unaware that they were provoking a character as strong as Manning's, waited until he was away in America during 1874–5 and opened a school against his expressed intent, claiming to be carrying out the wishes of Propaganda.[180] On his return to England Vaughan contested every inch of the ground. The fundamental point at issue was whether regulars were to be subject to, or independent of, episcopal control. Before the restoration of the hierarchy, the Jesuits had been supported and sustained in England by the Catholic gentry, and they did not always take kindly to finding themselves under diocesan authority. The Society had been experiencing similar difficulties in the United States; it now determined to force the issue and gain a ruling from Rome in its favour. Vaughan thought that the Society had deliberately chosen to do battle with the English bishops rather than face their American counterparts, 'who are Irish and more violent'.[181] If that was indeed the Jesuits' reasoning, they were making an egregious error.

Manning leapt into the fray. He described the issue at stake as he was wont to describe any contest in which he unreservedly engaged himself – the ousting of Errington, the Westminster succession, the control of seminaries – as 'a crisis next to the restoration of the Hierarchy'.[182] As always he sought not just victory but a complete kill. It would, he explained, be for the Jesuits' own good. 'I have long felt', he told Vaughan in March 1875, 'that the English province is altogether abnormal, dangerous to themselves, mischievous to the Church in England. I have seemed to see it and feel it with more than natural intellect and natural discernment. I am now convinced that I am right, and I propose to go through the whole work or warfare which has now been begun – for their sakes as much as for ours.'[183] There could hardly be a more revealing account of Manning's thought processes. But, no less typically, he underestimated the strength of the opposition which was to have this great good done to it. At first he reckoned that the affair would present no difficulties. 'I mean to bring the whole relation of the Jesuits to the Church in England before the Bishops, and to lay it before the Holy See,' he wrote from Rome in March 1875. 'I had a full conversation with Cardinal Franchi, and today with Rinaldi, about the Jesuit college in Manchester. I hope the business is at an end.'[184]

The business was in fact only just beginning. The Jesuits were strongly entrenched in Rome, and they lacked nothing in determination or political sagacity. Constant vigilance was necessary if they were to be held at bay. At one point they succeeded in convincing the aged Pius that it would be perfectly fair if they had a school in Manchester, since Vaughan had complete control in Salford. They did not mention, nor did the Pope divine, that Salford was just a name for the poorer regions of Manchester.[185] In 1877 Manning decided that it would be necessary, beside his own regular annual visits to Rome, to have Vaughan, and perhaps one other bishop, permanently stationed at the Vatican in order to counter such dastardly designs. Then the accession of Leo XIII threw the whole controversy back to its beginnings. The new Pope gravely announced, a year after the matter had been raised at Rome, that it would be necessary to have the questions at issue most carefully examined.[186] Manning began to worry: procrastination, he thought, would favour the Jesuit schemers. Moreover, Propaganda, which was adjudicating the case, was largely composed of regulars, an ominous circumstance.

It was therefore a decisive breakthrough for Manning when, in 1879, he secured that the dispute should be taken out of Propaganda's jurisdiction and entrusted to a special commission of cardinals. Thenceforth the Jesuits concentrated all their hopes on delay, a tactic which they pursued with consummate skill. As long as the decision could be postponed there was always hope. The Pope might die, or Manning might fatally overplay his hand. Leo would survive until 1903; the second possibility, however, proved better founded. Manning alarmed the Pope with his warnings that the Jesuits threatened to 'diminish the power of an authority higher than that of the bishops as well as theirs'.[187] By contrast, to raise the secular clergy was to raise the Church throughout the world. The case 'is no less than this', Manning wrote home to Ullathorne in July 1880, 'who is to form the clergy and educate the laity in England?'[188] That year he left Rome gladly, 'sick of the heat and intrigues'. Vaughan may have been no less glad to see him go; he was finding his chief's support a mixed blessing. 'They say Manning talks too much – lets his feelings be seen,' he recorded in his diary.[189] Yet Manning had shown himself capable of sinking his own vanity in so important a cause. In January 1880 he read a newspaper report that his presence in Rome might be doing more harm than good. 'If it be so,' he told Vaughan, 'the more falls on you and Clifford.'[190] And, notwithstanding

Vaughan's doubts, Manning did valuable service in persuading the heads of other orders not to take a stand with the Jesuits. In consequence the bishops were united; the regulars were not.

That was a vital factor in the victory that eventually crowned Manning's campaign. The bull *Romanos Pontifices*, published in 1881, six years after the opening of Manning's offensive, left the bishops firmly in control of their dioceses. The regular orders were required in future to obtain consent both from the ordinary and the Holy See before establishing any residence, church, convent, college or school in a diocese, and even before altering already existing institutions. 'It shows . . . that we have been right,' Manning concluded, crowing triumphantly about his 'great victory over the most powerful conspiracy in the Church'. The decision has had considerably more practical influence on the Church's development than the infallibility definition, which subsequent popes have handled with the greatest caution. Yet Manning's celebration was tinged with relief that the long contest was over. 'God grant that it may be the last internal conflict of the Church in England.'[191]

His prayer was answered in the sense that he never again felt called upon to attack his co-religionists with quite such rigour. Emotions which have been aroused over many years, however, are difficult to still. That had been made clear by the affair of Newman's cardinalate in 1878–9.

The accession of Pope Leo XIII had brought hope to some of Newman's better-connected lay friends – the Duke of Norfolk, Lord Petre, the Marquess of Ripon – that it might now be possible to gain for him this supreme mark of recognition at Rome. Protocol demanded, however, that any approach to the Pope on this matter should be made through Cardinal Manning as head of the Catholic Church in England. Purcell stated in his biography of Manning, though without mentioning any source, that when the Catholic lords waited on their Metropolitan with their proposal he 'bent his head and remained silent for some moments'.[192] That makes a good story, even better if, as in more elaborated versions, Manning is heard to whisper '*Fiat voluntas tua.*' All that is certainly known, however, is that Manning transmitted the request in the most generous possible terms, reproducing to the letter the sentiments with which the Duke of Norfolk had urged the case.

Newman, Manning wrote to the Pope's Secretary of State, had rendered 'singular and unequalled services: . . . In the rise and revival of the Catholic Faith in England, there is no one whose name will stand out in history with so great a prominence.' That last sentence, indeed, was so lavish that it inspired a tactful demurrer from Lord Petre. Manning also transcribed for Rome's benefit the Duke's feeling that Newman had been unjustly neglected:

He has continued for thirty years without any token or mark of confidence of the Holy See; and this apparent passing over of his great merits has been noted both among Catholics and non-Catholics as implying division amongst the faithful in England, and some unexplained mistrust of Dr. Newman. It is obviously not only most desirable that this should be corrected, but obviously right that Dr. Newman should be cleared of any unjust suspicion.

And Manning concluded on a personal note: 'I have felt it to be a duty, very grateful to myself, to convey to your Eminence this expression of the desires of the distinguished Catholic laymen in whose names I write, and of those whom they represent.'[193]

This letter was written in the summer of 1878, but as a result of the peregrinations of Cardinal Howard, to whom its delivery was entrusted, did not reach Rome until the end of the year. The Pope gladly agreed to make Newman a cardinal, and in January 1879 Manning was able to forward the joyful tidings to Ullathorne for communication to Newman.

There the matter should have ended, and would have ended, but for a tedious display of over-sensitivity by Newman. Naturally he was deeply touched by the honour done to him: 'The cloud is lifted from me for ever,'[194] he would remark to a fellow Oratorian. No less naturally he wished to accept, but it was not in his nature to be able to receive his new dignity without a prior display of fine feeling. He knew that there was an obligation laid upon cardinals without episcopal sees to reside in Rome, and that was a fate which he wished to avoid at all costs. He knew also, if not from his own judgement, at least after conversation with Ullathorne, that Rome could most likely be prevailed upon to make an exception in his case. Nevertheless, as Ullathorne kindly put it, 'Dr. Newman has far too humble and delicate a mind to dream of thinking or saying anything which would look like hinting at any kind of terms with the Sovereign Pontiff.'[195] The two men therefore concocted a scheme whereby Newman should address Ullathorne a long letter intended for Roman eyes, in which he would express his gratitude and set forth his difficulty without either accepting or refusing the honour, while Ullathorne should send a covering letter to Manning explaining that what Newman *really* meant was, perish the vulgar thought, 'Yes, please.' It was the kind of device that two conscientious old spinsters might have dreamt up, with much implied self-congratulation on the refinement of their sentiment. It was also an example of what Charles Kingsley had objected to in Newman, his slithery way with the truth. Would it really have been any less 'humble and delicate' if Newman had frankly and openly stated his desire to accept and asked for a ruling on the residence issue? To establish the will of a superior and submit is hardly to make terms. It does, however, involve the possibility of submitting to an adverse decision.

In any case, Newman's letter to Ullathorne made a pathetic plea that he might be allowed to die where he had so long lived, at the Oratory in Birmingham, and ended with a parade of disinterest that might very well be taken as a refusal of the cardinalate. 'Since I know now and henceforth that His Holiness thinks kindly of me, what more can I desire?'[196] It was left to Ullathorne, in his letter to Manning, to suggest the not-quite-so-noble answer to that moving enquiry: 'I am thoroughly confident that nothing stands in the way of his grateful acceptance except what he tells me greatly distresses him, namely the having to leave the Oratory at a critical period in its existence . . . and the impossibility of his beginning a new life at his advanced age.'[197] Both Newman's letter and Ullathorne's rider were forwarded to Manning, who now committed the unpardonable sin of taking Newman at his own word. That is, he sent Newman's letter on to Rome, but not Ullathorne's explanation. The Holy See should be allowed to make its own interpretation of Newman's obfuscations.

Of course this action of Manning's was quite inexcusable. No doubt a strong case might be made for him in terms of understandable human weakness. Newman's serpentine manoeuvrings *were* acutely irritating, while his contribution to English Catholicism was, by Manning's assessment, almost wholly negative. It would be quite wrong, however, to rest any defence of Manning on grounds which imply that he consciously and deliberately set out to prevent Newman's becoming a cardinal. Had that been his intention he could surely have acted far more effectively. He might, for instance, have sent an equivocal letter to Rome in the first place, and then used his influence to block the plan; he could have put up a formidable resistance if he had chosen. His failure to communicate the contents of Ullathorne's letter, on the other hand, made no sense at all as a stratagem; it must eventually be discovered and rebound to his own discredit. Those very detractors who lose no opportunity to accuse Manning of Machiavellian cunning are all too ready on this occasion to believe him capable of the most ridiculously crude and useless tactic.

Yet if Manning's withholding of Ullathorne's letter is taken out of the immediate context of his relations with Newman and referred instead to his general mode of proceeding it becomes as typical as Newman's prevarication. Had Manning been aware of harbouring illwill towards Newman he would have repressed it. He was not, however, conscious of any such motive. The key to his conduct lies rather in his infinite capacity for self-illusion. Newman's equivocating letter gave him grounds for believing what he wanted to believe, that Newman had refused; and thereafter Newman's refusal was his version of reality. Ullathorne's covering letter could be discountenanced because Manning never permitted extraneous facts to interfere with fundamental beliefs. Kingsley had once written of Newman that 'he is utterly unconscious, not only that he is deceiving others, but that he is deceiving himself'. The judgement was far more applicable to Manning, for whom truth had become simply an artefact of the will.

And so, in February 1879, the news seeped out of Archbishop's House that Newman had been offered, and refused, the cardinalate. On 18 Ferbuary an article in *The Times* appeared to that effect. This occurrence quickly persuaded Newman to show his true hand. He dispatched a letter to his friend the Duke of Norfolk denying his refusal and strongly implying that Manning was responsible for the rumours that had been flying about:

As to the statement of my refusing a Cardinal's Hat, which is in the Papers, you must not believe it, for this reason. Of course, it implies that an offer has been made me, and I have sent my answer to it. Now I have ever understood that it is a point of propriety and honour to consider such communications *sacred*. The statement therefore cannot come from me. Nor could it come from Rome, for it was made public before my answer got to Rome – It could only come then from some one who, not only read my letter, but, instead of leaving the *Pope* to interpret it, took upon himself to put an interpretation upon it, and published that interpretation to the world. A private letter, addressed to Roman authorities, is *intercepted* on its way and *published* in the English Papers. How is it possible that anyone can have done this? And besides, I am quite sure that, if so high an honour was offered to me, I should not answer it by a blunt refusal.[198]

The Duke, with true aristocratic insouciance, forwarded this letter to Manning, who had lately left for Rome. Whatever the emotions with which Manning scanned Newman's imputations of dishonourable conduct, he acted immediately to set matters straight. 'I have not a second time failed to understand your intention,' he wrote to Newman on 8 March. He still could not, with the best will in the world, detect any error on his own part. 'I fully believed that, for the reasons given in your letter, you declined what might be offered. But the Bishop expressed his hope that you might under a change of conditions accept it. This confirmed my belief that as it stood you declined it.'[199] Wonderful logic!

Newman, meanwhile, was busy accepting the Hat by every post. Of course there was no difficulty at all about his not residing at Rome; nobody could seriously have imagined that there would be. Newman's initial letter to Manning (4 March) gratefully accepted the permission which the Pope gave him to remain in Birmingham. But then he realized overnight that he had said nothing about the cardinalate itself. What might Manning make of that? Another letter was sent off on the morrow to set the matter absolutely straight. He also deemed it advisable to inform Cardinal Howard of his willingness to receive the purple. The episode had certainly improved Newman's powers of positive decision making. When, later in the year, he went to Rome for the ceremony that made him a prince of the Church he gave an affecting address explaining how he had always opposed the spirit of liberalism in religion. The more cynical, however, observed that it was just as well Rome had never read his works or he surely would not have been made a cardinal.[200]

Manning was left to endure the pointed celebrations in the English press. When rumours had been circulating that Newman had refused the proffered dignity, *Punch* had delivered itself of the following:

> A Cardinal's Hat! Fancy Newman in *that*,
>   For the Crown o'er his grey temples spread!
> 'Tis the good and great head would honour the hat,
>   Not the hat that would honour the head.
>
> There's many a priest craves it: no wonder *he* waives it
>   Or that we, the soiled headcover scanning,
> Exclaim with one breath, *sans* distinction of faith,
>   Would they wish Newman ranked with old Manning?[201]

That might be dismissed as ignorant Protestant malice, but the Jesuit journal *The Month* also went out of its way to imply the same invidious distinction. Cardinal Newman, it announced, was 'the most distinguished and the greatest Englishman who will ever have worn the Roman Purple'.[202]

10 Private Life and Public Character

Anchorite, who didst dwell
With all the world for cell. . . .

FRANCIS THOMPSON, *To The Dead Cardinal of Westminster*

Manning was seventy-two in 1880. Three of his family died that year: his sister Anna Maria and his brothers Charles and Frederick. 'Dear brother, I never knew how much he cared for me,'[1] reflected Manning as he leafed through the two handsome volumes in which Frederick had kept his letters. As Frederick had strenuously avoided meeting him for the previous twenty-nine years this ignorance was excusable. Still, the death of this highly principled brother was a sharp reminder. 'This will shake us all down,' Manning told hs sister Caroline. 'Some people do not like to talk about their end. I do: it helps me to make ready, and it takes away all sadness and fear.'[2] Caroline, however, was more than a match for her younger brother in sententiousness. 'I wonder why you and I are left the last,' he wrote to her in 1882. 'Is it because we have most need of time to make ready?' 'It is not time that is of importance, but what use we make of it,'[3] the redoubtable sister riposted, in a vein that recalled the lessons of their Evangelical upbringing.

Her admonition was singularly ill-directed. Manning's whole career had been one of phenomenal activity, and now, with no more faith to swallow, and no more worldly ambitions to achieve, his decks were cleared for the run into harbour with all sails hoisted. The last break that he took from his labours was a few days in Penzance in 1869; thereafter the nearest he came to a holiday was summer temperance campaigning in the industrial towns of the north. As he grew older he increasingly tended to stay put in Archbishop's House, whence issued forth his staggering daily output of words. The volume of his correspondence alone would have occupied every waking moment of any ordinary mortal. Day after day Manning sat before the fire, covering the paper on his knees with a script that retained its clarity to the very end of his life. There were letters to Cabinet Ministers, letters to fellow ecclesiastics, letters to Rome, letters to old acquaintances, letters to the newspapers, letters of spiritual counsel to the illustrious and obscure alike. 'Never hesitate to write,' he told one of the latter category, 'it does not take up my time.'[4]

There were no doubts, no hesitations about what to say or how to phrase it; he knew the truth and his pen had always been the willing servant of his brain. His books and articles, indeed, were now dictated. 'In my youth, and when beginning to write, I took great pains with my style. I am ashamed of this. It was unworthy.'[5] There were those like Döllinger (excommunicated now) who considered that Manning's writing declined after his conversion, but the Archbishop of Westminster wrote to immediate practical purpose and not to satisfy intellectuals. 'A book can only last until Christ's coming, and will then be burned up.'[6] How unfortunate for Cardinal Newman. It was impossible, Manning considered, to imagine the Apostles studying the rules and graces of literary style; what mattered for effective writing, as for effective preaching, was the man himself. 'In the measure in which we realise the world of faith, the eternal truths, the nature of sin, the love of souls, their danger of perishing, we shall find no difficulty in speaking of them with sincerity and simplicity. It is the desire to be eloquent and to shine as orators that causes unreality, vain-glory and emptiness.'[7]

This prescription certainly appeared to work in Manning's own case. The last quotation came from his book *The Eternal Priesthood*, which he published in 1883 and which became a classic, translated into several languages and even today still used in seminaries. The work reflected his concern to hold out the highest possible standards to the clergy and to shake off for ever the idea that the regulars had in any sense a more special calling. Manning wrote two further volumes on the same theme, but they were not fated to be widely read. The manuscript of the third book was conclusively lost by its bearer during a transatlantic crossing. The second, *The Pastoral Office*, was sent for correction to Ullathorne, who taxed the author with nursing a prejudice against the regulars. Manning denied this. He was merely filling a need. 'Regulars have authors, friends, preachers, books, prestige, tradition always working for their elevation. The pastoral clergy has none of these things. . . . I feel that our humble, hard-working, hard-worked, self-denying, unpretending, self-depressing pastoral clergy need and deserve to be encouraged, cheered, and told of their high and happy state.'[8] On a later occasion Manning described himself as having been 'set over a body of clergy better than myself';[9] and he liked to think of his writings on their behalf as a token of his gratitude and respect. Nevertheless, he also saw the point of Ullathorne's criticism, which he accepted in the most admirable spirit, even to the extent of leaving *The Pastoral Office* unpublished, though a few copies were run off for private circulation. Very few authors have as little literary vanity as that.

Besides these books and his sermons, Manning in his last decade produced dozens of articles on all kinds of topics, from educational policy to papal history, from impassioned social protest to treatises upon the immortality of the soul. One of the last of these articles, written in 1888, dealt with the origin of faith in terms that recalled how the young Henry Manning had escaped from the toils of frustration in 1830–32. 'The act of faith is an imperative of the will, founded and justified by the process and conviction of the intellect. Hitherto I have been a critic; henceforward, if I will, I become a disciple.'[10] In his own life Manning had never swerved a hair's breadth from that commitment. It was not, he admitted, that the objective evidence for or against Catholicism could be made weaker or stronger by the will. What could be changed, however, was the subjective approach to that evidence. Manning elucidated the point in a passage that recalls his early debt to Newman. 'What is good or bad, high or mean, lovely or hateful, ennobling or degrading, must attract or repel men as they are better or worse in their moral sense; for an equilibrium between good and evil, to God or to man is impossible.'[11]

His convert zeal never attached itself to the outward shows of Catholicism. When, exceptionally, Bodley came across him arrayed in full panoply, Manning passed the matter off in the style of an English public schoolboy: 'Forgive these togs, but it's the Immaculate Conception, and I have to go to Farm Street.' Normally the Cardinal's robes were threadbare.[12] For the intricacies of ceremonial he cared so little that they had called him 'Mgr Ignorante' in Rome owing to his casual way with ritual.[13] 'Manning . . . was very unrubrical,' recalled Bishop Patterson, 'and never obeyed his Master of Ceremonies, but argued the points at issue then and there, which was characteristic but embarrassing, as one never knew what he was going to do next.'[14] Yet internally Manning's faith was so secure that he could afford generous views of other denominations. His social work continually brought him into contact with Protestants whose goodness and effectiveness he had neither will nor need to deny. 'You know that I see the truth differently from you,' a charitable lady of extreme Protestant opinions told him when he showed signs of proselytising, 'and I have what satisfies me.' 'The Church has a doctrine of intention of the heart,' the old man replied; 'you have that intention of the heart. God bless you. God bless you.'[15] He had always admired fervent Dissenters, rather more, since his conversion, than he admired fervent Anglicans, who he considered ought to be Catholic; and this disposition became increasingly marked. He expressed respect for the work and achievements of the Salvation Army.[16] Even towards Anglicans his polemical zeal slackened as time went on. 'When the world is drifting to chaos and suicide I have no will for controversies,'[17] he told Canon Jenkins, his Anglican confidant. The English were not heretics; they had never rejected the Catholic religion; it had been wrested away from them.[18] And although they would never be forced back into the light, they might conceivably be wooed.

The complement to this open-minded approach to members of other denominations was a tough awareness of the failings of his co-religionists. Try as he might he never gained wide support from English Catholics for his social work, and their bland indifference left him exasperated. 'All the great works of charity in England', he was obliged to reflect, 'have had their beginning out of the Church.'[19] No one knew this better than the son of William Manning. The point was always being forced upon him. On one occasion he burst out in frustration: 'The Jews are taking better care of their people in the East End than we are. What are our people doing? Oh, I forgot; they have no time. They are examining their consciences or praying (with dear Mrs. Craven) for success in finding a really satisfactory maid.'[20] There was a great deal more to being a Catholic, he insisted, than accepting the decrees of the Council of Trent. 'That is only a very small part of it. Becoming a Catholic really means becoming again as a little child and having a new heart.'[21] Even his priests, whose qualities he would in genial mood generously praise, were found at other times to be woefully deficient. 'In the catacombs the candlesticks were of wood, but the priests were of gold. Now the candlesticks are of gold,'[22] he remarked, echoing Savonarola's strictures upon the clergy of his day.

English Catholics, Manning came to feel, were so much on guard against Protestant defilement that they failed to emulate Protestant virtues. They might learn from the Salvation Army, he mordantly observed, that the Holy Scriptures were not on the Index.[23] His criticism embraced practice as well as precept. Would that Catholics might take up congregational hymn-singing with the same fervour as Protestants. If there was any serious intention of converting England it would be better to bawl hymns in the streets than say the Rosary there, which only put Protestants off.[24] Always Manning set himself against the bloodless, comfortable, 'civilized' religion in which so many English Catholics delighted. As to their worship, 'I am wickedly in the habit of saying that the three maladies which hinder piety are fanciful books of devotion, theatrical music in church, and pulpit oratory.'[25] As he grew older Manning became capable of writing appreciatively of English Catholic families which had held to the faith through centuries of persecution. 'No more beautiful Catholic homes ever existed; no more chivalrous Catholic laymen; no more devoted Catholic priests could be found than those who shone here and there in the gloom of our times of depression.'[26] Nevertheless he hoped, in vain as it turned out, that Vaughan, already by 1880 his obvious successor at Westminster, would resist the influence of the Old Testament, as he termed traditional English Catholicism:

When I am gone [he told Vaughan], do not let the Old Testament close over you and bury you in the sacristy. I have held and, I hope, acted upon this law. Everything I did as an Englishman and a member of our Commonwealth with imperfect truth, I am bound to continue and to do all the more with perfect faith, save only where that faith forbids. The Old Testament taught, or rather acted as if it taught, that having a perfect faith we are to do nothing for the Commonwealth but to say Rosaries for it.[27]

Manning admired Vaughan's sterling character, but he could not resist rallying him upon his hidebound Catholic principles. Vaughan, who was an instinctive Tory, disapproved of much of Manning's social work and in particular disliked his enthusiasm for the Salvation Army. 'I know you would labour and love out of mere humanitarian motives,' he told Manning. 'That would be enough for you, but not for me. I could do it only as a duty, the duty of a Christian bishop.' 'God so loved the world that He sent His only-begotten Son – but that is a detail,' was Manning's swift, ironic response.[28] His efforts to humanize Vaughan included the unlikely expedient of sending him a copy of Sheridan's plays. 'You would be holier and happier if you would enter into such things and learn to laugh. You are grim and truculent.'[29] Manning was irritated with Vaughan over his impenetrably philistine reaction to an exhibition which they had visited together. Nevertheless, Sheridan's plays were an odd recommendation from someone who had forsworn the theatre at the age of twenty.

Many considered that it was Manning himself who was in need of the human touch. Fifty years previously he had complained that Newman treated religion as a system of requisitions. Now the outlook of the two men appeared to be reversed. It was Newman who thought of Catholicism as providing a climate within which, through tender care, the soul might spontaneously acquire health, and Manning who saw the necessity of harshly training the soul's growth in the required direction. If Newman's system ran the risk of allowing its exponents to let themselves off rather too easily, Manning's could result in an unnatural forcing of virtue, a process in which not merely sin but also much that makes for sympathy and affection is destroyed. Something of this kind happened to Manning himself; he seemed imprisoned in virtue, beyond the reach of ordinary fellow feeling. Gladstone's remark that no priest's shirt ever took such a quantity of starch will be recalled. The impression of Manning's isolation was heightened in his

last years by evidences of an inextinguishable inner need to leap the barriers
of archiepiscopal dignity back into the cosier commonplaces of existence.

'Our perfection of His friendship will vary in the measure in which we
maintain our liberty from all unbalanced human attachment,' he pronounced in *The Eternal Priesthood*. 'If we be weak and wander to human
friendships, we shall soon find that there is no rest anywhere else.'[30] That
might be an orthodox religious precept, but it was a bleak philosophy to live
by. Manning had underlings, not intimates; he attended functions, not
parties; he multiplied acquaintances, not friends. This, of course, was all of a
piece with the life-style that he deemed appropriate. 'A bishop must not be
dependent on the Upper Ten Thousand, nor a diner-out, nor a waster of
time, nor a joker of jokes, nor a reader of newspapers, nor a centre of
favourites.'[31]

To an extraordinary degree Manning kept to that rule. Yet he never, as he
himself claimed and certainly believed, lived entirely out of society. His
interest in the great world, especially the world of government, remained
intense. Political memoirs were his favourite non-spiritual reading;
politicians were his preferred non-spiritual companions. In the 1870s and
1880s he struck up a friendship with Sir Charles Dilke, another radical from
a plutocratic background, who seemed destined to succeed Gladstone as
leader of the Liberals. Dilke did not find it unduly difficult to lure Manning
to his dinners – to meet Baron Rothschild or Bismarck's son: the Archbishop
accepted as 'yours is a Cabinet dinner'.[32] It was just the kind of justification
that William Wilberforce might have given.

There were other events that could hardly be avoided, but which were
none the less welcome for that. The Prince of Wales, whose love of France
emancipated him from the Victorian prejudice against Catholicism, began
to invite Manning to his garden parties. Sometimes the Queen was there. 'I
never approached her. I might have done so, for I have the full right. In the
year 1844 I think I was presented, and used to attend both levees and
drawing-rooms. Therefore I need no presentation now. But I do not know
whether it would be acceptable to her; and I owe it to my office and to myself
not to allow a shadow of misunderstanding.' On 13 July 1881 this dilemma
was happily resolved:

In the garden at Marlborough House, the Prince and Queen passed me: I saw that
she turned to the Prince on recognising me. The Prince sent an equerry to say that the
Queen wished to see me, if I would stay where I was. I waited and they came. She
seemed embarrassed how to begin, so I said: 'It is a great happiness to see Your
Majesty again. The last time was six and thirty years ago at Buckingham Palace.'[33]

However gratifying such occasions might be, they hardly satisfied any deeper social instincts. Likewise the receptions which Manning held at Archbishop's House afforded scant opportunity for relaxation. The guests nervously sipped sherry and hoped that this dereliction would escape the eye of their host. Cigarettes were strictly forbidden.[34] Ruskin, it is true, reported to a sceptical female friend in September 1880 that he had enjoyed lunching with the Archbishop. 'Now you're just wrong about my darling Cardinal. See what it is to be jealous! He gave me lovely soup, roast beef, hare and currant jelly, puff pastry like Papal pretensions – you had but to breathe on it and it was nowhere – raisins and almonds, and those lovely preserved cherries like kisses kept in amber. And told me delicious stories all through lunch. *There!*'[35]

That is the sole extant testimonial to the cuisine at Archbishop's House, although it may be true that Manning's private habits were less austere than legend and his appearance suggested. Another visitor, G. W. E. Russell, reported that the Cardinal 'had a hearty appetite for his mid-day meal' and 'enjoyed his tea'.[36] (As Manning's staple noontide fare was mutton and mustard[37] these two assertions are by no means incompatible.) Russell, a Liberal MP, had got to know Manning when he came to Archbishop's House on some educational business, and found himself pressed to stay. It was almost as if the old man could not endure to be left once more alone. And when such occasions went well they invariably ended with another invitation, none the less urgent for its casual delivery – 'Come and see me again.' Late-night visitors were also encouraged: 'Come to me with the bats,'[38] the Cardinal would say. Perhaps it was the pressing need to share the drama of his own story that helped to deliver Manning into the hands of his biographer Purcell. 'Dear Mr. Purcell,' ran a note in June 1888, 'I have just received an important letter from Mr. Gladstone. Come this evening, I want to talk the matter over with you.'[39]

The appeal of George Russell was quite different: from him Manning *received* information about the world which he had forsworn. Russell, who was a connoisseur of society, diagnosed Manning as 'essentially a man of the world',[40] which in his mind was probably the highest accolade he could bestow. Of course this judgement was a ludicrous overstatement: even Russell saw that the Cardinal's every conscious thought was for the furtherance of his religion, but it was true that a streak of social sophistication had survived in Manning. He would never have inflicted religious conversation on a guest of Russell's type. The persona he displayed to such people was more likely to baulk at a split infinitive than at a heretical proposition. His crisp comments, intended rather to cap than to stimulate conversation, recalled the negligent elegance of the Regency period of his boyhood. 'An English gentleman should know his Aristotle and ride to hounds'[41] was typical of the kind of crusty apophthegm that this crusader for social justice could deliver when he found himself in appropriate company. Russell described him as a 'beautifully mannered, well-informed, sagacious old gentleman, who, but for his dress, might have passed for a Cabinet Minister, an eminent judge, or a great county magnate'. He never seemed to put himself forward, Russell noted, but he always contrived to be the most conspicuous character in any company.[42] It was all just as John Foster had recommended in those essays that Manning had read some sixty years before.

Yet there was one characteristic that Foster would not have approved. The Cardinal was decidedly partial to tittle-tattle about the chief actors in Vanity Fair. 'I was amused by finding how much he cared for gossip and even scandal,' wrote Dilke. 'He insisted upon talking to me about Sarah Bernhardt, and Gambetta, and the Prince of Wales, and all sorts and conditions of people.'[43] In 1885 Dilke himself gave the Cardinal matter for consideration when he was cited as co-respondent in a particularly seamy divorce suit. Manning rounded angrily on a tactless acquaintance who suggested that he knew nothing of this 'painful agitation': 'I have been hearing confessions in London for thirty years, and I fancy more people have confided their secrets to me than to you, Mr. –.'[44] In fact, Manning was probably the only person apart from the principals to know the truth about this famous case. Dilke, though not a Catholic, told him all (or so Dilke claimed) and remained a friend. Mrs Crawford, the woman who ruined Dilke, became a convert and one of Manning's spiritual charges. His treatment was notably successful. Mrs Crawford gave the rest of her life to social work, and died on Campden Hill as a woman of exemplary virtue in 1948. She always remained devoted to Manning, whose nature, she decided, drew its goodness from matrimonial springs: 'The celibacy of half a century did not mould his character as much as those three years of ideal home life and married happiness.'[45] No doubt Mrs Crawford would have appreciated the irony, if such it be, that there is now a Charles Wentworth Dilke who is Father Superior at the London Oratory.

Throughout his seventies Manning liked to drop in at the Athenaeum, always a likely place for a political chat. The unfortunate Goschen, Chancellor of the Exchequer, was cornered there and berated for Tory Government policy.[46] The Bishop of Londonderry remembered Manning in the Athenaeum, how he would sit in a big armchair with his hat pulled down over his eyes, apparently leafing through some magazine, but always searching out incomers in the hope of recognizing some acquaintance from his Anglican years.[47] The Cardinal's penchant for being in the know did not, however, incline him to judge kindly those who shared this harmless human weakness. The Jesuit community at Farm Street was derisively dismissed as 'the worst gossip-shop in London'.[48] And when, at the very end of his life, Manning discovered someone he had employed to put his papers in order understandably engrossed in Mgr Talbot's letters, he delivered a harsh verdict on his erstwhile ally in the Vatican – 'the most imprudent man who ever lived'.[49]

Manning was not imprudent; he perfectly understood the codes under which the ruling classes exchanged confidences. Yet his urbane manner was really no more than a useful medium for the conduct of business, or for social contacts with the Protestant establishment. The Regency man of the world shared his corporeal tenement with a raging medieval fanatic. W. H. Mallock gives a fascinating glimpse of the latter persona in his *Memoirs of Life and Literature*. He met Manning at a lunch party given in the Cardinal's honour at Chiswick House by the Marquess of Bute. The public event was like a scene from *Lothair*, with the great Catholic ladies vying with each other in the humility of their reverence to the Cardinal. Later in the afternoon Mallock was invited by his host to stay on for a private talk with Manning:

Under the Cardinal's guidance the conversation almost immediately – how and why I cannot remember – turned to the subject of spiritualism, and he soon was gravely informing us that, of all the signs of the times, none was more sinister than the multiplication of spiritualist seances, which were, according to him, neither more nor less than revivals of black magic. He went on to assert, as a fact supported by ample evidence, that the Devil at such meetings assumed a corporeal form – sometimes that of a man, sometimes that of a beautiful and seductive woman, the results being frequent births, in the prosaic world around us, of terrible hybrid creatures half-diabolic in nature, though wholly human in form. On this delicate matter he descanted in such unvarnished language that the details of what he said cannot well be repeated here. Of the truth of his assertions he obviously entertained no doubt, and such was his dry, almost harsh solemnity in making them that, as I listened, I could hardly believe my ears.[50]

Later, when Mallock met Manning again at Archbishop's House, he encountered the cool Balliol intellectual, with whom he had a most interesting discussion on the difficulties which prevented the modern mind from assenting to Catholicism. Nevertheless, the fervour of his innermost convictions made ordinary friendship with Manning exceedingly difficult. Nor did his manner invite intimacy. His clothes might be threadbare, his coach shabby; there was, all the same, as another visitor found, 'an atmosphere of Royalty about him which might well be missing in the Courts of this world'.[51] Russell recalled that 'the most Protestant knee instinctively bent'.[52] Should the Archbishop be caught unawares by some unexpected

intruder the benign old gentleman was nowhere in evidence. A philanthropic lady called Sarah Sheldon Amos recalled how on one of her visits
to Archbishop's House Manning came across her before her arrival had
been announced. His approach was 'as severe and distant as could be', until
he recognized her and extended the friendliest of welcomes.[53] His eyes were
always penetrating, but when they lit with delight it was easier to forget the
impression of ruthless purpose that emanated from the prominent jaw and
the thin, tightly-pursed lips.[54] The handsome young Oxonian had been
transmogrified into the alarming apparition he himself described as a
'death's head in a skull-cap'. No doubt the scarifying Manning whom Sarah
Sheldon Amos caught with her first glance was the only character whom
unwelcome visitors were permitted to meet. Vaughan wrote of how the
doorstep of the Cardinal's house became worn with the footsteps of the
fatherless and the widowed, the poor, the forlorn, the tempted and the
disgraced, who came to him in the hours of their trouble and sorrow.[55]
Inevitably, though, the outcasts who made it into Manning's presence were a
carefully selected band. Many of his own priests, for whom he theoretically
kept open house, would have been scared stiff to march into the inner
sanctum to confront their formidable chief. If they met him at all it was far
more likely that they had been summoned for some dereliction of duty than
that they had deliberately sought an interview. These erring priests soon
discovered, moreover, that nothing but abject contrition served to moderate
the Archbishop's accusatory stare.

Cut off by character, principle and position from any relations that
admitted sentiment, Manning turned back to his past as a source of
emotional satisfaction. Again and again in these last years he went through
the journals and notebooks that he had kept throughout his career. Passages
that he did not care to leave behind, including, it seems, much that related to
his marriage, were excised; other pages received further comment in the
light of passing years. He loved to talk over his extraordinary life as well,
giving commendation where commendation was due. On hearing that Sir
James Stephen had referred to him as 'the wisest man I ever knew', he
conceded that Sir James had been 'a man of excellent judgement'.[56] There
was also praise for Sir James Graham, who had spoken favourably of some
letters which Manning had written in the early 1840s. This Sir James had
been 'a man of profound judgement'.[57]

In 1881 Manning suddenly dreamt of his sister Harriet,[58] who had died
fifty-five years before. That summer he made an expedition to his childhood
home in Totteridge, where he astonished the owner of Copped Hall, a Mr
Boulton, with the accuracy and detail of his memory for scenes which he had
not visited for sixty-six years. 'He pointed out the room where he was born,'

Mr Boulton recorded, 'told me correctly where certain doors formerly stood, the position of which I had altered, also the suppression of a door into the Tapestry Room. He pointed out the spot whereon his uncle, when he was a child, read to the assembled family the first news of the battle of Waterloo.' Manning also paid his respects to his brother William and his grandfather William Coventry in Totteridge churchyard. Next day he wrote excitedly about the visit to his sister Caroline, telling her of the oaks that their father had planted for each of the children: 'True enough; there are seven, the eighth is gone.' He had remembered also how one of the servants had fallen out of a tree which he had climbed in search of an owl's nest: there was still a family of owls in that tree. 'So we go, and owls remain.'[59]

After that Manning returned more than once to Totteridge, and Mr Boulton, a financier, became an acquaintance with whom he conducted gentlemanly arguments about economics and social affairs. The son of the house had been at Balliol, another point of contact: Manning once undertook an hour's journey to see him when he was ill.[60] Boulton junior reciprocated by raising a subscription to present a portrait of the Cardinal to Balliol. Manning's fierce determination that Catholics should not go to Oxford did not prevent his taking an interest in his old college, to which he dispatched a handsome edition of St Thomas Aquinas's works. The aesthetic reputation of Balliol caused him some anxiety: 'It used to create men; I hope it will not end in a race of Mysians*.'[61] No doubt Manning felt more in his element at the Eton-Harrow cricket dinner that he attended (after the dinner) in 1888.[62] Oxford, he complained in 1889, 'has become a moral wreck and has admitted women'. Even so, he wrote in friendly fashion to Jowett, the renowned Master of Balliol and a man of liberal religious views: 'There are many things I should like to hear from you, for I think that if the North and the South Pole could sit over a good fire they could interchange many things of their long experience.'[63]

Manning also renewed his association with Lavington. After Samuel Wilberforce's death, the estate passed to his son Reginald, whose wife used to send flowers to Archbishop's House. When Manning dedicated a Roman Catholic church in Sussex, he seized the occasion to revisit his old parish. For several minutes he stood in silence beside the unmarked grave of his wife.[64] Why had he placed no stone upon it, Reginald Wilberforce was bold enough to ask. 'Because I could not put on it the inscription that I should have wished,' the Cardinal enigmatically replied.[65] Although not normally given to gratuitous proselytizing he pursued his rivalry with Samuel Wilberforce

---

* For once Manning's classical knowledge seems to have let him down. The Mysians, who inhabited what is now north-west Turkey, appear in the *Iliad* as a hardy and warlike race, in contrast to their effeminate neighbours the Phrygians.

beyond the grave by striving to bring his sons into the Catholic fold. 'It would give me much pleasure to see you all,' Uncle Henry wrote to Basil Wilberforce, 'though you are a sad medley of schism, nationalism, and ambition. . . . There are but two paths. There is or there is not a Divine teacher in the world. We are either disciples or critics. There is no third path. Make haste and go over the bar, or the Herodians will take away the little faith you and Charlotte have left.'[66] But Basil Wilberforce's faith proved quite sufficient to make him Archdeacon of Westminster.

Another symptom of Manning's obsession with the past, which grew stronger as the years gradually carried off his generation, was his meticulous observance of anniversaries. He had not communicated with Gladstone since 1875, but the fiftieth anniversary of Gladstone's entry into political life at the Newark election of 1832 did not pass unnoticed in Archbishop's House. It was an occasion to be linked with his own first sermon, preached at Cuddesdon on Christmas Day 1932. Nor did Manning shrink from a further comparison. 'His has been a great career of public service. . . . Mine has been a life of fifty years out of the world as Gladstone's has been in it. The work of his life in this world is manifest. I hope mine may be in the next. I suppose Our Lord called me out of the world because He saw that I should lose my soul in it. Separation from it greater than the last thirty years could hardly be.' Manning's conviction, maintained in the face of constant contact with Cabinet Ministers, that he had lived wholly out of the English world was one of his strangest delusions. Yet, he comforted himself, there was a sense in which he had laboured for a wider cause than any Gladstone could embrace. 'I remember saying that I had "given up working for the people of England to work for the Irish occupation in England". But that occupation is part of a Church throughout the world, of an Empire greater than the British.'[67]

The death of the Evangelical philanthropist Lord Shaftesbury and the *Life* that appeared in the following year presented a still more challenging comparison than Gladstone's career. '29 December 1886: I have just ended Lord Shaftesbury's "Life". It was a noble and unique Christian manhood. What a retrospective of work done. It makes me feel that my life has been wasted. He began with every advantage and facility the world could give him: I began absolutely with nothing in the world.' Even allowing for his father's bankruptcy, Manning's reference to his deprived beginnings was a less impressive feat of memory than his recall of his childhood at Copped Hall. Shaftesbury's achievement obviously bothered him. His journal once more referred to the Irish occupation of England, but it seemed that in this instance something more was required to square accounts:

The last six and thirty years I have worked for the building up again of the Catholic, and even of Christian Truth which was wrecked in the great revolt. And truth or faith are the conditions of the whole moral and spiritual life of the people. I have lived out of the world [at least he was consistent] and yet the Catholic Church tells upon public opinion and upholds what still remains of Christianity in England. I hope that in this I may not have lived in vain. So also I hope that I may have helped to bring the Catholic Church once more into open relations with the people and public opinion of England.[68]

At other times, however, Manning would glory in the *isolation* of the Church in England, urging that its poverty and unpopularity would help to keep its faith and practice unsullied by the world. 'I sometimes think that we are even too well thought of in England,'[69] he told Stead. The truth was that he could produce arguments for every occasion, but he never managed to martial his *ad hoc* pronouncements into a coherent vision of the place of the Church Militant in a predominantly Protestant and irreligious society.

The evolution of the Church fascinated Manning, but scarcely more than the part he himself had played in its unfolding history. Whatever his later moderation towards Protestants, he did not look back on his past conflicts within the Church with any mellow objectivity. On the contrary, emotion boiled over uncontrollably as he relived his battles. The more he considered matters, the more evident it became that his enemies had been the enemies of the Church of God upon earth. The opposition to the definition of papal infallibility at the Vatican Council now appeared no better than the instrument of Satan. How wickedly his adversaries had schemed. 'Their Parliamentary whipping, and canvassing, and boasting, and defiance, and I must add intrigue, to sway Pius IX, and to bring the pressure of the Civil Powers upon the Pope and the Council, were well known to me.' It had been horrible. Yet by some miracle the policy of these ecclesiastical Machiavellis had proved powerless against the innocent advocacy of divine truth:

The world worshipped them [the inopportunists], and every word they spoke or wrote. They were 'the greatest theologians of the day', the 'leaders of Catholic thought', the 'independent and manly characters who redeem the Catholic Church from servility and meanness'. But the Church decided against them. . . . We, the ignorants, the fools, the flatterers, the empty pates, were right after all. An Œcumenical Council justified us, and the Catholic Church believes and teaches what we said; and we said it because the Church taught us. . . . It has turned out that the wise men were always blundering, and the fools were always right . . . in truth, the main characteristic of these men was vanity – intellectual or literary. They had the inflation of German professors, and the ruthless talk of undergraduates.[70]

Literary vanity was now high on Manning's list of sins. He had started an autobiography, cast in the form of letters to a friend. Second thoughts were better. 'I was too busy a man; such a work would have been a waste of time and thought.'[71] It might also have invited comparisons with Newman's *Apologia*. Manning was quite aware that posterity would judge his reputation beside that of Newman and he made his dispositions accordingly. A note written in 1877 set out his view of what he described as his 'variance' with Newman. 'I began with a great admiration, a true affection, a warm friendship. I always regarded him as so far above me in gifts and culture of every kind that I never had a temptation to rivalry or jealousy.' Unfortunately, 'that Newman has a morbid sensitiveness is well known'. Differences had arisen over issues – the temporal power of the Pope, Oxford, infallibility – upon which

Newman was not in accord with the Holy See. I am nobody, but I spoke as the Holy See spoke. But almost every newspaper in England abused and ridiculed me. My name was never mentioned, but his was brought in to condemn me; his name was never mentioned, but mine was brought in to despite me. If only we had stood side by side and spoken the same thing, the dissension, division and ill-will which we have would never have been, and the unity of Catholic truth would have been irresistible. But it was not to be so. There is only one person who has kept Dr. Newman back from the highest office – himself. He is the sole cause.[72]

Manning's defence that he had simply followed the papal line would be somewhat undermined by the delicious irony of his later discovery that there might be certain conditions under which it was appropriate to limit the application of the Pope's authority. Nevertheless, his general position was more straightforward than that of Newman. If it strains credulity to accept the claims of the Catholic Church, it tests the intellect still more to make such a commitment and then hedge it about with reservations. Newman's mind, it may be reckoned, was equal to the task, but then Newman's mind had been able to see the Thirty-Nine Articles as a repository of Catholic doctrine. The man leaves the impression that he could have proved whatsoever he wished, which leaves the sceptic all the more wary of being convinced.

In his old age, however, Newman achieved something that eluded Manning: he became lovable. Perhaps he had always been lovable, but now his spell was no longer reserved for confessed disciples. His elevation to the cardinalate banished the sense which had haunted him that he was not properly appreciated or used by his fellow Catholics. He was still capable of astonishing pettiness: witness his refusal in 1884 to attend the opening of the new Brompton Oratory because the letter of invitation had unintentionally stirred memories of his quarrel with the London Oratorians thirty years before.[73] But while Manning, as age hardened the arteries, still waxed impatient and bitter against his Catholic opponents, Newman, now that honour and reverence surrounded his name, at last lost his zest for earthly conflict. 'You must not think that these little affairs of mine will be on the *tapis* in the courts of the next world,'[74] he observed to someone who spoke of the trials which he had undergone. Manning ceased to be a foe who was worth his reckoning. The two Cardinals met once or twice, notably when Newman finally went to the Brompton Oratory in 1886 for the funeral of the Dowager Duchess of Norfolk, an occasion definitely not to be missed. It was noticed how careful Manning was not to assert any precedence in the procession. He showed all the respect due to a fellow Cardinal. 'What do you think Manning did to me?' an astonished Newman said afterwards. 'He kissed me.'[75]

So Newman moved gracefully to the wings, while his old antagonist was left champing in the centre of the stage, a torn figure in whom neither rage nor resentment, nor yet charity or compassion, would ever be stilled. Lear-like, Manning had put the world from him and found no peace in the sacrifice. The saddest aspect was that he had no need whatsoever to fear comparisons with Newman, whom he had outstripped in practical achievement as conclusively as Newman outstripped him as a Catholic thinker. In his Lenten pastoral of 1890, Manning looked back upon his work in education. In 1889 there were 18,912 Catholics in parish elementary schools in the Westminster diocese compared with some 11,000 in 1865. (The number would be 21,776 by Manning's death.) During the same period more than 10,000 children had been rescued from the workhouses, in which such education as existed was of the most blinkered Protestant variety, and sent to Catholic schools. In addition, over 4,500 waifs, strays and outcasts had been housed and educated in Catholic reform and industrial schools.[76]

Such statistics will not impress those who imagine that a Catholic revival in England must depend on the conversion of a few intellectuals rather than on the establishment of a solid popular base; they will appeal still less to those who prefer their Catholicism to be of the *Brideshead Revisited* ('How I lived in a very big house and discovered God') variety. Very few, if any, among the thousands of children who owed their Catholic education to Manning wrote books descriptive of their remarkable spiritual progress. They were, nevertheless, souls who had been saved for the Church. Beside this one great fact the criticism which Manning has attracted from Catholic exquisites appears as irrelevant carping. It was as though his work constituted a rebuke which nothing but assumptions of superiority could allay.

Protestants, at least, may condescend to be generous to Manning's educational work, for he did more than anyone else to ensure the survival of denominational schools (or 'voluntary' schools as they were known after the 1870 Education Act) by excluding them from receipt of the school rate paid to the non-denominational board schools, had left them heavily dependent on private charity. Voluntary schools did receive Privy Council grants, it will be recalled, but only in places where there was no alternative provision in board schools. Moreover, these grants, even when available, were proportionate to private contributions. In theory the board schools had originally been created merely 'to fill the gaps' in the voluntary system, but with the financial advantage which they enjoyed from the rates it now looked as though they would eventually swamp the denominational schools, a prospect which radicals viewed with equanimity. By 1884 more than a thousand voluntary schools had given up the unequal struggle and surrendered to the local education boards, forfeiting their distinctive religious character in return for receiving rate assistance. Yet the extraordinary fact was that not one of these schools had belonged to the poorest denomination of all, the Catholics, who had indeed contrived to build hundreds of new schools without any grant whatever.[77]

Manning was quite determined that this heroic achievement, largely financed out of the pennies of impecunious Irish labourers, should not be set at risk by the encroachment of the board schools. He remained adamant that there could be no proper education without religion. The 1870 Act, with its provision of rates for non-denominational schools, 'spreads an abundant feast', he observed, 'but in platters and bottles where we cannot touch it'. He was not at all impressed that the Bible was read in board schools. 'Religion without doctrine is like mathematics without axioms, or triangles without bases and sides. I heartily rejoice that the life, and words, and works, and death of the Divine Saviour of the world should be read by children. But that is not the teaching of religion, unless the true meaning and the due intrinsic worth of all these things be taught.'

The solution which Manning now proposed, contrary to his lobbying before the 1870 Act, was that the voluntary schools should also be granted rate aid. 'If the Government may tax the whole people for education, the whole people have a right to share in the beneficial use of such taxation. . . . If any one form of education can be found in which all the people are content to share, let it be adopted; if no one such form be possible, let there be as many varieties as can with reason be admitted.' Manning was positively eager to concede that the Protestant denominations had as much right as the Catholics to share in the education rate. The chances of saving the voluntary schools would be immeasurably strengthened if all the denominations campaigned on the same platform. Manning carefully framed his arguments to achieve this end, serving up resolutely general principles with a dash of patriotic seasoning. The national character, he claimed, had been formed in religious schools: 'How can this English and Christian character be perpetuated or formed when the schools have ceased to be Christian?'[78] It had been clear since the Maynooth grant that the State must be neutral between different religions: the question at issue was how that neutrality should be interpreted. Did it mean that the State should use its power to enforce secular education? That was what Chamberlain and the radicals were plotting to accomplish. That was the policy of 'tyrannous malevolence' being pursued in France, to the ruin of 'that once great people'.[79] Manning believed, however, that the vast majority of Englishmen had never intended that the State should arrogate to itself such rights over *their* children.

What a consummate politician he would have been! Yet like a politician he was inclined to sacrifice consistency in his eagerness to seize the most convenient argument to hand. Even while he was campaigning for his interpretation of the neutrality of the State in education, he was demanding that atheists should be kept out of parliament. This issue arose from the refusal to allow Charles Bradlaugh, a declared atheist elected to the Commons in 1880, to make an affirmation instead of taking a parliamentary oath. Manning produced a spate of articles opposing his right to affirm. 'Deny the existence of God, and nine thousand affirmations are no more than nineteen or ninety thousand words. . . . If there be no God there is no eternal distinction of right and wrong; and if not, then no morals; therefore truth, purity, chastity, justice, temperance are names, conventions, impostures.'[80] Manning's argument certainly moved swiftly, and doubtless he would have been equally quick to claim that the twentieth century has borne out his prophecy. Nevertheless, in logic his refusal to countenance an atheist in parliament was the Christian equivalent to the secularists' demand that the State should not support denominational education. It was hardly possible to oppose State indifferentism in the Bradlaugh case and lobby for it in primary education.

Fortunately Manning lost the Bradlaugh argument and not the educational one. Together with Vaughan he created the Voluntary Schools' Association, an organization which deliberately solicited the participation of other denominations. As Vaughan put it: 'The Catholic schools may be the iron head to the spear, but the iron head will make a poor weapon unless it have the weight of the wooden shaft behind it.'[81] Manning regarded the plight of the voluntary schools as an issue of such importance that in 1885 he broke his rule of political neutrality and published an article, 'How Shall Catholics Vote at the Coming Parliamentary Elections?' in the *Dublin Review* of November that year. The answer, it appeared, was not for Gladstone and the Liberals.

It is conceivable that Manning's appeal, together with Parnell's recommendation to the Irish in England to vote Tory, may have swayed some
twenty to thirty seats against Gladstone at the election. At all events a hung
parliament resulted, and the Tories took power with Irish support. The
subsequent news of Gladstone's conversion to Home Rule swiftly ended
both this strange alliance and the Tory ministry, but not before Lord Cross,
the Home Secretary, had appointed a commission to investigate the working
of the 1870 Education Act. Manning was a prominent member of this
commission, which recommended in 1888 that voluntary schools should
receive aid from the local boards. People called it Manning's report, and
undoubtedly it represented a check to radical hopes that the denominational
schools would simply wither away. Nevertheless, the Tory Government,
which had been returned with a huge majority in the wake of Gladstone's
failure with Home Rule, declined to put Rome on the rates. The Anglican
bishops also backed away from so alarming a principle, even though it would
have benefited Church of England schools as well as Catholic ones. Manning
reacted by producing 'Fifty Reasons why the Voluntary Schools of England
ought to share the School Rates' (1888), which he referred to as 'fifty stripes
for the backs of those cowardly Anglican bishops'.[82] Copies were distributed
to Gladstone and Salisbury alike, but Anglican politicians proved as hard to
convince as Anglican bishops.

Catholic politicians could be equally obtuse. Lord Ripon, the first
Catholic Cabinet Minister since the Reformation, wrote to Manning in
November 1888 that the urging of rate aid to Catholic schools risked
provoking a reaction that would sweep them away for ever.[83] Manning's
more courageous instinct would eventually be proved the sounder:
voluntary schools were put on the rates by the Education Act of 1902.
Oddly, though, Manning showed no enthusiasm at all for the 1891
Education Act, which greatly helped voluntary, and particularly Catholic,
schools by providing a ten shillings per pupil grant towards the cost of fees.
In Manning's opinion this was blood money, acquired at the cost of
surrendering the principle that parents, and not the State, were ultimately
responsible for education. Manning's fear was that a State which controlled
all the purse-strings would find it easier to inflict its shapeless version of
Christianity on English children.[84]

If upper-class Catholics could not be relied upon to support Manning over
voluntary schools, it may be imagined that their hostility to his universities
policy never abated. A trickle of Catholics continued to attend Oxford and
Cambridge. In 1883 Bishop Hedley of Newport and two laymen, armed with
a letter from Cardinal Newman arguing the case for ending the ban, tried to
persuade the Pope to change the policy. Leo XIII listened with the greatest

attention and announced that he would place Newman's letter before Cardinal Manning![85] That was the end of the matter. Manning was not at a loss to explain the means by which his position had been maintained. 'How easily I might have been blinded and biassed by my love of Oxford and England. But I have been saved in this and other things by nothing less than the Holy Ghost.'[86]

Just as he took an increasingly harsh view of his opponents at the Vatican Council, so he did not incline to more generous judgements of those Catholics who wished to send their sons to Oxford and Cambridge. 'In truth, nobody cared for higher studies,' he wrote in 1888. 'Certain Catholic parents wished to get their sons into English society, and to have the latch-keys to Grosvenor Square. Nevertheless, a great noise was made about the need of higher studies.'[87] Alas, in the very next year the Duke of Norfolk, who might perhaps be acquitted of any overpowering interest in the latchkeys of Grosvenor Square, wrote to say that the Bishop of Southwark had granted permission for his nephew, the son of Hope Scott who had converted with Manning, to go to Oxford. Manning left the Duke in no doubt that it was possible to struggle more successfully with temptation. 'Every personal feeling I have is and always has been powerfully, and perhaps more powerfully than in most men, on the side of sending Catholic youth to Oxford. But every conviction I have as a Catholic and for the Catholic Church in England, confirmed by all I have learned and seen in eight-and-thirty years, compels me to suppress all personal feeling.'[88]

Perhaps it would have been more accurate to say that one personal feeling had been replaced by another. Emotion not logic was always at the root of Manning's attitudes; and although, as a brilliant man, he always discovered logic to sustain his emotion, his thinking rarely amounted, save in theology where the Church provided system, to any coherent philosophy. The impression of policy lines which, if not actually conflicting, were never absolutely reconciled, is particularly strong in his approach to Irish affairs. He sympathized with the violent Land League, but deplored the use of violence.[89] He railed against the injustice of English rule in Ireland,[90] but considered Gladstone tardy in dealing with Irish boycotters and law-breakers.[91] He accepted that the Irish were ruled by politicians, but longed to see 'the Irish Episcopate leading and uniting the people as in old times'.[92] He subscribed to the aims of Irish MPs, but deplored their obstructionist methods.[93] He admired Parnell, but distrusted the anti-clericalism of his followers.[94] In each case it would be possible to argue that these positions were not necessarily opposed to one another. Yet the impression remains that his wisdom was spread too broad and thin to be of much practical use. He stood outside the parliamentary battle, so his views were never tested in the fire. The politicians to whom he was so prodigal with his counsel may have been forgiven a touch of irritation at the ease with which Manning found remedies.

Yet his *feelings* were unequivocal in their strength. An Irish priest remembered meeting him just after Gladstone had locked up Parnell and many other Irish leaders:

When dinner was over and the visit to the Blessed Sacrament, the Cardinal drew me into the corridor and said: 'Oh, I fear every link of affection between the two countries is broken.' 'Yes,' I said, 'all but one.' 'What one is that?' said the Cardinal. 'Our love for you,' said I. I shall never forget how he looked at me when he answered: 'Do you mean that?' I said: 'You are the last man in England to whom I would say that if I did not believe it to be true.' And the dear old man burst into tears. After a bit, almost under his breath, 'It is what I have prayed for, it is what I have prayed for.'[95]

Presumably his prayers were also directed towards less subjective aspects of the Irish crisis. Certainly the direction of his sympathy was never in doubt. Gladstone recognized this when he wrote to Newman in December 1881, asking *him* to get the Pope to condemn Irish atrocities. Newman tactfully replied that the Prime Minister overrated the Pope's power in political and social matters.[96]

The limitations of Manning's Irish sympathies were evident in his attitude to Home Rule. He claimed, with some justice, that he had been in the van of Englishmen who realized that Ireland must be given legislative independence. But in practice the support which he gave to Home Rule was diminished by his unwillingness to contemplate the loss of the Irish Catholic MPs from Westminster. The problem, as he pointed out in the early 1880s, was that 'the whole constituency of England, Scotland and Wales does not return a single Catholic to Parliament'.[97] This situation marginally improved in the 1885 and 1886 elections, but it was still reasonable to suppose that Cabinet Ministers would be very much less inclined to heed Manning's representations on behalf of English Catholics if he could not rely, as he had relied in the battle for voluntary schools, upon the support of the Irish members. In February 1885 Manning wrote to Leo XIII in order to impress this point, citing Michael Davitt, the Irish leader. 'He . . . say[s] that, considering such a concession [a Parliament in Dublin] from the point of view of the head of the Catholic Church, the transference of forty or fifty Catholic members from the highest Protestant assembly of the world . . . cannot be a victory for the cause of the Catholic Church.'[98]

Manning was therefore well-disposed towards the scheme which Chamberlain advanced in the first part of 1885, that Ireland should be governed by creating a new system of local government with powers over land, education and communications, while retaining national represent- ation at Westminster. (An additional advantage of this plan was that its author, the godless Chamberlain, would thereby be prevented from meddling with Irish education.) Once more Manning was drafted in as an intermediary not just between Chamberlain and the Irish bishops but also between Chamberlain and Parnell. Manning's interventions in high politics always seemed to induce a sanguine mood, and soon he was reporting back that his interview with the Irish leader about the local government plan had been 'satisfactory, and as the Irish bishops are of the same mind two conditions of acceptance for the scheme appear to be secure'.[99] Unhappily the third, and most vital; condition was lacking: Chamberlain failed to get Cabinet approval and his project foundered. Thereafter he was more than a little sour to discover that when Gladstone's Government fell (June 1885) Manning immediately transferred his attention to the new Tory Irish Secretary Lord Carnarvon, even to the extent of refusing to give his erstwhile Liberal friends letters of introduction to Irish bishops.[100] Chamberlain resolved never again to trust the Archbishop. He took a severely practical view of politics. 'I do not see what Cardinal Manning has to offer. The majority of English Catholics are [sic] Conservative, and no concession that is within our power to make would secure their support for the Liberal Party.'[101]

The last months of Gladstone's administration had produced another issue that poisoned Manning's relations with the Liberals. On the death of the Archbishop of Dublin in February 1885, the Foreign Secretary, Lord Granville, had mounted a campaign to secure a moderate successor rather than Dr Walsh, the President of Maynooth, who was considered the best qualified candidate by the Church's standard. Manning described Walsh as no more a Nationalist than himself, but that was quite Nationalist enough to alarm the Government, as well as old Catholics like the Duke of Norfolk and the Bishop of Clifton.[102] Aware of the hopelessness of trying to press his case through the Archbishop of Westminster, Granville sent George Errington, a member of the same Catholic family as Manning's former rival, to lobby the Roman authorities on behalf of the Government.

Manning disliked this move intensely, both because he felt it would be fatal for the Vatican's reputation in Ireland if Walsh was set aside as a result of pressure from the English Government, and because he resented any interference with the appointed channel for communication between Rome and the Cabinet, namely himself. For this reason he had always objected to the idea of a papal nuncio in England.[103] Now he wrote to Leo XIII stressing the extreme danger of even *seeming* to be swayed by English and Protestant influence in the appointment of a Roman Catholic Archbishop of Dublin.[104] His letter was so strong that he feared he might have vexed the Pope.[105] At the same time he leant on Chamberlain and Dilke, who were then seeking his good offices over the Irish local government plan, to ensure that the case against the Errington mission was argued in Cabinet. His alliance with Chamberlain, who was a formidable and avowed enemy of the voluntary schools, was always a strange one, but Manning never searched for eternal verities outside theology, least of all in politics, which he knew well to be the art of the possible. In this case he was entirely effective: Walsh was duly appointed Archbishop of Dublin.

In November 1885 Gladstone suddenly broke his ten-year silence towards Manning and sent him a copy of his latest pamphlet, entitled 'The Dawn of Creation', a subject gratifyingly far removed from the controversy about papal infallibility. Whether the Liberal leader had experienced a sudden surge of affection for the ecclesiastic who was then implicitly urging his flock to vote Tory, or whether he dimly discerned that the Archbishop of Westminster's friendship might be useful in forthcoming Irish broils, his gesture was instantly reciprocated. Manning thanked him for the pamphlet – '. . . still more for your words, which revive the memories of the old days. Fifty-five years are a long reach of life in which to remember each other. We have been twice parted, but as the path declines, as you say, it narrows, and I am glad that we are nearing each other as we near our end. . . . If we cannot unite in the realm where "the morning stars sang together" we should indeed be far off.'[106] As it became evident that Gladstone would be attempting to carry some form of Home Rule, Manning's letters to him soon reverted to a more workaday level, with the Cardinal taking up once more that pedagogic tone in which he had been wont to address the great statesman in former times. Although Manning shrewdly told the Pope (4 January 1886) that he did not think that Gladstone would succeed in carrying Home Rule, he was never the type to withhold counsel from an old friend. 'I hope no deliberation will be spared to find an extension of the English constitution in Ireland. No paper schemes, no new Constitutions, no Colonial chambers or Hungarian Parliaments will live a twelvemonth.'[107] It was advice which Gladstone might easily have dispensed with at this most critical juncture in his career. He knew very well that what Manning really meant was: keep the Irish MPs at Westminster. The Archbishop now insisted that a parliament in Dublin was 'not suited to the Irish'.[108]

A Prime Minister, however, can rarely afford to indulge such clear-cut opinions. As Gladstone explained to Lord Granville at the end of April 1886, 'I scarcely see how a Cabinet could have been formed, if inclusion of Irish members [at Westminster] had been insisted on; and now I do not see how the scheme and policy can be saved from shipwreck if the exclusion is insisted on.'[109] The Home Rule Bill which he had introduced into the Commons earlier in the month had altogether excluded Irish MPs from Westminster. Manning had been in the Distinguished Strangers' Gallery to hear one of Gladstone's great oratorical performances in defence of his Bill, but the Prime Minister's arguments left him unimpressed. 'You must all stay here,'[110] the Archbishop told the Irish members as he left Parliament. The measure was 'bad Home Rule at a cost of a breach in the Empire',[111] he said on another occasion. Gladstone, fighting to the last, offered to amend the Bill if only it passed its second reading, so that Irish members would come to Westminster to vote upon imperial legislation. The opportunity never arose: on 8 June the Bill was defeated by thirty votes.

It would be giving Manning too much importance to contend that anything which he did or did not do affected that result. Nevertheless, he can hardly be said to have won a share in the glory of defeat. When it came to the crunch his concern for Catholic representation at Westminster proved stronger than his much vaunted love for Ireland. Not that he seemed disposed to surrender a jot or a tittle of that love. The same Irish priest who had made him weep at the realization of Ireland's affection was rash enough to tell the Cardinal at the time of Home Rule that the Irish were 'all blessing Mr. Gladstone'. Manning 'seemed quite nettled and answered: "But *I* was a friend of Ireland before Mr. Gladstone." ' The good priest added that this burst of human nature moved him almost more than the tears that had been shed on the former occasion.[112] It must be said, however, that the crushing of Ireland's and Gladstone's hopes in the July 1886 election caused Manning remarkably little emotion. He merely explained the result, as he explained everything else, in the light of his own convictions. 'I do not interpret this election as a refusal to Ireland, but as a rejection of the mutilation of the Imperial Parliament by the removal of the representatives of Ireland.'[113] The wounds which Home Rule inflicted on Gladstone's party seemed almost a matter of relief. 'I have been watching with great interest the break up of the Liberal Party,' he wrote to Lord Cross, Minister for Ireland in the new Tory Government. 'If it had held together it would have become an aggressive Liberalism – Chamberlain an English Gambetta.' That, of course, would no more have suited the Catholic cause than the removal of the Irish MPs from Westminster. So the Tory Ministry received the radical Cardinal's blessing. 'I wish you a long life and a strong local government for the three kingdoms, on common principles, with local adaptations.'[114]

This enthusiasm did not last long. Manning very soon lost patience with the Tory Government's failure to take any constructive initiative in Ireland, and as the dreary cycle of violence and repression renewed itself the gap between the opinions of the Archbishop and those of his spiritual subjects among the English landholding classes widened more than ever. 'They think me past praying for,' he told Gladstone in 1887 apropos the old Catholic families, 'because I would not denounce Parnell and I would defend Archbishop Walsh.'[115] Influential Catholic laymen pressed the Vatican to uphold the rule of law in Ireland, but their efforts, it seemed, were of no avail. 'The Pope sees that your views and mine about Ireland do not agree,' the Duke of Norfolk told Manning in 1887, 'and I am sorry to say that he trusts yours rather than mine.'[116] It was not that Manning defended the violence – indeed he urged Archbishop Walsh to 'vindicate the law of God against English and Irish wrong-doers'.[117] His anxiety, as over Walsh's appointment, was that Rome should on no account appear to the Irish as a cipher for English interests. It was all very well to talk, as the Tories talked, of upholding the law of landlord and tenant, but how could there be any genuine freedom of contract between wealthy English landlords and desperately poor Irish peasants?

The Duke of Norfolk may have carried more weight with Leo XIII than he gave himself credit for. At all events the Pope, who possessed the instincts of a diplomat, decided to send a mission under a Mgr Persico to investigate English charges that the Irish hierarchy was encouraging the men of violence. Manning, who was always suspicious of the least threat to episcopal authority, cannot have much appreciated this decision, though he hotly denied a *Times* report that he had tried to get the mission revoked.[118] He did, however, closely and anxiously follow Mgr Persico's progress through Ireland in the second half of 1887. Everything appeared satisfactory. Mgr Persico wrote from Cork on 21 December: 'Your Eminence understands the Irish question thoroughly; I wish others in Rome understood it as your Eminence does. As far as I am concerned, I shall not fail to make a proper *exposé* of things.' By February 1888 Mgr Persico's opinions had progressed even further in the required direction. 'I am entirely of your Eminence's opinion that the people of Ireland have had no defenders but the priests, and I firmly believe that the clergy in Ireland must be the guides and protectors of the people.' The English were coldblooded, but always with one shining exception – 'Oh, how I wish that your Eminence could be entrusted with everything.'[119]

No doubt Mgr Persico felt this wish even more sharply when, in April 1888, Leo XIII suddenly issued a decree condemning the Irish 'Plan of Campaign' against landlords. Mgr Persico discovered that the Irish Capuchins with whom he was staying no longer relished his company, and was compelled to move his abode. 'It is known to Your Eminence that I did not expect at all the said Decree', he wrote pathetically to Manning, 'and that I was never more surprised in my life than when I received the circular.'[120] Manning was no less surprised, but typically he immediately set himself to limit the damage. As a result of his representations a second letter came from Rome explaining how badly the Pope's original statement had been misinterpreted and misunderstood. Even so, the episode had been a shock, one that forced Manning two years later into the uncharacteristic position of determining the proper limits of papal infallibility:

The Decree of Leo XIII was absolutely true, just, and useful. But in the abstract. The condition of Ireland is abnormal. The Decree contemplates facts which do not exist. . . . Pontiffs have no infallibility in the world of facts, except only dogmatic. The Plan of Campaign is not a dogmatic fact, and it is one thing to declare that all legal agreements are binding, and another to say that all agreements in Ireland are legal.[121]

It is never wise to jump too quickly to conclusions, but it rather looks as though Manning may have been saying that the Pope had made a mistake.

11 *The Pitcher at the Fountain*

I remember how often I have said that my chief sacrifice in becoming Catholic was 'that I ceased to work for the people of England, and had thenceforth to work for the Irish occupation in England'. Strangely all this is reversed. If I had not become Catholic I could never have worked for the people of England, as in the last year they think I have worked for them.

MANNING'S JOURNAL, 9 NOVEMBER 1890[1]

The last decade of Manning's life was a time when the plight of the poor, to which he had always been sensitive, forced itself on his attention with especial urgency. German and American competition was beginning to destroy Britain's industrial supremacy, just as cheap American corn had previously afflicted the English countryside. Manning, with his natural proclivity for sensing catastrophe, was one of the first to recognize that Britain was in relative economic decline. 'For the last many years', he wrote to Wyndham in 1888, 'I have been afraid that we have passed the highest point in our prosperity, which seems to me to have been the result of transient causes.'[2] Other countries now had the steam power and machinery on which Britain's manufacturing supremacy had rested. Manning stressed the need for better technical education in terms which are still heard frequently a century later, to equally little effect. 'Though our great productive supremacy has in time past been attained without systematic technical instruction, we can hardly hope to retain it in competition with foreign countries which are now systematically instructing their youth in the principles and the practices of arts and manufactures. It is of absolute necessity that we should keep pace with them in this also.'[3]

The destitution of the urban slums bore out Manning's warnings. It did not stem from the fact that wages were depressed; on the contrary, overall purchasing power increased during the 1880s. The worst hardship was caused by the cyclical nature of the economy, the alternation of boom and slump. In times of severe recession like 1879 and 1886 unskilled labourers, often Irish Catholics and Manning's particular charge, were the first to be thrown out of work. Families which existed on the edge of survival at the best of times were swiftly reduced to actual starvation in the worst. Manning, in Archbishop's House, lived in the midst of appalling suffering, and in his case familiarity brought neither contempt nor indifference.

What he saw and heard of this misery reinforced the conviction which he had held since the 1840s, that England was on the brink of some terrible insurrectionary disaster. In his view the social order was fragile in the extreme: what passed for civilization lay thin upon violent destructive forces. Even the best conceived legislation, he had told a temperance meeting in 1868, was 'no more than the beauty of a country lying upon the volcano. There is beneath it a power so ungovernable, a moral and spiritual power so terrible, that at any moment the justest and best laws may be scattered to ruin.'4 The episode of the Paris Commune, in which, among many others, the Archbishop of Paris had been slaughtered, had been a terrible warning of what might be in store for England. Now in the 1880s he discerned portents that the volcano was about to erupt. On 7 February 1886, Black Monday, a procession of unemployed ran riot in Pall Mall, and even the windows of the Athenaeum were not spared. Next year on 13 November, Bloody Sunday, a demonstration in Trafalgar Square degenerated into a vicious encounter with the police. Manning delivered a stern rebuke to those who had allowed themselves to get involved in the violence.5 But could mere rebuke, even from the Archbishop of Westminster, long hold back the fury that was to come?

Manning recognized clearly that private charity could never suffice to alleviate distress on such a scale. He himself had been so generous in his almsgiving that by the 1880s he had wholly exhausted his means.6 While his compassion drove him to help the victims, his practical nature searched for ways of eradicating the disease. He exhorted the rich to give, but he discouraged the notion that they might salve their consciences or solve the problem by throwing money at misery from a comfortable distance. All classes had contributed to the 'social wreckage' which he saw around him; all classes must involve themselves actively in the work of reparation. 'If, through faults of ours, however remotely or indirectly, by commission or omission, they [the destitute] are outcasts, let us now begin and try to bring them back to what they once were.'7

Society should be organized to preserve the full potential of man. Manning possessed a Rousseauesque belief in the innate goodness of the human species, a theory perhaps only maintainable by those who, whether through celibacy, science or the Foundling Hospital, spare themselves the joys of parenthood. Manning, who only occasionally saw the young, never

began to exhaust his belief in their virtue. When he visited schools his
daunting face would soften with sympathy and tenderness.[8] 'I like to go into
the parks on Sunday to see the children and talk with them,' Manning told a
Non-Conformist visitor, adding on a typical note, 'No one can say that I am
proselytising in that.'[9] In *The Eternal Priesthood* he recorded his conviction
that 'children come round a priest not only by a natural instinct, drawn by
kindness, but by a supernatural instinct as to one who belongs to them by
right'.[10] Children, however, have a tiresome habit of getting a bit too
proprietorial. Legend has it that at some function or other a child informed
the fully rigged Cardinal that he looked like 'an old silly'. But this event,
even if not apocryphal, left intact both Manning's charitable intentions and
his social determinism:

There is no doubt that in every great city there will be a refuse of the population who,
through their own perverse will, blind conscience, and evil passions, gather together
in a demoralised and dangerous horde. But it is also certain that each one was once an
innocent child. The bloated and brutal man, if he had been nurtured by a loving
mother in a pure home fit for a man to live in; if he had grown up in the consciousness
of a Divine law and presence; if he had lived in honest labour . . . would not have
become the wreck in body, mind, and speech, which we may see in our streets every
day.[11]

It followed that 'the care of children is the first duty after, and even with,
the salvation of our own soul'.[12] Those who engaged in the work of saving
children from the streets could be sure of his support and encouragement
whatever their religion, although there were some wrangles with Dr
Barnado about the rights and capabilities of Catholic rescue workers to look
after their own.[13] One Non-Conformist who became discouraged that all his
labours had yielded but seventy young charges in care recorded that the
Cardinal's response to his plaints gave him new strength. 'Only seventy
cases! Small result! Think of seventy little children's tears dried, and seventy
little children's tears stopped. We can never say that is nothing. It is glorious.
A child's needless tear is a blood-blot upon the earth.'[14] Again, anyone who
has lived with children knows that a child's needless tear may just as well be a
means of gaining attention. On the other hand, anyone tempted to such a flip
reflection is unlikely to have achieved for the children outside his immediate
charge one thousandth part of what Manning achieved.

The existence of abandoned children distressed him so deeply not only as
a tragedy in itself but also as a symptom of the breakdown of family life. He
regarded the family as the surest defence against the kind of social disaster
which he so readily prognosticated. Conversely, 'a commonwealth in which
domestic life is perishing has a settlement in its foundations'.[15] The most

appalling of all the dire consequences of pauperism was that it destroyed or rendered unattainable the humanizing amenities of hearth and home, and guaranteed that the next generation also would grow up without any hope, principle, religion or purpose beyond the blind struggle for survival. If there was one predominating and unifying aim in all Manning's social work, it was his determination to break into this circle of despair by doing everything in his power to create and sustain opportunities for the poor to lead a settled family existence.

This ambition did not always cast him in the forefront of radical thought. To say the least, he was never an advocate of Women's Liberation. It was not that he was so naïve or obtuse as to deny feminine potential: he protested that women were 'more courageous than men . . . stronger in good things than men'.[16] These virtues, however, had been divinely allotted to one particular sphere. 'Wives and mothers have neither right nor duty to bind themselves for such and such a number of hours per day,' he wrote in 1890, 'in violation of their previous engagement as mothers and wives. Such a bond is *ipso facto* illegal or null . . . without domestic life there is no nation.'[17] Really the only choice before women was marriage or the convent. He believed that the Catholic Church was 'the only power which had known how to make full use of its women and that when Catholic women wanted to work they became nuns and all their efforts were disciplined and directed'. He did admit that 'a great many women, and some of the best women too, are quite unfitted by nature for marriage or for the cloister', but that was a problem for which he offered no solution. In his more abandoned moments he was prepared to concede that women whose means and circumstances permitted might serve as Poor Law Guardians, or even on County Councils, but permissiveness stopped well short of allowing that they might become MPS. The legislation which men passed in parliament was bad enough. There was, for example, the law enabling a man to marry his deceased wife's sister. Manning considered that this measure was a most dangerous attack on family stability.[18] This opinion involved him in a telling exchange with the Prince of Wales, who met the Cardinal shortly after voting for the Bill in the House of Lords. 'I have been doing something you disapprove, sir!' the Prince remarked. 'I know you have, sir!' returned Manning. 'But I did what was right, sir,' the Prince rashly persisted. 'I know you think so, sir!'[19] the prince of the Church responded.

An aspect of Manning's work that deserved the respect of men and women alike was the support which he gave to W. T. Stead in his campaign against the prostitution of young girls. Earlier in his life Manning had occasionally been able to help Gladstone find a home for rescued prostitutes,[20] but this had been done quite out of the public eye. Stead was a journalist who relied upon publicity as the means of furthering his ends, even delighting to go to prison when he exposed in his own person how easily juveniles might be procured. Both the man and his work were phenomena from which the spiritually fastidious tended to recoil with shock and disdain. Manning claimed that he was 'literally denounced by Catholics'[21] for associating himself with such a cause, but he was ferociously and magnific-ently unrepentant. 'I should forget all the laws of proportion and fitness if I took notice of the gross impertinence of Abraham's children. If, and when, I saw fit to issue a Pastoral, twelve tribes of Pharisees and Scribes would not hinder me. What do they take me for, and what do they imagine themselves to be?'[22] Manning had the satisfaction of seeing Stead's campaign, however brashly urged, succeed: the age of consent was raised from thirteen to sixteen.

Manning's crusade against drink may also be seen in the context of his defence of family life. There could be no domestic content so long as precious pennies were thrown away on stupefaction. As Manning aged, he saw the temperance issue in more and more simplistic terms as a straight fight between good and evil. As a result his line became increasingly harsh and extreme. On the one side were the innocent exploited poor; on the other the wicked drink interest. 'Shall five hundred be enriched and the nation perish?'[23] he dramatically demanded of a temperance meeting at Oldham in 1881. Brewers and publicans deserved no quarter at all. At the end of the 1880s Manning strongly opposed the Tory Government's attempts to ensure that publicans should be compensated for the loss of their licence, arguing that such a measure would constitute a form of protection for the evil drink trade.[24]

He had long since ceased, in his temperance work, to hope or to look for any assistance among the more influential of his own flock. 'I have piped and they have not danced; there is not one gentleman who will give up one glass of sherry to help me in the battle.'[25] He denounced aristocrats who would shriek with indignation if a pub should appear at the end of their drive, but looked on with calm indifference as pubs were built in the slums, where they did infinitely more harm.[26] Manning himself would continue to be 'a fool for Christ's sake' in his temperance work.[27] The old Catholics could sneer as much as they liked in the correspondence columns of the *Tablet*; they were victims of 'the fine gentleman heresy'.[28] It did not signify either that the Bishop of Nottingham, otherwise a radical ally, should in the summer of 1884 attack his own Metropolitan in that journal. 'A small minority of the clergy', the Bishop wrote under the pseudonym of 'Senex', 'has formed a league to promote teetotalism. A majority, quite equal with them in zeal, and more than equal in experience, do not believe that any good is to be expected from the League.'[29] Manning did not condescend to notice such things. 'If others think to save more souls by suing their liberty to drink wine, let us wait for the last day.'[30]

Pending that event, Manning has paid dearly for his principles. Vaughan, formerly his staunchest ally, bitterly offended him by attending a Licensed Victuallers' dinner in Manchester. Next time the Bishop of Salford visited London he was taxed severely for his dereliction. The discussion grew heated. 'I saw he was a bit put out,' recalled Vaughan, 'but what do you think he did? He went upstairs, took out his will, and struck his pen through my name as executor. It was a mistake; if I had been his executor, his private papers would never have fallen into the hands of Mr. Purcell.'[31] And without Purcell where would Lytton Strachey have scavenged the means for his pernicious essay? Yet Manning, surely, would have been proud to forfeit reputation in the cause of temperance. When he had lain so ill in Paris during the autumn of 1877 his greatest comfort, he said, had been in the reflection that he had saved so many drunkards.[32] And his temperance work did gain him one gratifying admirer. The brilliant Francis Newman, who never missed an opportunity to make a point against his detested elder brother, openly declared his respect. 'I see Christian sects vying in *good works*, and of late even Catholics joining with Protestants. That is the way to improve the world, and to improve one another. As initiator of the good movement, I with delight signalise Cardinal Manning.'[33]

Sobriety was one prerequisite for domestic content; adequate leisure was another. The restriction of working hours was a cause to which Manning eagerly lent his authority and influence. 'The humblest workman, no less than the man who is rich and literate, has need of certain hours wherein to cultivate his mind and soul; and if such hours are not permitted he is cowered to the state of a machine.'[34] This was a case which he had first made when trying to improve the lot of the shepherds and ploughmen at Lavington. Now in London it was the shop and factory workers who benefited from his advocacy. He rejoiced when, in the last year of his life, an Act raised the age of half-timers in factories from ten to eleven. 'I was so pleased I positively couldn't eat my breakfast.'[35]

Domesticity was also impossible without tolerable housing. As long as families of five to ten people were each being herded together in one or two rooms it was idle to speak of the elevating effects of home life. 'What moral influence or formation of the life and character of children is possible in overcrowded dens where all is misery and confusion?'[36] Manning demanded. So he accepted with enthusiasm when, in 1884, Dilke invited him to become a member of the Royal Commission on the Housing of the Working Classes. It was a star-studded committee, with the Prince of Wales and Lord Salisbury among the other members. Before tackling the problems of the working classes it was necessary to resolve the tricky issue of precedence. Eventually the prince of the Church was allotted a position after the Prince of Wales but before the Marquess of Salisbury, whose family had helped to consolidate the Protestant Reformation in England.

Manning's views on the matter in hand, however, remained wholly radical. 'Would it not be advisable', he suggested, 'to remove out of the streets into the suburbs the following: Prisons, infirmaries, certain hospitals, ironworks, all factories not needed for daily or hourly work?'[37] Such an idea might be orthodox today, but it proved far too sweeping for Manning's fellow commissioners. The Cardinal 'is our only revolutionary',[38] commented Dilke, who thought his notions totally impractical and ill-conceived. Manning further expressed the view that extortionate rents should destroy the right of the landlord in the property concerned: 'some authority might be created to pronounce what is extortionate.'[39] His eloquent pleas on behalf of the poor prompted the Secretary of the Commission to remark that 'if there had been some half dozen Mannings England would have run some risk of being converted to Christianity'.[40] The Housing Commission constituted no threat in this direction. Manning described the report as 'evidently pale from fear',[41] although it was forthright enough to deter the Tory Government from taking any action. Manning thereafter concentrated his hopes of effective action on the establishment of better local government, and this at least was achieved with the creation of the London County Council in 1888.

As a man of the Church Manning claimed to be independent of politics,[42] but then he also said that if he were not a Cardinal he would be standing for Westminster in the radical interest.[43] What a rascal he would have become (he further reflected) if he had achieved his political ambitions.[44] His way of preserving official neutrality without sacrificing any of his opinions was to call himself 'a Mosaic radical',[45] a phrase which repeatedly appears in his later writings and which carried in his mind the meaning 'For God and People'. 'My Radicalism I learned of Moses and St Paul,' he told the Duchess of Buccleuch in 1869, 'and I may say my politics are summed up in the words, "I have compassion on the multitude, for they have nothing to eat." '[46] For Manning political and moral decisions were inseparable: that is what he meant when he told the young Hilaire Belloc that 'all human conflict is ultimately theological'.[47] For fifty years and more he insisted that the welfare and interests of the people at large must always come before the exigencies of more sophisticated social theories. 'We must admit and accept calmly and with good will that industry and profits must be considered in second place; the moral state and domestic condition of the whole working population must be considered first.'[48]

Manning fought for the victims of the recession in any way that he could. In 1887–8 he was a member of the Lord Mayor's Committee to relieve distress in London, and he led a deputation to Downing Street to persuade the Prime Minister to provide some temporary relief. Above all, he fiercely resisted the 'heartless and headless'[49] notions of *laissez-faire* theorists who found it so easy to tolerate conditions which they were not called upon to suffer:

We have been for years so tutored with warnings against alms and doles and private charities [Manning wrote to *The Times* in 1886], that Mr. Ruskin has said he never dares to give anything in the streets without looking on all sides to see whether there is a political economist coming. . . . The Good Samaritan did not delay to pour oil and wine into the wounds of the man half-dead until he had ascertained whether he was responsible for his own distress. Necessity has no law, nor has present distress, except a claim for prompt relief.[50]

The Times was always incurring Manning's scorn in his last decade, whether over Irish or social affairs. Manning urged that the suffering of the destitute presented the Government with claims prior to its concern to maintain an open market; and he had no patience with journalists who informed him that in his pleadings for the poor he was mistaking effect for cause. 'That is the sort of criticism that an undergraduate makes', remarked the Cardinal, 'and thinks himself very clever. But I am told that in the present day *The Times* is chiefly run by undergraduates.'[51] *The Times* sneered that the Archbishop was 'destitute of the rudiments of the science upon which he poses as an authority', but Manning was far too confident intellectually to be impressed by that line. 'This is hardly reasoning,' he commented, 'but by some it may be mistaken for it.'[52]

In 1887 he did battle in the paper's correspondence columns with an economist named Giffin, who had stated the *laissez-faire* case in its most rigid form. 'The only way to make more work for the unemployed,' Giffin believed, 'is for the employed to produce as much profit as they can – i.e. as much surplus as they can – over the cost of producing: for all that profit *must* be spent on employing somebody in some way or other.' Both that argument and Manning's riposte have a familiar ring today. 'But if there is no surplus?' the Cardinal demanded. 'Theories of the gradual accumulation of surplus will not feed hungry men, woman and children; and hunger cannot be sent to Jupiter or to Saturn.' Capitalists were free to do what they liked with their money: it might be sunk into land or invested abroad or

spent in a thousand ways that never reach such a distress as is now weighing upon London. . . . Finally I would ask, what number of years may be required to raise the level of surplus and employment over the surface of the country? And, in the meanwhile, how many hundreds of thousands may die off by a death of which a jury the other day found that it was accelerated by want. . . . A universal surplus is a dream.[53]

Manning detested the nineteenth-century Poor Law which forced men into the workhouse if they were to receive relief from the want into which they may have fallen not from their own fault but through the vicissitudes of the trade cycle. 'The workhouse test implies that he is a culprit or unworthy of help, and classes him with loafers, idlers and vagabonds.'[54] Manning's dislike of the workhouse system was such that he adopted the standpoint, rare for a Catholic ecclesiastic, of praising the social legislation of Elizabeth I, in which he discerned both a more charitable and a more effective spirit than that exemplified by the Poor Law of 1834. In particular, he appreciated the Elizabethan injunction that in every town and city the justices of the peace should order 'a competent stock of wool, hemp, flax, iron and other stuff – by taxation of all – so that every poor and needy person, old and young, able to work and standing in need of relief, shall not, from want of work, go abroad begging, or committing pilferings, or living in idleness'.[55] Manning's relish for such paternalism was absolutely in character, as was the highly selective use which he made of history. He conveniently ignored the fact that many of the sixteenth-century poor had preferred to wander the countryside rather than submit to beating hemp under the eye of the local magistrate, even though the penalty for persistent vagrants was whipping until 'their backs be bloody'.

Manning's outspoken comments on social issues led opponents to label him a socialist. It was a charge which he neither rejected nor accepted. As he pointed out, no one really had any idea what socialism meant: it was just 'a party cry'[56] used by reactionaries against anyone who demanded change. Yet it is easy to see why the term stuck to Manning, who was occasionally capable of statements that would not have sounded amiss in the works of Marx and Lenin. At the end of his life he became the *doyen* of the Catholic social movement that flourished in France under the leadership of Count Alfred de Mun and Léon Harmel, and he seemed determined to demonstrate to continental audiences that the unyielding advocate of papal infallibility lacked nothing in progressive instincts where the material welfare of the people was at stake. Writing to the *XXe Siècle*, the journal of Action Catholique de la Jeunesse Française founded by Sylvio de Monléon and Alexandre Bergasse, Manning used phrases which give off a somewhat hollow ring to those reading them with the benefit of hindsight. 'We have been, up to now, hampered by an excessive individualism, and the next century will show that mankind is greater and more noble than any individual thing.'[57] That was an odd sentiment to issue from a prince 'of the Church: it conveys a hint of 'systems so perfect that no one will need to be good'.[58]

Of course Manning intended nothing of the kind; he believed in State intervention, not State control, and it was blunt common sense, not sophisticated political theory, that determined his thought and action. Obviously, if people were starving, it was the duty of Government to provide for them; 'and in my opinion the best relief in such cases would be in the form of employment upon works of public utility.'[59] Wherever there were wrongs to be righted, the Government should act. Regarding housing, for example, Manning told Dilke that 'without a high-handed executive nothing will be done until another generation has been destroyed'.[60] It was equally clear that Government should assist emigration as a means of countering unemployment; and Manning appeared both puzzled and a trifle irritated that the pig-headed multitude did not see the obvious advantages of forsaking their homeland.[61] Worse, Manning's views of emigration earned him a rebuke from the pioneer socialist H. M. Hyndman, who accused him of wanting to export unemployment to countries where the problem was as grave as in Britain.[62]

An instinctive authoritarian, Manning envisaged his high-handed executives acting like latter-day Robin Hoods to redress inequities wherever they occurred. He never showed any awareness that State intervention might shade into State control, which he abhorred. In his view, though individualism might *become* excessive, collectivism was flawed of its very nature. When he met Henry George, the American advocate of land nationalization, he hastened to make his position absolutely clear:

Before we go further, let me know whether we are in agreement upon one vital principle. I believe that the law of property is founded on the law of Nature, and that it is sanctioned in Revelation, declared in the Christian law, taught by the Catholic Church, and incorporated into the civilisation of all nations. Therefore, unless we are in agreement upon this, which lies at the foundation of society, I am afraid we cannot approach each other.[63]

Fortunately George managed to improvise some remarks about Christ being an example for rich and poor alike, which provided a satisfactory basis for further conversation. Manning was radical, however, in that he did not limit the idea of property to material possessions. 'Labour and skill are as true capital as land or money':[64] that was why he regarded unemployment as a species of theft, which the State had a duty to prevent.

Though the State might, and ought to, intervene in order to protect this capital of labour, Manning was firm that it should possess absolutely no rights in toil and sweat. To make the State a public employer, he thought, was

an exaggeration of the worst danger in politics – namely, exaggerated centralis-ation. . . . To make the state – that is, the Government of the day – the only employer of an unlimited number of the populace at large, who must necessarily be the least skilled, successful, and to some extent trustworthy of the people, would be a public danger, fatal, sooner or later, to any Commonwealth, and in such a Commonwealth as ours of certain and speedy disorder.[65]

Government must serve society as a kind of doctor with a strictly limited role:

Whenever social evils, by the growth of tradition and custom, and the vicissitudes of the time, shall arise in any Commonwealth, the correction of such social evils, like the practice of healing, is conservative of the life and health of society. . . . Socialism . . . identifies social evils with society itself, and kills the patient to cure his maladies. For example: the accumulation of property, whether in capital or land, in a few hands is to the socialist the chief evil of the times. To cure it, some socialists deny the right of property in individuals, which is founded radically in the law of nature.[66]

So the modern Left, no less than the modern Right, might find much to regard as objectionable in Manning's political thought. Manning, in fact, prided himself on the conservatism of his attitude towards institutions.[67] He wanted the existing system to work better, not that it should be overturned. 'Socialism is to society what rationalism is to reason,'[68] he pronounced, and no one ever accused him of favouring rationalism. The apophthegm was typical of his debating style: it was clever, it sounded good, it hardly admitted of any speedy reply, and it obviated the necessity for any deeper thought. To attempt to set Manning up as a valuable social theorist would be quite fruitless. His sharp mind anticipated many twentieth-century problems, but his solutions tended to be facile. In 1890, for instance, in his role of leading social guru to European Catholics, he wrote to a meeting at Liège of his conviction that harmonious relations between employer and employed would never be 'safely and solidly secured until the just and due proportion between profits and wages shall have been fixed, recognised, laid down, and publicly known to govern all free contracts between capital and labour'.[69] What a forward-looking concept that seems. Yet when the Liège conference respectfully enquired who should do the fixing of this just proportion, the Cardinal could only reply that it should be arranged between management and workers,[70] an answer that begged the entire question.

To some extent, then, *The Times* had a point when it referred to the 'confusion' of Manning's thought. But it would be quite wrong to suggest that this in any way invalidated his pleadings on behalf of the outcasts of society. Feeling is a far more effective advocate than intellect, and Manning's appeal only gained in power because it sprang so evidently from deeply experienced emotion. Lady Dilke, a shrewd observer, saw that this was the secret of his hold upon the imagination. Commenting on a remark that misery and suffering always caused Manning the most acute anguish, she wrote:

This was true in a degree that I have known in hardly any other man. I have heard him speak with a sound in his voice and a light in his eyes which meant depths of restrained passion. 'Give all yourself to London, it is the abomination of desolations' or 'No one knows the depth of the sufferings of women save the doctor or the priest.' That he was so pained by your pain was the chief cause of his great power. He could never have been a great doctor of the Church, a great theologian, for his metaphysics were of the weakest, but his brilliant understanding and his unrivalled practical instincts coupled with this passionate capacity for feeling made him one of the most striking personalities I have known.[71]

Manning's political ideas, such as they were, came from the New Testament, not from any blueprint for establishing Utopia on earth. He delighted to quote St Jerome: 'Man without God is cattle.'[72] When someone taxed him with advocating socialism, he sharply riposted: 'I do not know whether it means socialism to you. To me it means Christianity.'[73] Similarly, when Huxley, whose influence he detested, accused him of spreading the 'mischievous' doctrine that the poor had a *right* to work, it was enough for Manning to reply: 'I am very sure what Our Lord and His Apostles would do if they were in London.'[74]

His insistence that the Church's teachings should put it on the side of the people at large, of the governed against the governors, tied up happily with his conviction that such a stance represented the best hope of recovering the lost masses of England and of maintaining Catholicism everywhere. 'I do not believe that the English people will be won back through the intellect,' he wrote at the end of his life. 'Their will has been lost by the sins and miseries of the past. But their will is already changing and may be won by finding sympathy and care in the bishops and priests of the Church.'[75] On this point he enjoyed the full sympathy and support of Leo XIII, with whom he had many long and satisfactory conversations on his last visit to Rome in 1883.[76] In many ways Manning had much more in common with Leo XIII than with his adored Pius IX, who in his old age used to react like a startled hare at the least suggestion of political radicalism. It has been said that Manning helped to guide Leo XIII towards involving the Catholic Church in social questions. The claim ignores the Pope's prior interest in such matters when he was

Bishop of Perugia; besides, the kind of action which both men advocated had been outlined by the Congress of Mainz in 1848, before Manning was even a Catholic.

The Archbishop of Westminster did, nevertheless, acquire a reputation for being able to influence Rome against adopting too reactionary a stance in social affairs. His renown had now spread across the Atlantic. When Cardinal Gibbons of Baltimore was struggling to prevent a condemnation of the Knights of Labour, a predominantly Irish Catholic organization of working men that had incurred the suspicions of the Church authorities both for being too radical and for indulging in quasi-masonic secret rites, he naturally turned to Manning for help. Manning also pleaded, at Gibbons's behest, that the works of Henry George should not be put on the *Index*. In both cases his efforts were successful. 'I cannot sufficiently express to you', Gibbons wrote to Manning in March 1887, 'how much I felt strengthened in my utterances on the claims of the working man to our sympathy. . . . We are indebted more than you are aware to the influence of your name in discussing these social questions and in influencing the public mind.'[77]

At home Manning's long record of concern for the unfortunate gave him the moral authority without which he could never have achieved his greatest English triumph, the resolution of the London Dock Strike of 1889. The strike also demonstrated how far Manning had travelled from his roots. His father and his brother Frederick, Tories to the backbone, had both been directors of dock companies, but it was Ben Tillett, the trade union leader who had striven to organize unskilled labour in the docks, with whom Manning had the closest contacts. Tillett had written to him in March 1888[78] about the difficulties and disappointments of his work, and had received a most encouraging reply. Next year, as the economy gradually came out of recession, Tillett determined that the dock workers should have their share from the improving conditions. He had two principal demands: that the basic wage in the docks should be sixpence an hour instead of the fourpence or even threepence which was sometimes paid, and that casual workers, whose contracts had hitherto been determined almost entirely at the employers' whim, should be hired for a minimum period of four hours. These demands not being met, the strike became effective from 14 August 1889. Within a week the London docks, through which so much of the nation's shipping then passed, were entirely paralysed.

Historians are wont to discern in the strike an event of great significance, one of the first occasions on which unskilled labour effectively combined. The powers at the time, however, seemed entirely unaware that they were witnessing the dawn of a revolution. Parliament broke up for the recess on 30 August without so much as a mention of the strike. The Home Secretary, the Lord Mayor, and the head of the London police all retired for their summer holidays. Perhaps somewhat angered by their failure to make an impression, labour leaders began to talk in terms of a general strike of the whole London labour force, while radical journalists anticipated the historians with articles about the revolutionary, if peaceful, changes that were imminent.[79]

Manning had been closely in touch with dockland politics from the very beginning of the strike through the intermediary of a journalist named Margaret Harkness, who wrote for the radical newspaper *The Star*.[80] Whatever the sang-froid, or pigheadedness, shown by the ruling class, the Cardinal found no difficulty in grasping the nature of the threat. Images of destruction and chaos were never far from his mind; now, it seemed, reality might at last be matching up. The mental state which the strike induced in Manning is evident in an account which he wrote afterwards:

For a month the streets of London were choked day by day with processions of tens of thousands. Disorder and horseplay, which at any moment may turn to collisions with the people or the police, were imminent; these were sharpened by disappointment, and irritated by refusal of an additional penny an hour. At any moment a drunkard, or a madman, or a fool might have set fire to the docks and warehouses. The commercial wealth of London and the merchandise of the world, the banks and wharves of the Thames might have been pillaged, and the conflagration might have spread for hours before order, at unimaginable loss, could be restored.[81]

Manning naturally resolved that it was his duty to do everything within his power to prevent these horrors. There is a story, indicative at least of the kind of character the Cardinal held in dockland, that he presented himself early on in the strike at Ben Tillett's lodgings. When Tillett returned, his landlady informed him that a priest had been waiting in his rooms all afternoon. Manning had passed the time reading Sherlock Holmes in the *Strand* magazine. His line of questioning, however, owed nothing to the great detective. Were the strikers in a state of grace, he demanded. Tillett replied that he could not answer for the grace, but they were certainly in a state of hunger. Yet on 29 August the strikers' position was immeasurably strengthened by the arrival of funds from Australian trade unionists, who would eventually provide a total of £30,000.[82] The strikers also enjoyed much popular sympathy, as well as the support of many newspapers, always excepting the redoubtable *Times*.

Manning realized that justice by itself was not enough to win the strike: what was needed, if a prolonged struggle was to be avoided, was some conciliation procedure to make the employers see reason. On 1 September he wrote to Sir John Lubbock, President of the London Chamber of

Commerce, asking for his help in finding a solution to the strike.[83] Four days later, on 5 September, Manning acted on his own account. By this stage of his life he rarely left Archbishop's House, but now he drove both to the Home Office and to Mansion House, only to discover that the Home Secretary and Lord Mayor were still out of town. Finally he tracked down the Deputy Mayor and the acting head of police, whom he persuaded to accompany him on a visit to the Joint Committee of dock company directors. The meeting was not a success. The directors were unimpressed by Manning's assurance that revolution was at hand.[84] To the Cardinal's entreaty that the employers should on no account, as had been rumoured, use imported labour from Holland to break the strike, the President of the Joint Committee retorted that he was free to employ whomsoever he pleased. Neither Manning's presence nor his moralizing tone were appreciated. He left without having achieved anything, complaining that 'I never in my life preached to so impenitent a congregation.'[85] It had been a full day for an eighty-one-year-old.

Nothing daunted, he next day sat on a committee of conciliation which the now returned Lord Mayor had hastily convened at Mansion House. Dr Temple, the Bishop of London, was also a member, along with Sidney Buxton, MP for Poplar, Sir John Lubbock and Lord Brassey. These worthies patched together a compromise whereby the dockers should receive their sixpence an hour, but only with effect from 1 March 1890. Tillett and his fellow strike leader John Burns, summoned before the conciliation committee, refused to countenance such a long delay. They were prepared, however, to recommend the terms to the strike committee provided they took effect from 1 January 1890. Next day, 7 September, the Joint Committee of dock directors agreed, after a stormy debate, that they would accept this settlement. It seemed that the strike was over. Tillett and Burns discovered to their surprise, however, that their colleagues utterly refused to consider the 1 January date. Some of the dockers had wrung out of the wharf owners an agreement starting from 4 September, and the rest were in no mood to settle for less.

At this point the Bishop of London threw in his hand. Manning alone made a serious effort to keep negotiations going. On Sunday 8 September he saw Tillett, fresh from a Hyde Park rally, at Archbishop's House, and understood that the strikers were now demanding that 1 October should be the date when the settlement took effect. On Monday the Lord Mayor's conciliation committee (minus Dr Temple) tried to persuade Tillett and Burns to accept the 1 January date which they had previously countenanced, but met with an adamantine refusal. Manning declared that he would not bow to this verdict without meeting the entire committee of strike leaders.

The Lord Mayor was only too glad to delegate this task to the Cardinal, who was given powers to act on behalf of his fellow conciliators. So it came about that on 10 September the ancient Archbishop, accompanied only by Sidney Buxton, drove down to the East End to try and bring the men to terms.

The meeting took place in the austere surroundings of a classroom at Kirby Street school, the strikers' usual headquarters at the *Wade's Arms* presumably being deemed unsuitable for an encounter with the teetotal Cardinal. At first the atmosphere was hostile to any kind of concession. Buxton later described the mood of the men as 'excited and obstinate, angry and suspicious'.[86] Manning proposed 4 November (St Charles's Day, surely not a coincidence) as the compromise date from which the terms should apply. Tillett advanced his objections, which Manning answered with the ease of a practised debater. After two hours of argument, however, there was still no sign of an agreement. Then Manning pulled out all the stops in an impassioned plea, the last great speech of his life. He begged the men to recognize his impartiality, as one who now had accounts to give to no one but God. He dwelt upon the danger to the nation in general and upon the likely sufferings of the strikers' families in particular if the strike was allowed to drag on.[87] It was now late in the evening, and according to the legend it seemed to some of the men that as the saintly-looking Cardinal spoke the tawdry image of the Virgin on the classroom wall shone with a radiance quite beyond the meagre power of the school's gas lighting. The legend founders on the fact that the Kirby Street school was not Catholic; even so, there was no resisting such an appeal. The militants continued to resist, but everyone knew in his heart that the battle was over. By twenty-eight votes to fifteen, with some abstentions, the meeting accepted the 4 November date and authorized Manning to negotiate a settlement with the Joint Committee on that basis. Driving home in his carriage from a gathering now overwhelmed with religious emotion, the Cardinal, with the resolution signed by the strike leaders tucked safely away in his pocket, permitted himself a secular reflection: 'This shows the perpetual advantage of acting upon that aphorism, If you want a thing done – go; if you want it neglected – send!'[88]

The strike was now virtually resolved, although there were four more days of negotiation before a final settlement was reached. Manning's triumph was complete. The Pope, and even Cardinal Newman,[89] sent congratulations. The English press hailed him as the hero of the hour, the *Daily Telegraph* observing that it was through such men as Manning that the English would learn to look upon Catholics with other eyes. The Church, the one true Church, was well and truly in the forefront of the nation's affairs: people spoke of 'the Cardinal's peace'.[90] For a while, as *The Times* recorded with disgust, 'there was not a strike in the south of England but that somebody said something about the Cardinal'.[91] Manning's role in the dock strike was contrasted with that of the Bishop of London, who had so readily abandoned the task of conciliation. 'Cardinal Manning has done well in London,' the Archbishop of Canterbury confided to his journal, 'but why has my dear Bishop of London gone back and left it to him?'[92] The question sprang easily to the mind of an Anglican archbishop who knew that many were now referring to Manning as the real Primate of All England.

The Cardinal's popularity among working men was now at its zenith. In 1890 his portrait appeared beside that of Karl Marx on banners in the May Day procession,[93] a rare and perhaps not altogether enviable distinction for a Roman Catholic ecclesiastic. The dockers raised a subscription and presented him with £160, which he used to endow a bed for them at the London Hospital. The Revd James Adderley, an Anglican who worked in the East End, considered that if Manning had cared to follow up his triumph with a mission to dockland he would have gathered a rich harvest for Rome.[94] 'This seems like the latter end of Job, greater than the beginning,' the Cardinal reflected a year later, adding characteristically: 'I hope it is not the condemnation when all men speak well of me.'[95]

He had no need for worry upon that score. His success spawned the inevitable brood of envious nit-pickers. The *Manchester Guardian* observed, as though this somehow tarnished the whole undertaking, that he had owed his influence to the fact that many of the dockers were Catholics; to which W. T. Stead riposted in the *Pall Mall Gazette* that, whether or not this had been true before the strike, he would not be surprised if it were true now.[96] Actually none of the principal leaders of the strike was Catholic, though that did not in any way inhibit their devotion to the Cardinal. When the *Saturday Review* accused Manning of popularity hunting, John Burns publicly threatened to beat up the editor.[97] In contrast, there were English Catholics who remained resolutely unimpressed by their Archbishop's intervention. 'Even in more sober quarters,' the *Tablet* commented on 14 September 1889, 'there seems to be an uneasy feeling that it would have been better if the peacemaker had been another.'[98] The remark reflected Vaughan's influence on that paper. He was of the opinion that Manning had no right to drag down the great office of a priest into a squalid dispute about wages.

Manning, not a whit abashed, looked for further fields of action. *The Times* obituary writer would find deep satisfaction in the failure of his attempt to intervene in a gas workers' dispute. His chief concern, however, was to establish some permanent conciliation procedure for resolving such disputes. He eagerly joined a committee of enquiry which the London Chamber of Commerce set up to explore this possibility. The suggestion, put to him by Mr Boulton of Copped Hall, that 'arbitration applied by one eminent individual, however disinterested and benevolent, was not the method which should normally be applied to the settlement of Labour disputes', did not in the least dim his enthusiasm. He agreed that it was not the business of a prelate to fix wages.[99] Even so, he continued to find it monstrous that the nation might be held to ransom by industrial disputes, and he rejected absolutely the view that strikes were simply matters between masters and men. In the dock strike, for instance, there had been 'two other parties interested besides masters and men, the multitude of suffering women and children, and the whole peaceful population of London. At a certain stage of such a conflict, either or both of these parties have a social, civil and natural right to intervene to protect the public safety.'[100]

These remarks should not be taken to imply that Manning adopted a neutral stance in the eternal struggle between employers and their workers. 'I have been turning over the Strike matters,' he wrote at the end of 1889, 'and the more I think, the more I am on the side of labour.'[101] He had no doubts at all as to the legitimacy of the strike weapon. 'A strike is like a war. If for just cause a strike is a right inevitable, it is a healthy constraint imposed upon the despotism of capital. It is the only power in the hands of the working men.'[102] Manning also knew, however, that the strikers themselves were often the worst losers by a strike,[103] which was another reason for preferring arbitration. The idea of a purely political strike, which seemed to be gaining ground on the continent, horrified him. Equally, though, to expect men to accept exploitation without complaint was ludicrous. 'Where there is no proportion, or no known proportion, between enormous and increasing profits, and scanty and stationary wages, to be contented is to be superhuman.' Manning objected to company accounts being kept secret, so that it became impossible to discover just how much management was taking out of the business. Justice must not merely be done; it must be *seen* to be done.[104] He knew, however, that the capitalists would never surrender without a struggle. 'There is no justice, mercy, or compassion in the Plutocracy: that is my creed.'[105]

After the dockers' strike Manning hardly ventured again out of Archbishop's House. 'How I wish I could take Henry to see the shops in Regent Street,'[106] exclaimed his sister Caroline, who tried in vain to lure him from his fastness. He did not for a moment consider, however, that his work was finished. 'My active life is over,' he had written in 1888 (before the dockers' strike), 'but much may still be done by word and by writing. If it be the will of my good Master, I should hope not to outlive my faculties.'[107] This hope was fulfilled quite beyond the ordinary human lot. The energy and clarity of his mind were preserved to the very end, and the only one of his senses that seriously deteriorated was his hearing, which had given problems since the

1850s.[108] No one but Vaughan, who equated temperance crusades and radical politics with mental decline, ever nurtured doubts about the keenness of Manning's mind. Vaughan considered that in his last years the Cardinal 'lost his old power of judging men aright' and that 'the process of senile decay had set in'.[109] By that he meant that journalists like Stead and social outcasts like Mrs Crawford were welcome at Archbishop's House. Others might consider that Manning's refusal to restrict his acquaintance to the beautiful and the good was one of his more endearing characteristics. Another was the complete lack of presumption he showed in assessments of his own character. When Mrs Crawford tactfully suggested that he bore a resemblance to St Charles, Manning would have none of it. 'No,' he said, 'St. Charles was meek.'[110] And on another occasion he cut short a toady who remarked after some display of irritation how consoling it was to find a Cardinal with ordinary human sensitiveness: 'No, no, it is very disappointing.'[111]

The Archbishop of Westminster was still at the centre of affairs. As it happened, he found himself involved, immediately after the dock strike, in a private event of ultimately far greater public significance. At that time it seemed, on the evidence of by-elections, that the English electorate might be ready to give Gladstone a clear mandate to carry Home Rule in conjunction with Parnell's Irish Nationalist party. On 19 October 1889, however, Manning received advance warning of a potentially shattering blow to this hope. Captain O'Shea, who was married to Parnell's mistress, called at Archbishop's House and announced his intention of suing for divorce, citing Parnell as co-respondent.[112] It was a critical moment. Manning obviously knew that the prospective suit would destroy Parnell, and although he could not have been expected to foresee that Parnell would be prepared to split his Party to save his leadership, he must have realized that the loss of so dominant a personality would do nothing to help the cause of Home Rule. His first instinct, then, was to temporize, to insist upon definite proof of Mrs O'Shea's infidelity. (One might have thought that Mrs O'Shea's children by Parnell would have constituted evidence enough, but after all Manning only had O'Shea's word for their paternity.) In November Manning wrote to O'Shea deprecating a separation and once more stressing the need for further evidence. It is intriguing to speculate how different the relations of England and Ireland might have been if Manning had contrived to stave off this divorce. By upholding a matrimonial fiction he might have performed his greatest service for Ireland. At least he tried. O'Shea, however, took umbrage that the Archbishop of Westminster appeared more concerned to screen Parnell than to defend marital honour,[113] although the pose of outraged husband would have been more convincing if he had not concealed his wrong for years in the hope of receiving a rich legacy from his wife's aunt.

Manning might privately attempt to ward off O'Shea's determination to divorce; he took a much more rigorous line when the scandal broke in November 1890. 'From the moment of this deplorable divorce case', he declared, 'I have held Mr. Parnell to be excluded from the leadership not on political but on moral grounds.'[114] This elevated tone did not, perhaps, consort altogether happily with his previous efforts to sweep the affair under the carpet, but Manning had espied a providential chance in the episode. Now the blow had fallen, the tragedy of Parnell's ruin and the danger to Home Rule appeared to affect him less than the realization that the split in the Irish Nationalist Party presented the Church with an opportunity to re-establish its authority over the Irish people. Manning had never relished either the Protestantism of Parnell or the anti-clericalism of some of his supporters. Now he badgered Archbishop Walsh with advice on the need to stand by principle against the temptation to uphold Parnell simply for reasons of expediency. 'This is a supreme moment to convince Rome that you do not put politics before faith and morals.'[115] The Irish hierarchy, however, only knew that this was not the moment to commit themselves against the man who had been the idol of the Irish nation. When Manning wrote an open letter stating that 'Ireland by its fidelity has outlived all that politics can do against it: and by the same Christian and Catholic fidelity of its Pastors and People it will win all the rights it has so long striven by suffering to obtain',[116] Walsh deemed it advisable to leave this message unpublished.

It was stimulating for Manning to find himself once more at the centre of a political crisis. In November 1890 he fired off almost daily letters of advice to Gladstone. No danger was ignored – 'take care of this sudden cold and do not walk without your hat'[117] – but his main burden was to urge Gladstone to insist, as a condition of his future co-operation with the Irish Nationalists, that Parnell should be removed from the leadership of their Party. The Liberal leader should not even countenance negotiations if they were designed to save Parnell. 'I hope that your one pledge will be, I will endeavour to frame a scheme of Home Rule which shall be acceptable to the people of Ireland. If they refuse to accept I will relinquish the work to other hands and leave public life.' The tone of Manning's letters suggested that he was addressing a political novice rather than the greatest Prime Minister of the nineteenth century. Perhaps he felt this, for the letter from which the above extract comes ended: 'Excuse my intrusion. I could not be silent.'[118]

Justice for Ireland had been one of the main themes of Manning's archiepiscopate. To the end of his life he spoke of his love for that country.

'It was forunate for my neck that I was not born in Ireland,' he told a visiting American. 'Had the Land of Saints given me my birth, I would have been hung long ago.'[119] Bold words. Yet in the last analysis a settlement of the Irish problem never seemed quite so important to Manning as fostering the cause of the Church, which he regarded as the essential precondition of any real progress. The fall of Parnell, with its adverse consequences for Home Rule, caused him remarkably little distress. No doubt there was nothing he could have done to save the Irish leader after he had failed to persuade O'Shea from prosecuting his divorce. Nevertheless, the cold righteousness with which he upheld the cause of morality after it had become a public issue was no more attractive for his eagerness to exploit the situation to the Church's advantage. The impression left by Manning's behaviour over the affair was not enhanced by an interview he gave to a French journalist, in which, with a notable exhibition of English Tartuffery, he dwelt upon the noble qualities of the Irish leader whom he had been bent on destroying.[120] Parnell, broken by the strain of trying to maintain his position, died in 1891 at the age of only forty-five. Manning's optimism remained unquenchable. 'I am most hopeful about Ireland,' he wrote cheerily to Stead on 21 December 1890. 'For ten years Ireland has been dragged by the politicians. It will now, I hope, return to its old guides.'[121] These old guides, of course, were the bishops and priests. A year later, in November 1891, he was regaling Gladstone with a confidence that few others felt. 'This year, beginning and ending with poor Parnell's tragic fall and death, has transformed Ireland. It is no longer revolutionary, Fenian, sanguinary, and hostile to England. The two peoples have a mutual goodwill.'[122]

This was one of the last letters Manning ever addressed to Gladstone, who was now entirely restored to favour. In 1887 he had graciously informed the Liberal leader that he was now as isolated for having given up all for Ireland as he, Manning, had been when he had given up all for the Church in 1851.[123] This was not a comparison which Gladstone can have greatly relished, but neither man had any taste for wrangling on the brink of eternity. On 23 July 1889, the day before another anniversary that must have been in his mind, the death of his own wife fifty-two years before, Manning wrote to congratulate Mrs Gladstone on her golden wedding. 'You know how nearly I have agreed in William's political career: especially in his Irish policy of the last twenty years. . . . We have had a long climb up these eighty steps, for even you are not far behind: and I hope we shall not "break the pitcher at the fountain".'[124] There was no longer a fault to be found in the great foe of papal infallibility. It was wonderful, Manning told George Russell in 1890, in flat contradiction to what he had once said to Disraeli, how Gladstone never bore a grudge, no matter how fierce disagreements might be.[125]

The note of oblivious affection proved more elusive in the case of the other great adversary friendship of Manning's life, that with Newman. To the very end Manning's irritation with his fellow Cardinal was always liable to burst to the surface. When Bodley made some favourable reference to Newman, Manning immediately set him right. 'From an observation you have made', Bodley was told, 'I gather you are under the impression that Newman is a good Catholic. . . . Either you are ignorant of the Catholic doctrine, or of the works of Dr. Newman.'[126] Manning's last meeting with Ullathorne, who died in 1889, provided occasion for a similar outburst. The two venerable Archbishops (Ullathorne had been made Archbishop of Casaba upon his retirement in 1888) clashed with such heat on the subject of Newman that Ullathorne's anger spilled over immediately after Manning's departure in a conversation with Canon John Caswell. 'What do you think?' Ullathorne exclaimed. 'He lectured me as though I had been a boy for suggesting Newman's promotion to the Cardinalate, and urging it so strongly. Manning said to me: "You do not know Newman as I do. He simply twists you round his little finger; he bamboozles you with his carefully selected words, and plays so subtly with his logic that your simplicity is taken in. *You are no match for him*." ' Ullathorne, who had come to revere Newman, and who considered himself with some reason to be a match for anyone, reciprocated the compliment, telling Manning roundly that he had completely misjudged his man.[127]

Newman lived into extreme old age. Although he remained alert, his faculties were not spared to the same extent as Manning's. When Vaughan visited the Oratory in 1889 he reported back to Manning that Newman's mind was much impaired and his memory for names curiously gone. 'He said Provost Manning had seen him a short time ago and that he, the Provost, was able to read much, which he could not do.'[128] Ever since 1851 Newman had been writing of his death as imminent, and at last it was evident that the prophecy was about to be fulfilled. Always fascinated by every detail of his own existence, he had written in younger days of passing each year unknowing over the date of death, 'as if walking over one's own grave'.[129] The date in question turned out to be 11 August; the year, 1890. He was eighty-nine.

To Manning fell the duty of delivering the address at the Requiem Mass for Newman in Brompton Oratory. As he really believed that Newman's influence on English Catholicism had been almost wholly detrimental, it was a task of some delicacy, akin to that which Gladstone had faced when he found himself obliged to deliver a parliamentary tribute to Disraeli. Manning showed equal generosity and skill. He looked back over 'the memories of an affectionate friendship . . . of more than sixty years', with never a suggestion that a cloud had passed over it. His testimony to Newman's work was magnanimous. He could hardly, by his own lights, refer to Newman as a dedicated upholder of Catholic dogma or of Roman authority. He therefore made much of his services to the Church of England which Newman, almost alone, had saved from complete domination by the spirit of Erastianism and Rationalism. As for Newman's influence upon the Catholic Church in England:

No one who does not intend to be laughed at will henceforward say that the Catholic religion is fit only for weak intellects and unmanly brains. . . . But beyond the power of all books has been the example of his humble and unworldly life; always the same, in union with God, and in manifold charity to all who sought him. He was the centre of innumerable souls, drawn to him as Teacher, Guide and Comforter through long years, and especially in the more than forty years of his Catholic life. To them he was a spring of light and strength from a supernatural source. A noble and beautiful life is the most convincing and persuasive of all preaching, and we have all felt its power. Our Holy Father Leo xiii knew the merits and the gifts, both natural and supernatural, which were hidden in his humility, and to the joy of all he called him to the highest dignity next his own. The history of our land will hereafter recall the name of John Henry Newman among the greatest of our people, as a confessor for the faith, a great teacher of men, a preacher of justice, of piety, and of compassion. May we all follow him in his life, and may our end be painless and peaceful like his.[130]

It was more than Manning could manage to sustain this elevated tone in private, and at least once in the eighteen months before his own death the mask of friendship slipped. A former Oratorian called Arthur Hutton, who had lost his faith and gained a wife almost in one fell swoop, marked Newman's death by publishing three articles bitterly attacking his conduct of the Oratory. Newman was accused of indifference to the welfare of the community and favouritism towards particular members. George Russell asked Manning if he had seen the articles. 'He replied that he had, and thought them very shocking; the writer must have a very unenviable mind, etc; and then having sacrificed to propriety, after a moment's pause he added: "But if you ask me if they are like poor Newman, I am bound to say — *a photograph*." '[131]

There were now hardly any of the old set left, he remarked in the wake of Newman's death: 'It is very sad to be one of the last to be called.'[132] Yet, though he spoke of a 'slowing into the terminus',[133] his appetite for work remained insatiable. When Newman died, Manning was in the middle of a lengthy paper designed for his successor, in which he set forth the 'Hindrances' that were working against the spread of Catholicism in England.[134] The content and style of this work show him still at the height of his powers, at the height of his prejudices too, since the Jesuits once more appear as bogy men, while bishops are sternly admonished against encouraging theatricals in convents and schools. The paper contained some devastatingly frank criticism of the failings of Catholicism in England. The clergy was an uneducated body compared to its Anglican counterpart and its preaching was often shallow; the contents of the Bible were unknown; priests relied overmuch on their sacramental power instead of making themselves fit in their own persons. The controversial spirit of so much Catholic writing and preaching was deplored, an odd criticism from the man to whom W. G. Ward had once written that 'there is nothing you have more earnestly taught us than that the interests of truth come before those of peace'.

It appeared that Manning still had not resolved his conflicting ideas on the place of the Church in English society. On the one hand, he urged the need to mix in the institutions of the country: 'The whole civil and political life of England is open to us if we know how to enter and how to bear ourselves.' On the other hand, he continued to glory in the freedom of action which the Church gained from being outside the English establishment. 'We are happily as independent and detached from the world, from its titles, wealth, classes, and privileges as the Church of the Apostles.' It might be argued that the counsel of involvement was addressed to the laity, and the enthusiasm for disinvolvement to the clergy, but what of these anathemas which he called down upon his own past? 'Woe to the man who entangles the Church with governments and politics. And woe to the bishop who is of any party or prejudice within the Church.'

Apparently Manning was at last learning the virtue of moderation. Yet one side of his nature had always been moderate. His theological extremism had always been matched with a severely practical streak in the affairs of this world. His fanatical upholding of the Pope's temporal power had not long survived its actual extinction. Similarly in England he had rarely, save in the case of papal infallibility, allowed his dogmatic fury to sweep away all lesser considerations:

Looking back I am conscious of how little I have done [he had written in 1889], partly from want of courage, partly from over-caution. And yet caution is not cowardice. For the highly sensitive state of England and of London, one step too fast is worse than ten steps too slow, and somehow the steady and peaceful gain and growth of the Catholic Church in the last twenty-four years – for I am speaking only of my reckoning – has been very sensible.[135]

That was a fair judgement. The Catholic advance should not be measured only by the increase in numbers, which was steady rather than sensational:

there were some 1.25 million Catholics in England and Wales at Manning's death. The striking point was how much better they were integrated into English life. Whereas in 1850 the least sign of papistry had been liable to provoke a riot, by Manning's death Catholics could process through the streets on feast days without attracting hostility. Manning for his part expressed the most generous reciprocal sentiments towards his fellow countrymen in his 'Hindrances' paper. The doctrine *Nulla salus extra Ecclesiam*, so grateful to some Catholic minds, no longer appealed to the Archbishop of Westminster. It applied only to those who understood and deliberately rejected the law:

I have received into the Church I do not know how many souls in whom I could find no mortal sin. They were evidently in the grace of their Baptism. . . . How with these facts can men go on speaking of those who are out of the Church in England as in a state of nature and in bad faith, and to be avoided as immoral? There are no doubt such persons among them. But what is the state of France, Italy, Spain, South America? All the light and grace of the Catholic Church is in vain for multitudes in those Catholic nations.[137]

Another year passed and still Manning worked indefatigably on. In February 1891 he was busy concocting plans for a Catholic mission to the slums. Curiously, given his long history of fighting for the parish priest, he envisaged the organization of this mission in almost Wesleyan terms, with priests to be sent out in teams to gather in the non-believers quite independently of any pre-existing Church structure. In view of these plans it was annoying to discover that a kind of Catholic Toynbee Hall had already been established in the East End – by 'some young idiots, no doubt',[138] as the Cardinal snorted.

The wider Catholic horizon proved more rewarding. In May 1891 Leo XIII produced his great encyclical *Rerum Novarum*, in which he set out the bases for Catholic action in social affairs while rejecting full-blooded socialist theory. Manning understandably rejoiced, regarding Leo's message as a vindication of his own work and beliefs. 'All of a sudden', he wrote in presenting the encyclical to English Catholics, 'they [the civil powers] find that the millions of the world sympathise with the Church, which has compassion on the multitude, rather than with the State or plutocracy which has weighed so heavily upon them.'[139] A. N. Wilson, in his biography of Hilaire Belloc, states that *Rerum Novarum* 'was really written by Manning'.[140] Certainly the encyclical expressed many of Manning's sentiments; certainly also Leo XIII, in sending a copy to the Archbishop of Westminster, declared himself 'grateful for the important communications' which Manning had made to him. Nevertheless, to foist authorship of the document upon Manning alone is to take too parochial a view of a Catholic social movement that had eloquent spokesmen in France, Italy and Germany, as well as at Westminster. The error is the more easily made because the Pope instructed Manning to help with the English translation of *Rerum Novarum*, which gave him the opportunity to make a version in which some of the phrasing echoed his own writings. But it was the earlier encyclical on slavery that Leo referred to as Manning's work;[141] even then, however, he may have been making a gallant papal gesture rather than a strict statement of fact.

Events in England still aroused Manning's interest, if rarely his approval. He ended his life as he had lived it, prophesying doom and disaster. Modern society, he told Mrs Crawford, was 'quite as corrupt and luxury-loving and selfish as the old French *noblesse*, and it will all go smash of a sudden. I shall not see it, but you will.'[142] Mrs Crawford knew exactly how to treat Manning, sensing the loneliness that lay behind the old man's gruff, laconic manner. 'I think he feels very much the sort of hidden antagonism to all his views which exists among the Catholic Upper Ten Thousand. He knows quite well that they only just tolerate him because they must and because they hope for better things when he is gone.'[143] Mrs Crawford's secret was to be open and unabashed, even to the point of a little gentle teasing. Seeing him after a visit to Paris she recorded:

The Cardinal, I am afraid, regards me as somewhat contaminated by the inevitable wickedness of the place. He didn't want me to go at all and from his point of view no doubt he was right, for Paris always makes me feel dreadfully frivolous. However, he was very nice about it and let me have my own way. And yesterday, when he asked me what I had been doing, he tried to be stern but couldn't help being amused at my lively descriptions. I sometimes think the Cardinal's greatest grace is his sense of humour.[144]

Manning's humour was not equal, however, to Mrs Crawford's information that dancing in short skirts was now the fashion for young girls in private houses. 'The dear Cardinal had never heard of such a thing and nearly stood on his head with horror.'[145] Mrs Crawford was so fond of her dear Cardinal that she agreed never again to sully herself by reading a French novel.

When she saw Manning on New Year's Eve 1891, he was in especially good form, bright and vigorous, an old man in the pink of health. He congratulated her on her persistence with the religious exercises he had prescribed, and reiterated his view that religious fervour does not mean acting on sporadic bursts of enthusiasm, but rather in patiently and determinedly doing one's duty to God every day, the more especially in periods of dryness. Yet this counsel, which his whole life had so conspicuously illustrated, was accompanied by an unexpected statement that Mrs Crawford would henceforth need a new spiritual adviser. 'My life may be measured by months and weeks, perhaps even by days,' he declared, 'and I should not like to die feeling that you had no one to turn to.'[146] These words seemed in odd contradiction to his evident well-being, especially as Manning, unlike Newman, had never been given to making regular references to the imminence of his death, not since 1847 anyway.

His premonition proved accurate. On 9 January 1892, a Saturday, he had a feverish çold, and Vaughan, who happened to arrive that day, advised him to go to bed. 'When you hear I have taken to my bed you can order my coffin,' Manning had warned.[147] Yet there was no immediate surrender. His doctor, Sir Andrew Clarke, was greeted with a clear and crisp, 'Come in,' when he knocked at the door of the tiny bedroom on the Monday. Sir Andrew diagnosed broncho-pneumonia and announced that he would return on the morrow. 'Be sure you do,' came the firm command.[148] Deterioration set in apace, however, and by Wednesday morning there were signs of heart failure. The Cardinal was attired in his rochet and mitre, and the Westminster canons, docile successors of those canons with whom Manning had quarrelled so bitterly thirty years before, were summoned to witness the final ceremonies of his life. The Provost recited the Profession of Faith, and Manning himself rehearsed the definitions of the Vatican Council. 'It is pleasant to have been able to do everything,' he remarked.[149]

Nevertheless the proceedings had exhausted him. It was clear that the end was near, though he still retained sufficient strength to refuse indignantly the suggestion of an alcoholic stimulant. That night of 13–14 January Vaughan, Canon Johnson, and Dr Gasquet, who had married his niece, watched and prayed beside the bed: '*Dulcissime Jesu, non sis mihi Judex sed Salvator*' ('Sweetest Jesus, be not to me a Judge but a Saviour'). Very near the end – so the story goes – the dying man fumbled under his pillow and pulled out a small, worn volume which he handed to Vaughan. 'I know not to whom to leave this,' he said, 'I leave it to you. Into this little book my dearest Wife wrote her prayers and meditations. Not a day has passed since her death on which I have not prayed and meditated from this book. All the good I may have done, all the good I may have been, I owe to her. Take precious care of it.'[150] Dying men rarely make such pretty speeches, yet Vaughan, from whom the story derives, was the soul of honour and truth.

Manning's last coherent words were in Latin: '*Deposui jugum, opus meum consummatum est*' – 'I have laid down the yoke, my work is done'. In his prime he had spoken of his terror at the punishments to be inflicted in Purgatory, but now death came as the gentlest of guides. The Cardinal lay like a tired child in a quiet sleep.[151] During the night the difficulty in breathing increased; at about six in the morning Vaughan left the room to say Mass for him. Manning murmured something, but for the first time in eighty years his words were not clear. Before the return of Vaughan, he had passed insensibly into the eternity upon which he had staked his conscious being.

Epilogue

The ultimate test of religious values is nothing psychological, nothing definable in terms of *how it happens*, but something ethical, definable only in terms of *what is attained*.

PROFESSOR G. A. COE, QUOTED IN WILLIAM JAMES, *The Varieties of Religious Experience*

Even before he was buried the backbiting began. On the morrow of his death *The Times* took up what was already a well worn theme for Manning denigrators, though somehow they never seem to tire of reiterating the point: 'Cardinal Newman . . . will stand out in history as a more impressive figure, a loftier intellect, and a more lovable nature.' Manning's interventions in industrial affairs, *The Times* continued, 'were not seconded by tact and conciliatory methods, and his interference, not unjustly, aroused the inbred English jealousy of sacerdotal authority'. In Rome also, it appeared, he was 'never entirely trusted'. In sum, 'to his countrymen he was a picturesque and interesting figure, both in his personal and in his ecclesiastical character, though he was no nearer when he died than he was when he became Archbishop to commanding their religious allegiance'. No wonder that *The Times* was surprised by the scenes that attended his lying in state and funeral. According to its obituary column he had quite forfeited the regard of the great British public: 'The part which the Cardinal, together with an exalted prelate of the Church he had left, played some years ago in connexion with an unsavoury and sensational operation, which resulted in a sentence of imprisonment for Mr W. T. Stead, did not enhance his reputation with his countrymen. Nor were they greatly edified when they saw him associated with an Anglican Bishop, the First Mayor of the City, and an ambitiously philanthropic member of Parliament in an endeavour to settle the dock strike in 1889.'[1]

The more intellectual specimen of English Catholic was likewise seized with a sorrowful awareness of Manning's shortcomings. 'Poor Cardinal!' reflected the poet Coventry Patmore. 'It is wonderful how he imposed on mankind by the third-century look of him, and his infinite muddleheadedness, which passed for mystery. I knew him well, and am convinced that he was the very minutest soul that ever buzzed in so high a place.' Patmore strove for generosity. 'He was a good man according to his *capacity*; but he hated all whom he suspected of being able to take his measure; and latterly I was not at all in his good books.'[2] No doubt the intensely egocentric Patmore's real complaint was that the (second) Angel in his House was that same Marianne Byles who had worshipped Manning at Lavington and never lost the habit of her earlier devotion even under lofty poetic influence. Yet Patmore's contemptuous dismissal of Manning is only an extreme example of a line that had become almost *de rigueur* among Catholics with intellectual pretensions, albeit those pretensions left them well short of Manning in energy and clarity of thought. 'Your having known Manning intimately quite explains why you never became a Catholic,' Father Forbes Leith, a Jesuit, kindly explained to J. E. C. Bodley.[3]

The dislike which some English Catholics felt for Manning conveys as much about them as it does about him. They believed that to be Catholic and English implied a conservative and anti-Roman bias; Manning urged them, on the contrary, not just to be Roman in sympathy, but to set that Romanism at the service of a wider brand of patriotism, one which looked beyond the confines of national reputation to the welfare of the people at large. To some extent the hostility which Manning encountered was a reflex reaction from a sect appalled to discover that the powerful ecclesiastic who led them considered the New Testament ethic to be a practical proposition. Manning's willingness to brave such antagonism does him nothing but credit. There have always been enough priests of the opposite kind, those who feel themselves called to minister to the spiritual agonies of the rich, a vocation which easily attracts encomia for wisdom and humility. Manning was quite prepared to concede the rich their spiritual problems; indeed, he considered their religious state to be far more precarious, and no more interesting, than that of the poor. He also took the view that in this life the rich were more than capable of looking after themselves. It was the poor who needed a spokesman, not the flatulent children of privilege. It was the poor who would revive Roman Catholicism in England, not self-complacent intellectuals or the spiritually stunted scions of the old recusant families.

Such were the calculations which, together with his heartfelt concern for all suffering, underlay Manning's social work, and surely his diagnosis was as correct as his advocacy was brave and his action effective. All the same, to rest a defence of Manning exclusively on such grounds, however valid, does not entirely meet the case. Those who reacted against him were not all narrow and selfish bigots incapable of understanding the wide sympathies and deep charity of a great ecclesiastical statesman. There is no point in denying the fact: there were aspects of Manning that invited dislike.

For example, while he was innocent of the grosser charges of ambition that Purcell and Strachey levelled against him, there was something in Newman's jibe that he had a great power of winning superiors. His slavish devotion to Pius ix and Cardinal Wiseman, though justifiable in terms of obedience to ecclesiastical authority, is open to less charitable interpretation. This does not mean that he consciously schemed for promotion; consciously, indeed, he strove to discipline the desire for elevation that he knew himself to possess. It was a blind instinct conferred in his upbringing that, allied to his great abilities, propelled him irresistibly towards the heights of influence. Even so, an interloper who consistently ingratiates himself with the powers that be does not win friends, least of all when he behaves towards less well connected opponents with unbending *hauteur*.

On the other hand, if Manning knew himself qualified for high ecclesiastical office, he knew no more than the self-evident truth. To forswear his intimacy with his superiors would have been to bury a great administrative talent. There was no better way in which he could serve the Church than through his promotion. Always eager, perhaps over-eager, to vindicate himself, and only too aware of the kind of attack to which he was vulnerable, he made a note in 1881 about the charge of ambition:

If it be ambition to desire to see work done that ought to be done, and to be done as it ought to be done, and when ill done to be done better; and to be done without being the doer of it, if only it be done at all – or to be impatient when, with the evils and wants and miseries of the people before them, men, and above all those who bear the office to do what is needed, do nothing; and if they will not work, but make mountains of excuses and fictitious impossibilities, it be ambition to say let me try them, I acknowledge to ambition, and I hope to die in it.[4]

This is perfectly acceptable as a piece of self-justification. It does not, however, suggest a man who is likely to be loved by his colleagues.

These later notebooks, which Manning so assiduously prepared in his own defence, often produce the counter effect of making it easier to understand the recoil which he inspired. The combination of self-assurance and self-assertion, the easy way in which he identifies his own actions with the divine purpose, the unwillingness to admit error, the unremitting self-absorption – these characteristics live on to stifle the generosity of posterity just as the man himself laid a cold hand on some of his contemporary associates. It is important to remember, however, that these notes which he scribbled in his old age, for all their fluency, are the outpourings of a nature that had become finally set in its authoritarian mould. His earlier records of spiritual struggle – the 1865 retreat diary, for instance – present a completely different picture, that of a man almost morbidly aware of his failings, and clinging all the more determinedly to his faith for that very reason. The faith remained with him to the end, and so did his compassion for all suffering, but he lost that sense of vulnerability which helps to draw sympathy and warmth. He was immensely, and rightly, admired, even reverenced, but he was *loved* only by the unloved and the distant poor. That is a huge congregation, it may be said, and one which any prince of the Church should be proud to own. The fact remains that it did not suffice to save his reputation. When after his death his name was blackened, there was not a single English Catholic prepared to undertake the labour of writing a full-scale book in his defence.

Yet it is not by their allure, but by their fruits that ye shall know them, the true servants of the Lord. That his own generation both recognized and venerated his achievement was proved beyond all contradiction at his funeral. Today it is hard to form a true estimate of his work. The power and subtlety of a great mind like Newman's can still be appreciated in his books. Manning produced books too, shelves of them, but as he himself observed they were 'written in and for action'; on the whole their relevance has passed. He knew that this would happen and dreamt of a more lasting memorial: 'I wish I could say: "You are my Epistle, written in my hand, and known and read of all men", poor children, poor drunkards, and perhaps a few other souls.'[5] A hundred years on, though, that Epistle has been entirely lost to human sight.

Equally, however much Manning contributed to the integration of Catholics into English life, it is difficult to measure that influence with any precision. One can say that he hob-nobbed with Cabinet Ministers, that he shook the old Catholics out of their paralysis, that he fostered acceptance of the Irish, that he won Catholicism credit among the working classes. The problem is to separate his part in these developments from more general trends, such as the better assimilation of second-generation Irish or (what Manning foresaw and abhorred) the rise of religious indifference. On the other side of the case, moreover, Manning's uncompromising ultramontanism undoubtedly brought his faith much contempt from his fellow countrymen.

The doctrine of papal infallibility remains, but in practice has been treated with the greatest caution, and never used in the way Manning envisaged, as a challenge thrown in the face of the modern world. It is rather Manning's vision of Church and people crusading together for justice that retains contemporary relevance, and many a priest in Latin America would subscribe to the spirit of his writings on social affairs. *Would* subscribe, be it emphasized, for it is extremely doubtful that they *have* read him, or that they have even heard of him. As for Manning's own country, the attempt to inject

Evangelical fervour into English Roman Catholicism was sustained by nothing save his own formidable will. When he died, his hopes in this direction died with him. It is easy to imagine the stand he would have taken in the 1926 General Strike. Yet from the Catholic hierarchy of the day there was hardly a radical squeak.

Ultimately, it is not in the success or failure of this or that endeavour, however admirable or misconceived, that Manning's claim to our respect and attention lies. It is rather in the witness to the beneficent power of Christianity that his whole life affords.

His faith was far removed from the temper of the present age, which seems prepared to extend its credulity to almost anything but Christian dogma. The enemies of Christianity like to imagine that reason has triumphed over superstition. In fact the new orthodoxies are as blindly supported as the old. Millions make acts of faith in Marx and Freud without attempting to read a single word of those great unreadables, even while clinging to the conviction that anyone who believes in a divinely revealed religion must be soft in the head. This is not so much the triumph of philosophy as the expression of a desperate longing to shuffle off the burden of individual responsibility. The search is on for creeds that demand nothing and excuse everything. The faith by which Manning lived, on the contrary, demanded everything and excused nothing. Determinism was a salve to be applied to other people, not to oneself.

Like the devotee of any creed, he set experience to work in the service of his faith. All his perceptions were filtered through the prism of his prior religious commitment. Many, like Stevie Smith, will think that this is to act 'as if truth were a convenience'.[6] Manning rather saw it as rooting and fostering moral intuitions that were the deepest of all realities. If the mind were not provided with firm premises from which to proceed it would soon lose its way in unending circles of argument. 'Except in figures and numbers there is no conviction which excludes the possibility of the contrary being true,' he told Robert Wilberforce in 1854. 'It is not impossible even that Jesus Christ is not come in the flesh. I mean it does not involve a contradiction in its terms to suppose that the Christian History is a myth. It is only contrary to the moral laws which govern mankind, and the evidence of the past.'[7]

A severely practical man, who needed a firm basis for action, Manning was not disposed to forgo the system of absolute values that he craved temperamentally just because water-tight logical proof was lacking. 'I fancy that you are looking for what God does not give,' he wrote in that same letter to Robert Wilberforce, 'I mean a conviction which precludes the exercise of faith.' Manning's own acceptance of the challenge, what Newman called 'the ventures', of faith certainly did not make his existence in this world any more convenient. He was drawn into the harsh and painful way of Christian obligation, a path which he followed according to his lights with a dedication and determination that can only be called heroic. There was no attitudinizing or posing about Manning's religion: its beginning, middle and end were moral action, at no matter what personal cost. He did not entirely change his character (who can?), but he did most comprehensively change his life. The elegant Harrovian adopted the vulgar temperance crusade; the ferocious Jingo crusaded against the English wrongs to Ireland; the First Class Balliol man became the champion of the common people; the eager friend of Cabinet Ministers became the leader of a despised sect. These were not transformations to be achieved without suffering. Nevertheless, his supposedly narrow attachment to his faith yielded sympathies infinitely fuller and broader than might have been expected of the cocksure young Harrovian.

When the last sneer has been sneered at his careerist instincts, and the last *frisson* of intellectual superiority extracted from consideration of his theological extravagances, consider the bare fact that remains. A man of rare ability, ruthless will, dominating temperament and high ambition began his life as the slave of secular glory and ended it as the hero of the poor, the weak, the outcast and the despised. That is a noble progress to be achieved by devotion to . . . to what, to a chimera? Would that many more great men had been similarly deceived.

And if the chimera were, after all, reality? Then, if Henry Manning is not saved seventy times seven times, God help the rest of us.

Source Notes

Key to references

The titles of the following works have been abbreviated:

B   Butler, Perry *Gladstone: Church, State and Tractarianism* (1982)

BC   Butler, Dom Cuthbert *The Vatican Council* (1930) 2 volumes

BU   Butler, Dom Cuthbert *The Life and Times of Bishop Ullathorne 1806–89* (1926) 2 volumes

C   Chadwick, W. O. *The Victorian Church* (1966 and 1970) 2 volumes

CR   'Reminiscences of Cardinal Manning', *Contemporary Review* (February 1982)

DR   *Dublin Review*

DNB   *Dictionary of National Biography*

L   Leslie, Shane *Henry Edward Manning, His Life and Labours* (1921)

LD   Dessain, C. S. and others (editors) *The Letters and Diaries of John Henry Newman* (1961–   )

ME(1) Oldcastle, J., pseudonym of Meynell, Wilfrid (editor) 'Letters on Subjects of the Day' (by Manning) *Merry England* (July 1891)

ME(2) Oldcastle, J. 'Memorials of Cardinal Manning', *Merry England* (February 1892). Pages unnumbered

ME(3) Oldcastle, J. 'Sayings of Cardinal Manning', *Merry England* (March 1892). Pages unnumbered

NS   Newsome, David *The Parting of Friends* (1966)

P   Purcell, E. S. *Life of Cardinal Manning* (Second edition February 1896) 2 volumes

SC   Snead-Cox, J. G. *The Life of Cardinal Vaughan* (1910) 2 volumes

T vol. 1 Trevor, Meriol *Newman, The Pillar of the Cloud* (1962)

T vol. 2 Trevor, Meriol *Newman, Light in Winter* (1962)

W   Ward, Wilfrid *The Life of John Henry Cardinal Newman* (1912) 2 volumes

WW   Ward, Wilfrid *The Life and Times of Cardinal Wiseman* (1897) 2 volumes

In addition the names of correspondents have been abbreviated in the following three cases:

G   Gladstone
M   Manning
N   Newman

Prologue

1 *The Times*, obituary of Manning 15 January 1892 and reports of obsequies 15 to 22 January 1892

2 G to Wilfrid Meynell, 25 January 1892, ME(2)

3 M to Vaughan 1880, SC vol. 1, p. 461

4 L p. ix

5 Purcell, E. S. 'Poisoning the Wells of Catholic Criticism', *The Nineteenth Century* (March 1896), p. 515

6 *Notes and Queries*, 9th series, vol. xi (1903), p. 86

7 L p. x

8 Bodley, J. E. C. *Cardinal Manning and Other Essays* (1912), p. 50

9 Ryder, H. I. D. 'Purcell's "Life of Cardinal Manning" ', *Essays* (1911) p. 273

10 *ibid.* p. 276

11 P vol. 1 'Advertisement'

12 L p. x .

13 Ryder *op. cit.,* p. 271

14 Vaughan, Herbert 'The Life of Cardinal Manning', *The Nineteenth Century* (February 1896), p. 249

15 G to Purcell 6 February 1896, *The Nineteenth Century* (March 1896). Also L p. xiii

16 *The Nineteenth Century* (February 1896), p. 249

17 Holroyd, M. *Lytton Strachey* (1967) vol. 1, p. 456

18 Holroyd *op. cit.* vol. 2, p. 703

1: A Decided Character

1 *Notes and Queries*, 8th series, vol. ix (1896), p. 164–5

2 M to Caroline Austen 26 August 1890, P vol. 2, p. 712

3 P vol. 1, p. 6

4 P vol. 2, p. 712

5 Gasquet, J. R. *Cardinal Manning* (1896), p. 2

6 *Notes and Queries*, 8th series, vol. ii (1892), p. 56

7 W vol. 1, p. 27

8 *Notes and Queries*, 8th series, vol. ii (1892), p. 56

9 P vol. 1, p. 6

10 Checkland, S. G. 'Finance for the West Indies' *Economic History Review*, Second Series, vol. x, No. 3 (April 1958), p. 464

11 *ibid*

12 L p. 6

13 P vol. 1, p. 3

14 P vol. 1, pp 13–14

15 Brown, F. K. *Fathers of the Victorians* (1961), pp 507–8

16 Brown *op. cit.*, p. 357

17 Wilberforce, R. I. and S. W. *The Life of William Wilberforce* (1838) vol. 2, p. 10

18 Hazlitt, W. *The Spirit of the Age* (1825), p. 359

19 Ashwell, A. R. *Life of Samuel Wilberforce* vol. 1 (1880), p. 19

20 P vol 1, p. 712

21 Gasquet *op. cit.*, p. 2

22 DNB vol. xxviii, p. 286

23 Barratt, S. G. R. *History of Totteridge*, p. 144 (Parish Records)

24 P vol. 1, p. 7

25 DNB vol. iii, p. 462

26 P vol. 1, p. 7

27 P vol. 1, p. 9

28 L p. 6

29 P vol. 1, p. 9

30 P vol. 1, p. 4

31 P vol. 2, p. 634

33 P vol. 1, p. 10

34 Augier, F. R. *The Making of the West Indies* (1961) pp 130–1

35 Wordsworth, C. *Annals of My Early Life* (1898), p. 8

36 *Strand Magazine* (July 1891)

37 P vol. 1, p. 11

38 P vol. 1, p. 12

39 P vol 1, p. 13

40 Soloway, R. A. *Prelates and People 1783–1852* (1969), p. 84

41 B p. 17

42 P vol. 1, p. 12

43 DNB vol. xxx, p. 273

44 Bready, J. W. *Lord Shaftesbury and Social-Industrial Progress* (1928), p. 19

45 Howson, E. W. and Townsend Warner, G. *Harrow School* (1891), p. 67

46 *ibid.*

47 P vol. 1, p. 19

48 P vol. 1, p. 17

49 *Tablet* 16 February 1892, p. 81

50 Merivale, C. *Autobiography* (1898), p. 48

51 Oxenden, A. *History of My Life* (1891), p. 13
52 Merivale *op. cit.*, p. 49
53 Wordsworth *op. cit.*, p. 18
54 P vol. 1, p. 12
55 L p. 14
56 Ashley Cooper, F. S. *Eton v. Harrow at the Wicket* (1922)
57 Overton, J. H. and Wordsworth, E. *Christopher Wordsworth* (1888), p. 33
58 *Weekly Register* 13 February 1892, p. 214
59 M to Charles Wordsworth 12 September 1825, Wordsworth *op. cit.*, p. 25
60 Thornton, P. M. *Harrow School and Its Surroundings* (1885), p. 246
61 Laborde, E. D. *Harrow School* (1948), pp 90–92
62 Chapman, R. *Father Faber* (1961), pp 12–13
63 P vol. 1, pp 27, 19
64 P vol. 1, p. 27
65 P vol. 1, p. 7 ('the parson'), L p. 14 ('the general')
66 Oxenden *op. cit.*, p. 13
67 Chapman *op. cit.*, pp 12–13
68 Anderdon to M 1826, L p. 15
69 M to Anderdon June 1827, L p. 23
70 Anderdon to M 7 November 1826, L p. 16
71 M to Anderdon 1826, L p. 16
72 M to Anderdon 7 November 1826, P vol. 1, p. 22
73 P vol. 1, p. 26 (written 1882)
74 Anderdon to M 30 July 1827, M to Anderdon (reply), L pp 23–4
75 M to Anderon June 1827, L p. 23
76 M to Anderdon June 1827, L p. 22
77 M to Anderdon 1 September 1827, P vol. 1, p. 50
78 DNB xx, p. 58
79 Foster, J. *Essays* (1835), pp 89, 115, 139, 140, 151
80 M to Anderdon 1826, P vol. 1, p. 21
81 M to Anderdon 13 February 1829,

P vol. 1, pp 50–51
82 Pattison, M. *Memoirs* (1885), p. 74
84 Wordsworth *op. cit.*, p. 95
84 P vol. 1, p. 57
85 M to Anderdon 1826, P vol. 1, p. 21
86 P vol. 1, p. 59
87 *ibid.*
88 P vol. 1, p. 25
89 Doyle, Sir Francis H. *Reminiscences and Opinions* (1886), p. 107
90 Milnes Gaskell, J. *Records of an Eton Schoolboy* (1939), p. 168
91 Mozley, T. *Reminiscences* (1882) vol. 1, pp 424–5
92 P vol. 1, p. 34
93 Doyle *op. cit.*, pp 112–13
94 P. vol. 1, p. 67
95 P. vol. 1, p. 63
96 Debate of 14 May 1829
97 Pares, R. *A West India Fortune* (1950), p. 311
98 William Manning to M 18 August 1829, L p. 34
99 J. Milnes Gaskell to his mother 9 February 1830, Gaskell *op. cit.*, p. 172. Also M to Anderdon 18 September 1830, P vol. 1, p. 53
100 M to Anderdon October 1830, P vol. 1, p. 55
101 P vol 1, p. 71
102 L p. 35
103 M to Anderdon 13 March 1831, P vol. 1, pp 73–5
104 *ibid.*
105 *ibid.*
106 M to Anderdon P vol. 1, p. 72 (no date given)
107 P vol. 1, p. 77
108 P vol. 1, pp 80–81
109 M to Anderdon 3 April 1831, P vol. 1, p. 76
110 *ibid.*
111 M to Anderdon 13 June 1831, P vol. 1, pp 82–3
112 P vol. 1, p. 94
113 M to Anderdon, L p. 29 (no date

given)

114 P vol. 1, p. 49

115 N 12 September 1830, LD vol. ii,
p. 290

116 P vol. 2, p. 749. See also M to N
31 March 1866 LD xxii, p. 198

117 Newman, J. H. *Parochial and
Plain Sermons* (1878 edition)
vol. viii, No. 9, preached 12
September 1830

118 L p. 37

119 Miss Bevan 24 November 1831, L
p. 37

120 Fielding, H. *Tom Jones*, Book
One, chapter 10

121 Miss Bevan's account of M 9
February 1832, L pp 39–42

122 Gasquet, *op. cit.*, p. 12

123 P vol. 1, p. 93

124 P vol. 1, p. 94

125 Newman, J. H. *Apologia pro Vita
Sua* (1864), p. 56

126 P vol. 1, p. 69

127 Foster *op. cit.*, p. 165

128 L p. 38

2: Marriage and Churchmanship

1 Chapeau, A. 'Manning the
Anglican', Fitzsimons J. (editor),
Manning: Anglican and Catholic
(1951), p. 17

2 B, p. 50

3 Wade, J. *The Extraordinary Black
Book* (1831), p. 5

4 Bowen, D. *The Idea of the
Victorian Church* (Montreal 1968),
p. 10

5 Carpenter, S. C. *Church and
People 1789–1889* (1933), p. 57

6 Bowen *op. cit.*, p. 9

7 Overton, J. H. *The English
Church in the Nineteenth Century*
(1894), p. 7

8 C vol. 1, p. 39

9 Abbey, C. J. and Overton, J. H.
*The English Church in the
Eighteenth Century* (1878) vol. 2,
p. 12

10 Hare, A. *The Story of My Life*
(1896) vol. vi, p. 177

11 Vulliamy, C. E. *John Wesley*
(1931), p. 95

12 Abbey and Overton *op. cit.*, vol.
2, p. 15

13 Kegan Paul, C. *Confessio Viatoris*
(1891), p. 14

14 Gladstone, W. E. *Gleanings of
Past Years* (1879) vol. vii, p. 220

15 Sydney Smith to Mrs Beach 26
August 1798, No 22 in *Letters* (ed.
Nowell-Smith) (1953)

16 P vol. 1, p. 93

17 C vol. 1, p. 88

18 C vol. 1, p. 32

19 Wood, A. *Nineteenth Century
Britain* (1960), p. 84

20 C vol. 1, p. 27

21 Bell, A. *Sydney Smith* (1982),
p. 176

22 Thomas Arnold to Rev J. E. Tyler
10 June 1832, Stanley, A. P. *Life
and Correspondence of Thomas
Arnold* (1881) vol. i, p. 278

23 Halévy, E. *The Triumph of
Reform* (1961), p. 150

24 M to Anderdon 9 March 1832, P
vol. 1, p. 88

25 M to Anderdon, P vol. 1, p. 89
(no date given)

26 M to Mrs Manning 9 April 1832, P
vol. 1, p. 97

27 M journal 28 March 1852, P
vol. 2, p. 13

28 Manning, H. E. *England and
Christendom* (1867), p. liv

29 P vol. 1, p. 89

30 M to Anderdon 2 March 1832, P
vol. 1, p. 90

31 Forster, E. M. *Marianne Thornton*
(1956), p. 138

32 N to Henry Wilberforce 9 March
1833, LD iii, p. 247

33 Henry Wilberforce to Robert
Wilberforce 30 November 1832,
NS p. 116

34 Wilberforce, A. M. *Lavington:
The History of a Sussex Family*
(1919), p. 34

35 Wordsworth *op. cit.*, p. 335

36 Wilberforce, A. M. *op. cit.*, p. 43

37 Horsfield, T. W. *The History, Antiquities and Topography of the County of Sussex* (1835) vol. ii, p. 95 (Graffham) and p. 170 (Lavington)

38 William Wilberforce to Mary Smith 1804, NSP. p 121

39 *vide* NS facing p. 83

40 Wilberforce, A. M. *op. cit.*, p. 42

41 Hobsbawm, E. J. and Rudé, G. *Captain Swing* (1969), p. 111

42 Manning, H. E. 'The Dignity and Rights of Labour' (1874), *Miscellanies* vol. ii (1877), p. 77

43 Caroline Sargent to Emily Wilberforce 1830, NS p. 127

44 Wilberforce, R. G. 'Cardinal Manning in the Church of England', *The Nineteenth Century* (February 1892), p. 281

45 Wood to M 1833, P. vol. 1, p. 103

46 L p. 47

47 Wilberforce, A. M. *op. cit.*, p. 43

48 Henry Wilberforce to Robert Wilberforce 11 May 1833, NS p. 147

49 P vol. 1, pp 103–4

50 M journal 28 March 1852, P vol. 2, p. 13

51 M to Mrs Sargent 8 November 1833, NS pp 150–51

52 Mozley, T. *op. cit.*, vol. 1, p. 186

53 Newman, J. H. *Lectures on Justification* (1838), p. 388

54 Battiscombe, G. *John Keble* (1963), p. 111

55 Samuel Wilberforce to William Wilberforce 21 June 1823, NS p. 73

56 M journal 1878–82, P vol. 1, p. 112

57 *Tracts for the Times 1833–4* (1839), pp 1–2

58 Henry Wilberforce to N 8 November 1833, LD vol. iv, p. 92

59 Brilioth, Y. *The Anglican Revival* (1925), p. 43

60 Manning, H. E. *England and Christendom* (1867), pp xxxvii–xxxviii

61 T vol. i, p. 83

62 Newman, J. H. *Apologia* (1864), p. 380

63 Newman, J. H. *Fifteen Sermons preached before the University of Oxford* (1980 edition), p. 183

64 Newman, J. H. *Parochial and Plain Sermons* vol. i (1879 edition), no. 15, p. 202

65 Newman, J. H. *Parochial and Plain Sermons* vol. vi (1881 edition), p. 114

66 Newman, J. H. *The Via Media of the Anglican Church* vol. i (1888), pp 135–6

67 N to Mrs Newman 28 February 1833, LD vol. iii, pp 224–5

68 Newman, J. H. *Parochial and Plain Sermons* vol iv (1839), p. 199

69 Newman, J. H. *Tract 10*

70 Newman, J. H. *Parochial and Plain Sermons* vol i (1879), p. 320

71 Newman, F. W. *Contributions, chiefly to the early history of the late Cardinal* (1891), p. 72

72 Newman, J. H. *Parochial and Plain Sermons* vol. iii (1881), no. 13 'Jewish Zeal, a Pattern to Christians', p. 187

73 Brémond, H. *Newman* (Paris 1906), p. 65

74 Bodley *op. cit.*, p. 16

75 Manning, H. E. *England and Christendom* (1867), p. xxxviii

76 Manning, H. E. *The English Church, its succession and witness for Christ* (1835), p. 18

77 M to Samuel Wilberforce 18 October 1836, NS pp 232–3

78 Mozley, T. *op. cit.*, vol. 1, pp 425–6

79 Manning, H. E. *Sermons* vol. 1, (1844), p. 207

80 Ellman, E. B. *Recollections of a Sussex Parson* (1925), p. 41

81 M to Samuel Wilberforce 12 January 1834, NS p. 232
82 N to Henry Wilberforce 3 August 1834, LD vol. iv, p. 316
83 Bowden to N 4 February 1836, LD vol. v, p. 237
84 M to Samuel Wilberforce 15 September 1835, NS p. 201
85 M to Samuel Wilberforce 3 January 1837, NS p. 201
86 *ibid.*
87 *The Nineteenth Century* (February 1892), pp 285–6
88 L p. 54
89 M to Samuel Wilberforce 3 January 1837, NS p. 233
90 L p. 46
91 P vol. 1, p. 111
92 *The Nineteenth Century* (February 1892), pp 283–4
93 *The Nineteenth Century* (February 1892), p. 280
94 L pp 45–6
95 Battiscombe *op. cit.*, p. 178
96 L p. 46
97 *Weekly Register* 30 January 1892, p. 137
98 Manning, H. E. *The English Church, its succession and witness for Christ* (1835), p. 27
99 N to M 8 September 1835, LD vol. v, pp 136–7
100 *ibid.*
101 M to N 15 September 1835, LD vol. v, p. 137
102 Chapeau *op. cit.*, p. 7
103 N to M 6 March 1838, LD vol. vi, pp 210–11
104 M to N 16 March 1838, P vol. 1, p. 231
105 M to N 15 September 1835, P vol. 1, pp 219–20
106 N to M 9 October 1836, LD vol. v, p. 370
107 N to Pusey 21 January 1836, LD vol. v, p. 208
108 Samuel Wilberforce to Louisa Noel 1 April 1836, NS p. 169
109 M to Samuel Wilberforce 15 December 1834, NS p. 202
110 P vol. 1, p. 116
111 G to M 5 April 1835, B p. 71
112 N to M 4 September 1836, LD vol. v, pp 348–9
113 N to M 4 September 1836, LD vol. v, p. 349
114 *The Nineteenth Century* (February 1892), p. 286
115 P vol. 1, p. 118
116 N to M 4 September 1836, LD vol. v, p. 349
117 N to M 12 April 1837, LD vol. vi, p. 54
118 Mrs Sargent to Sophia Ryder 23 July 1837, NS p. 251
119 P vol. i, p. 124
120 *The Nineteenth Century* (February 1892), p. 281
121 P vol. i, p. 124
122 Manning, H. E. *Sermons*, vol. iv (1850), p. 77
123 Mrs Sargent to Emily Wilberforce 3 August 1838, NS p. 252
124 Ryder *op. cit.*, p. 301
125 M to N, P vol. 1, p. 123 (no date given)
126 M to Samuel Wilberforce 25 September 1837, NS p. 253
127 Longford, E. *A Pilgrimage of Passion: the Life of Wilfrid Scawen Blunt* (1979), p. 7
128 Champneys, B. *Memoirs and Correspondence of Coventry Patmore* (1900) vol. 1, p. 210
129 P vol. 1, p. 395
130 P vol. 2, p. 684
131 M to G 27 July 1837, L p. 48
132 M to Samuel Wilberforce 22 April 1841, NS p. 263
133 L p. 49
134 Mrs Sargent to Emily Wilberforce July 1839, P vol. 1, pp 159–60
135 L p. 50
136 *ibid.*
137 *ibid.*

3: Promotion and Powerlessness

1 P vol. 2, p. 686
2 C vol. 1, pp 98–9

3 Ziegler, P. *Melbourne* (1976),
p. 216

4 C vol. 1, p. 219

5 Manning, H. E. *The Principle of
the Ecclesiastical Commission
Examined in a letter to the Bishop
of Chichester* (1838), pp 9, 33,
37–8, 40–41, 42

6 N to M 12 January 1838, LD vi,
pp 186–7

7 C vol. 1, p. 337

8 Manning, H. E. *National
Education, A Sermon* (1838)
pp 17, 23, 25–6, 27, 29

9 *ibid.*, p. 32

10 Manning, H. E. *The Rule of Faith*
(1838), pp 52, 9, 71, 50

11 N to M 9 August 1838, P vol. 1,
p. 137

12 Samuel Wilberforce to Miss Elliott
18 May 1842, P vol. 1, p. 139

13 Bishop Otter to M 1838, P vol. 1,
pp 135–6

14 P vol. 1, p. 139

15 P vol. 1, p. 136

16 J. W. Trower to M 26 December
1838, P.vol. 1, p. 138

17 Manning, H. E. *The Rule of Faith*,
p. 115

18 Manning, H. E. *The Rule of Faith*,
p. 134

19 P vol. 1, p. 147

20 Wood to M 9 November 1838, P
vol. 1, p. 148

21 Bishop Otter to M 1838, P vol. 1,
p. 136

22 L pp 54–5

23 Ashwell, A. R. *Life of Samuel
Wilberforce* vol. 1 (1880), p. 130

24 N to M Autumn 1838, P vol. 1,
p. 153

25 M to Frederick Manning 23
December 1838, P vol. 1, p. 158

26 *ibid.*

27 P vol. 1, p. 49

28 L p. 56

29 P vol. 1, p. 156

30 L pp 58–9

31 L p. 73

32 NS p. 267

33 M to Laprimaudaye 16 June 1847,
P vol. 1, p. 472

34 N to M 1 September 1839, P vol.
1, pp 233–4

35 Williams, N. P. and Harris, C.
(editors) *Northern Catholicism*
(1933), pp 29–30

36 Newman, J. H. *Apologia* (1864),
pp 209–10

37 N to Rogers 22 September 1839,
W vol. 1, p. 68

38 N to M 1 September 1839, P
vol. 1, p. 234

39 M to N 23 October 1839, P vol. 1,
p. 232

40 M to Archdeacon Hare 11
November 1840, P vol. 1, p. 167

41 M to G 1841, Chapeau *op. cit.*,
p. 11

42 Manning, H. E. *The Preservation
of Unendowed Canonries* (1840),
pp 11, 12

43 M to Archdeacon Hare 20
November 1840, P vol. 1, p. 175

44 M to Archdeacon Hare 28 August
1840, P vol. 1, p. 171

45 Dean Chandler to M, P vol. 1,
p. 170 (undated)

46 Melbourne to Russell 27 August
1840, C vol. 1, p. 124

47 DNB vol. lii, p. 176

48 M to Archdeacon Hare 11
October 1840, P vol. 1, pp 174–5

49 P vol. 1, p. 180

50 G to M 2 January 1841, P vol. 1,
pp 185–6

51 DNB vol. lii, p. 176

52 Faber, G. *The Oxford Apostles*
(1974), p. 429

53 Manning, H. E. *Charge 1845*, p. 9

54 P vol. 1, p. 445

55 Manning, H. E. *Charge 1841*,
pp 16, 46, 47

56 L p. 46

57 P vol. 1, p. 442

58 *Weekly Register* 23 January 1892,
p. 121

59 P vol. 1, p. 444

60 G to M 22 April 1841, P vol. 1,
   p. 265
61 Ornsby, R. *Memoir of James
   Robert Hope-Scott* (1884) vol. 2,
   p. 74
62 P vol. 1, p. 261
63 Maurice to Strachey 15 September
   1843, Maurice, F. (editor) *The
   Life of Frederick Denison Maurice*
   (1884) vol. 1, p. 350
64 Sterling to Richard Trench 16
   March 1839, L p. 59
65 Lockhart, William 'Some Personal
   Reminiscences of Cardinal
   Manning when Archdeacon of
   Chichester' DR (April 1892),
   p. 372
66 Aubrey de Vere to Lady de Vere
   14 August 1850, Ward, W. *Aubrey
   de Vere* (1904), p. 162
67 De Vere, Aubrey *Recollections*
   (1897), pp 290, 288, 306
68 Wilberforce, R. G. *Life of Samuel
   Wilberforce* vol. 2, (1881) p. 266
69 P vol. 1, pp 331, 332–3; vol. 2,
   p. 688
70 M 31 May 1865, L p. 163
71 M to Archdeacon Hare 24 August
   1840, P vol. 1, p. 167
72 M 15 January 1883, P vol. 2,
   p. 678
73 M's 1865 Retreat journal, DR
   (January 1920), p. 7
74 P vol. 1, p. 511; vol. 2, p. 45
75 M to Samuel Wilberforce Easter
   Eve 1850, NS p. 313
76 P vol. 1, p. 274
77 Manning, H. E. *Sermons* vol. 1
   (1842), p. 340
78 *ibid.*, pp 69–70
79 *ibid.*, p. 63
80 *ibid.*, p. 272
81 Trower to M 26 November 1838, P
   vol. 1, p. 138
82 Newman, J. H. *Parochial and
   Plain Sermons* vol. ii (1880),
   pp 343–57
83 *ibid.*, p. 356
84 Manning, H. E. *Charge 1841*,

p. 15
85 Newman, J. H. *Apologia* (1864),
   p. 379
86 Newman, J. H. *Lectures on
   Anglican Difficulties* (1850),
   No. viii
87 N to Froude 7 November 1833,
   LD vol. iv, p. 90
88 L p. 44
89 Manning, H. E. *Charge 1845*,
   pp 25, 26
90 Manning, H. E. *Charge 1846*,
   pp 45, 46
91 Manning, H. E. *Charge 1845*,
   p. 43
92 Manning, H. E. *Sermons* vol. 1,
   p. 205
93 Blake, R. *Disraeli* (1966),
   pp 171–2
94 P vol. 1, p. 161
95 Manning, H. E. *Charge 1842*,
   p. 24
96 *The Nineteenth Century* (February
   1892), p. 283
97 Manning, H. E. *Charge 1842*,
   pp 23–4
98 *ibid.*, pp 9–10, 12
99 Hutton, A. W. *Cardinal Manning*
   (1892), pp 27–8
100 M to G 7 March 1843, L p. 62
101 Manning, H. E. *The Unity of the
    Church* (1842), pp 250, 2, 102
102 M to G 11 November 1841, L
    p. 69
103 P vol. 1, p. 198
104 Manning, H. E. *The Unity of the
    Church*, pp 365, 361, 363
105 Chapeau *op. cit.*, p. 14
106 M to G 1842
107 N to M 14 October 1843, J. H.
    Newman *Apologia*, p. 350
108 *Rheinische Zeitung* July 1842
109 N to M 14 October 1843, J. H.
    Newman *Apologia*, pp 350–51
110 M to N October 1843, T vol. 1,
    p. 309
111 N to M 25 October 1843, J. H.
    Newman *Apologia*, p. 351
112 G to M 28 October 1843, Morley,

J. *Life of W. E. Gladstone*
(1903) vol. 1, p. 260
113 *ibid.*
114 L p. 60
115 M to G 16 May 1843, B p. 110
116 L p. 46
117 M to Pusey 1843, P vol. 1,
pp 251–2
118 Manning, H. E. *Sermons preached
before the University of Oxford*
(1844), pp 93, 95–6
119 *The Century* vol. xxvi (1883),
p. 129
120 N to M 24 December 1843, P
vol. 1, p. 254
121 G to M 31 December 1843, P
vol. 1, p. 255
122 *ibid.*
123 L p. 65
124 G to M 18 November 1843, P
vol. 1, p. 268
125 P vol. 1, p. 250
126 G to M 15 January 1844, P vol. 1,
p. 269
127 P vol. 1, p. 336

4: An Essay in Development

1 P vol. 1, p. 282
2 N to Northcote 8 February 1846,
LD vol. xi, p. 110
3 Manning, H. E. *Sermons* vol. 4
(1850), p. 323
4 Ellman, E. B. *op. cit.*, p. 130
5 DR (January 1920), p. 11
6 Manning, H. E. *Sermons* vol. 4,
p. 334
7 Ward, Wilfrid *W. G. Ward and the
Oxford Movement* (1889), p. 343
8 Newman, J. H. *The Present
Position of Catholics in England*
(1851), p. 254
9 Clark, K. *The Gothic Revival*
(1928), p. 158
10 Ward, Wilfrid *W. G. Ward and the
Catholic Revival* (1893), p. 3
11 Robson, R. (editor) *Ideas and
Institutions of Victorian Britain*
(1967), p. 127

12 Stephens, W. R. W. *The Life and
Letters of W. F. Hook* (1878)
vol. 2, p. 47
13 Newman, J. H. *Present Position of
Catholics in England* (1851),
pp 176–7
14 Newman, J. H. *Apologia* (1864),
pp 62–3
15 N to M 16 November 1844, P
vol. 1, p. 259
16 Manning, H. E. *Charge 1845*,
pp 46, 56
17 M to Robert Wilberforce 30 June
1845, P vol. 1, pp 503–4
18 M to Robert Wilberforce 6
October 1845, P vol. 1, pp 504–5
19 *ibid.*
20 Allies, Mary *Thomas William
Allies* (1907), p. 49
21 Norman, E. R. *Anti-Catholicism
in Victorian England* (1968), p. 27
22 *ibid.*, p. 127
23 G to M 26 April 1845, P vol. 1,
p. 301
24 M to Sidney Herbert 3 April 1846,
P vol. 1, pp 301–3
25 *ibid.*
26 N to M 8 October 1845, LD
vol. xi, p. 8
27 M to N 14 October 1845, P vol. 1,
pp 309–10
28 M journal November 1845, P
vol. 1, pp 323–4
29 M to Coleridge 28 October 1845,
NS p. 316
30 M to Robert Wilberforce 3
November 1845, P vol. 1, p. 310
31 M to G 29 October 1845, L p. 66
32 G to M 21 November 1845, P
vol. 1, p. 313
33 M to G 26 December 1845, L
p. 66
34 G to M 28 December 1845, P
vol. 1, p. 315
35 M 8 December 1845, P vol. 1,
p. 278
36 M December and January 1845–6,
P vol. 1, pp 279–81
37 M 30 January 1846, P vol. 1,

p. 281

38 Manning, H. E. *Sermons* vol. 3, p. 298

39 L p. 75

40 WW vol. 1, p. 314

41 B p. 62

42 Newman, J. H. *An Essay on the Development of Christian Doctrine* (1845), pp 38–9

43 G to M 23 December 1845, B p. 196

44 M to Robert Wilberforce 30 December 1845, P vol. 1, p. 311

45 Newman, J. H. *Development*, pp 127–8

46 M to Robert Wilberforce 22 January 1851, P. vol. 1, pp 600–601

47 Newman, J. H. *Development*, p. 138

48 M May 1846, P vol. 1, p. 484

49 M 5 July 1846, P vol. 1, pp 485–6

50 M 2 August 1846, L pp 77–8

51 M 4 August 1846, P vol. 1, p. 450

52 M 16 August 1846, P vol. 1, pp 451–2

53 M to G 28 August 1846, B p. 198

54 G to M 31 August 1846, B p. 198

55 M to G 1 December 1846, B p. 199

56 G to Hook 30 June 1847, B p. 206

57 *Quarterly Review* vol. lxxxi (June 1847), p. 151., B p. 208

58 M 5 July 1846, P vol. 1, p. 486

59 P vol. 1, p. 469

60 Lockhart, William 'Personal Reminiscences of Cardinal Manning' DR (April 1892), p. 378

61 NS p. 317

62 P vol. 1, p. 469

63 Gasquet *op. cit.*, p. 46

64 Maurice to Miss Hare 30 March 1849, Maurice, F. *op. cit.* vol. 1, p. 533

65 Battiscombe G. *op. cit.*, p. 304

66 Manning, H. E. *Sermons* vol. 3, p. 61

67 M 7 February 1847. P vol. 1, pp 330–31

68 P vol. 1, p. 547

69 P vol. 1, p. 341

70 Manning, H. E. *Sermons* vol. 1, p. 295

71 M 20 February 1847, L p. 78

72 P vol. 1, p. 333

73 M 25 March 1847, p vol. 1, p. 335

74 M 20 March 1847, L pp 78–9. M 26 March 1847, P. vol. 1, p. 335

75 G to M 15 March 1847, B p. 201

76 M to G 18 March 1847, B p. 201

77 G to M 20 March 1847, B pp 201–2

78 M 26 March 1847, P vol. 1, p. 335

79 P vol. 1, p. 445

80 Strachey, L. *Eminent Victorians* (Penguin 1948), p. 17

81 M 27 March 1847, P vol. 1, p. 336

82 M 24 June 1847, P vol. 1, p. 340

83 M Easter Day 1847, P vol. 1, p. 338

84 M Easter 1847, P vol. 1, pp 338–9

85 M 12 May 1847, P vol. 1, pp 452–3

86 M Whitsunday 1847, P vol. 1, p. 342

87 M to RW 11 May 1847, P vol. 1, pp 505–6

88 M 27 June and 5 July 1847, P vol. 1, p. 342

89 M 10 and 11 July 1847, P vol. 1, p. 349

90 M 20 July, 19 July, and 5 September 1847, P vol. 1, pp 352–6

91 P vol. 1, p. 357

92 *Notes and Queries*, 8th Series, vol. i (1892), p. 106

93 M 7 November 1847, P vol. 1, p. 359

5:*The One True Fold*

1 P vol. 1, p. 590

2 N to Mrs John Mozley 26 January 1847, LD vol. xii, p. 24

3 W vol. 1, pp 148, 156

4 N to Henry Wilberforce 12 January 1848, LD vol. xii, p. 154

5 Metternich, Prince *Mémoires*

(Paris 1883) vol. 7, p. 341
6 Mathew, D. *Lord Acton and his Times* (1968), p. 142
7 Hales, E. E. Y. *Pio Nono* (1954), p. 17
8 Mathew, D. *op. cit.*, p. 143
9 Hales *op. cit.*, p. 67
10 Manning, H. E. *Charge 1848*, p. 60
11 M to G 3 April 1848, L pp 83–4
12 P vol. 1, p. 396
13 P vol. 1, p. 388
14 P vol. 1, p. 395
·15 P vol. 1, p. 367
16 P vol. 1, p. 372
17 M to Dodsworth 28 January 1848, L p. 83
18 M 23 March 1848, P vol. 1, p. 375
19 M to Sydney Herbert 14 February 1848, P vol. 1, p. 377
20 M to Robert Wilberforce January 1848, P vol. 1, pp 507–8
21 M to Dodsworth 28 January 1848, L p. 83
22 M to Robert Wilberforce January 1848, P vol. 1, p. 508
23 M to Mrs Laprimaudaye 31 March 1848, P vol. 1, p. 382
24 L p. 82
25 P vol. 1, p. 417
26 M to Robert Wilberforce 11 March 1848, P vol. 1, p. 514
27 M to Robert Wilberforce 15 February 1848, P vol. 1, p. 512
28 M to Robert Wilberforce 11 March 1848, P vol. 1, p. 514
29 P vol. 1, p. 480
30 M to Robert Wilberforce 11 March 1848, P vol. 1, p. 514
31 L p. 85
32 G Diary 10 July 1848, B p. 203
33 P vol. 1, p. 570
34 Keble to Pusey July 1848, Battiscombe *op. cit.*, p. 304
35 Bodley *op. cit.*, p. 27
36 M to Henry Wilberforce 2 October 1848, NS p. 357
37 M to Mary Wilberforce 26 January 1849, NS p. 327

38 M to Sidney Herbert 24 November 1848, P vol. 1, p. 421
39 Lockhart *op. cit.*, p. 377
40 N to Henry Wilberforce 9 March 1848, LD vol. xii, p. 183
41 Manning, H. E. *Charge 1849*, pp 71, 70
42 Maurice *op. cit.* vol. 1, p. 545
43 M to Sidney Herbert 1849, P vol. 1, p. 424
44 M to G 12 January 1849, B pp 204–5
45 M to Phillpotts 16 February 1849, Davies, G. C. B. *Henry Phillpotts, Bishop of Exeter* (1954), p. 295
46 M to Mary Wilberforce Holy Week 1849, NS pp 326–7
47 M to Mary Wilberforce Advent 1849, L p. 88
48 M to Robert Wilberforce 28 December 1849, P vol. 1, pp 515–16
49 *ibid.*
50 M to Miss Maurice 5 August 1850, L p. 91
51 Greville, C. *Memoirs* (edited by Henry Reeve 1874) Part I vol. ii, p. 287
52 M to Phillpotts 10 February 1849, Davies *op. cit.*, p. 296
53 M to Samuel Wilberforce 24 January 1850, NS p. 350
54 M to Robert Wilberforce 12 January, 1850, P vol. 1, p. 518
55 Hope to M 29 January 1850, P vol. 1, p. 524
56 Robert Wilberforce to M 22 February 1850, NS p. 371
57 P vol. 1, p. 592
58 P vol. 1, p. 528
59 P vol. 1, pp 532–3
60 G to M 4 April 1850, P vol. 1, p. 536
61 C vol. 1, p. 263
62 M to Robert Wilberforce 22 May 1850, P vol. 1, p. 538
63 Samuel Wilberforce to Robert Wilberforce 8 September 1850, NS pp 362–3

64 G to Robert Wilberforce 28 April 1850, B p. 219

65 G to M 23 June 1850, B p. 232

66 M to G 25 June 1850, L p. 92

67 M to Robert Wilberforce Easter 1850, L p. 50

68 M to Robert Wilberforce 25 June 1850, P vol. 1, p. 558

69 M to Mary Wilberforce 6 May 1850, P vol. 1, pp 473–4

70 M to Caroline Austen 18 June 1850, P vol. 1, p. 546

71 M 11 July 1850, P vol. 1, pp 481–2

72 G to Mrs Gladstone 21 July 1850, B p. 219

73 Samuel Wilberforce to G 14 September 1850, NS p. 363

74 M to Robert Wilberforce 5 August 1850, P vol. 1, p. 559

75 M to Robert Wilberforce 10 May 1850, P vol. 1, p. 555

76 M to Hope 23 November 1850, B pp 220–21

77 G to M from Genoa 5 November 1850, P vol. 1, p. 581

78 M to G 17 November 1850, L p. 94

79 M to Samuel Wilberforce 20 October 1850, NS pp 364–5

80 M to Robert Wilberforce 22 October 1850, P vol. 1, pp 564–6

81 Fothergill, A. B. Nicholas Wiseman (1963), pp 293–7, where Wiseman's letter is printed in full

82 Norman, E. R. Anti-Catholicism in Victorian England, p. 56

83 Walpole, S. Life of Lord John Russell vol. 2 (1889), p. 121

84 Norman, Anti-Catholicism, p. 61

85 P vol. 1, p. 580

86 M to Robert Wilberforce 15 November 1850, P vol. 1, pp 578–9

87 M to G 6 December 1850, L p. 96

88 M to Robert Wilberforce 14 December 1850, P vol. 1, p. 589

89 M to Hope 11 December 1850, P vol. 1, pp 589–90

90 N to Capes 24 December 1850, LD vol. xiv, p. 174

91 M to Robert Wilberforce 14 December 1850, P vol. 1, p. 588

92 P vol. 1, pp 585–7, 624

93 Purcell, E. S. 'Cardinal Manning in his Anglican Days' DR vol. cx (April 1892), p. 382

94 M to Robert Wilberforce 27 February 1851, P vol. 1, p. 506

95 Foot, M. R. D. and Matthew, H. C. G. (editors) The Gladstone Diaries vol. iv (1974), p. 314

96 ibid. 30 March 1851, p. 319

97 P vol. 1, p. 617

98 G to M 1 April 1851, P vol. 1, pp 611–12

99 G to Mrs Gladstone 4 March 1851, Shannon, R. Gladstone (1982), p. 234

100 M to G 5 April 1851, L p. 98

101 Craven, Mrs A. Life of Lady Georgiana Fullerton, translated by H. J. Coleridge SJ (1888), pp 198–9

102 M to Robert Wilberforce 6 April 1850, P vol. 1, p. 620

103 L p. 101

104 Samuel Wilberforce to M (undated), L pp 100–101

105 Mrs Sargent to Mary Wilberforce 7 April 1851, NS p. 368

106 Sidney Herbert to M 14 April 1851, L p. 100

107 P vol. 1, p. 627

108 G 7 April 1851, The Gladstone Diaries vol. iv, p. 322

109 G to Robert Wilberforce 11 April 1851, Morley op. cit. vol. 1, p. 387

110 P vol. 1, p. 634

111 Shannon op. cit., pp 235–7

112 L p. 99

6: A Forward Piece?

1 Altholz, J. L. The Liberal Catholic Movement in England: the 'Rambler' and its Contributors, 1848–64 (1962), p. 212

2 M to Robert Wilberforce 14 April

1851, P vol. 1, pp 620–21

3 WW vol. 1, pp 209–10

4 Hughes, P 'The English Catholics in 1850', Beck, G. A. (editor) *The English Catholics 1850–1950* (1950), pp 42–85

5 WW vol. 1, p. 216

6 WW vol. 1, p. 512

7 Talbot to M 26 December 1865, P vol. 2, p. 267

8 Pius VII to the Primate of Poland 29 June 1816, Husenbeth, F. C. *The Life of the Right Rev. John Milner* (1862), p. 241

9 Ward, B. *The Sequel to Catholic Emancipation* (1915) vol. 1, p. 72

10 *ibid.* vol. 2, pp 256–7

11 Ullathorne, W. B. *From Cabin-Boy to Archbishop* (1941 edition), p. 226

12 Ward, Wilfrid *W. G. Ward and the Catholic Revival* , p. 75

13 P vol. 2, p. 631

14 Duke of Norfolk to Lord Beaumont 28 November 1850, WW vol. 2, p. 15

15 P vol. 2, pp 778–9

16 Ward, Wilfrid *The Catholic Revival*, p. 51

17 *ibid.* p. 75

18 Hale M. and Bonney, E. (editors) *The Life and Letters of John Lingard 1771–1851* (1911), p. 353

19 P vol. 1, p. 633

20 Charlton, Barbara *Recollections of a Northumbrian Lady* (1949), pp 244, 255

21 Chapman *op. cit.*, p. 233

22 Norman, E. R. *The English Catholic Church in the Nineteenth Century* (1984), pp 155–6

23 Hutton, A. W. *op. cit.*, pp 82–4

24 P vol. 1, p. 628

25 P vol. 1, p. 633

26 L p. 102

27 M to Robert Wilberforce 16 April 1856, P vol. 2, p. 47

28 Ward, Wilfrid *Aubrey de Vere* (1904), p. 170

29 M to Robert Wilberforce 28 August 1851, B p. 223

30 Hutton *op. cit.*, p. 8

31 Longford, E. *A Pilgrimage of Passion* (1979), p. 15

32 P vol. 2, p. 347

33 L p. 103

34 *The Venerabile* vol. xv (1951), p. 201

35 *ibid.* p. 201

36 Talbot to Wiseman 20 April 1866, McElrath, Damian *The Syllabus of Pius IX, Some Reactions in England* (Louvain, 1964), pp 135–6

37 P vol. 2, p. 226

38 BU vol. 1, p. 296

39 De Vere, A. *Recollections* (1897), p. 329

40 L p. 51

41 M journal 1879–82, P vol. 2, p. 19

42 P vol. 2, p. 11

43 P yol. 2, p. 13

44 M to Sidney Herbert 4 January 1849, P vol. 1, p. 423

45 Hales *op. cit.*, p. 279

46 M to Robert Wilberforce 19 May 1854, P vol. 2, p. 43

47 P vol. 2, p. 92

48 M to Robert Wilberforce 25 January 1852, P vol. 2, p. 26

49 M's journal 1878–82, P vol. 2, p. 19

50 M to Robert Wilberforce 16 April 1856, P vol. 2, p. 47

51 M to Robert Wilberforce 1 April 1856, P vol. 2, p. 680

52 P vol. 2, p. 680

53 ME(2)

54 L p. 123

55 WW vol. 2, p. 191

56 N journal 21 January 1863, W vol 1, p. 584

57 L p. 478

58 BU vol. 1, p. 197

59 M to N 14 August 1852, LD vol. xv, p. 181

60 Newman, J. H. *Sermons Preached on Various Occasions* (1875)

61 N to M 30 September 1857, LD vol. xviii, p. 134
62 N to M 25 June 1857, LD vol. xviii, pp 61–2
63 N Diary 20 January 1858, LD vol. xviii, p. 236
64 M to N 20 October 1857, L p. 270
65 WW vol. 2, p. 43; Fothergill *op. cit.*, p. 189
66 WW vol. 2, p. 193
67 WW vol. 2, p. 188
68 *ibid.*
69 WW vol. 2, p. 365
70 Wiseman to Faber 27 October 1852, P vol. 2, p. 8
71 ME(3)
72 W vol. 1, p. 155
73 ME(3)
74 WW vol. 2, p. 264
75 M Good Friday 1853, P vol. 2, p. 16
76 P vol. 2, p. 17
77 *ibid.*
78 Fothergill *op. cit.*, p. 211
79 L p. 111
80 M 21 December 1854, L p. 113
81 M to Miss Stanley 8 February 1855, L p. 116
82 L p. 118
83 Fothergill *op. cit.*, p. 239
84 M to Miss Stanley c. 1854–5, pp 120–21
85 M journal 1878–82, P vol. 2, p. 57
86 M to Pius ix February 1860, WW vol. 2, p. 360
87 M to Wiseman 14 April 1857, P vol. 2, p. 69
88 P vol. 2, p. 60
89 P vol. 2, p. 8
90 M to Wiseman 15 December 1856, P vol. 2, p. 61
91 L p. 166
92 M journal 1879, P vol. 2, p. 74
93 Ambrose St John to N 4 May 1867, WW vol 2, p. 167
94 W vol. 2, p. 358
95 Ward, Denis 'Manning and his Oblates' in Fitzsimons, J. *Manning: Anglican and Catholic*

(1951), p. 54
96 L p. 126
97 Fitzsimons, p. 54
98 Rev Dr Butler, ME(2)
99 Wiseman to Cardinal Barnabò 22 February 1860, WW vol. 2, p. 357
100 P vol. 2, p. 79
101 Lady Herbert to Purcell 8 June 1892, P vol. 2, p. 80
102 SC vol. 1, pp 454–5
103 P vol. 2, p. 79
104 SC vol. 1, p. 455
105 W vol. 1, p. 421
106 WW vol. 2, p. 259
107 WW vol. 2, p. 265
108 Fothergill, *op. cit.*, p. 232
109 M to Wiseman 8 April 1857, P vol. 2, p. 75
110 P vol. 2, p. 77
111 *ibid.*
112 M 1 June 1865, P vol. 2, p. 230
113 M to Wiseman 14 April 1857, P vol. 2, p. 69
114 Fothergill *op. cit.*, p. 240
115 *ibid.*, p. 241
116 N to Ambrose St John 22 November 1845, LD vol. xi, pp 39–40
    N to Dalgairns 16 December 1845, LD vol. xi, pp 64–5
117 SC vol. 1, p. 75
118 M to Talbot 17 September 1859, P vol. 2, p. 99
119 M to Talbot 17 June 1859, P vol. 2, pp 140–41
120 *ibid.*
121 M to Vaughan 7 October 1858, SC vol. 1, p. 88
122 M to Talbot 17 September 1859, P vol. 2, p. 99
123 M to Talbot 18 August 1859, P vol. 2, p. 99
124 M to Wiseman November 1850, WW vol. 2, p. 352
125 WW vol. 2, p. 274
126 WW vol. 2, p. 275
127 *ibid.*
128 M to Wiseman 7 August 1858, 'More Letters of Wiseman and

Manning', DR clxxii (January 1923), pp 107–8

129 Schiefen, R. J. 'Some Aspects of the Controversy between Cardinal Wiseman and the Westminster Chapter' *Journal of Ecclesiastical History* vol. 21, no. 2 (April 1970), p. 139

130 WW vol. 2, p. 383

131 Manning to Wiseman 3 December 1858, DR clxxii (January 1923), pp 109–10

132 Schiefen *op. cit.*, p. 140

133 M to Talbot 14 September 1860, P vol. 2, p. 101

134 WW vol, 2, p. 276

135 WW vol. 2, p. 283

136 M to Wiseman 6 March 1858, SC vol. 1, p. 75

137 Oakeley to Talbot 27 September 1860, Schiefen, *op. cit.*, p. 127

138 Fitzsimons *op. cit.*, p. 51

139 BU vol. 1, p. 242

140 Wiseman to Talbot 8 March 1859, Fothergill *op. cit.*, p. 252

141 Talbot to Wiseman 29 March 1859, WW vol. 2, p. 331

142 L pp 137, 135

143 Talbot to Searle 13 January 1859, WW vol. 2, pp 332, 607 (Italian)

144 Talbot to Errington 19 April 1859, WW vol. 2, p. 333, 619 (Italian)

145 P vol. 2, p. 98. See also P vol. 2, p. 101, and L p. 143

146 Talbot to Wiseman 4 November 1859, WW vol. 2, p. 343

147 M to Wiseman November 1859, WW vol. 2, p. 351

148 Wiseman to Barnabò 22 February 1860, WW vol. 2, pp 354–65

149 M to Patterson 13 July 1860, WW vol. 2, p. 375

150 M to Pius ix February 1860, WW vol. 2, pp 366, 368–9

151 WW vol. 2, p. 369

152 P vol. 2, p. 95

153 M to Ullathorne 20 November 1860, L pp 136–7

154 M to Patterson 1 June 1860 and 12

July 1860, WW vol. 2, pp 373, 375

156 Norman, E. R. *The English Catholic Church in the Nineteenth Century*, p. 257

157 BU vol. 1, p. 254

158 M to Talbot, SC vol. 1, pp 94–5 (no date given)

159 M to Talbot 4 October 1861, P vol. 2, p. 126

7: *The Unnamed Coadjutor*

1 L p. 142

2 Manning, H. E. *Pastoral on the Centenary* of St Peter (1867)

3 Manning, H. E. *The Temporal Power of the Vicar of Christ* (1862) xxiv et seq.

5 Manning, H. E. *The Temporal Power*, p. 163

6 *ibid.*, p. 115

7 *ibid.*, pp 163–4

8 G to M 4 September 1861, Clais J. *Le Cardinal Manning et La Question Sociale*, Thèse presentée á l'Université François Rabelais de Tours (1981), p. 249

9 M to G 5 February 1865, P vol. 1, p. 249
M to G 24 February 1865, L p. 204

10 G to M 17 February 1865, P vol. 2, pp 249–51

11 Manning, H. E. 'The Visit of Garibaldi to England,' an open letter to the Right Hon. Edward Cardwell, MP, 10 May 1864, *Miscellanies* vol. 1 (1877), p. 123

12 G to M 17 February 1865, P vol. 2, p. 251

13 M to Lady Herbert 21 April 1865, P vol. 2, p. 243

14 G to Lord Granville 25 November 1874, Morley *op. cit.* vol. 2, p. 519

15 L p. 190

16 G to M 1 August 1864, L p. 189

17 Talbot to M 6 July 1861, P vol. 2, p. 156

18 M to Talbot 19 July 1861, P vol. 2, p. 158

19 M to Talbot 13 June 1861, P vol. 2, p. 154
20 Talbot to M 6 July 1861, P vol. 2, p. 156
21 T vol. 2, p. 291
22 N 8 January 1860, W vol. 1, p. 578
23 N to Capes 1 February 1857, LD vol. xvii, p. 514
24 Chapman op. cit., p. 345
25 W vol. 1, p. 199
26 N to Lord Braye 29 October 1882, LD vol. xxx, pp 141–2
27 Wilson, A. N. Hilaire Belloc (1984), p. 18
28 Altholz op. cit., p. 63
29 M to Talbot 17 June 1859, P vol. 2, p. 141
30 N Memorandum 24 May 1882, W vol. 1, p. 494
31 M to N 22 September 1859, LD vol. xix, p. 175
32 N to Wiseman 19 January 1860, LD vol. xvii, pp 289–90
33 N to Father Whitty 12 April 1870, LD vol. xxv, pp 92–6
34 Ryder op. cit., p. 284
35 N to Acton 7 June 1861, LD vol. xix, p. 508
36 Ward, Wilfrid Catholic Revival, p. 14
37 Acton to N 19 June 1861, W vol. 1, p. 523
38 W vol. 1, p. 560
39 W vol. 1, p. 388
40 Manning H. E. 'The Subjects Proper to the Academia' (Session 1863–4), Miscellanies vol. 1, p. 95
41 M to N 22 June 1861, W vol. 1, p. 525
42 M Note 1887, P vol. 2, p. 349
43 N to Acton 20 June 1861, LD vol xix, p. 518
44 N to Acton 21 August 1861, LD vol. xx, pp 35–6
45 Holmes, J. D. More Roman than Rome: English Catholicism in the Nineteenth Century (1978), p. 121
46 M to Oakeley 14 August 1867, P vol. 2, p. 332
47 N to Ullathorne 31 January 1862, LD vol. xx, p. 145
48 M to Ullathorne 28 October 1862, 'Some Birmingham Bygones. Illustrated from the Correspondence of Manning and Ullathorne', DR vol. clxvi (April 1920), p. 207
49 Altholz op. cit., p. 170
50 N to Ambrose St John 7 August 1862, LD vol. xx, pp 253–4
51 M 10 May 1862 (from Italy), L p. 335
52 N Note of August 1875, LD vol. xx, p. 254
53 N to Wetherall 10 February 1865, LD vol. xxi, p. 413
54 T vol. 2, pp 419–20
55 Wiseman to M 10 March 1862, 'Unpublished Letters of Cardinal Wiseman to Dr Manning', DR vol. clxix (October 1921), p. 179
56 Vaughan to Talbot 6 May (no year given), Norman, E. R. The English Catholic Church in the Nineteenth Century, p. 256
57 M to Talbot c. 1860, P vol. 2, p. 135
58 Wiseman to M 17 June 1862, BU vol. 1, p. 247
59 Wiseman to the Rev William Burke 26 September 1858, WW vol. 2, p. 183
60 M to Talbot 21 March 1861, P vol. 2, p. 104
61 W to Talbot 26 June 1863, Fothergill op. cit., p. 276
62 WW vol. 2, p. 284
63 M to Wiseman, 25 January 1862, BU vol. 1, p. 232
64 Vaughan to Wiseman 22 February 1862, BU vol. 1, p. 236
65 M to Talbot 17 June 1859, P vol. 2, p. 141
66 M to Talbot 16 February 1862, P vol. 2, p. 128
67 M to Wiseman 30 July 1863, L p. 142
68 M to Wiseman 18 February 1864,

BU vol. 2, p. 124

69 M to Wiseman 26 April 1862, L
p. 512

70 M to Wiseman 7 February 1862,
'More Letters of Wiseman and
Manning', DR vol. clxxii (January
1923), p. 124

71 Talbot to Wiseman 11 May 1863,
L p. 142

72 Vaughan to Wiseman 10 January
1862, L p. xvii

73 Talbot to M 10 October 1863, P
vol. 2, p. 177

74 BU vol. 1, p. 258

75 Ullathorne to Brown 26 February
1864, BU vol. 1, p. 261

76 M to Wiseman 13 December 1861,
P vol. 2, pp 107–8

77 Vaughan to Wiseman February
1862, BU vol. 1, p. 259

78 Oakeley to Talbot 24 January
1861, Norman, E. R. *The English
Catholic Church in the Nineteenth
Century*, p. 257

79 Vaughan to Talbot 26 June 1863,
ibid., p. 259

80 BU vol. 1, p. 259

81 Talbot to Wiseman 3 November
1863, L p. 143

82 M to Wiseman 4 December 1863,
P vol. 2, p. 181

83 M to Wiseman 8 December 1863,
P vol. 2, p. 182

84 M to Wiseman 2 January 1864, P
vol. 2, p. 185

85 M to Wiseman 8 December 1863,
P vol. 2, p. 183

86 M to Talbot 1864, P vol. 2, p. 188
(undated)

87 M note 23 December 1883, P
vol. 2, p. 183

88 Neve to Clifford 13 February 1864,
L p. 145

89 M to Ullathorne 18 February 1864,
BU vol. 2, p. 124

90 M to Talbot 12 June 1863, P
vol. 2, p. 175

91 ME(3)

92 Purcell, E. S. and De Lisle, E.
*Life and Letters of Ambrose
Phillipps de Lisle* (1900) vol. 2,
p. 2 *et seq.*

93 Manning, H. E. 'The Work and
the Wants of the Catholic Church
in England' (1863) *Miscellanies*
vol. 1, pp 25–71, *vide* 56, 53

94 Gaisford to the Bishop of
Southwark 11 December 1864, W
vol. 2, p. 542

95 N to Pusey 17 November 1865, LD
xxii, p. 104

96 Newman, J. H. 'A Letter
addressed to the Rev E. B. Pusey,
D.D., on the occasion of his
Eirenicon' 7 December 1865,
*Certain Difficulties felt by
Anglicans considered* (1891
edition) vol. 2, p. 7

97 T vol. 2, p. 291

98 T vol. 2, p. 424

99 Beck *op. cit.*, p. 297

100 Grant to M, BU vol. 1, pp 364–5
(undated)

101 N to Bellasis 24 January 1864, LD
vol. xxi, p. 28

102 N to Acton 18 March 1864, LD
vol. xxi, p. 84

103 N journal 21 January 1863, W vol.
1, p. 583

104 T vol. 2, p. 294

105 Neville, W. P. (editor) *Addresses
to Cardinal Newman with his
Replies* (1905), p. 123

106 Newman, J. H. *Apologia* (1864),
p. 401

107 C vol. 2, p. 415

108 N to Baddeley 23 March 1864, LD
vol. xxi, pp 86–7

109 W vol. 2, p. 400

110 M to Wiseman, P vol. 2, p. 326
(undated)

111 SC vol. 1, p. 215

112 P vol. 2, p. 717

113 Monsell to N 29 January 1864, LD
vol. xxi, p. 40

114 N to Monsell 6 February 1864, LD
vol. xxi, p. 43

115 N journal 22 February 1865, W

vol. 2, p. 73

116 BU vol. 2, p. 4

117 N to Hope Scott 29 August 1864, LD vol. xxi, p. 211

118 M to Talbot 29 August 1864, LD vol. xxi, P vol. 2, p. 299

119 N to Gaisford 16 December 1864, LD vol. xxi, p. 28

120 N to Bellasis 24 January 1864, LD vol. xxi, p. 28

121 T vol. 2, p. 397

122 W vol. 2, p. 179

123 BU vol. 2, p. 12 (early 1865)

124 M note of 1879, P vol. 2, p. 192

125 M to Talbot 13 February 1865, P vol. 2, p. 193

126 M to Lady Herbert 16 February 1865, P vol. 2, p. 240

127 Ward, Wilfrid *The Catholic Revival*, p. 221

8: Archbishop of Westminster

1 P vol. 2, p. 257

2 *Catholic Revival*, p. 220

3 M to Talbot 24 February 1865, P vol. 2, p. 206

4 *Catholic Revival*, pp 220–21

5 M to Talbot 24 February 1865, P vol. 2, p. 206

6 M to Talbot 31 March 1865, P vol. 2, p. 210

7 M to Talbot 24 February 1865, P vol. 2, p. 206

8 M to Talbot 6 March 1865, L p. 151

9 M to Talbot 14 March 1865, L pp 151–2

10 M to Talbot 31 March 1865, P vol. 2, p. 209

11 L p. 153

12 Coffin to M 8 April 1865, P vol. 2, P. 213

13 BU vol. 1, p. 267

14 *ibid*.

15 Talbot to M 28 March 1865, P vol. 2, pp 210–11

16 M to Talbot 11 April 1865, P vol. 2, p. 214

17 M note 1882, P vol. 2, pp 217–18

18 Edward Hearne to M 25 April 1865, P vol. 2, p. 244

19 Grant to Clifford 29 April 1865, L p. 154

20 M to Talbot 9 May 1865, P vol. 2, p. 221

21 Fitzsimons, *op. cit.*, pp 58–9

22 Vaughan to M 24 May 1865, L p. 155

23 SC vol. 1, p. 152

24 Vaughan to M 6 June 1865, P vol. 2, pp 245–6

25 L p. 157

26 Talbot to M, P vol. 2, pp 220–21 (no date given)

27 Talbot to M 3 June 1865, P vol. 2, p. 227

28 M to Talbot 12 May 1865, P vol. 2, p. 224

29 *ibid*.

30 Ullathorne to M 10 May and 12 May 1865, BU vol. 2, pp 125–7

31 B vol. 2, p. 152

32 M to Ullathorne 3 June 1865, Ullathorne to M 4 June 1865, B vol 2, p. 128

33 M to Talbot 12 May 1865, P vol. 2, pp 223–4

34 Miss Bowles to N 10 May 1865, LD vol. xxi, p. 466

35 N to Miss Bowles 15 May 1865, LD vol. xxi, p. 466

36 Ullathorne to M 12 May 1865, BU vol. 2, p. 127

37 W vol. 2, p. 88

38 M to N 30 May 1865, W vol. 2, pp 88–9

39 N to M 31 May 1865, LD vol. xxi, p. 478

40 M to N 4 June 1865, W vol. 2, p. 89

41 Printed in DR vol. clxvi (January 1920), pp 1–21. Extracts in L pp 161–9

42 M to Talbot 27 January 1866, P vol. 2, p. 285

43 Fitzsimons *op. cit.*, p. 59

44 Fowler J. *Life of R. W. Sibthorpe*

(1880), p. 173

45 CR p. 175

46 Gasquet *op. cit.*, p. 60

47 Morris to Talbot 26 February 1866, Norman, E. R. *The English Catholic Church in the Nineteeth Century*, pp 268–9

48 M journal 1878–82, P vol. 2, p. 355

49 St John, E. *Manning's Work for Children* (1929), p. 32 ·

50 *The Month* 1866, pp 299–300

51 M to Talbot 14 June 1866, P vol. 2, p. 358

52 St John *op. cit.*, p. 66

53 Manning, H. E. *The Eternal Priesthood* (1883), p. 142

54 Manning, H. E. *Miscellanies* vol. i (1877), pp 66–7

55 N to Dalgairns 31 December 1846, LD vol. xi, p. 306

56 N to Mrs John Mozley 19 January 1837, LD vol. vi, p. 16

57 ME(I) p. 50

58 Quinquagesima Pastoral 1866, Clais *op. cit.*, pp 261–2

59 *The Times* 12 June 1866

60 St John *op. cit.*, p. 71

61 *ibid.*, pp 89–90

62 M to G 3 July 1868, Clais *op. cit.*, p. 229

63 *Tablet* 3 July 1869

64 P vol. 2, p. 287

65 Manning, H. E. *England and Christendom* (1867), pp 218–19

66 BU vol. 1, pp 346–7

67 Newman, J. H. 'A Letter addressed to the Rev. E. B. Pusey, D.D., on occasion of his Eirenicon' 7 December 1865, *Certain Dificulties felt by Anglicans Considered* (1841) vol. 2, p. 22

68 Talbot to M 20 February 1866, P vol. 2, pp 322–3

69 Ward to M 8 June 1865, P vol. 2, p. 309

70 N to St John 3 May 1867, LD vol. xxiii, p. 202

71 M to Ullathorne 24 March 1866, BU vol. 1, p. 364

72 M to N 8 February 1866, LD vol. xxii, p. 149

73 M to Ullathorne 14 February 1866, p. 274

74 M to Talbot 25 February 1866, P vol. 2, pp 322–3

75 N to Copeland 27 May 1866, LD vol. xxii, p. 241

76 N to Ullathorne 12 August 1866, LD vol. xxii, p. 277

77 N to Sir Justin Sheil 22 March 1867, LD vol. xxiii, p. 101

78 W vol. 2, p. 195

79 N to Miss Bowles 3 January 1867, LD vol. xxiii, p. 10

80 M to Talbot 26 June 1866, P vol. 2, p. 300

81 BU vol. 2, p. 16

82 St John to N 1 May 1867, LD vol. xxiii, p. 207

83 M to Oakeley 14 August 1867, P vol. 2, p. 333

84 T vol. 2, p. 398

85 T vol. 2, p. 400

86 W vol. 2, p. 183

87 N to Hope-Scott 16 August 1867, LD vol. xxiii, p. 302

88 T vol. 2, p. 403

89 W vol. 2, p. 544

90 Address of Laity to Newman 6 April 1867, W vol. 2, p. 143

91 Oakeley to N 16 May 1867, LD vol. xxiii, p. 232

92 Talbot to M 25 April 1867, P vol. 2, pp 317–19

93 N to Pusey 23 November 1865, LD vol. xxii, p. 109

94 L p. 182

95 *ibid.*

96 Ullathorne to Dr Johnson 17 September 1867, BU vol. 2, p. 134

97 M to Talbot 3 May 1867, P vol. 2, p. 319

98 N to Ullathorne 8 January 1867, LD vol. xxiii, p. 17

99 M to N 7 August 1867, P vol. 2, p. 329

100 N to M 10 August 1867, LD vol.

xxiii, p. 290

101 P vol. 2, pp 331–41

102 M to Ullathorne 2 January 1869, P vol. 2, p. 344

103 N to M 3 November 1869, P vol. 2, p. 346

104 M to Talbot 25 February 1866, P vol. 2, pp 323–4

105 Holmes, *op cit.*, p. 125

106 L pp 330–31

107 Manning, H. E. *Pastoral on Modern Society* (1871)

108 P vol. 2, p. 775

109 Newman, F. W. *Contributions, chiefly to the early history of the late Cardinal* (1891), p. 110

110 MR (3)

111 M's Pastoral for St Patrick's Day 1867, cited in Clais *op. cit.*, pp 371–2

112 Harrison, B. H. and Dingle, A. E. 'Cardinal Manning as Temperance Reformer', *Historical Journal* (1969), p. 489

113 *ibid.*, pp 494–5

114 M to Lady Herbert 10 December 1864, L p. 146

115 Manning, H. E. 'A Letter to Earl Grey' 12 March 1868, *Miscellanies* vol. i, p. 254

116 Stead, W. T. 'Cardinal Manning', *The Review of Reviews* vol. i, no. 6 (June 1890) p. 481

117 Gwynn, S. and Tuckwell, G. *Life of the Rt Hon Sir Charles Dilke* (1917) vol. 1, p. 292

118 M to G 24 February 1865, L p. 204

119 M quoting Peel, *Miscellanies* vol. I, p. 253

120 Manning, H. E. 'Pastoral for St Patrick's Day 1867', Clais, *op cit.*, p. 305

121 G to Samuel Wilberforce

122 cited Hardinge, Sir Arthur *Life of the Fourth Earl of Carnarvon* (1925), p. 160

123 M to Archbishop Cullen 5 February 1866, L p. 194

124 L p. 195

125 BU vol. 2, p. 142

126 L p. 196

127 Manning H. E. A Letter to Earl Grey', *Miscellanies* vol i, p. 218

128 M to Disraeli 21 May 1868, L. p. 198

129 P vol. 2, p. 519

130 Disraeli, B. *Lothair* (1870) chapters 2, 9, 28, 6

131 Disraeli, B. *Lothair* (edited by V. Bogdanov 1975), p. xvii

132 Manning, H. E. 'A Letter to Earl Grey', *Miscellanies* vol. i, pp 217, 226, 218, 243, 239, 251

133 Marsh, P. T. *The Victorian Church in Decline* (1969), p. 21

134 M to G 4 December 1868, L p. 201

135 G to M 24 July 1869, L p. 202

136 M to G 24 July 1869, Morley *op. cit.* vol. 2, p. 279

137 G to M 12 March 1870, Hammond J. L. and B. *Gladstone and the Irish Nation* (1938), p. 103

138 G to M November 1869, Morley *op. cit.*, p. 509

9: Infallibility at Rome and Westminster

1 Manning, H. E. *The Vatican Decrees in their Bearing on Civil Allegiance* (1875), p. 175

2 Manning, H. E. 'Caesarism and Ultramontanism' (1873), *Miscellanies* vol. 2, p. 135

3 Manning, H. E. *The Vatican Council and its Definitions* (1870), p. 121

4 Manning, H. E. *Rome and Revolution. A Sermon* (1867), pp 15–16

5 Manning, H. E. *The Oecumenical Council and the Infallibility of the Roman Pontiff* (1869), p. 52

6 BC vol. 1, pp 77,76

7 BC vol. 1, p. 147

8 P vol. 2, p. 420

9 BC vol. 1, pp 85–7

10 BC vol. 1, p. 147
11 BC vol. 1, p. 117
12 N to O'Neill Daunt 27 June, LD xxv, p. 150
13 T vol. 2, p. 378
14 N to Canon Jenkins 21 November 1869, LD vol. xxiv, p. 379
15 BC vol. 1, p. 174
16 BC vol. 1, p. 172
17 BV vol. 1, p. 174
18 P vol. 2, p. 457
19 BC vol. 1, p. 173
20 Ollivier, E. *L'Eglise et L'Etat au Concile du Vatican* (Paris 1877), vol. 2, p. 8
21 Althaus, F. (editor) *Roman Journals of Ferdinand Gregorovius 1852–74* (1911), p. 354
22 P vol. 2, pp 416–17
23 BC vol. 2, p. 272
24 Church to J. B. Mozley 29 January 1870, Church, M. *Life and Letters of Dean Church* (1897), p. 224
25 Pusey to Copeland 2 January 1870, Bowen *op. cit.*, p. 349
26 N to Ullathorne 28 January 1870, LD vol. xxv, p. 19
27 G to M 23 January 1870
28 M to G 6 April 1870, McClelland V. A. *Cardinal Manning: His Public Life and Influence 1865–92* (1962), p. 69
29 P vol. 2, p. 435
30 Morley *op. cit.* vol. 2 pp 509–11
31 G 2 January 1870, Morley *op. cit.* vol. 2, p. 510
32 G to M 16 April 1870, Lathbury, D. C. *Correspondence on Church and Religion of William Ewart Gladstone* (1910) vol. ii, p. 52
33 P vol. 2, p. 456
34 BC vol. 2, p. 50
35 BC vol. 1, p. 239
36 BC vol. 2, p. 69
37 BC vol. 2, p. 125
38 BC vol. 2, p. 157
39 P vol. 2, p. 547
40 Fitzsimons, *op. cit.*, p. 100
41 L p. 230
42 N to Miss Giberne 27 July 1870, LD vol. xxv, p. 167
43 N to O'Neill Daunt 23 June 1870, LD vol. xxv, p. 150
44 N to Canon McColl 11 November 1871, LD vol. xxv, p. 430
45 N to Mrs William Froude 8 August 1870, LD vol. xxv, p. 176
46 Mathew, D. *Lord Acton and His Times* (1968), pp 228 *et seq.*
47 Wilberforce, R. G. *Life of Samuel Wilberforce* vol. 3 (1882), pp 248–9
48 Earl of Granville to R. G. Wilberforce 25 September 1882, *Life of Bishop Wilberforce* vol. 3, p. 424
49 M 15 January 1883, P vol. 2, p. 680
50 G to M 2 August 1870
51 G to M 26 March 1870, McClelland *op. cit.*, p. 69
52 Ullathorne to his Vicar General 23 February 1870, Norman, E. R. *The English Catholic Church*, p. 285
53 Beck *op. cit.*, p. 373
54 McClelland *op. cit.*, p. 68
55 Ullathorne to O'Sullivan 23 February 1870, Selby, D. E. 'Henry Manning and the Education Bill of 1870', *British Journal of Educational Studies* vol. xviii, no. 2 (June 1970), p. 202
56 M to G 25 March 1870, McClelland *op cit.*, p. 68
57 M to Ullathorne September 1870, BU vol. 2, pp 146–7
58 P vol. 2, p. 494
59 *ibid.*
60 M's Education Pastoral 1872, Beck *op cit.*, p. 377
61 Harrison and Dingle *op cit.*, p. 491
62 *ibid.*, p. 492
63 *ibid.*
64 *Weekly Register* 23 January 1892, p. 122
65 M 1874, ME(3)

66 Hutton *op cit.*, p. 168
67 P vol. 2, p. 699
68 P vol. 2, pp 601–2
69 Manning, H. E. *Modern Society*,
    p. 4
70 Manning, H.E. *Charge 1846*, p. 33
71 Manning, H. E. *Modern Society*,
    p. 5
72 Manning, H. E. 'The Work and
    the Wants of the Catholic Church
    in England', *Miscellanies* vol. i,
    p. 69
73 Manning, H. E. *Pastoral on
    Modern Society*
74 Vaughan to Manning 10 February
    1873, L p. 349
75 M to G 21 December 1872, L
    p. 349
76 M to G December 1872, L p. 349
77 McClelland *op cit.*, p. 209
78 Manning, H. E. 'The Dignity and
    Rights of Labour' (1874),
    Miscellanies vol. ii (1877), pp 94,
    97
79 M to Ruskin 21 October 1873, L
    p. 326
80 Ruskin to M 25 January 1878,
    Ruskin J. *Works* (1903–12) vol.
    37, pp 240–41
81 Viljoen, H. G. (editor) *The
    Brantwood Diary of John Ruskin*
    (1971), p. 546
82 Ward, Wilfred *The Catholic
    Revival*, p. 309
83 N to Dean Church 11 January
    1876, LD vol. xxviii, p. 11
84 Ward, Wilfred *The Catholic
    Revival*, p. 306
85 G to M 1872, P vol. 2, p. 515
86 M to G 26 February 1873, L p. 211
87 M to G 7 March 1873, L p. 212
88 Manning, H. E. 'Letter to the
    Archbishop of Armagh' 31 August
    1873, *Miscellanies* vol. i, p. 377
89 M to G 5 February 1874, L p. 213
90 *ibid.*
91 Manning, H. E. 'Ultramontanism
    and Christianity', *Miscellanies* vol.
    ii, pp 165–99

92 G to M 22 January 1874, L p. 246
93 G Diary 11 March 1874, Morley
    op cit., vol. 2, p. 499
94 Gladstone to Lord Granville 25
    November 1874, Morley *op cit.*,
    vol. 2, p. 519
95 M to *The Times* 7 November 1874,
    P vol. 2, p. 475
96 M to *New York Herald* 10
    November 1874, P vol. 2, p. 476
97 L pp 247–8
98 G to N 15 January 1875, LD vol.
    xxvii, p. 192
99 N to Lord Blachford 2 October
    1874, LD vol. xxvii, pp 122–3
100 Newman, J. H. 'Letter to the
    Duke of Norfolk', *Certain
    Difficulties felt by Anglicans in
    Catholic Teaching* (1891), vol. 2,
    pp 297, 300
101 BU vol. 2, p. 104
102 M to Ullathorne 15 January 1875,
    L p. 247
103 M to Propaganda 1875 (translated
    from Italian) BU vol. 2, pp 101–2
104 M to G 24 February 1875, P vol. 2,
    p. 477
105 M to G 25 February 1875, P vol. 2,
    p. 479
106 M to Ullathorne 7 December
    1874, DR (April 1920), p. 216
107 Manning, H. E. *The Vatican
    Decrees*, p. 177
108 O'Callaghan to M 16 February
    1875, T vol. 2, pp 518–19
109 G Diary 6 February 1875, Morley
    op cit. vol. 2, p. 521
110 P vol. 2, p. 487
111 P vol. 1, p. 583
112 L p. 166
113 L p. 473
114 L p. 474
115 ME(2)
116 L p. 457
117 ME(2)
118 M to Canon Murname 22 April
    1890, ME(1)
119 ME(2)
120 M to Ullathorne 9 March 1883,

BU vol. 2, p. 155
121 Manning, H. E. *Miscellanies* vol. i, p. 59
122 BU vol. 2, p. 159
123 L p. 297
124 P vol. 2, p. 783
125 P vol. 2, p. 784
126 M Note of 1887, P vol. 2, p. 507
127 P vol. 2, p. 789
128 M to Ullathorne 9 March 1883, BU vol. 2, p. 155
129 M to Talbot 13 December 1860, P vol. 2, p. 135
130 Manning, M. E. 'The Work and Wants of the Church in England' (1882), *Miscellanies* vol. iii, p. 353
131 P vol. 2, pp 767–8
132 L p. 294
133 McClelland *op cit.*, pp 55 *et seq.*
136 L p. 294
135 P vol. 2, p. 767
136 N to St John 20 March 1857, LD vol. xvii, pp 541–2
137 William Anderdon to M Whitsunday 1875, L p. 299
138 M to William Anderdon 15 May 1875, L pp 299–300
139 Anderdon to M 1876, L p. 300
140 M to William Anderdon 24 July 1876, L pp 300–1
141 Holmes *op cit.*, p. 142
142 M to De Vere 26 March 1875, De Vere, A. *Recollections*, p. 295
143 M to Vaughan 14 March 1875, SC vol. 1, p. 292
144 Disraeli to M 31 December 1879, L pp 259–60
145 CR p. 183
146 L p. 161
147 Blake, R. *Disraeli*, p. 737
148 BU vol. 2, pp. 34–5
149 BU vol. 2, p. 304
150 M to G 1 March 1873, McClelland *op. cit.*, p. 112
151 N to M 24 November 1873, LD vol. xxvi, p. 390
152 M Note of 1887, P vol. 2, p. 502
153 SC vol. 2, p. 71
154 Manning, H. E. *Miscellanies* vol.

iii, p. 349
155 M Note of 1887, P vol. 2, p. 503
156 L. p. 189
157 M Note of 1887, P vol. 2, p. 503
158 Sir Augustus Paget to Lord Derby 21 December 1874, Rhodes, A. P. *The Power of Rome: the Vatican in the age of Liberal Democracies* (1983), p. 165
159 M. de Courcelle 28 April 1876, Rhodes *op. cit.*, p. 165
160 P vol. 2, p. 574
161 P vol. 2, p. 573
162 M to De Vere 21 September 1870, De Vere *op. cit.*, p. 297
163 M journal 4 December 1883, P vol. 2, p. 580
164 M to G 16 September 1870, L p. 236
165 Rhodes *op. cit.*, p. 165
166 P vol. 2, p. 615
167 Rhodes *op. cit.*, p. 165
168 P vol. 2, p. 615
169 M to De Vere 19 April 1888, De Vere *op. cit.*, pp 297–8
170 M 24 May 1889, P vol. 2, p. 616
171 P vol. 2, p. 576
172 P vol. 2, p. 548
173 P vol. 2, p. 553
174 P vol. 2, p. 549
175 M to Lane Fox 10 February 1878
176 M 1876, L p. 176
177 P vol. 2, p. 550. See also BU vol. 2, p. 107 note
178 Fitzsimons, *op. cit.*, pp 63–4
179 Hughes, P. *A Popular History of the Catholic Church* (1946), p. 276
180 SC vol. 1, pp 284–5
181 SC vol. 1, p. 337
182 M to Clifford 10 May 1877, SC vol. 1, p. 326
183 M to Vaughan 25 March 1875, SC vol. 1, p. 293
184 M to Vaughan 18 and 14 March 1875, SC vol. 1, p. 292
185 SC vol. 1, p. 294
186 SC vol. 1, p. 328
187 SC vol. 1, p. 338
188 M to Ullathorne 24 July 1880, L

p. 312
189 SC vol. 1, p. 336
190 M to Vaughan, SC vol. 1, p. 331
(no date given)
191 M to Vaughan 18 May 1881, SC
vol. 1, p. 354
192 P vol. 2, p. 555
193 M to Cardinal Nina summer 1878,
P vol. 2, pp 555–6
194 W vol. 2, p. 438
195 Ullathorne to M 3 February 1879,
BU vol. 2, p. 113
196 N to Ullathorne 2 February 1879,
LD vol. xxix, pp 18–19
197 Ullathorne to N 3 February 1879,
BU vol. 2, p. 113
198 N to Duke of Norfolk 20 February
1879, LD vol. xxix, pp 31–2
199 M to N 8 March 1879, P vol. 2,
p. 58
200 Dollinger cited by Vaughan,
Holmes *op. cit.*, p. 192
201 *Punch* 1 March 1879
202 *The Month* (April 1879) p. 465

10: *Private Life and Public
Character*

1 M to Caroline Austen 9 January
1882, P vol. 2, p. 711
2 M to Caroline Austen 1 February
1881, P vol. 2, p. 711
3 M to Caroline Austen 9 January
1882
Caroline Austen to M (January
1882, P vol. 2, p. 726
4 M 21 August 1885, L p. 490
5 De Vere *op. cit.*, p. 301
6 L p. 332
7 Manning, H. E. *The Eternal
Priesthood* (1883), p. 184
8 M to Ullathorne 9 March 1883,
BU vol. 2, pp 155–6
9 P vol. 2, p. 784
10 Manning, H. E. 'The Church its
own Witness' (1888), *Miscellanies*
vol. iii, p. 434
11 *ibid.*, pp 434–5
12 Bodley *op. cit.*, p. 7

13 Hutton *op. cit.*, p. 96
14 WW vol. 2, p. 193
15 CR p. 186
16 Manning, H. E. 'The Salvation
Army' (1882), *Miscellanies* vol. iii,
pp 189–205
17 M to Canon Jenkins, L p. 480 (no
date given)
18 Manning, H. E. *England and
Christendom* (1867), p. 68
19 P vol. 2, p. 781
20 L p. 485
21 M to Virginia Crawford 24
December 1891, 'Virginia
Crawford, Sir Charles Dilke and
Cardinal Manning', DR vol. ccclv
(Autumn 1967), p. 198
22 CR pp 181–2
23 L p. 483
24 P vol. 2, p. 791
25 M to Rev P. O'Keefe November
1887, ME(1) p. 58
26 Manning, H. E. 'William George
Ward' (1882), *Miscellanies* vol. iii,
p. 186
27 M to Vaughan December 1881, SC
vol. 1, p. 458
28 SC vol. 1, p. 482
29 M to Vaughan 24 September 1883,
SC vol. 1, p. 458
30 Manning, H. E. *The Eternal
Priesthood* (1883), p. 171
31 P vol. 2, p. 788
32 *Life of Dilke* vol. 2, p. 241
33 M 9 October 1881, P vol. 2, p. 687
34 CR pp 174–5
35 Cook, E. T. *The Life of John
Ruskin* (1911) vol. 2, p. 450
36 Russell, G. W. E. *Collections and
Recollections* (1898), p. 43
37 P vol. 2, pp 698–9
38 CR pp 185, 172
39 M to Purcell June 1888, Purcell,
E. S. 'Poisoning the Wells
of Catholic Criticism', *The
Nineteenth Century* (March 1896),
p. 520
40 Russell *op. cit.*, p. 45
41 ME(2)

42 Russell *op. cit.*, p. 44
43 *Life of Dilke* vol. i, p. 292 (July
    1879)
44 Russell *op. cit.*, p. 47
45 DR (Autumn 1967), p. 200
46 L p. 430
47 P vol. 2, p. 702
48 DR (Autumn 1967), p. 197
49 L p. xii
50 Mallock, W. H. *Memories of Life
    and Literature* (1920), pp 99–100
51 Katharine Tynan, ME(2)
52 Russell *op. cit.*, p. 44
53 CR p. 185
54 Russell *op. cit.*, p. 44
55 Fitzsimons *op. cit.*, p. 65
56 P vol. 1, p. 304
57 P vol. 1, p. 199
58 P vol. 2, p. 711
59 P vol. 1, pp 4, 5
60 CR p. 180
61 *Weekly Register* 30 January 1892,
    p. 149
62 *Weekly Register* 23 January 1892,
    p. 123
63 L pp 475, 472
64 *The Nineteenth Century* (February
    1892), p. 282
65 Wilberforce, A. M. *Lavington:
    The History of a Sussex Family*
    (1919), p. 52
66 Russell, G. W. E. *Basil
    Wilberforce* (1917), p. 48
67 M 13 December 1882, P vol. 2,
    pp 676–7
68 M 8 February 1887, P vol. 2,
    p. 678
69 *The Review of Reviews* vol. 1
    (1890), p. 479
70 P vol. 2, pp 455, 457–8
71 P vol. 2, p. 716
72 P vol. 2, p. 351
73 T vol. 2, pp 608 *et seq.*
74 T vol. 2, p. 640
75 T vol. 2, p. 613
76 M's Lenten Pastoral 1890, St John
    pp 125–6, 128
77 SC vol. 2, p. 88
78 Manning, H. E. 'Is the Education

    Act of 1870 a Just Law?' (1882),
    Miscellanies vol. iii, pp 10, 7, 5, 20
79 Manning, H. E. 'Is the
    Christianity of England Worth
    Preserving?' (April 1883),
    Miscellanies vol. iii, pp 60, 62
80 Manning, H. E. 'An Englishman's
    Protest' (August 1880),
    Miscellanies vol. iii, pp 101–2
81 SC vol. 2, p. 113
82 L p. 452
83 Lord Ripon to Manning, 18
    November 1888, Fitzsimons *op.
    cit.*, pp 108–9
84 DR (Autumn 1967), p. 196
85 W vol. 2, p. 487
86 M to Vaughan 1883, SC vol. 1,
    p. 469
87 M 15 November 1888, P vol. 2,
    p. 303
88 M to Duke of Norfolk 19 January
    1889, L p. 476
89 P vol. 2, p. 641
90 P vol. 2, p. 632
91 P vol. 2, p. 631
92 M to Archbishop Croke 13 July
    1881, L p. 385
93 *ibid.*
94 L p. 430
95 L pp 431–2
96 Morley *op. cit.* vol. 3, pp 62–3
97 Manning, H. E. 'The Catholic
    Church and Modern Society',
    Miscellanies vol. iii, p. 318
98 M to Leo XIII 17 February 1885,
    L pp 402–3
99 M to Chamberlain 4 May 1885,
    Lyons, F. S. L. *Charles Stewart
    Parnell* (1977), p. 273
100 L p. 397
101 *Life of Dilke* vol. 2, p. 191
102 McClelland *op. cit.*, p. 183
103 M to Cullen 31 July 1878, L p. 464
104 Fitzsimons *op. cit.*, p. 130
105 M to Vaughan 28 June 1885, L
    p. 392
106 M to G November 1885, Morley
    op. cit. vol. 3, p. 281
107 M to G 6 January 1886, L

pp 406–7

108 Wilfrid Scawen Blunt's Diary 23 February 1886, L p. 416

109 G to Lord Granville 30 April 1886, Morley vol. 3, p. 307

110 L p. 416

111 L p. 407

112 L p. 432

113 M to Walsh 14 July 1886, L p. 417

114 M to Lord Cross 9 December 1886, L p. 410

115 M to G 25 September 1887, L p. 411

116 Duke of Norfolk to M May 1887, L p. 419

117 M to Walsh 4 June 1887, L p. 419

118 M to *The Times* 27 June 1887, ME(1), p. 40

119 Persico to M 21 December 1887 and 12 February 1888, L pp 423, 424

120 Persico to M 9 May 1888, L p. 428

121 L p. 429

11: The Pitcher at the Fountain

1 P vol. 2, p. 801

2 M to Wyndham 12 December 1888, ME(1) p. 60

3 M's Report to Diocesan Education Fund May 1890, St John *op. cit.*, pp 140–41

4 Harrison and Dingle *op. cit.*, p. 504

5 *The Review of Reviews* (February 1892), p. 133

6 Holmes *op. cit.*, p. 175

7 Manning, H. E. 'A Pleading for the Worthless' (1888) *Miscellanies* vol. iii, p. 275

8 *Weekly Register* 23 January 1892

9 CR p. 191

10 Manning, H. E. *The Eternal Priesthood* (1883), p. 232

11 Manning, H. E. *Miscellanies* vol. iii, p. 273

12 St John *op. cit.*, p. 144

13 McClelland *op. cit.*, pp 48–9

14 CR p. 180

15 Manning, H. E. *Miscellanies* vol. iii, p. 274

16 Harrison and Dingle *op. cit.*, p. 507 (1884)

17 M to M. Descurtins July 1890, ME(1) p. 12

18 DR (Autumn 1867), pp 194–5

19 CR p. 180

20 L p. 61

21 P vol. 2, p. 781

22 P vol. 2, p. 654

23 M's notes for a speech at Oldham 15 September 1881, reproduced Clais *op. cit.*, between pp 390 and 391

24 Manning, H. E. *Compensation to the Drink Trade* (1888), *Miscellanies* vol. iii, pp 389–99

25 CR p. 176

26 Manning's speech at Newcastle 4 September 1882, Clais *op. cit.*, p. 395

27 Manning 1888, P vol. 2, p. 600

28 Manning 1890, P vol. 2, p. 604

29 *Tablet* 16 August 1884

30 M 1888, P vol. 2, p. 600

31 SC vol. 1, p. 475

32 P vol. 2, p. 603

33 Newman, F. W. *Contributions* (1891), p. 108

34 M to M. Descurtins July 1890, ME(1) p. 13

35 DR (Autumn 1867), p. 195

36 Manning, H. E. *Miscellanies* vol. iii, p. 261

37 M to Dilke, L pp 448–9

38 *Life of Dilke* vol. 2, p. 19

39 M to Dilke 13 February 1885, L p. 449

40 Fitzsimons *op. cit.*, p. 138

41 M to Dilke 13 February 1885, L p. 449

42 CR 174

43 *Life of Dilke* vol. 2, p. 292

44 L p. 472

45 P vol. 2, p. 676

46 L p. 382

47 Belloc, H. *Cruise of the Nona* (1925), p. 54

48 McClelland *op. cit.*, p. 22

49 ME(1) p. 3

50 M to *The Times* November 1886, ME(1) p. 27

51 Russell, G. W. E. *Collections and Recollections*, p. 47

52 M to *The Times* February 1888, ME(1) p. 2

53 *ibid.*, pp 2–3, 11

54 M to *The Times* 7 February 1888, ME(1). p. 9

55 Manning, H. E. 'Outdoor Relief' (1888), *Miscellanies* vol. iii, pp 369–76

56 M to Comte de Mun 25 January 1891, ME(1) p 22

57 M to Editor of *XXe Siècle* January 1891, ME(1) pp 22–3

58 Eliot, T. S. 'Choruses from The Rock', no. vi, *Collected Poems* (1958), p. 170

59 M's interview with the *Daily Chronicle* c. December 1890, ME(1) p. 20

60 M to Dilke October 1883, *Life of Dilke* vol. 1, p. 508

61 Manning, H. E. 'Why are Our People Unwilling to Emigrate?' (1887), *Miscellanies* vol. iii, pp 207–26

62 Hyndman to Manning 26 November 1886

63 M to *Brooklyn Review* 1 December 1996, ME(1) p. 30

64 M to *The Times* 7 February 1888, ME(1) p. 8

65 M to *The Times* 6 February 1888, ME(1) p. 6

66 ME(1) p. 23

67 P vol. 2, p. 636

68 L p. 378

69 M to Congress of Liege 2 September 1890, ME(1) p. 18

70 M to Van Overbergh 24 October 1890, ME(1) p. 13 (wrongly dated)

71 Fitzsimons *op. cit.*, p. 72

72 Manning, H. E. *Miscellanies* vol. iii, p. 263

73 Taylor, Ida A. *The Cardinal Democrat* (1908) p. 221

74 N to Tillet December 1890, ME(1) p. 17

75 P vol. 2, p. 792

76 P vol. 2, p. 577

77 G to M 14 March 1887, L p. 362

78 Tillet to M 1 March 1888, Clais *op. cit.*, p. 493

79 *Pall Mall Gazette* and *Labour Review* 31 August 1889

80 Leslie, S. 'Cardinal Manning and the London Dock Strike' DR vol. clxvii, no. 335 (Autumn 1920), p. 221

81 Manning, H. E. 'Leo XIII on "The Condition of Labour" ', DR (July 1891), p. 164

82 Llewellyn Smith, H. and Nash, V. *The Story of the Dockers' Strike* (1889), pp 186–7

83 M to Sir John Lubbock 1 September 1889, Clais *op. cit.*, p. 501

84 Buxton, Sydney 'Cardinal Manning. A Reminiscence', *Fortnightly Review* (1896), p. 581

85 *ibid.*, p. 586

86 *ibid.*, p. 586

87 Clais *op. cit.*, p. 504

88 Buxton *op. cit.*, p. 587

89 N to M 29 September 1889, LD vol. xxxi, p. 276 and W vol. 2, p. 534

90 *The Guardian* 18 September 1889

91 *The Times* 15 January 1892, p. 5

92 Archbishop Benson's Diary 17 September 1889, L p. 373

93 Fitzsimons *op. cit.*, p. 145

94 Adderley, J. *In Slums and Society* (1916), p. 198

95 M 9 November 1890, P vol. 2, p. 801

96 *Pall Mall Gazette* 13 September 1889

97 *Morning Post* 16 September 1889

98 *Tablet* 14 September 1889

99 P vol. 2, pp 664–5

100 DR (July 1891), p. 164

101 M to Buxton 27 December 1889, Buxton *op. cit.*, p. 591

102 DR (July 1891), p. 163

103 *Weekly Register* 27 February 1892, p. 283

104 ME(1) p. 13

105 M to Sydney Buxton 21 January 1890, Buxton *op. cit.*, p. 592

106 *The Nineteenth Century* (February 1896), p. 252

107 P vol. 2, p. 800

108 DR (Autumn 1967), p. 188. Rev Dr Butler's Memoir, ME(2)

109 Vaughan, Herbert 'The Life of Cardinal Manning', *The Nineteenth Century* (February 1896), p. 252

110 DR (Autumn 1967), p. 197

111 CR p. 177

112 O'Shea, Katharine *Charles Stewart Parnell: his love story and political life* (1914) vol. 2, pp 221–3

113 Lyons, F. S. L. *The Fall of Parnell* (1960), pp 58–9

114 Hutton, A. W. *op. cit.*, p. 185

115 M to Walsh 29 November 1890, Walsh P. J. *William J. Walsh* (1928), p. 424

116 M to Walsh 4 December 1890, Walsh *op. cit.*, p. 426

117 M to G 27 November 1890, McClelland *op. cit.*, p. 198

118 M to G 5 December 1890, L p. 439

119 *Weekly Register* 20 February 1892

120 Taylor, Ida A. *op. cit.*, pp. 228–9

121 M to Stead 21 December 1890, L pp 440–41

122 M to G 26 November 1891, L p. 494

123 M to G 18 September 1887, L p. 410

124 M to Mrs Gladstone 23 July 1889, Drew, M. *Catherine Gladstone* (1919), p. 187

125 Russell, G. W. E. *Collections and Recollections*, p. 51

126 Bodley *op. cit.*, pp 16–17

127 BU vol. 2, pp 158–9

128 Vaughan to M March 1889, T vol. 2, p. 639

129 T vol. 2, p. 645

130 P vol. 2, pp 749–52

131 Russell, G. W. E. *Collections and Recollections*, p. 56

132 DR (Autumn 1967), p. 189

133 P vol. 2, p. 798

134 P vol. 2, pp 772–96, see especially pp 775, 792–3

135 P vol. 2, p. 801

136 Inglis, K. S. *Churches and the Working Classes in Victorian England* (1963), p. 123

137 P vol. 2, p. 781

138 DR (Autumn 1967), p. 193

139 DR (July 1891), p. 167

140 Wilson, A. N. *Hilaire Belloc* (1984), p. 27

141 Vaughan to M 17 October 1880, McClelland *op. cit.*, pp 150–51

142 DR (Autumn 1967), p. 197

143 *ibid.*, p. 196

144 *ibid.*, p. 194

145 *ibid.*, p. 197

146 *ibid.*, p. 198

147 CR pp 183–4

148 *Weekly Register* 23 January 1892

149 L p. 495

150 Von Hugel, Baron Friedrich *Selected Letters* (1927), p. 256

151 L p. 495

Epilogue

1 *The Times* 15 January 1892

2 Patmore, D. *The Life and Times of Coventry Patmore* (1949), pp 133–4

3 Bodley *op. cit.*, p. 37

4 P vol. 2, p. 685

5 P vol. 2, p. 730

6 Smith, Stevie 'How Do You See?', *Collected Poems* (1975), p. 521

7 M to RW 20 January 1854, P vol. 2, pp 36–7

Index

Abel Smith, Elizabeth, 11
Academy of the Catholic Religion, 183
Accademia Ecclesiastica, 152
Acton, Lord, 179, 181, 182, 183, 184, 231, 236
Agricultural Labourers' Union, 243
Anderdon, Anna Maria (M's sister), 12, 13, 19, 268
Anderdon, John (M's brother-in-law), 19–22, 26–30, 34, 35, 110
Anderdon, Father William (M's nephew), 253–4
Anglicanism, *see under* Church of England
anti-Catholicism, 78, 100–101, 136–7; moderation of, 318; *see also under* Gladstone, William
Antonelli, Cardinal, 199
Apologia Pro Vita Sua, 194, 195, 282
Archbishop's House, 250, 269, 295
Arnold, Thomas, 40–41
Association for the Promotion of the Unity of Christendom, 210–11
Athenaeum, the, 276
Austen, Caroline (M's sister), 13, 28, 75, 120, 135, 139, 269, 279, 311

Balliol, 23, 31, 279
baptismal regeneration, 131–2
Barnabò, Cardinal, 169, 171, 186, 196, 197, 200, 201, 216
Barnardo, Dr, 296
Basevi, George, 10
Belloc, Hilaire, 300
Bergasse, Alexandre, 302
Bevan, Favell Lee, 31–5, 42, 61
Black Monday, 295

Blomfield, Bishop, of London, 75, 132, 134
Bloody Sunday, 295
Blunt, Mary, 65
Bodley, J. E. C., 4, 315, 323
Boulton, S. B., 278–9, 310
Bradlaugh, Charles, 285
Brock, Revd William, 104
Brompton Oratory, 2, 147, 282, 315
Brown, Bishop, 180, 215
Brownbill, Father, 140
Buccleuch, Duchess of, 153, 300
Burns, John, 308, 310
Bute, Marquess of, 223, 277
Butler, Bishop, 38
Butler, Father, 4
Butler, Revd George, 16
Buxton, Sidney, 308–9
Byles, Marianne, 65, 323
Byron, Lord, 16, 17, 25

Capel, Mgr, 223, 257
Captain Swing riots, 46–7
Carnarvon, Lord, 289
Castelfidardo, 174
Catholic Bible Society, 144
Catholic devotions, 144–5, 162, 166; *see also under* M (3)
Catholic Emancipation, 25–6, 53, 101, 142–3
Catholic schools, 207–10, 238–40, 252–3, 262–4, 283–6; *see also under* M (3) Education
Chamberlain, Joseph, 285, 288–9, 290
Chapeau, Abbé Alphonse, 7–8
Charlton, Barbara, 146
Church of England, condition in 1830,

36–41; doctrinal fuzziness, 42;
Newman's hopes for, 52–3; relation
to State, 53, 68–70, 104–5, 132, 238;
escapes radical reform, 67–8; Peel's
Ecclesiastical Commission, 68–9;
evangelical bias in, 69, 132;
functional impotence, 71, 90–91;
Ward's criticism, 99; Pius IX on, 126;
see also under M (3) and Newman,
John Henry
Church, R. W., 232
Clais, Jacqueline, 8
Clarence and Avondale, Duke of, 1, 2
Clark, Sir Andrew, 320
Clifford, William, Bishop of Clifton,
197, 198, 234, 289
Cobbett, William, 40
Coffin, Robert, 18, 160–61, 200
Coleridge, Edward, 106
Collegio di Propaganda, 121, 182, 195,
196, 197, 199, 200, 213, 214, 216,
248, 262, 263
Collegio Romano, 153
Combe Bank, 15
confession, 100; see also under M (3)
converts to Catholicism, 142, 145–7;
see also under M (3)
Copped Hall, Totteridge, 10–11, 15,
278–9
Cornthwaite, Bishop, of Beverley, 198
Cox, Dr, 195
Crawford, Virginia, 276, 312, 319–20
Crimean War, 157–8
Cross, Lord, 286, 290
Cullen, Archbishop, of Dublin, 219
Cunningham, Revd John, 18

Darwin, Charles, 110, 227
Davitt, Michael, 288
Dean and Chapter Act (1840), 68
Decision of Character, 21–2, 50
Defell, Miss, 29
De La Salle brothers, 253
De Profundis, 207
Deputatio de Fide, 230–31, 234
De Vere, Aubrey, 84, 149, 150–51
Dilke, Lady, 305
Dilke, Sir Charles, 220, 274, 276, 290,
300, 303

Disraeli, Benjamin, 10, 222–3, 245,
255–6, 314, 315
Dollinger, Dr, 148, 227, 270
Doyle, Sir Francis, 24
Dupanloup, Bishop, of Orleans, 229

education, see under M (3)
Education Acts (1891, 1902), 286
Endymion, 255–6
English Catholicism, 142–7; see also
anti-Catholicism and M (3) –
Catholic Church in England
Errington, George, Archbishop of
Trebizond, 161–4, 166–73, 188, 198–
9, 202
Errington Mission, 289–90
Essay on the Development of Christian
Doctrine, 107, 110–11
Essays and Reviews, 192
Eton College, 16
Evangelical revival, 38, 39–40; in
decline, 48–9; and Oxford
Movement, 50–51
Extraordinary Black Book, 36

Faber, Frederick, 18, 19, 147, 179, 193
Farm Street, 140, 198, 202, 251, 252,
277
Fenianism, 219–20, 221
Ffoulkes, Edmund, 217
Fielding, Henry, 32
Fisher, Canon, 20
Forbes Leith, Father, 323
Forster, W. E., 238
Foster, John, 21–2, 35, 50, 276
Froude, Hurrell, 49, 88
Fry, Elizabeth, 126
Fullerton, Lady Georgiana, 140

Gallwey, Father, 251, 252
Garden of the Soul, 144
Garibaldi, Guiseppe, 176
Gaskell, James Milnes, 24
Gasquet, Dr, 10, 320
Gathercole, Revd Augustus, 100–101
George, Henry, 303
Gibbons, Cardinal, 306
Gilbert, Bishop, of Chichester, 81
Gioberti, Vicenzio, 122

Gladstone, William Ewart, *see, chiefly*, M (4); 15, 36, 58, 61, 62, 64, 65, 123, 171, 221, 244, 256, 288, 315; book on Church and State, 104; anti-Catholic prejudice, 113–14, 134, 210, 246–7
Goderich, Lord, 28
Gorham Case, 131–3, 135–6
Goschen, G. J., 276
Goulburn, Henry, 130
Graffham, 43, 45, 57
Graham, Sir James, 278
Grant, Bishop, of Southwark, 157, 193, 198, 199, 230
Granville, Lord, 237, 247, 289, 290
Gregorovius, F., 231–2
Gregory XVI, Pope, 75–6
Greville, Charles, 101, 132
Grey, Lord, 67

Hallahan, Margaret, 162
Hamilton, Walter, 153
Hammersmith Reformatory, 171
Hammersmith Seminary, 252
Hampden, R. D., 61, 126–7
Hare, Archdeacon, 66
Harkness, Margaret, 307
Harrow School, 15–18, 279
Hazlitt, William, 12
Hedley, Bishop, of Newport, 2, 286
Herbert, Lady Elizabeth, of Lea, 153, 160–61, 176
Herbert, Sidney, 24, 105, 128, 140, 152, 171
Hooker, Richard, 42, 57
Hope (Scott), James, 24, 83, 133, 138, 140, 141, 208, 287
Housing Commission, 299
Howard, Cardinal, 265, 268
Howley, Archbishop, of Canterbury, 40, 67
Humphreys, Father, 253
Hunter, Sir Claudius, 12–13
Hutton, Arthur, 316
Huxley, T. H., 244–5, 305
Hyndman, H. M., 303

industrial schools, 209
Ireland, *see under* M (3)
Irish Catholics in England, 142–3,

146–7, 155, 159; *see also under* M (3)
Irish Church Act (1869), 225
Irish Land Act (1870), 225, 237
Irish University Bills, 222, 245
Italian unification, 122–3, 124–5, 174, 236

Jenkins, Canon, 272
Johnson, Canon, 320
Jowett, Dr, 122, 279

Keate, Dr, 16
Keble, John, 58, 59, 114–15, 128, 133, 153, 233
Kensington University, 256–8
Kingsley, Charles, 194, 198, 265
Knights of Labour, 306

Lamennais, Abbé Félicité Robert de, 75, 123
Laprimaudaye, Charles, 117, 160
Lavington, 43–6, 57, 59, 85, 118–19, 126, 135, 138, 151, 184, 279
League of the Cross, 241
Lendon, Revd Abel, 15
Leo XIII, Pope, 231, 261–2, 263, 264, 286–7, 288, 289–90, 292–3, 305, 309, 316, 318–19
Licensing Bills, 240, 241–2
Lincoln's Inn preachership, 96–7
Lingard, John, 146
Lockhart, William, 84
London County Council, 300
London dock strike, 306–10, 311
Lothair, 222–3, 277
Loughborough, Lord, 12
Lubbock, Sir John, 307–8
Luther, Martin, 32
Lyte, H. F., 120
Lythgoe, Father, 251

McClelland, V. A., 8
Maguire, Canon John, 201
Mainz, Congress of, 306
Mallock, W. H., 277
Maltby, Bishop, of Chichester and Durham, 48, 61, 137
Manners, Lord John, 89
Manners-Sutton, Archbishop, of

Canterbury, 37

Manning, Anna Maria (M's sister), *see* Anderdon

Manning, Caroline (M's sister), *see* Austen

Manning, Caroline, *née* Sargent, (M's wife), 45–8, 56, 63–6, 116, 128, 134, 151, 214, 278, 279, 314, 320

Manning, Charles (M's brother), 10, 13, 16, 149, 269

Manning, Charlotte (M's sister), 13

Manning, Frederick (M's brother), 13, 27, 29, 138–9, 269, 306

Manning, Harriet (M's sister), 13, 23–4, 278

Manning, Henry Edward:

(1) *Career*:
previous biographies, 4–8; background and childhood, 9- 15; Harrow, 15–19; private tuition, 19–22; Oxford, 22–6; clerk in Colonial Office, 28–9; frustration and inner struggle, 29–35; takes Orders, 35, 41; Fellow of Merton, 41–2; engagement and marriage, 47–8, 63–6; Rector of Lavington, 47- 50, 55–9, 83; Archdeacon of Chichester, 81; Lincoln's Inn failure, 96–7, 109; spiritual turmoil, 102–20; Rome, indecision and conversion, 119–41; Roman Catholic priest, 147–8; study in Rome, 151–3, 155–6; at Farm Street, 153, 158; superior of Oblates, 155, 158- 60, 164–73; prospective bishop, 156–8, 187–8; Provost of Westminster, 163; Protonotary Apostolic, 172; Archbishop of Westminster, 197–200; Cardinal, 254–5; death, 320–21; funeral, 1–3; *The Times* obituary, 322; summing up, 323–7

(2) *Characteristics*:
abilities, 17, 20, 33, 83–4, 129, 157, 159–60, 171, 210
ambition and counter-ambition, 19, 22, 27, 29–35, 85–7, 108–10, 117, 150, 153, 156, 158, 163, 170–71, 190, 198, 199, 203–6,

312, 324
appearance, 16, 17, 23, 59, 83, 84, 121, 206, 222–3, 231–2, 271, 276, 277–8
ascetic, 83, 218, 231, 250, 275
authoritarian, 18–19, 49, 56, 160, 165–6, 230, 231, 243, 256, 257, 303
children, love of, 58, 295–6
cricketer, 17–18, 19, 58
divided nature, 30–31, 33, 86, 206, 283
extremist, 14, 34, 175–6, 228–35, 258
faith, 34–5, 69, 71–2, 135–6, 148–9, 271
fanatic, 175–6, 233–4, 254, 277
hard worker, 15, 21, 75, 171, 205, 206, 255, 269–70, 316
ill health, 15, 43, 75, 114, 115–17, 120, 121, 258, 260
isolation, 24, 64–5, 273–5
jealous, 117
man of the world, 17, 83, 153, 275–6
natural speaker, 24–5
need for certainty, 96, 135–6, 148–9, 204, 205
obsessed by own past, 278–82
paternalist, 89–90, 243, 302, 303
pragmatist, 129, 173, 239, 243, 259, 316
preacher, 59, 87, 156
pride, 33, 97
political instincts, 24–7, 157, 219, 221, 222, 230–6, 245, 258, 274, 285, 289, 290, 300
repellent effect, 114–15, 160–61, 169, 185, 200, 204, 324
reserve, 47, 64, 114–15, 169, 217
self-assurance, 24, 25, 50, 56, 167
self-control, 86
self-criticism, 110, 115, 117, 118, 203–6, 312
self-discipline, 15, 20, 23, 151
sense of crisis, 166, 262
sense of useful people, 11–13, 150, 152, 164
social conscience, 87–91, 191, 218,

294–306
strong feelings, 288, 305
writer, 19–20, 270–1
(3) *Views and policies*:
Antichrist, 175–6, 260
Apostolic Succession, 50, 55–7, 59
Catholic Church (M's Anglican
   view), 62–3, 73–7, 79, 92,
   94–5, 98, 100, 111, 112–14,
   119–20, 123–4, 125
Catholic Church in England, 165,
   273, 281, 316–18; uniting, 201–
   2, 212, 215–16, 248–9
Catholic devotions, 77, 98, 119,
   130, 272
Catholic integration, 218, 240,
   281, 284–5, 318
Catholics at Oxford, 191–2, 212–
   14, 256, 285–6
charity, 90, 208–9, 272, 277
Church and people, 123–4, 305–6,
   318, 325
Church of England, 35, 41, 42,
   56–7, 59, 68–73, 76–7, 80, 82,
   91, 92, 94–9, 102–20 *passim*,
   127–38 *passim*, 192, 211, 271–2,
   317
Church union, 130, 210–11
clerical marriage, 65, 124, 278
confession, 58, 92, 116
conversions, 77, 103, 114, 135,
   149, 153–4, 161
daily service, 56
Darwin, 227
Education:
   achievement, 283
   Act of 1870, 237–40, 284, 286
   Acts of 1891 and 1902, 286
   Anglican politics, 129
   higher education, 191–2, 195–6,
     212–14, 251, 245–6, 256–8,
     286–7
   Pastoral 1866, 207–10
   saving voluntary schools, 238–9,
     284–6
   spiritual trust, 70–71, 207
   technical, 242, 253, 295
   workhouse problem, 209
   see also under Jesuits

emigration, 303
England, 119, 125, 175, 220, 225,
   242, 255, 285, 305, 323
Evangelical sympathies, 11, 14,
   30–31, 41–2, 49, 61, 204, 207,
   242
friendship, 23–4, 163–4, 274
Gorham case, 131–5
Hampden as bishop, 126–8
hatred of cold theory, 88, 224,
   300–2
Hell, fear of, 14, 99, 203, 320
Holy Ghost, devotion for, 204
Home Rule, *see under* Ireland
housing, 299–300
Irish in England, 207, 217–18, 280
Ireland, 124, 155, 176, 219–25,
   255, 287–93; Home Rule, 220,
   246, 288–91, 312–14
Jesuits, 124, 153, 158, 198, 202,
   251–3, 256; battle over schools,
   262–4, 317
Liberal Party, 246, 291
literary vanity, 270, 281–2
materialism, 87, 207, 242
Maynooth, 104–5
music, 2, 250, 272
Non-Conformists, 211, 246, 271–2
old Catholics, 165, 166, 201, 207–
   8, 272–3, 292
papal infallibility, 73–4, 113, 148,
   226–36, 246–9, 293
priesthood, 34, 59, 69, 164–5,
   251–2, 272, 277
prophesying doom, 14, 128–9,
   242–3, 295, 307–8, 319
property, 88, 224, 303, 304
Protestantism, 79–80, 119, 271,
   272
radical, 25, 88, 123, 300
religious orders, 130, 251–3, 270
socialist or not, 302–5
strikes, 310–11
succubi, 277
suffering, 86–7, 115, 204–5
temperance, 218–9, 240–2, 298–9,
   320
temporal power of pope, 125,
   175–6, 227, 258–60

theatre, 31, 273
Ullathorne, 189–90
unemployment, 303
Vatican Council, 281
violence, 295
women, 64, 250, 297, 305
working hours, 89–90, 299
worldly Catholicism, 192, 212, 218
(4) *Works mentioned in text*:
   Charges to Chichester clergy:
      1841, 82; 1845, 102; 1848, 123,
      128; 1849, 128–9
   Dignity and Rights of Labour,
      The, 243
   Eternal Priesthood, The, 208, 270,
      274, 296
   Grounds of Faith, The, 153
   Pastoral Office, The, 270–71
   Present Crisis of the Holy See, 181
   Public Letters: against
      Ecclesiastical Commission, 68;
      in defence of canonries, 80; to
      Dr Pusey, 192; to Earl Grey,
      223–4; to Archbishop of
      Armagh, 246
   Sermons: The English Church,
      58–9; National Education, 70-
      71; The Rule of Faith, 71–3
(5) *Manning-Gladstone relations*:
   G on M's obsequies, 3; on M's
   life, 6; G and Purcell, 4, 5; first
   meeting, 23; Oxford Union, 24–5;
   similar backgrounds, 25; career
   prospects, 25; G finds a seat, 27;
   establishment of friendship, 62;
   Rome, 75–6; social life, 83;
   Newman, 93–4, 96; mutual
   compliments, 93; Lincoln's Inn,
   96–7; Maynooth, 104–5; answering
   Newman, 107, 111; G ignores M's
   doubts, 115; differences over
   confession, 116; G satisfied by M's
   views 1848, 127; Gorham, 133–4;
   M's conversion, 134–41; M on G's
   future, 138; re-encounter, 176;
   temporal power of pope, 176–7,
   247; co-operation, 209–10; G's
   impatience, 221; Ireland, 222,
   224–5; G Prime Minister, 224–5;

   Vatican Council, 233–4, 237;
   Education Act, 237–9; Irish
   University, 245–6; 1874 election,
   246; pamphlet warfare, 246–9;
   second break, 248–9; M and
   Disraeli gossip about G, 255, 256;
   G's fifty years in politics, 280; 1885
   election, 285–6; reconciliation,
   290; rescuing prostitutes, 297–8;
   Home Rule, 290–91, 312–14; last
   contacts, 314–15
(6) *Manning-Newman relations*:
   M more widely mourned, 3;
   similar background, 9, 12; Oxford
   exams, 26; early contacts, 31; M
   under N's spell, 31, 50–63 *passim*,
   69, 72; M on N's sermons, 61; Mr
   Osburn, 62; Roman fever cases,
   77–8; N's Roman sympathies, 93–
   4, 102; M's 5 November sermon,
   95–6; effect of N's conversion on
   M, 97, 106; Doctrine of
   Development, 107–8; M finds N
   sceptical, 111; Roman meeting,
   121; N and M's conversion, 128,
   138, 140; M visits N, 149; N offers
   Vice-Rectorship to M, 149;
   converts, 153, 193; Second Spring
   sermon, 154; expressions of
   esteem and affection, 36, 60, 63,
   69, 72, 75, 79, 95–6, 102, 106, 154,
   179, 181, 183–4; Oblates and
   Oratorians, 158, 159–60; decline
   of friendship, 177–84; *Rambler*,
   179; N's missing letter to Rome,
   181; ultramontanism, 182; Oxford,
   193–6, 212–14; N attacks ultras,
   194; M on *Apologia*, 194;
   Barnabò's tactful comment, 196;
   N and Westminster succession,
   198, 202; N declines bishopric,
   203; M's consecration, 203;
   Wesley, 209; N's Letter to Pusey,
   211–12; M's critical view of N,
   212; animus grows, 214–17;
   Catholic laity's address to N, 215;
   Vatican Council, 229–30, 233, 236;
   lots compared, 232–3;
   Metaphysical Society, 244–5; N's

Letter to Duke of Norfolk, 248–9; Kensington University, 256–7; N's cardinalate, 264–8; writers, 270; M sums up relations, 282; differing achievements, 283; final meetings, 283; Oxford ban, 286–7; London dock strike, 309; N's death and M's sermon, 315–16; always compared, 322

(7) *Manning-Pius ix relations*, 121, 125, 126, 148, 152, 156, 164, 169, 171–2, 200, 205, 214, 227–8, 235, 236–7, 241, 254–5, 258, 260–1, 305

(8) *Manning-Wiseman relations*, 63, 76, 147–8, 155, 156, 158, 162–73, 177, 178, 185, 186, 188, 189–90, 196, 198, 205

Manning, William (M's father), wealth, 9, 10, 14–15; Governor of Bank of England, 10; first marriage and Evangelicalism, 11; paternal duty, 13; pays for crammer, 20; and Oxford, 23; bankruptcy and death, 26–7; 306

Manning, William (M's brother), 13, 279

Manning, William (M's nephew), 200

Manning, William Coventry (grandfather), 9–11, 279

Marx, Karl, 93, 302, 310

Maurice, F. D., 83, 114, 129

Maynooth seminary, 104–5

Melbourne, Lord, 53, 67–8, 69, 80

Merivale, Dean, 17, 18

Merton, 28, 41–2

Metaphysical Society, 244–5

Metternich, Prince, 122, 123

Milner, Bishop, 143–4

Mirari Vos (1832), 76

Moberly, George, 127, 128

Monléon, Sylvio de, 302

Month, The, 207, 268

Morris, Father, 168, 186, 199, 253

Mozley, Thomas, 49, 56

Napoleon iii, Emperor, 174

Neve, Frederick, 215

Newcastle, Duke of, 171

Newman, Francis, 299

Newman, John Henry, Cardinal, *see also, and chiefly, under* M (6); 23, 43–4, 49; on faith and authority, 51–4; fanatic, 54; anti-Roman prejudice, 53, 55, 102; his *Via Media*, 53–4; prickly, 55, 178–9, 282; loses faith in Church of England, 78–9, 93–4, 102; resigns St Mary's, 92; on treatment of Catholic priests; conversion, 106; on Romans, 121; failure and depression, 177–9, 184, 193; delated to Rome, 180; views on temporal power, 181–2; on Pius ix, 182–3; gossip at Oratory, 193; *Apologia*, 194; under suspicion, 211–12; papal infallibility, 229–36; mellows, 282–3; G consults over Irish atrocities, 288; death, 320

Nice, 120, 174

Nightingale, Florence, 157

Norfolk, 13th Duke of, 145

Norfolk, 14th Duke of, 264, 267, 287, 289, 292

Oakeley, Frederick, 249

Oblates of St Charles, 155, 158–60, 164–73

O'Callaghan, H., 215

old Catholics, 142–6, 160, 194, 208–9, 225, 253, 256, 257, 310; *see also under* M (3)

Ollivier, Emile, 231

Oratory school, 178, 193

Oriel, 22–3

Orme, Garton, 44

orphanages, 209

Oscott, Synod of (1852), 154

Oscott, Synod of (1859), 167, 170

O'Shea, Captain and Mrs, 312, 314

Otter, William, Bishop of Chichester, 68, 72–3, 75, 80

Oxenden, Bishop, 17, 18

Oxford Movement, 50–55

Oxford University, 22, 100, 221; Union, 24–6; Catholics at, 190–6, 212–14, 286–7

Paget, Augustus, 258
Palmerston, Lord, 199, 220
papal infallibility, *see under* M (3);
   definition, 235
papal nuncios, 289
Papal States, 75; reforms in, 122; 123,
   124–5, 174, 236, 247
Paris, 260, 295, 319
Parnell, Charles Stewart, 287, 288, 289,
   312–14
Patmore, Coventry, 322–3
Patterson, James, Bishop of Emmaus,
   173, 271
Peel, Sir Robert, 68, 85, 104
Pelham, George, Bishop of Lincoln,
   13, 15
Persico Mission, 292–3
Phillpotts, Henry, Bishop of Exeter,
   83, 131–2, 134
Pitt, William, 11
Pius v, Pope, 143
Pius vii, Pope, 144
Pius ix, Pope, 121–5, 150, 151–2, 160,
   172, 174, 182–3, 186, 187, 192, 193,
   196, 199, 213–14, 227, 231, 236, 305;
   see also under M (7)
Prince of Wales (later Edward vii),
   274, 297, 299–300
Prior Park, 145
propaganda, *see* Collegio di
   Propaganda
Pugin, Augustus Welby, 100
Punch, 268
Purcell, Edmund Sheridan, 3–4, 4–6,
   275, 299
Pusey, Edward Bouverie, 60, 81, 94,
   98, 107, 133, 211, 233; his *Eirenicon*,
   192, 211

Rambler, the, 179, 180, 182, 183
Record, The, 61, 73
reformatories, 171, 207
Reform Bill, 25, 40
Richmond, Duke of, 88
Richmond, George, 18, 45, 83
Ripon, Marquess of, 264, 286
Rerum Novarum, 318–19
Romanus Pontifices, 264
Rome (city), 236, 258–9; M in, 75–7,

121–7, 151–3, 155–6, 196, 258, 260
Ruskin, John, 244, 275, 301
Russell, Lord John, 67, 126, 137, 139
Russell, G. W. E., 275–6, 314, 316
Russell, Odo, 233, 236
Ryan, Elizabeth (M's grandmother), 9,
   10
Ryder, George, 48, 61, 112
Ryder, Ignatius (M's nephew), 5, 64
Ryder, Sophia, *née* Sargent (M's
   sister-in-law), 45, 48, 63, 64, 112

St Charles Borromeo, 127, 159
St Charles's College, 252, 258
St Edmund's, Ware, 162, 165–7, 169,
   173, 252
St Patrick's Day, 218, 219
St Paul's, Knightsbridge, 133
Salisbury, Lord, 286, 300
Salvation Army, 241, 271, 272, 273
Sargent, Mary, *née* Abel Smith (M's
   mother-in-law), 45, 63, 64, 65, 140
Sargent, Revd John, 43, 44–7
Searle, Mgr, 163, 167, 170, 186, 201,
   209
Senestrey, Bishop, of Ratisbon, 228,
   235
Shaftesbury, Earl of, 18, 20, 220, 280
Shelley, Percy Bysshe, 25
Sheridan, Richard Brinsley, 273
Shuttleworth, Philip Richard, Bishop
   of Chichester, 80–81
Sidmouth, Viscount, 13
Simeon, Charles, 44
Sloane, Sir Hans, 13
Sloane, Mary (M's grandmother), 13
Smith, Sydney, 39, 40, 142
Social Catholicism, 75–6, 123, 318–19,
   325; *see also under* M (3) Church
   and People
Society for the Propagation of
   Christian Knowledge, 61–2
Southwark Cathedral, 139, 153
Spectator, The, 225
Stead, W. T., 220, 281, 297–8, 310,
   312, 322
Stephen, Sir James, 278
Sterling, James, 84

Strachey, Lytton, 6–7, 54, 63, 116, 190, 299
sugar trade, 14–15, 26
Syllabus Errorum, 174, 192
Tablet, the, 3, 210, 298, 310
Talbot, Mgr George, 149–50, 156–7, 158, 162, 164, 170, 172–3, 174, 177, 179, 185, 186, 187, 188, 190, 194, 197–201, 208, 211, 213, 215–16, 217
temperance, *see under* M (3)
Temple, Bishop, of London, 308, 310
temporal power of pope, 122–3, 174, 181–2; *see also under* M (3)
Tennyson, Lord, 1, 244
Throckmorton, Sir John, 143
Tierney, Father, 251
Tillett, Ben, 306–9
Times, The, 1–2, 209, 301, 307, 322
Tracts for the Times, 50, 54, 60; Tract 90, 79
Trent, Council of, 53, 74, 127, 230, 272
Trevelyan, Charles, 124, 152
Trollope, Anthony, 16

Ullathorne, William Bernard, Bishop of Birmingham, 184–5, 186–7, 189–90, 193, 198, 203, 212, 215–16, 217, 228, 230–31, 233, 237, 239, 249, 251, 263, 265–6, 315
Ultramontanism, 145, 165, 182, 183, 198, 214–15, 226–36
United Kingdom Alliance, 219, 240–41
Univers, 227
Upwalden, 43, 44

Vatican Council, 226–36, 281
Vaughan, Father Bernard, 257
Vaughan, Herbert (M's successor at Westminster), 6, 161, 165–6, 185, 186–7, 194, 200–201, 214, 262–4, 273, 285, 299, 310, 312, 315, 320–21
Ventura, Father, 123, 124
Veuillot, Louis, 227
Victoria, Queen, 137, 274
voluntary (denominational) schools, *see under* M (3) Education; Voluntary Schools Association, 285

Walsh, William J., Archbishop of

Dublin, 289–90, 292, 313
Ward, W. G., 47, 99–100, 145–6, 162–3, 165, 182, 193, 196, 197, 211–12, 229, 232, 244, 317
Ward, Wilfrid, 10, 145
Watson, Edward, Bishop of Llandaff, 37
Webber, Archdeacon, 80–81
Wesley, John, 35, 37, 209
West Indies, 9–11
West London Protestant Institute, 160, 168
Westminster Cathedral, 206–7
Westminster Chapter, 163, 166–9, 198–9, 200, 201, 215
Westminster Gazette, 3
Whewell, W., 83
Wilberforce, Basil, 280
Wilberforce, Emily, *née* Sargent (M's sister-in-law), 43, 45, 85
Wilberforce, Henry, 24, 31, 43–4, 47–8, 56, 58, 103, 104, 128, 133, 135
Wilberforce, Mary, *née* Sargent (M's sister-in-law), 45, 64, 115, 130, 135
Wilberforce, Reginald, 279
Wilberforce, Robert, 31, 43, 103, 108, 111, 115, 118, 125, 126, 127, 131, 132, 133, 134, 135, 137, 138, 142, 149, 152, 153, 160
Wilberforce, Samuel, Bishop of Oxford and Winchester, 12, 24, 25, 43, 49, 61, 63, 72, 85–6, 103, 108, 109, 110, 132, 134, 136, 140, 153, 221, 236–7, 256, 261, 279–80
Wilberforce, William, 11–12, 16, 38, 45, 274
Wilberforce, William (son of above), 43
William IV, King, 67, 68
Wiseman, Nicholas, Cardinal, 62; Flaminian Gate Letter, 136–7; Romanising policy, 145, 165; 146, 149, 150, 151, 153; character, 154–5; 158; and Errington, 162–5 *passim*; opinion of M, 155, 171, 178; 180, 181, 186, 191, 192, 196, 201, 252; *see also* M (8)
Wood, S. F., 47
Wordsworth, Charles, 15, 17, 18, 23,

24
Wordsworth, Christopher, 15
wordsworth, Christopher (son of
above), 15

Wordsworth, William, 101
workhouses, 171, 207, 209–10, 302

Young England, 89